Bible Studies
Genesis Exodus
Second Edition

James Malm

ISBN: 978-1-7753510-7-8

Copyright © 2019 James Malm

All Rights Reserved

Dedication

This work is dedicated to the Great God whose house is eternity; the Father and Sovereign of all that exists, and the sum of all Truth, Wisdom, Love, Justice and Mercy.
May God's house be filled with children whose chief joy is to be like Him!

Visit Our Website

theshininglight.info

Table of Contents

Genesis 7

- Introduction 8
- Genesis 1 13
- Genesis 2 21
- Genesis 3 31
- Genesis 4 45
- Genesis 5 50
- Genesis 6 53
- Genesis 7 59
- Genesis 8 63
- Genesis 9 67
- Genesis 10 72
- Genesis 11 87
- Genesis 12 91
- Genesis 13 94
- Genesis 14 97
- Genesis 15 100
- Genesis 16 104
- Genesis 17 108
- Genesis 18 112
- Genesis 19 117
- Genesis 20 123
- Genesis 21 126
- Genesis 22 132
- Genesis 23 137
- Genesis 24 139
- Genesis 25 146
- Genesis 26 151
- Genesis 27 155
- Genesis 28 163
- Genesis 29 167
- Genesis 30 171

Genesis 31	176
Genesis 32	182
Genesis 33	187
Genesis 34	190
Genesis 35	194
Genesis 36	197
Genesis 37	203
Genesis 38	208
Genesis 39	212
Genesis 40	217
Genesis 41	220
Genesis 42	227
Genesis 43	232
Genesis 44	236
Genesis 45	240
Genesis 46	244
Genesis 47	248
Genesis 48	252
Genesis 49	258
The Ten Tribes Removed From the Line of David	264
The Tribes of Israel Today	269
Possession of the Promised Land	279
Genesis 50	282
Exodus	**287**
Prophecies of the Exodus	288
Exodus 1	295
Exodus 2	300
Exodus 3	310
Exodus 4	314
Exodus 5	319
Exodus 6	324
Exodus 7	328
Exodus 8	332

Exodus 9	337
Exodus 10	343
Exodus 11	348
Exodus 12	351
Exodus 13	363
Exodus 14	367
Exodus 15	372
Exodus 16	379
Exodus 17	384
Exodus 18	387
Exodus 19	391
Exodus 20	395
Exodus 21	399
Exodus 22	405
Exodus 23	409
Exodus 24	414
Exodus 25	418
Exodus 26	422
Exodus 27	425
Exodus 28	428
Exodus 29	434
Exodus 30	441
Exodus 31	445
Exodus 32	448
Exodus 33	454
Exodus 34	459
Exodus 35	465
Exodus 36	469
Exodus 37	472
Exodus 38	477
Exodus 39	480
Exodus 40	484

Genesis

Introduction

Genesis [beginnings] is full of basics on creation and the history of the world up to the day that Joseph went down into Egypt.

The creation is covered in only the most succinct detail and is therefore subject to misunderstanding by those who are not close to God and have a basic knowledge of science and organization.

For example God was not one individual doing all this work himself. God the Father was the Chief Executive who approved the final plans and gave the order of execution, while the God Being who became Jesus Christ was the Implementing Creator and had millions of angels to carry out His commands.

In the beginning there were two Beings revealed to us by the term Elohim [meaning Mighty One's] who had full executive authority, and one of these Beings [who became the Father] approved everything and then entrusted the other [who became the Son] to carry out the actual creation on the earth, while God the Father oversaw the rest of the universe.

The Creator

The God Being who became God the Father has Executive Authority over the entire universe!

The One who became God the Father is the Executive Authority over the creating of all things; while the one who later gave up his Godhood to become flesh as Jesus Christ, had Implementing Authority carrying out the actual creating!

The one who became the Son was a part of the God Family from the very beginning along with the one who became the Father. The one who became the Father was the Executive Authority; the Decider: and the one who became the Son, was the Implementing Authority in the creating process.

John 1:1 In the beginning was the Word, and the Word was with God, and the Word was God. **1:2** The same was in the beginning with God. **1:3 All things were made by him; and without him was not any thing made that was made.**

Colossians 1:13 "Who hath delivered us from the power of darkness, and hath translated US into the kingdom of his dear Son: **1:14** In whom we have redemption through his blood, EVEN the forgiveness of sins: **1:15** Who is the image of the invisible God, the firstborn of every creature: **1:16 For by him were all things created, that are in heaven, and that are in earth, visible and invisible**, whether they be thrones, or dominions, or principalities, or powers: **all things were created by him, and for him**: **1:17** And he is before all things, and by him all things consist. **1:18** And **he is the head** of the body, the church: who is the beginning, **the firstborn from the dead**; that in all things he might have the preeminence."

The two Beings in the God family first created the spirits [angels] and then they planned the physical creation together.

Then the one who became the Father commanded, as the Executive Authority; "Lets do this:" and the one who later became the son acted as the Implementing Authority, and with the help of the billions of angels which he had created; created the physical universe including the earth.

Of course all things were made by God. God first made the angels and then they, working at God's command and according to God's plan assisted God, but God was the Being who was the responsible authority.

Ford made a car, but it was his workers who put it together. When we say that Ford made the car we mean that Ford designed, planned, organized, financed, provided the workers and in every way was responsible for the car being made.

God made all things in that God designed, planned, organized, financed, provided the workers by creating them and in every way was responsible for the worlds being made.

God has angels who fight for him (Rev 12:7), angels who deliver messages to people from God (Dan 10), angels who pour out correction on the earth (Rev 15), and God even has angelic living transportation (Ezek 1); is it so hard to believe that God also had angels assisting him in creating physical things at God's command?

We know that the scripture refer to angels in the following verse, simply because **no man was present at the creation of the physical universe!**

> **Job 38:3** Gird up now thy loins like a man; for I will demand of thee, and answer thou me. **38:4** Where wast thou when **I laid the foundations of the earth**? declare, if thou hast understanding. **38:5** Who hath laid the measures thereof, if thou knowest? or who hath stretched the line upon it? **38:6** Whereupon are the foundations thereof fastened? or who laid the corner stone thereof; **38:7 When the morning stars** [created angels] **sang together, and all the sons of God** [by creation] **shouted for joy?**

The process of creating the physical universe began with the creation of the heavenly bodies which we see today, but that was only the beginning of the creation process for the universe. At that time the process of creating a perfect universe had not yet been completed or accomplished, it had only begun with the creation of the physical bodies in the heavens.

After the initial creation of matter and the physical planets, stars etc in space, the two God Beings came to the earth; which was also not a completed creation being without form and void.

The term "without form" referred to the fact that the earth was a round ball of water and had no earthly form of mountains, valleys, plains etc. The term "void" referred to a complete emptiness and lack of life.

No light did not mean no sun, for the star we call the sun had been created with the universe and the first existence of the earth, but the light of the sun did not reach the earth in the sense that the earth was not rotating so light could not reach the whole planet.

We see that that a God family of "Mighty Ones" created the spirits [amgels] BEFORE creating physical things; who together with the Mighty Ones in full control, created the present physical universe.

Then at some unknown time later, the God family of Elohim [Mighty Ones] came to a formless earth to accomplish the creation week and finish the creation of the earth and all life upon it.

Earth's destruction and re-creation

After making the rough creation of the universe, God perfected the earth FIRST, but then Satan rebelled taking one third of the angels with him and destroying the earth..

- There is no way to determine the age of anything on the earth accurately beyond a few hundred years.

- The creation of the universe has not yet been completed and the universe is NOT in the state of perfection that God plans, therefore God perfected the earth first.

- After having made the physical universe the work to perfect the earth came first, but at some point Satan rebelled destroying the earth. At this point the creation week of Genesis begins with the God family of Elohim [Mighty Ones] coming to the earth to re-create the planet.

While in the flesh the Son told us that he had already beheld the fall of Satan from heaven, long before he gave up his Godhood to be made flesh (Luke 10:18); that means that Lucifer had already rebelled and was cast down to the earth before the physical birth of Christ; it also implies that Christ existed before his physical birth.

This statement also reveals that Lucifer fell, BEFORE the Genesis creation week; since he was already in rebellion against God and tempting Eve to rebel against God in the garden.

> **Luke 10:18** And he said unto them, I beheld Satan as lightning fall from heaven.

Since Satan would have fought this fall, it also strongly indicates that we would find immense destruction in the area of the battle as is now clear in the state of the moon and various planets in this solar system.

> **2 Peter 2:4** For if God spared not the angels that sinned, but cast them down to hell [tartaros], and delivered them into chains of darkness, to be reserved unto judgment; Please note that "hell" is on the earth, and that the word Tartaros [often translated as the grave]

but actually **means a place of incarceration or restraint** which means that they were confined to the earth.

I accept the likelihood that the earth was completed by God and after existing for a time was then destroyed, and that the creation week story is about a second or re-creation of the earth. This **"Gap Theory"** is understood by many.

While Elohim [the family of Mighty Ones] came to the earth with the angels to accomplish the creation week, there is nothing to indicate that other events did not take place on the earth at some point between the creation of the physical universe and the creation week.

This issue of dinosaurs is not revealed in the Holy Scriptures and while we might speculate, we must not become closed minded on our pet explanation; and we must wait to ask Christ at his coming.

Genesis 1

Verse one speaks of the ultimate beginning [creation] of the physical universe.

Genesis 1:1 In the beginning [of the physical universe] God created the heaven and the earth.

Since the entire universe is in an unfinished state today, we can understand verse 1 as meaning only a rough first creation which needed to be polished off and completed.

> The word "was" indicates the condition at the time that God arrived on the earth, it says nothing about what had taken place before God arrived to begin the creation week, and it is entirely possible that things could have happened on this earth between its original initial creation and the beginning of the creation week!

In any case we know that the earth was created along with the universe; and that the earth either was or became formless and void, empty of life.

We cannot know the age of the earth or universe since there is NO scientific way to measure that age and God has not revealed it.

There is no scientific way to measure more than a few hundred years into the past; all so called dating methods are full of serious problems and are NOT scientific at all, even carbon dating has some serious assumptions built in and cannot be relied upon for more than a few hundred years; even tree rings are not reliable because they do not measure years at all, they measure wet and dry cycles of which there could be many in any given year.

Where do they get their billions of years from? They simply assume that it would take that long for their theories to work out; these billions of years are assumptions and NOT science!

Here is a little fact they close their eyes to: The sun is a great fire which like all fires, consumes its fuel; Even 50 million years ago the sun would be far larger and hotter than it now is; In fact the surface of the earth would have been hotter than Mercury is now, and neither Mercury or Venus could have existed and no life on earth have existed only 50 million years ago!

Neither the earth nor the universe are billions of years old; but they could be much older than a few thousand years.

Genesis 1:2 And the earth was [or possibly became] without form, and void; and darkness was upon the face of the deep. And the Spirit of God moved upon the face of the waters

The word "was" indicates the condition of the earth at the time that God arrived on the earth; it says nothing about what had taken place before God arrived to begin the creation week.

Now we come to the moment that God [Elohim; Mighty Ones] came to the earth to begin their re-creation week plan. A large amount of time may have gone into the planning and now God [the two members of Elohim] is ready to re-surface the earth and fill it with physical life.

So God [the two Elohim] come down to the surface of the earth and they found it covered with water.

The First Day

This verse need not suppose that the sun was created at that point; in reality it shows the light of an already existing sun being revealed on all the earth by setting the earth in rotation on its axis.

1:3 And God said, Let there be light: and there was light.

There was darkness and God caused the light to shine on the earth

The first day of creation week began when the light of the [already existing] sun was made to shine on ALL of the earth by setting the earth in rotation on its axis.

Once the earth began to rotate God called the lighted portion of the earth day and God called the dark portion of the earth the night. The earth being set in rotation to bring the present day and nght cycles over the entire planet.

1:4 And God saw the light, that it was good: and God divided the light from the darkness. **1:5** And **God called the light Day, and the darkness he called Night**. And **the evening and the morning were the first day.**

The term "evening" refers to sunset as the law reveals

> **Deuteronomy 23:11** But it shall be, **when evening** cometh on, he shall wash himself with water: and **when the sun is down**, he shall come into the camp again.

The Second Day

The KJV English word "firmament" came from the Late Latin firmamentum "support". The English word "firmament" is a mistranslation from the Hebrew word "raqiya."

The actual Hebrew noun is raqiya which is derived from the verb raqa, which means "to spread abroad, stamp out, or stretch."

The terminology of many other verses, such as Psalm 104:2 and Isaiah 40:22 speak of the stretching out of the heavens.

The Hebrew word used in these verses for heaven is shamayim (literally "heavens"); and in Genesis 1:8 God explicitly calls the firmament "heaven, (shamayim)" thus equating raqiya [expanse, stretching out] with shamayim [the heavens].

Since the stretched out nature of the shamayim [the heavens] is the intended meaning, the word "expanse" [instead of firmament] is the correct translation from the Hebrew.

Definitions:

> The Hebrew word "raqiya" mistranslated as "firmament" in the Vulgate and KJV in Genesdis means a vast space or expanse called a "shamayim" or heaven.
>
> 1. The first heaven "shamayim" is the space or vast expanse "raqiya" between the surface of the earth and the clouds above where the birds fly (Gen 1:6-8, 20).

2. The second heaven "shamayim" is the space or vast expanse "raqiya" in deep space where the stars have been placed (Dan 12:3, Psalm 19:1).
3. The third heaven "shamayim" is the place "raqiya" outside of the physical universe where God dwells (Rev 3:12, 16:17, 21:2-3).

In certain other places the word "raqiya" is properly translated as "firmament" meaning a solid platform (Ezek 1).

The Creator then ordered the creation of an atmosphere [expanse] between the surface waters and the clouds.

1:6 And God said, Let there be a firmament [an expanse or atmosphere between the surface waters and the clouds] in the midst of the waters, and let it divide the waters from the waters.

Then God made the atmospheric expanse or sky, between the surface of the earth and the clouds.

1:7 And God made the firmament [atmospheric expanse], and divided the waters which were under the firmament [the waters on the surface of the earth] from the waters which were above the firmament [the clouds]: and it was so.

There are three places called heaven in the scriptures; the place of God's throne, the expanse of space and the atmospheric expanse of the earth.

1:8 And God called the firmament [expanse] Heaven. And the evening and the morning were **the second day**.

The Third Day

Then God caused upthrusts to raise up land and also would have made openings in the sea bed to drain water lower, and dry land and surface features appeared on the earth. Unimaginably vast quantities of water would have drained rapidly from this land as it was lifted up from the sea.

1:9 And God said, Let the waters under the heaven be gathered together unto one place, and let the dry land appear: and it was so. **1:10** And God called the dry land Earth; and the gathering together of the waters called he Seas: and God saw that it was good.

Then on the third day the Implementing Creator, who later gave up his Godhood to become Jesus Christ; commanded billions of angels and all kinds of vegetation was created on the earth. Indeed many such kinds have gone extinct over the millennia; at creation the numbers of plants and animals was many times greater than today!

1:11 And God said, Let the earth bring forth grass, the herb yielding seed, and the fruit tree yielding fruit after his kind, whose seed is in itself, upon the earth: and it was so. **1:12** And the earth brought forth grass, and herb yielding seed after his kind, and the tree yielding fruit, whose seed was in itself, after his kind: and God saw that it was good. **1:13** And the evening and the morning were **the third day**.

The Fourth Day

The Creator then established the annual movement of the earth around the sun to measure years, and the monthly cycles of the moon to make months.

Here the Creator is not making the sun and moon as is commonly supposed; because God had already brought the light to ALL the earth by setting the earth in rotation on the first day; and the light on the earth comes from the sun which was made when the universe was created; before the first day of the creation week.

On the fourth day God set the orbit of the earth around the sun at 360 days to establish years, and the moon's orbit around the earth at 30 days to make months.

This cycle was later disrupted in the days of Hezekiah; please see "The Biblical Sabbath and Calendar" book.

1:14 And God said, Let there be lights in the firmament [expanse] of the heaven to divide [lights for the day and the night] the day from the night; and **let them be for signs, and for seasons** [the first light of the new moon was to be used to start months], **and for days** [days are included here because of Genesis 1:4-5, in that the sun's light and the periods of darkness due to the earths rotation constituted days], **and years: 1:15** And let them be for lights in the firmament [expanse] of the heaven to give light upon the earth: and it was so.

We know that the sun and moon already existed since God created the heavens and the earth BEFORE the first day of the creation week, therefore we know that the following refers to setting the bodies in motion and is not a reference to original creation.

1:16 And God made [Strong's 6213 to make, to attend to, to put in order] two great lights; the greater light to rule the day, and the lesser light to rule the night: he made the stars also.

1:17 And God set them [Lexicon 5414 appointed them, established them as signs of the days, months and seasons] in the firmament [expanse] of the heaven to give light upon the earth,

Remember that God gave the lights of the sun and moon to shine on ALL the earth on the first day by setting the earth in rotation on its axis; so this refers to God setting the earth's rotation around the sun, and the moon's rotation around the earth to establish years and months.

1:18 And to rule over the day and over the night, and to divide the light from the darkness: and God saw that it was good. **1:19** And the evening and the morning were **the fourth day**.

The Fifth Day

Salt and fresh water life and birds were created.

1:20 And God said, Let the waters bring forth abundantly the moving creature that hath life, and fowl that may fly above the earth in the open firmament of heaven. **1:21** And God created great whales, and every living creature that moveth, which the waters brought forth abundantly, after their kind, and every winged fowl after his kind: and God saw that it was good. **1:22** And God blessed them, saying, Be fruitful, and multiply, and fill the waters in the seas, and let fowl multiply in the earth. **1:23** And the evening and the morning were **the fifth day.**

The Sixth Day

All land creatures including mankind were created.

1:24 And God said, Let the earth bring forth the living creature after his kind, cattle, and creeping thing, and beast of the earth after his kind: and it was so. **1:25** And God made the beast of the earth after his kind, and cattle after their kind, and every thing that creepeth upon the earth after his kind: and God saw that it was good.

Then the two Elohim [Mighty Ones, plural] make physical mankind in their own image and likeness. Man looks like and is made in the same general shape of God but is only physical and not yet spirit.

Here it is revealed that TWO separate members of the God Family were involved in the creation; first the one who became the Father, and also the one who became the Son!

1:26 And God said, Let **us** make man in **our** image, after **our** likeness: and let them have dominion over the fish of the sea, and over the fowl of the air, and over the cattle, and over all the earth, and over every creeping thing that creepeth upon the earth.

Chapter 1 is a general overview of the establishment of the earth as a suitable habitat for physical life and the creation of physical life. On the sixth day God made both man and woman.

> In chapter two Moses goes back to begin the history of man by explaining the creation of man and woman in greater detail.

1:27 So God created man in his own image, in the image of God created he him; male and female created he them.

The Creator then gave man authority over the earth and commanded men to learn to rule [and replace Satan as ruler of the earth] by ruling the earth well.

1:28 And God blessed them, and God said unto them, Be fruitful, and multiply, and replenish the earth, and subdue it: and have dominion over the fish of the sea, and over the fowl of the air, and over every living thing that moveth upon the earth.

The Creator gave all physical life vegetation as their food at that time. For physical sin and death had not yet entered the world. We see then that God had intended that all creatures including humanity be vegetarian in diet. It was later when sin entered the world that God cursed the earth with killing.

> We know today that God could have changed the nature of creatures by changing their genetic structure, and that God can reverse this process to make all wild beasts tame and vegetation eaters once again when Christ comes.

1:29 And God said, Behold, I have **given you every herb bearing seed, which is upon the face of all the earth, and every tree, in the which is the fruit of a tree yielding seed; to you it shall be for meat** [food]. **1:30 And to every beast of the earth, and to every fowl of the air, and to every thing that creepeth upon the earth, wherein there is life, I have given every green herb for meat** [food]: **and it was so. 1:31** And God saw every thing that he had made, and, behold, it was very good. And the evening and the morning were **the sixth day.**

Genesis 2

Genesis 1 shows that the universe was created and fell into catastrophe and later God [Elohim the Mighty Ones] re-created the earth and made all physical living things in six days.

Genesis 2:1 Thus the heavens and the earth were finished, and all the host of them.

The Implementing Creator then rested from his activity of preparing the earth for man and making man; and he sanctified [Set Apart] the seventh day for man to rest from his physical activities and join with his Creator in learning spiritual things.

Here we see that the seventh day Sabbath was a memorial that God had created all things and was a time for Adam and all humanity to rest and take time out from physical activities to spend that time with God.

The Sabbath had nothing to do with being Jewish and was for Adam the father of all humanity and for ALL of his descendants! No man has any authority to change this perpetual memorial of the earthly physical creation, and the perpetual seventh day cycle of assembling with our Creator.

See our Ecclesiastical Authority book.

2:2 And on the seventh day God ended his work which he had made; and he rested on the seventh day from all his work which he had made. **2:3**

And God blessed the seventh day, and sanctified it: because that in it he had rested from all his work which God created and made.

The Sabbath Day

It was the Creator who later became Jesus Christ who made the Sabbath so that he might have a Set Aside Time to be with and teach his creation; mankind. The seventh day was sanctified [made holy] and was to be a time set aside for man to rest from physical activities and to learn of God in the presence of man's Creator.

Since Adam was the father of all humanity, and Judah did not even exist for several thousand years after creation; the seventh day Sabbath was created by the Creator Jesus Christ for Adam and ALL of Adam's descendants! For all of humanity!

This six days of physical creation followed by a weekly seventh day Sabbath is a memorial of the physical creation and the awesome power and greatness of the Implementing Creator who later gave up his God-hood to be made flesh as Jesus Christ. It is also a day to set aside physical pursuits to learn the ways of God and life eternal.

Later the Feast of Unleavened Bread was instituted to represent six days or six thousand years, of a SPIRITUAL creation.

A kind of first fruits of salvation were called out by God the Father to come to him through Messiah the Creator over six thousand years. Their resurrection would be followed by a seventh day High Holy Day Millennial Sabbath of rest in the presence of the Creator.

No man has any authority to change this perpetual memorial of the earthly physical creation, and this perpetual seventh day cycle of assembling with our Creator.

Since the biblical Sabbath is a weekly memorial remembering that God is, and what God has done; it must be observed on HIS commanded seventh day [Friday sunset to Saturday sunset] and NOT on any other day.

Genesis 2:2 And on the seventh day God ended his work which he had made; and he rested on the seventh day from all his work which he had made. **2:3** And God blessed the seventh day, and sanctified it [Set it apart for Holy Use]: because that in it he had rested from all his work which God created and made.

Thus was the history of creation explained by Moses:

First the creation of the universe Genesis 1:1; after this the earth was fashioned and then fell into disaster.

Then God [the two members of the God [Elohim] family] came to a water covered earth and re-created the earth, created physical living creatures and finally create the seventh day Sabbath as a memorial. to be a day of rest from all physical work; dedicated to assembling with God and learning of God and the way to life eternal.

The very Implementing Creator of all things, the one who gave up his God-hood to become flesh, Jesus Christ [Hebrew: Yeshua Mashiach]; also created the seventh day Sabbath! Therefore he could rightly claim that he was the Lord of the Sabbath!

> **Matthew 12:8** For the Son of man is Lord even of the sabbath day.

Jesus Christ on that occasion reminded us that the seventh day Sabbath was created for all mankind! The seventh day Sabbath was created for Adam and Eve and for ALL of their descendants at the first week of creation! The seventh day Sabbath was NOT made two thousand years after the creation, just for the Jews!

In saying that: **Mark 2:27** And he said unto them, The sabbath was made for man, and not man for the Sabbath: Jesus revealed that the Sabbath was made for all men at the Creation!

Which day is God's Sabbath? Why the very day that the Creator made the Sabbath by the majesty of his authority: The seventh day of the week which is sunset Friday to sunset Saturday!

How do we know this? Because in the flesh Jesus Christ the very Creator of the Weekly Sabbath, himself kept the seventh day Sabbath from Friday sunset to Saturday sunset, the same as the Jews of his day!

Some professing Christians actually reject the seventh day Sabbath that Jesus Christ created and himself kept, thinking that they honor Christ by disobeying him and observing the first day of the week Sunday instead of the day that Christ created and commanded his people to observe. This is rebellion against Jesus Christ.

What do the prophets say? In the millennium when Jesus Christ rules as King of kings; he will require ALL humanity to keep HIS seventh day Friday sunset to Saturday sunset Sabbath

> **Isaiah 66:23** And it shall come to pass, that **from one new moon to another, and from one sabbath to another, shall all flesh come to worship before me, saith the Lord.**

The very Creator of the universe and of humanity, also created the weekly Sabbath for Adam and Eve and ALL their descendants, ALL of humanity!

Then he commanded all flesh to rest from their labors and spend the seventh day Sabbath, from Friday Sunset to Saturday sunset; with God.

The seventh day Sabbath is a gift of love to all humanity so that we might have rest from our labors and a time to commune with God to learn of God and the way to life eternal in peace and harmony with God and with each other.

As the Implementing Creator of the entire universe this Being of incredible power and glory, who made man and all things; set aside the weekly seventh day Sabbath for man; and most men today reject this incredible opportunity to learn the way to eternal life.

This incredible being of glory and power, gave his seventh day Sabbath to be with us and teach us; He gave up his God-hood to be made flesh and to be placed in the womb of a woman to grow up and to be sacrificed to reconcile repentant humanity to God the Father! Crowning his immense power with humility and godly love!

It is to our immense shame that we are not zealous to keep his Word; which is for our good and brings eternal life!

The Sabbath was instituted by our Creator on the seventh day after the completion of six days of physical creative activity (Gen 2:2-3). The Sabbath was made for man (Mark 2:27) so that man could follow the example of his Creator and rest from his physical labors. It is not reasonable to think that God should need to rest, therefore he rested as an example for us.

It is lawful to do those things that God has commanded for us to do on the Sabbath, since God is also the maker of the Sabbath and can therefore tell us what he wants done on HIS Sabbath. For this reason the Priests may fulfill their God commanded duties on the weekly Sabbath.

Since the Sabbath was made for the good of man, we may also do acts of compassion and mercy. We are NOT to use the "emergencies" to justify and excuse habitual Sabbath breaking. We are not to travel on the Sabbath to the extent that it becomes a tiring labor, nor are we to burden others by buying gas, food, drink and lodgings on Sabbath. We are to use the Preparation Day to properly prepare for the Sabbath.

We are not to do any cooking on the Sabbath (Ex 16:22-24) nor to do our own thing nor to even think our own thoughts. We are to be totally dedicated to our God on his Holy Sabbath Day (Is 56 and Is 58).

We are to do no work at all on God's Holy Sabbath except for that which God himself commands to be done, and acts of mercy for the health of others; nor shall we be responsible for any others doing any work.

To pay others to serve us in a restaurant is no different than to pay others to work at any other service. To pay anyone else to do what we would not do ourselves is HYPOCRISY! We are to avoid all appearance of sin.

> **Exodus 20:10** But the seventh day is the sabbath of the LORD thy God: in it thou shalt not do any work, thou, nor thy son, nor thy daughter, thy manservant, nor thy maidservant, nor thy cattle, nor thy stranger that is within thy gates:

Cooking, Buying and Work on Sabbath and Holy Days

> **Exodus 12:15** And in the first day there shall be an holy convocation, and in the seventh day there shall be an holy convocation to you; no manner of work shall be done in them, **save that which every man must eat, that only may be done of you**.

This statement that food may be prepared during the Feast of Unleavened Bread has been used to justify for preparation on all subsequent and all other Holy Day Annual Sabbaths. Is that a valid assumption?

This verse actually refers to the very First Feast of Unleavened Bread: and its two High Holy Days when Israel was in the process of marching out of Egypt as God had commanded them . Allowing food to be prepared and eaten was due to that particular and very special arduous circumstance. Some extrapolate from this verse that food may also be prepared and eaten on all subsequent Feasts of Unleavened Bread and all other High Holy Days.

It is necessary to understand that this particular scripture is a history of Israel coming out of Egypt.

After that FIRST Passover all leftovers had been burned, there was no prepared food available. As a singular act of mercy, God permitted food to be prepared and eaten on this one exceptional emergency occasion. Nowhere else in all scripture is such a liberty [to prepare food on a Sabbath or High Day] mentioned. This is simply a record of a special allowance, an act of mercy; made for a special situation.

This one time act of mercy is an exception to the rule and does NOT justify breaking the commandments for the weekly Sabbath and annual High Day Sabbaths!

Brethren we have sinned against God and His weekly and annual Sabbaths! We must quickly repent and turn from this sin of using Holy Time for our own purposes and pleasures before we are corrected as physical Israel / Judah were corrected for the same sin!

The fact that the Passover was the preparation day for the first annual Sabbath of the Feast of Unleavened Bread on which it was well understood that no work including cooking was to be done, is made clear by the faithful who rushed to entomb Jesus BEFORE the High Day of Unleavened bread began at sunset that evening.

> **John 19:31** The Jews therefore, **because it was the preparation,** that the bodies should not remain upon the cross on the sabbath day, (for **that sabbath day was an high day,**) besought Pilate that their legs might be broken, and that they might be taken away.

The Weekly Sabbath and the Annual Holy Days are Holy Time. No work of any kind is to be done on them. That means no food preparation and cooking and no buying of food or drink.

Food and drink are to be prepared on the previous day which is the Preparation Day for the Weekly and Annual Sabbaths.

On the weekly and annual Sabbaths we are to do what God has specifically commanded for those days, in addition, acts of mercy are to be done and the days are to be observed by convoking with God as Adam and Eve did and by doing so with other like minded persons. The Sabbaths are God's time, not our time; and the Sabbaths are for our good to teach us the way to peace and life eternal

Genesis 1 shows that the universe was created and fell into catastrophe and later God [Elohim the Mighty Ones] re-created the earth and made all physical living things in six days.

Genesis 2:4 These are the generations of the heavens and of the earth when they were created, in the day that the LORD God made the earth and the heavens, **2:5** And every plant of the field before it was in the earth, and every herb of the field before it grew:

In the beginning of the new earth God watered the earth by means of evaporation and then condensing the vapor into dew on the land, and there was no rain with its rainbow until the days of Noah.

. . . for the LORD God had not caused it to rain upon the earth, and there was not a man to till the ground. **2:6** But there went up **a mist from the earth, and watered the whole face of the ground.**

Moses now goes back to the sixth day to explain in more detail the creation of the man and woman and to begin the history of mankind.

The breath of life was the air and also the spirit in man which is neutral. Man is born knowing nothing until he learns to do good from evil by good or evil influences. And without God's Spirit and having only the spirit of man, humanity cannot resist the spirit of evil from Satan.

Therefore the man and woman were of a neutral spirit until Satan came along and enticed them to turn away from trusting and obeying the Creator.

2:7 And the LORD God formed man of the dust of the ground, and breathed into his nostrils the breath of life; and man became a living soul.

When he made the man, God planted a wondrous garden for him; which was an allegory of the paradise that humanity could have if they only obeyed God. Revelation 22 is the real thing that the Garden in Eden was meant to picture.

2:8 And the LORD God planted a garden eastward in Eden; and there he put the man whom he had formed. **2:9** And out of the ground made the LORD God to grow every tree that is pleasant to the sight, and good for food; the tree of life also in the midst of the garden, and the tree of knowledge of good and evil.

One river of water went out of Paradise and then split into four parts to water the earth. It is quite possible that the legends are correct and that in the world before the flood of Noah there was only one large continent. In future a river of life will flow out of the millennial throne of God in the new physical Temple in Jerusalem! This river will be restored when God the Father comes down to live with men on a new earth (Rev 21:1).

This river of the water of life represents the Holy Spirit and the whole Word of God which is life eternal for those who keep it.

> **John 4:14** Jesus answered and said unto her, Whosoever drinketh of this water shall thirst again: but whosoever drinketh of the water that

I shall give him shall never thirst; but the water that I shall give him shall be in him a well of water springing up into everlasting life.

John 7:37 In the last day, that great day of the feast, Jesus stood and cried, saying, If any man thirst, let him come unto me, and drink. **7:38** He that believeth on me, as the scripture hath said, out of his belly shall flow rivers of living water. **7:39** (But this **spake he of the Spirit**, which they that believe on him should receive: for the Holy Ghost was not yet given; because that Jesus was not yet glorified.)

Revelation 22:1 And he shewed me a **pure river of water of life,** clear as crystal, proceeding out of the throne of God and of the Lamb.

Revelation 22:17 And the Spirit and the bride say, Come. And let him that heareth say, Come. And let him that is athirst come. And whosoever will, let him take **the water of life** freely.

This river of water that was in Eden was divided into four parts and went out to water the whole earth before the flood of Noah; picturing the great river of living water that will also water the whole earth when God the Father comes; and this physical water is symbolic of the Holy Spirit and the whole Word of God. Since only one river divided into four parts watered the whole earth, the earth must have consisted of one land mass.

Genesis 2:10 And a river went out of Eden to water the garden; and from thence it was parted, and became into four heads.

The four rivers named

2:11 The name of the first is Pison: that is it which compasseth the whole land of Havilah, where there is gold; **2:12** And the gold of that land is good: there is bdellium and the onyx stone.

2:13 And the name of the second river is Gihon: the same is it that compasseth the whole land of Ethiopia.

2:14 And the name of the third river is Hiddekel: that is it which goeth toward the east of Assyria.

And the fourth river is Euphrates

The man was placed in Eden and told to care for it. Thus the lordship of man was coupled with responsibility.

2:15 And the LORD God took the man, and put him into the garden of Eden to dress it and to keep it.

The tree of the knowledge of good and evil represented deciding for ourselves what is right and wrong, instead of living by every Word of God.

This tree may have been any tree and its fruit physically may well have been good; but the command not to eat of this tree was a TEST to see if the man would obey God in all things or follow his own desires.

Today we are also failing this same TEST by standing on the traditions of men and deciding according to our own thoughts, instead of being zealous to live by every Word of God.

2:16 And the LORD God commanded the man, saying, Of every tree of the garden thou mayest freely eat: **2:17** But of the tree of the knowledge of good and evil, thou shalt not eat of it: for in the day that thou eatest thereof thou shalt surely die.

God had made man incomplete, to need woman; and we now come to the details of the creation of the woman. This is all still part of the in depth explanation of the sixth day.

2:18 And the LORD God said, It is not good that the man should be alone; I will make him an help meet for him.

Previously in creation week God had made every bird and beast, and after making man out of the same earth; God presented these creatures to the man on the sixth day and the man was permitted to name them.

2:19 And out of the ground the LORD God formed every beast of the field, and every fowl of the air; and brought them unto Adam to see what he would call them: and whatsoever Adam called every living creature, that was the name thereof. **2:20** And Adam gave names to all cattle, and to the fowl of the air, and to every beast of the field; but for Adam there was not found an help meet for him.

The world's first surgery. If you have a rib removed today will your children have fewer ribs? Of course not! Because a rib was removed from Adam does not mean that his descendants would have fewer ribs.

2:21 And the LORD God caused a deep sleep to fall upon Adam, and he slept: and he took one of his ribs, and closed up the flesh instead thereof; **2:22** And the rib, which the LORD God had taken from man, made he a woman, and brought her unto the man. **2:23** And Adam said, This is now bone of my bones, and flesh of my flesh: she shall be called Woman, because she was taken out of Man.

Woman was made from the flesh and DNA of man; all that was needed was for God to make a slight change in the DNA of Adam's rib to make woman, by adding the X chromosome to the existing human genetic material.

Remember that God had already made all other animals male and female! God, who had created man, understood the things which man is now only beginning to understand. It was the Creator's intention that one man join with one woman to become one couple as long as they live.

> **Matthew 10:3** The Pharisees also came unto him, tempting him, and saying unto him, Is it lawful for a man to put away his wife for every cause?
>
> **10:4** And he answered and said unto them, Have ye not read, that he which made them at the beginning made them male and female, **10:5** And said, For this cause shall a man leave father and mother, and shall cleave to his wife: and they twain shall be one flesh? **10:6** Wherefore they are no more twain, but one flesh. What therefore God hath joined together, let not man put asunder.
>
> **10:7** They say unto him, Why did Moses then command to give a writing of divorcement, and to put her away?
>
> **10:8** He saith unto them, Moses because of the hardness of your hearts suffered you to put away your wives: but from the beginning it was not so. **10:9** And I say unto you, Whosoever shall put away his wife, except it be for fornication, and shall marry another, committeth adultery: and whoso marrieth her which is put away doth commit adultery.

Genesis 2:24 Therefore shall a man leave his father and his mother, and shall cleave unto his wife: and they shall be one flesh.

There is absolutely nothing wrong with being naked with one's spouse, and sex was created by God to make two into one; therefore sex between married couples is Very Good, completely godly, and absolutely nothing to be ashamed of. Married couples should take full advantage of this blessing and consolation from all our sorrows in this life without any sense of guilt.

People should not be naked before third parties including their own children.

2:25 And they were both naked, the man and his wife, and were not ashamed.

Genesis 3

In Genesis 3 God gave a command in order to test the man and the woman to see if they would be faithful to their Maker or if they would follow another or decide right and wrong for themselves.

Satan the Adversary of God appears on the scene and begins to entice the woman by bringing up the subject of the forbidden fruit.

The term translated "serpent" is from the word "hiss" H 5172, considered to be the flying serpent dragon or Satan from other scriptures. Satan was referred to as a dragon [flying serpent" in Rev 12:3-17, Rev 13:2 and 13:4, Rev 16:13, Rev 20:2].

This was not a literal physical serpent, it was Satan the spirit cherub being described in terms of a serpent.

This description "serpent" does not refer to any physical snake. It referred to the spirit being Satan who because of his appearance was worshiped as the winged serpent Quetzalcoatl in Latin America and a dragon in the orient where he is considered a good luck [good fortune] bringer.

Satan begins to entice the woman by bringing up the subject of the forbidden fruit.

Notice very carefully here, God did not say that the fruit would kill; he said that the act of eating the fruit would kill: for the wages of sin [living contrary to the way that brings life] is death. The nature of this fruit had nothing to do with the issue which issue is: Will we zealously live by every Word of God or will we decide for ourselves as to what we regard as good and evil? Please read our book on Ecclesiastical Authority.

Any departure, watering down, or compromising with any part of the whole Word of God is sin and brings the end result of death. Whether it is eating a fruit or some meat that God has forbidden to eat, or idolizing the words of men above the Word of God to follow men and turn away from any zeal to live by every Word of God.

The woman and the man lost their zeal for keeping and obeying the Word of God; just like we have done today! They decided right and wrong for themselves instead of obeying the Word of God! Just like the latter day Ekklesia, who reject much of the Word of God to remain faithful to their idols of men and false traditions! The very same TEST and the very same failure has come to many of those who call themselves the people of God today!

Since that day in Eden, mankind has rejected living by the Word of God for millennia. The "wisdom" of man has destroyed the planet and brought endless bloodshed, pain and misery on humanity and all other creatures.

WE NEED GOD! Like any young child needs its parents!

Like a little child we may think that we are able, but we simply lack the experience, the wisdom, and the ability; to take care of ourselves and this good earth which God has given to us.

WE NEED A FATHER to lead and guide us and teach us how to live and get along with each other.

Eve and Adam thought that they could decide things for themselves and so rejected their Father Creator.

All history since then has been a bloody and graphic demonstration of how wrong they were. Mankind cannot find the way to peace or life eternal.

We cannot discern between right and wrong on our own, we need HELP, we need someone to show us the way. Only when all peoples realize this and are ready to humble themselves before their Creator will they begin to follow His instructions leading to peace.

Any departure from what God has commanded us is a rejection of the wisdom of God

Eating a fruit that God forbade him to eat, was not simply about the fruit itself; it was about rejecting obedience to God by not doing what God had said.

In the garden Eve and then Adam turned away from obeying their Creator to decide right and wrong for themselves, rejecting the Word of their LORD!

Ever since that time the vast majority have rejected the Word of God to remain faithful to their idols of men and their false, contrary to scripture traditions!

Genesis 3:1 Now the serpent [Satan] was more subtil than any beast of the field which the LORD God had made. And he said unto the woman, Yea, hath God said, Ye shall not eat of every tree of the garden? **3:2** And the woman said unto the serpent, We may eat of the fruit of the trees of the garden: **3:3** But of the fruit of the tree which is in the midst of the garden, God hath said, Ye shall not eat of it, neither shall ye touch it, lest ye die.

Satan told the woman that she would not die if she rejected the Word of God to decide right and wrong for herself!

This is the same lie being told to the brethren by Satan through their leaders today! They say: "God doesn't mind if we are lax for his Word and zealous for our own ways! We are God's people and whatever we do, must be right, because God left us in charge. Obey us and do not question us by God's Word for we are leaders in place of God, between God and the brethren."

Taking advantage of the fact that death would not be immediate Satan told the lie that in deciding for ourselves we would not die. He added that we would be like God [exalt ourselves as equals with God] if we decided right from wrong for ourselves instead of letting God decide right from wrong for us.

3:4 And the serpent said unto the woman, Ye shall not surely die: **3:5** For God doth know that in the day ye eat thereof, then your eyes shall be opened, and ye shall be as gods, knowing good and evil.

Deciding for ourselves always looks good to those who have no love to live by every Word of God. We love self more than we love God, and because of this self- love and self-exaltation and pride; we are led away from our zeal to live by every Word of God just as Eve and Adam were.

3:6 And when the woman saw that the tree was good for food, and that it was pleasant to the eyes, and a tree to be desired to make one wise, she took of the fruit thereof, and did eat, and gave also unto her husband with her; and he did eat.

The following is literal and is also figurative, for they knew that they had disobeyed their Maker and were physically and spiritually naked; devoid and empty of the righteousness of obeying God; just like today's Laodicean Ekklesia which is spiritually wretched and naked. Without the righteousness of God because of exalting their own ways above the Word of God: Instead of running to God in sincere repentance they tried to cover up for themselves.

Eve and Adam were not ashamed of seeing each other: They were already one flesh and "knew" one another fully.

Adam and Eve were afraid of being seen by God, for they knew that they had sinned and disobeyed him. They were moved by fear and shame to try and hide their physical and spiritual nakedness by making clothing and hiding from God in the bush.

3:7 And the eyes of them both were opened, and they knew that they were naked; and they sewed fig leaves together, and made themselves aprons.

The Creator came to see his creation; and they hid from him because their sin had separated them from God. They had rebelled and decided for themselves what would be right or wrong in their own eyes; instead of obeying their Creator.

Consider when we were all little children; did most of us not at some time or other, do something that we knew our parents had forbidden or taught us was wrong? Were we not ashamed and afraid that our parents would find out and correct us?

Adam and Eve, although fully physically developed were full of that same fear and shame because they knew that they had acted against the Word of their Creator.

Today we who claim that we have God's Spirit should be full of fear and shame also, because of our departure to follow idols of men and false traditions, instead of being passionately zealous to live by every Word of God.

3:8 And they heard the voice of the LORD God walking in the garden in the cool of the day: and Adam and his wife hid themselves from the presence of the LORD God amongst the trees of the garden.

Adam knew that he was naked of faithfulness to keep the Word of God and that he did not have on the garments of the righteousness of the whole Word of God. He feared the anger of his Creator for his sin.

It would be well with us if we also understood our sin and feared our God, turning to sincere repentance instead of justifying ourselves.

3:9 And the LORD God called unto Adam, and said unto him, Where art thou? **3:10** And he said, I heard thy voice in the garden, and I was afraid, because I was naked; and I hid myself.

Such is human nature. Adam blamed his wife instead of taking responsibility for his own actions. This is partly why man was given authority over woman; so that he would be forced to take responsibility for his own actions.

Friends, the authority of the husband over his wife is 90% about being responsible for his own conduct! Each husband is going to have to answer God for his own conduct, no matter what his wife or anyone else says.

The same is true in the Ekklesia; there are very many out there who feel safe in justifying themselves by blaming the organization or its elders for their own sins like Adam did with Eve. "I was only following the minister" they will say.

Brethren, this Nazi excuse that we were only following others; WILL NOT WORK WITH Almighty God! Each and every human being is completely responsible for their OWN conduct; regardless of what others may say or do.

It did not work for Adam and it will not work for anyone else: We shall each be accepted into or denied the paradise of eternal life based on our OWN personal conduct.

> **Revelation 20:12** And I saw the dead, small and great, stand before God; and the books were opened: and another book was opened, which is the book of life: and **the dead were judged out of those things which were written in the books, according to their works. 20:13** And the sea gave up the dead which were in it; and death and hell delivered up the dead which were in them: and they were judged every man **according to their works.**

Adam admitted that he had sinned and disobeyed God and then he blamed someone else for his actions.

Genesis 3:11 And he said, Who told thee that thou wast naked? Hast thou eaten of the tree, whereof I commanded thee that thou shouldest not eat? **3:12** And the man said, The woman whom thou gavest to be with me, she gave me of the tree, and I did eat.

Eve admitted that she had sinned and disobeyed God and then blamed Satan; yes Satan had tempted her but she believed him above believing God and she disobeyed God. Both the woman and the man were personally responsible for listening to the temptation and deciding for themselves to disobey the Word of God.

So it is today as the Ekklesia falls to the temptation to be zealous for idols of men; and turns away from zealous obedience to the whole Word of God!

3:13 And the LORD God said unto the woman, What is this that thou hast done? And the woman said, The serpent beguiled me, and I did eat.

Every person is responsible for their own conduct, yet there is a very heavy responsibility of guilt for the original deceiver as well. Because of this sin, Satan was cursed and our elders and leaders who teach men to follow themselves and not to be zealous to live by every Word of God are facing a most severe correction.

Because they use their office to deceive and have not fulfilled their responsibility to teach zeal to live by every Word of God; they will be rejected from being shepherds of God's flock and prevented from the gift of eternal life, unless they quickly repent (Hos 4:6, Ezek 34, Jer 25, Isaiah 56:11).

3:14 And the LORD God said unto the serpent, Because thou hast done this, thou art cursed above all cattle, and above every beast of the field; upon thy belly shalt thou go, and dust shalt thou eat all the days of thy life:

The spirit cherub [serpent, dragon] Satan, shall bruise a man [Christ] and then he will ultimately be destroyed by the Son of a woman even the resurrected Jesus Christ.

3:15 And I will put enmity between thee and the woman, and between thy seed and her seed; it [Jesus Christ] shall bruise [crush] thy head [permanent destruction], and thou shalt bruise his heel [temporary death for three days and three nights].

Because of her sin the woman was given the monthly cycle and pain in childbirth which no animal has, and Christ here sets the man to rule [to learn to rule responsibly and lovingly] over his wife.

3:16 Unto the woman he said, I will greatly multiply thy sorrow and thy conception; in sorrow thou shalt bring forth children; and **thy desire shall be to thy husband, and he shall rule over thee**.

Adam is judged for listening to the woman and not listening to and keeping the Word of God, for letting himself be led into sin instead of leading in godliness; and we shall all be judged for listening to anyone other than our Mighty God!

3:17 And unto Adam he said, Because thou hast hearkened unto the voice of thy wife [and followed her into sin], and hast eaten of the tree, of which I commanded thee, saying, Thou shalt not eat of it:

The man and woman were then cast out of paradise and made to struggle against all manner of adversity, so that they might learn through many sorrows that our own ways apart from God are not good.

Adam and his descendants are being forced to see the difference between godliness, which brings life,peace and paradise and deciding for themselves what is right and wrong, which brings all manner of adversity, decay and finally death.

. . . cursed is the ground for thy sake; in sorrow shalt thou eat of it all the days of thy life; **3:18** Thorns also and thistles shall it bring forth to thee; and thou shalt eat the herb of the field; **3:19** In the sweat of thy face shalt thou eat bread, till thou return unto the ground; for out of it wast thou taken: for dust thou art, and unto dust shalt thou return.

3:20 And Adam called his wife's name Eve; because she was the mother of all living.

Then because of the sins of the woman and man death entered the world and the necessity of a sacrifice came into existence.

The Creator then made cloaks of skins for the man and woman; which skins are examples of the fact that death had entered the world and that their sincerely repented sins might be covered by the sacrifice of Christ, as represented by the sacrifice of animals.

In the beginning all creatures including humans were to eat only vegetation but from that time forth, death reigned in the world and men were to sacrifice clean animals for sin: and the offerer's of sacrifices must partake

[eat] the sacrifices; the sacrificial animals picturing the sacrifice of the Lamb of God for sin and the partaking, picturing the internalizing of the nature and Spirit of God.

3:21 Unto Adam also and to his wife did the LORD God make coats of skins, and clothed them.

Satan said that man could become God, simply by deciding right and wrong for himself. And while man could be the decider for himself just as God decides things; mankind living that way could not have eternal life! Only faithful passionate obedience to the way of life that God has ordained can bring eternal life.

Because the man would now decide what was wrong and right for himself, instead of listening to the words of eternal life; the man was rejected from eternal life and the paradise of God. The Creator denied man eternal life as long as man decided for himself what was right and wrong.

As Adam rejected the Word of God to decide for himself; today's spiritual Ekklesia rejects any zeal to live by every Word of God, in order to live by their own ways and false traditions.

Just as Adam was rejected from eternal life and eternity with God; so the unrepentant who have rejected zeal to passionately keep the whole Word of God, shall also be kept from entering the Promised Land of eternal life.

3:22 And the LORD God said, Behold, the man is become as one of us, to know [to decide for himself] good and evil: and now, lest he put forth his hand, and take also of the tree of life, and eat, and live for ever: **3:23** Therefore the LORD God sent him forth from the garden of Eden, to till the ground from whence he was taken.

The way into eternal life and the eternal paradise of God has been shut up and closed by the command of God; except for those specifically called out by God the Father.

3:24 So he drove out the man; and he placed at the east of the garden of Eden Cherubims, and a flaming sword which turned every way, to keep the way of the tree of life.

The Tree of Life

In Genesis 3 two trees are described. The first tree was the Tree of the Knowledge of Good and Evil and it was forbidden to the man and woman.

This tree was symbolic of deciding right and wrong for ourselves and the command forbidding eating from this tree was a test command to see if the man and woman would obey God or decide right and wrong for themselves.

Disobeying God in eating from this tree [or in anything else] represents and consists of deciding for ourselves what us right and wrong instead of living by every Word of God; and the ultimate fruits of this tree is death.

To decide for ourselves to act and live contrary to what God has commanded, is to exalt ourselves above the Word of God and the end of this decision is death. Therefore this tree could also be called the Tree of Death.

A second tree, the Tree of Life, was the exact opposite of this symbolic tree of death. The Tree of Life brought LIFE; just as rejecting obedience to God and taking of the forbidden fruit brought death.

The river of water of life coming out from the throne of God is a picture of the Holy Spirit of life eternal flowing out from God.

> **Revelation 22:1** And he shewed me a pure river of **water of life**, clear as crystal, proceeding out of the throne of God and of the Lamb.

The tree of life nourished by the water was a type of eternal life coming from the waters of the Holy Spirit.

> **22:2** In the **midst of the street** [growing up out of the river and overspreading to both sides is the tree of eternal life] of it, and on either side of the river, was there the tree of life, which bare twelve manner of fruits [figurative of the fruits of the Holy Spirit], and yielded her fruit every month [the trees bore a new kind of fruit each month]: and the leaves of the tree were for the [spiritual] healing of the nations.

A natural tree has a trunk which here is used to represent Jesus Christ and branches representing the faithful who are in Christ. It would also have leaves which turn the light of the sun into energy giving strength and life to the whole tree. The leaves would therefore represent the Holy Spirit which takes in the LIGHT [every Word of God] of God and turns it into spiritual energy, pouring spiritual health and life through the branches and producing the fruits of the Holy Spirit and healing the nations.

There are twelve Fruits of the Spirit: Love, Joy, Peace, Longsuffering, Gentleness, Goodness, Faith, Meekness, Temperance (Gal 5:22), a Sound Mind which is the ability to absorb and retain the nature of God as defined by the whole Word of God (2 Ti 1:7), Wisdom which is the correct application of God's Word and Eternal Life.

22:3 And there shall be no more curse [sin or the decay and death that sin brings]: but the throne of God and of the Lamb shall be in it; and his servants shall serve him:

22:4 And they [the people now changed to spirit] shall see his face; and his name shall be in their foreheads [the nature of God will dwell in the minds of all people who are changed to spirit; absolutely no sin allowed].

The Wages of Sin

Romans 6:23 For the wages of sin is death; but the gift of God is eternal life through Jesus Christ our Lord.

What is this sin that brings death?

1 John 3:3 Whosoever committeth sin transgresseth also the law: for sin is the transgression of the law.

What is this law which brings long life then? It is it not the Ten Commandments of God? and what do the Ten Commandments say?

Exodus 20:12 Honour thy father and thy mother: that thy days may be long upon the land which the Lord thy God giveth thee.

Who then is our father? Ultimately our Father is our Creator; first God the Father as the Executive Authority of the creation and then Jesus Christ as the Implementing Authority of the creation. The one who became Jesus Christ called God in heaven his Father and commanded us to live by every Word of that God the Father.

Matthew 4:4 But he answered and said, It is written, **Man shall not live by bread alone, but by every word that proceedeth out of the mouth of God.**

Matthew 4:10 Then saith Jesus unto him, Get thee hence, Satan: for it is written, **Thou shalt worship the Lord thy God, and him only shalt thou serve.**

Deciding right and wrong for ourselves as Eve and Adam did when they failed the test in the garden, is sin and brings death. While diligently living by EVERY WORD of God is life eternal!

Therefore as the fruit or end result of partaking of the Tree of the Knowledge of Good and Evil by rejecting God's Word for our own ways is death. Living by EVERY WORD of GOD brings life eternal.

Satan said that man could become God, simply by deciding right and wrong for himself. And while man could be the decider for himself as God decides things; man living by his own ways could not have eternal life! Only faithful passionate obedience to the way of life that God had and that man outside of God cannot have, can bring eternal life.

Because the man would now decide what was wrong and right for himself, instead of listening to the words of eternal life; the man was rejected from eternal life and the paradise of God. The Creator denied man eternal life as long as man decided for himself what was right and wrong.

As Adam rejected the Word of God to decide for himself; today the Ekklesia reject any zeal to live by every Word of God in order to live by their own ways and false traditions. As Adam was rejected from eternal life and eternity with God; so the unrepentant who have rejected zeal to passionately live by every Word of God, shall also be kept from entering the Promised Land of eternal life.

> **Psalm 3:22** And the LORD God said, Behold, the man is become as one of us, to know [to decide for himself] good and evil: and now, lest he put forth his hand, and take also of the tree of life, and eat, and live for ever: **3:23** Therefore the LORD God sent him forth from the garden of Eden, to till the ground from whence he was taken.

The way into eternal life and the eternal paradise of God has been shut up and closed and man has been cut off from God by the command of God; except for those specifically called out by God the Father as a kind of early first fruits to God.

Man was cut off from repentance and from turning back to obey God, so that man could learn a lesson through experience, that the way of God is the way of life and that any other way brings death.

This cutting off of mankind from God was essential to prevent the man from repenting and after being changed to spirit with eternal life, sinning again in future. The whole purpose of cutting man off from God was to allow man to live by his own ways until he had thoroughly learned that there is no other way to eternal life in peace other than the way of God.

God cut man off from himself, or rather it was the sins of man that cut man off from God

> **Isaiah 59:1** Behold, the Lord's hand is not shortened, that it cannot save; neither his ear heavy, that it cannot hear:**59:2** But your iniquities have separated between you and your God, and your sins have hid his face from you, that he will not hear.

When mankind was cut off from the Tree of Life and rejected from the presence of God, God's plan for salvation started up. That plan was for the Implementing Creator Jesus Christ to give up his God-hood and be made flesh and to live a perfect sinless life at the end of which he would give his life as the sacrificial Lamb of God for humanity, so that he could be a DOOR through which man could be reconciled to God the Father.

We are to live by EVERY WORD of GOD the Father, which is eternal life; but the door to reconciliation to God the Father is our sincere repentance after thoroughly learning that God is the ONLY way to life; a commitment to go and sin no more and to live by every Word of God from henceforth and forever more; and then the Door of Reconciliation which is the sacrifice of the Lamb of God will be applied to us and we shall be reconciled to God our Father in Heaven receiving the gift of the Holy Spirit, and if we continue and overcome we shall inherit the gift of eternal life.

From Adam to the ascension of Christ on Wave Offering Sunday in 31 A.D., mankind was cut off from God except for a very few called out in faith that Christ would fulfill his mission; and from 31 A.D. to today mankind has been cut off from God except that more have also been called out to have faith in the efficacy of that sacrifice and to live by every Word of God; this is the early Spring Harvest to eternal life. The Fall Festivals picture another harvest, the main of all humanity who has lived through the past being cut off from God and from the tree of Life.

> **John 10:9 I am the door: by me if any man enter in, he shall be saved**, and shall go in and out, and find pasture.

> **John 5:11** And this is the record, that God hath given to us [those faithful to live by every Word of God] **eternal life, and this life is**

> in his Son. **5:12 He that hath the Son hath life; and he that hath not the Son of God hath not life.**

The bread of manna was another allegory of the true Bread of Life, Jesus Christ; who came down from heaven to give himself as our Bread of Life, for our salvation.

Salvation is not just saying "I repent" and consenting to being dunked in a pool of water, or attending some organizational meetings, while continuing in sin.

Salvation requires the internalization of the nature of God; through diligent study, and the practical application of the whole Word of God in our own minds and in all our deeds! It i s essential for us to OVERCOME and to "Go and sin no more," and for us to live as Christ lived!

> **John 6:47** Verily, verily, I say unto you, He that believeth on me [and lives as Christ lives] hath everlasting life.

Jesus Christ being ONE in full unity with God the Father, was sent by the Father as the Bread of Life, for all God the Father would call.

Carefully consider these words given just before Passover and Unleavened Bread.

6:48 I am that bread of life. 6:49 Your fathers did eat manna in the wilderness, and are dead. 6:50 This is the bread which cometh down from heaven, that a man may eat thereof, and not die. 6:51 I am the living bread which came down from heaven: if any man eat of this bread, he shall live for ever: and the bread that I will give is my flesh, which I will give for the life of the world.

Jesus explains what the wine and unleavened bread of Passover and the Feast of Unleavened Bread mean.

> **6:52** The Jews therefore strove among themselves, saying, How can this man give us his flesh to eat? **6:53** Then Jesus said unto them, Verily, verily, I say unto you, Except ye eat the flesh of the Son of man, and drink his blood, ye have no life in you.
>
> **6:54** Whoso eateth my flesh, and drinketh my blood, hath eternal life; and I will raise him up at the last day. **6:55** For my flesh is meat indeed, and my blood is drink indeed. **6:56** He that eateth my flesh, and drinketh my blood, dwelleth in me, and I in him.

We are to take the nature of Christ into ourselves and we are to live as Christ lived; We are to live by God the Father's Word as Jesus did!

6:57 As the living Father hath sent me, and **I live by the Father**: so he that eateth me, even he shall live by me. **6:58** This is that bread which came down from heaven: not as your fathers did eat manna, and are dead: he that eateth of this bread shall live for ever.

6:59 These things said he in the synagogue, as he taught in Capernaum.

John 14:6 Jesus saith unto him, I am the way, the truth, and the life: no man cometh unto the Father, but by me.

John 17:3 And **this is life eternal, that they might know** [be one with] **thee the only true God, and Jesus Christ, whom thou hast sent.**

Jesus used the example of a tree, like the example of the Tree of Life [which is to live by EVERY WORD of God] to teach that HE is the way to God the Father and to eternal life.

Genesis 4

Cain was the firstborn of humanity.

Genesis 4:1 And Adam knew Eve his wife; and she conceived, and bare Cain, and said, I have gotten a man from the LORD.

Other daughters and sons were also born but Cain and Abel are specifically mentioned for this story. Tradition has it that Eve bore 56 children over several hundred years.

4:2 And she again bare his brother Abel. And Abel was a keeper of sheep, but Cain was a tiller of the ground.

Over time Cain and Abel each brought offerings to the Creator. This strongly implies that Christ had not left them alone but continued to teach them of God's ways as the Father's High Priest called Melchisedec, and that the sacrifice of clean animal sacrifices and the subject of salvation by sacrifice and sincere repentance was being taught.

It is also evident that the nature of the desired sacrifice was known, otherwise Cain's sacrifice would not have been rejected; further this clearly implies that the law of clean and unclean had been put into play, otherwise the nature of an acceptable sacrifice would be unknown, and Cain's sacrifice would not have been rejected.

The sacrifice of a lamb which represented the Creator himself as the true Lamb of God was accepted; but the offering of the produce of the earth, which represented earthy carnal things was not accepted.

This incident again illustrates that we must follow the whole Word of God to be covered by the application of the sacrifice of Christ, the Lamb of God; to be reconciled to God the Father in heaven; and that doing what we decide for ourselves is right is not acceptable to God.

At Sinai a fuller sacrificial system was commanded by God, but its beginnings came when sin came into the world.

4:3 And in process of time it came to pass, that Cain brought of the fruit of the ground an offering unto the LORD. **4:4** And Abel, he also brought of the firstlings of his flock and of the fat thereof. And the LORD had respect unto Abel and to his offering:

> **Hebrews 11:4** By faith Abel offered unto God a more excellent sacrifice than Cain, by which he obtained witness that he was righteous, God testifying of his gifts: and by it he being dead yet speaketh. [His example of faithful obedience was recorded for us.]

Genesis 4:5 But unto Cain and to his offering he had not respect

Cain was very angry because what he had decided for himself was NOT acceptable to God; and Christ explained to him that if he did right according to the Word of God he would also be accepted.

. . . And Cain was very wroth, and his countenance fell.

4:6 And the LORD said unto Cain, Why art thou wroth? and why is thy countenance fallen? **4:7** If thou doest well [keeps the whole Word of God], shalt thou not be accepted?

If we do well and are zealous to learn and to live by every Word of God, we are acceptable to God; but if we decide for ourselves what is right or wrong, sin rules over us.

and if thou doest not well [if we decide for ourselves what is right, instead of keeping the Word of God; it is sin], sin lieth at the door. And unto thee shall be his [sin's] desire, and thou [properly IT] shalt rule over him [sin will rule over us].

> **Romans 6:16** Know ye not, that to whom ye yield yourselves servants to obey, his servants ye are to whom ye obey; whether of sin unto death, or of obedience unto righteousness?

> **John 8:34** Jesus answered them, Verily, verily, I say unto you, Whosoever committeth sin is the servant of sin.

Cain was jealous of Abel because he was accepted by God, and Cain was convicted of his sin of doing what he wanted instead of what God had commanded; but instead of repenting he persecuted and killed his righteous brother. In the same way, many today are convicted of their sins by the faithful example of the zealous and turn to persecute the godly.

Genesis 4:8 And Cain talked with Abel his brother: and it came to pass, when they were in the field, that Cain rose up against Abel his brother, and slew him.

Christ then cursed Cain for his shedding of the blood of the innocent.

4:9 And the LORD said unto Cain, Where is Abel thy brother? And he said, I know not: Am I my brother's keeper? **4:10** And he said, What hast thou done? the voice of thy brother's blood crieth unto me from the ground.

Does this mean literally that the blood cried out? No, it is a figure of speech that the evidence of the blood makes the crime known. Then Jesus Christ judged Cain and cursed him so that the land would not yield its increase for him and he become a nomad, a wanderer, vagabond and fugitive for his shedding of innocent blood.

4:11 And now art thou cursed from the earth, which hath opened her mouth to receive thy brother's blood from thy hand; **4:12** When thou tillest the ground, it shall not henceforth yield unto thee her strength; **a fugitive** and a vagabond shalt thou be in the earth.

Cain instead of repenting, complains of his punishment.

4:13 And Cain said unto the LORD, My punishment is greater than I can bear. **4:14** Behold, thou hast driven me out this day from the face of the earth; and from thy face shall I be hid; and I shall be a fugitive and a vagabond in the earth; and it shall come to pass, that every one that findeth me shall slay me.

Then Christ the merciful, gave his protection to the physical Cain as long as he would live on the earth.

4:15 And the LORD said unto him, Therefore **whosoever slayeth Cain, vengeance shall be taken on him sevenfold**. And the LORD set a mark upon Cain, lest any finding him should kill him.

The Family of Cain

Then Cain went east from the presence of God

4:16 And **Cain went out from the presence of the LORD,** and dwelt in the land of Nod, on the east of Eden.

Cain had a family and he built them a city; this may have started as a small farm village but living and reproducing for hundreds of years they would later have eventually become quite a large number of people.

4:17 And **Cain knew his wife; and she conceived, and bare Enoch**: and he builded a city, and called the name of the city, after the name of his son, Enoch. **4:18** And unto Enoch was born Irad: and Irad begat Mehujael: and Mehujael begat Methusael: and Methusael begat Lamech.

In the fifth generation of Cain Lamech was born and he became the father of the pre Noah flood nomads, musicians and metal workers. These were all destroyed by the flood and this is probably mentioned to inform us that mankind did develop before the flood.

4:19 And Lamech took unto him two wives: the name of the one was Adah, and the name of the other Zillah.

4:20 And Adah bare Jabal: he was the father of such as dwell in tents, and of such as have cattle. **4:21** And his brother's name was Jubal: he was the father of all such as handle the harp and organ.

4:22 And Zillah, she also bare Tubalcain, an instructer of every artificer in brass and iron: and the sister of Tubalcain was Naamah.

Lamech the descendant of Cain also murdered someone, like his forefather Cain.

4:23 And Lamech said unto his wives, Adah and Zillah, Hear my voice; ye wives of Lamech, hearken unto my speech: for I have slain a man to my wounding, and a young man to my hurt.

God had decreed that Cain was not to be killed by men for his crime and Lamech knowing that, desired the same protection for himself and said:

4:24 If Cain shall be avenged sevenfold, truly Lamech seventy and sevenfold.

The Righteous Line

After Abel died Adam had another son, whom he considered a replacement for righteous Abel. God the Father called Seth to himself through Jesus Christ to keep the righteousness of the Word of God on the earth just as he had called out Abel.

There is no indication of when Seth was born in relation to Cain and Abel, but Seth was born when Adam was 130 years old.

Genesis 4:25 And Adam knew his wife again; and she bare a son, and called his name Seth: For God, said she, hath appointed me another seed instead of Abel, whom Cain slew.

Seth called upon God and was righteous like Abel; Seth was faithful to the Creator and taught his own son Enos to be likewise. And Enos his son did likewise; so that there were godly persons again on the earth after the death of Abel.

4:26 And **to Seth, to him also there was born a son; and he called his name Enos: then began men to call upon the name of the LORD** [after righteous Abel had died].

Genesis 5

The generations [descendants of] Adam, as counted through Seth; the father of the righteous on the earth before the flood of Noah

Humanity and all higher creatures were created male and female, each kind to reproduce after its own kind: with humanity being created after the God kind. Physical humans are embryonic children of God and have the capacity to be changed from the physical state to spiritual composition by God at the resurrection; if they are faithful to God their Father and his Word.

Genesis 5:1 This is the book of the generations of Adam. In the day that God created man, in the likeness of God made he him; **5:2** Male and female created he them; and blessed them, and called their name Adam, in the day when they were created.

Regardless of when Cain and Abel were born and grew up, Seth was born 130 years after the creation of Adam.

5:3 And **Adam lived an hundred and thirty years, and begat a son in his own likeness, and after his image; and called his name Seth:**

5:4 And the days of Adam after he had begotten Seth were eight hundred years: and **he begat sons and daughters**: **5:5** And all the days that Adam lived were **nine hundred and thirty years**: and he died.

5:6 And **Seth lived an hundred and five years**, and **begat Enos**: **5:7** And Seth lived after he begat Enos eight hundred and seven years, and begat sons and daughters: **5:8** And all the days of Seth were **nine hundred and twelve years**: and he died.

5:9 And Enos lived **ninety years, and begat Cainan**: **5:10** And Enos lived after he begat Cainan eight hundred and fifteen years, and begat sons and daughters: **5:11** And all the days of **Enos were nine hundred and five years:** and he died.

5:12 And **Cainan lived seventy years and begat Mahalaleel: 5:13** And Cainan lived after he begat Mahalaleel eight hundred and forty years, and begat sons and daughters: **5:14** And all the days of **Cainan were nine hundred and ten years:** and he died.

5:15 And Mahalaleel lived **sixty and five years, and begat Jared: 5:16** And Mahalaleel lived after he begat Jared eight hundred and thirty years, and begat sons and daughters: **5:17** And all the days of Mahalaleel were **eight hundred ninety and five years**: and he died.

5:18 And Jared lived **an hundred sixty and two years, and he begat Enoch: 5:19** And Jared lived after he begat Enoch eight hundred years, and begat sons and daughters: **5:20** And all the days of Jared were **nine hundred sixty and two years:** and he died.

Because of his faith Enoch was translated from one place to a refuge by God when some sought to destroy him; however he later eventually died (Heb 11:13).

> **Hebrews 11:5** By faith Enoch was translated [transported or removed to another place] that he should not see death [was saved from being murdered for his righteousness]; and was not found, because God had translated [removed him from the danger to anther place] him: for before his translation he had this testimony, that **he pleased God**.
>
> **Hebrews 11:13 These all died in faith, not having received the promises,** but having seen them afar off, and were persuaded of them, and embraced them, and confessed that they were strangers and pilgrims on the earth.

Genesis 5:21 And Enoch lived **sixty and five years, and begat Methuselah: 5:22** And Enoch walked with God after he begat Methuselah three hundred years, and begat sons and daughters: **5:23** And all **the days**

of Enoch were three hundred sixty and five years: **5:24** And Enoch walked with God: and he was not; for God took him.

Enoch was a prophet of God whose book is no longer in existence. There is a fraudulent claim of a Book of Enoch having been found in Ethiopia, but that book is filled with scriptural errors and is now understood to be the creation of a western explorer trying to make a name for himself.

This fraudulent book supposedly found in Abyssinia, is a main source for the gross error that angels copulated with men to produce giants; Jesus Christ told us that angels do not reproduce (Mat 22:30, Mark 12:25 and Luke 20:35).

5:25 And Methuselah lived an **hundred eighty and seven years, and begat Lamech.**

Note that this was a completely different Lamech being of the line of Seth, than the Lamech who descended from Cain. In the past some have confused the two Lamech's.

Methuselah did not live for 1,000 years as some have supposed.

5:26 And Methuselah lived after he begat Lamech seven hundred eighty and two years, and begat sons and daughters: **5:27** And **all the days of Methuselah were nine hundred sixty and nine years: and he died.**

5:28 And **Lamech lived an hundred eighty and two years, and begat a son: 5:29 And he called his name Noah, saying, This same shall comfort us concerning our work and toil of our hands, because of the ground which the LORD hath cursed.**

5:30 And Lamech lived after he begat Noah five hundred ninety and five years, and begat sons and daughters: **5:31** And all the days of **Lamech were seven hundred seventy and seven years:** and he died.

5:32 And **Noah was five hundred years old: and Noah begat Shem, Ham, and Japheth.**

Genesis 6

This chapter begins with God's condemnation of inter-religious marriage, just as the sons of God [called and converted men desired unconverted women] intermarried with unbelievers in those days; and the unconverted partners led the converted astray.

This resulted in the men being subverted from God as Solomon was. The term "son's of God" is also applied to the angels in Job, but that is not the case here as I will shortly prove.

Genesis 6:1 And it came to pass, when men began to multiply on the face of the earth, and daughters were born unto them, **6:2** That the sons of God [converted men] saw the daughters of men [unconverted women] that they were fair; and they took them wives of all which they chose.

The sorrow that these mixed marriages brought, besides turning the called out away from God; caused Christ to give up on striving with wicked humanity and to decide to put an end to men with a flood 120 years in the future.

It is clear that many post flood life spans surpassed 120 years of age. Every descendant in the line of Shem from his son Arphaxad down to Jacob lived more than 120 years, therefore this 120 years refers to the warning period before the flood.

6:3 And the LORD said, My spirit shall not always strive with man, for that he also is flesh: **yet his days shall be an hundred and twenty years**.

6:4 There were giants [tyrants] in the earth in those days; and also after that, when the sons of God came in unto the daughters of men, and they bare children to them, the same became **mighty men which were of old, men of renown.**

These tyrants dominated followings of people; just like the Nicolaitanes of the today's spiritual Ekklesia. Then these groups fought with each other just as the nations did after the flood until this day.

There is great confusion here, as some have taught that angels married women and reproduced to create some kind of giants.

Let us put the facts together on this.

    1. Angels do not marry and they do not reproduce.

    2. Each kind reproduces after its own kind and spirit kinds cannot reproduce with physical kinds.

Man was made after the God kind and has the potential to be born of God; the angels were created in multiple kinds of angels none of them of the God kind.

    3. These giants were pre-flood and were completely destroyed in the Noah flood. Therefore they were not the progenitors of any giants that existed post-flood.

    4. The word "giant " here does not necessarily mean being physically huge at all. It means being a mighty man, a man of renown; a bully, tyrant, dominator of others.

> **Strong's Lexicon Genesis 6:4** There were giants 5303 in the earth 776 in those days 3117; and also after 310 that 3651, when 834 the sons 1121 of God 430 came in 935 8799 unto the daughters 1323 of men 120, and they bare 3205 8804 [children] to them, the same 1992 [became] **mighty men** 1368 which [were] of old 5769, **men** 582 **of renown** 8034.

God the Father and Jesus Christ loved mankind and were very sorrowful over all of the sufferings of humanity; and it was decided to stop the suffering.

Then later they would bring these folks up in a physical resurrection to a new world without Satan for their only opportunity of salvation and receiving the gift of eternal life.

6:5 And God saw that the wickedness of man was great in the earth, and that every imagination of the thoughts of his heart was only evil continually. **6:6** And it repented the LORD that he had made man on the earth, and it grieved him at his heart. **6:7** And the LORD said, I will destroy man whom I have created from the face of the earth; both man, and beast, and the creeping thing, and the fowls of the air; for it repenteth me that I have made them.

Then he found Noah who had remained faithful to the whole Word of God from among all of humanity.

6:8 But Noah found grace in the eyes of the LORD.

The generations of Noah referred to here; are simply Noah, his wife and their three sons and their wives; and the time period in which they lived. This term is used to begin the story of Noah just as we might say: "The beginning of the story of Noah."

Moses writes under inspiration, that Noah walked with God and that Noah was just and perfect before God. The term "perfect in his generations" simply means that Noah was perfect in his love for God and in his learning and living by every Word of God, throughout his lifetime; that is, during the generations in which he lived Noah was found faithful to God throughout his lifetime.

This has nothing to do with racism, for the whole earth was of the one race of Adam until God confused humanity at Babel.

Noah was saved because of his faithfulness to God and the Word of God, not because he was of some race or other. The Creator later created ALL races at Babel.

The word "generations" always refers to the passage of time in which one or more persons live, and never refers to race.

> We will find Genesis 6:9 explained by **Genesis 7:1** And the LORD said unto Noah, Come thou and all thy house into the ark; **for thee have I seen righteous before me in this generation.**

Genesis 6:9 These are the generations of Noah: Noah was a just man and perfect in his generations, and Noah walked with God. **6:10** And Noah begat three sons, Shem, Ham, and Japheth.

6:11 The earth also was corrupt before God, and the earth was filled with violence. **6:12** And God looked upon the earth, and, behold, it was corrupt; for all flesh had corrupted his way upon the earth.

The Elohim Member who later gave up his God-hood to become flesh as Yeshua Mashiach [Jesus Christ], decided to destroy all of humanity and save Noah and his immediate family. WHY? Could he not have rebuked Satan and delivered these people at that time instead of destroying them?

Of course he could have! Then why not do so?

All scripture is for our learning and instruction! This was to be an allegorical lesson that ONLY those who are zealously faithful to God will be changed to spirit and given life eternal; while all of those who reject a zeal to learn and to live by every Word of God, deciding for themselves what is right and wrong: will perish.

This was an object lesson for us, and in due time those people will be raised back to physical life and given their opportunity, and at that time they will understand that lesson!

Today, we also need to learn the lesson that deciding right and wrong for ourselves and not being zealous to learn and live by every Word of God, brings destruction!

ONLY those who are perfect in their generations; that is. through their converted lives to learn and to zealously keep the whole Word of God will receive the promise of eternal life in the resurrection to spirit!

Jesus commanded us to be perfect like God the Father is perfect; which is to live as God the Father lives and as Jesus Christ lives. We are to become like God and to live according to his Word, as God the Father and Jesus live!

> **Matthew 5:48** Be ye therefore perfect, even as your Father which is in heaven is perfect.

Genesis 6:13 And God said unto Noah, The end of all flesh is come before me; for the earth is filled with violence through them; and, behold, I will destroy them with the earth.

The word "Gopher" is not translated to English but is the original word in Hebrew. "Gopher" does not necessarily mean a species of tree, which may or may not be in existence today. It most probably means pitched [tarred] or waterproofed wood.

Due to the similarity between a "g" and a "k" in the Hebrew alphabet (both resemble a backwards "C"), some have suggested that the first letter in the word "gopher" could be a scribal error, and that the word should be "*kopher.*" *Kopher* is a Hebrew word translated as "pitch [tar]" in Genesis 6:14. Pitch is a waterproof covering.

As long as wooden ships have been used for long distance sailing it has been the practice to coat them with pitch [tar] to prevent water logging.

This seems quite possible since the word "gopher" in nowhere else in the Bible.

6:14 Make thee an ark of gopher wood; rooms shalt thou make in the ark, and shalt pitch ["Kofer"] it within and without with pitch ["Kofer'].

The following dimensions are based on an 18 inch cubit.

6:15 And this is the fashion which thou shalt make it of: The length of the ark shall be three hundred cubits [450 feet; 135 meters], the breadth of it fifty cubits [75 feet, or 22.5 meters], and the height of it thirty cubits [its three stories totaled 45 feet, or 13.5 meters].

6:16 A window shalt thou make to the ark, and in a cubit shalt thou finish it above; and the door of the ark shalt thou set in the side thereof; with lower, second, and third stories shalt thou make it.

Each deck was equivalent in area to 20 standard college basketball courts or 36 lawn tennis courts. The rectangular dimensions of the Ark show an advanced design in ship-building. Its length of six times its width and 10 times its height would have made it amazingly stable on the ocean. Remember it was made more for floating than for sailing, because it wasn't headed anywhere. The Ark was made to withstand a turbulent sea, not to be at a certain place at a certain time.

6:17 And, behold, I, even I, do bring a flood of waters upon the earth, to destroy all flesh, wherein is **the breath of life,** from under heaven; and every thing that is in the earth shall die.

A covenant of peace and salvation is made between the Creator and Noah and his family because of his faithfulness to live by every Word of God.

Those who break their baptismal covenant to keep the whole Word of God zealously, will not be saved from destruction, nor will they be changed to spirit to inherit eternal life.

6:18 But with thee will I establish my covenant; and thou shalt come into the ark, thou, and thy sons, and thy wife, and thy sons' wives with thee.

Of each UNCLEAN species [not of each different creature within a species] one male and one female are to be taken into the ark. That would not necessarily include water creatures since verse 17 qualifies this by using the term breathing creature.

6:19 And of every living thing of all flesh, two of every sort shalt thou bring into the ark, to keep them alive with thee; they shall be male and female. **6:20** Of fowls after their kind, and of cattle after their kind, of every creeping thing of the earth after his kind, two of every sort shall come unto thee, to keep them alive.

Noah is also told to stockpile food for his family and for the animals. One could easily speculate that many of the animals would hibernate for much of the time.

6:21 And take thou unto thee of all food that is eaten, and thou shalt gather it to thee; and it shall be for food for thee, and for them.

Noah never having known rain or flooding before since the earth was watered by misting and dew; still believed and obeyed God.

Soon God will command that His people go to a refuge which he has prepared, a kind of an ark of safety; and those who obey God will be spared the correction that will come upon those who refuse to obey God. God will warn us and clearly announce the consequences of each course of action, then the choice of whether to obey God or not will be ours.

6:22 Thus did Noah; according to all that God commanded him, so did he.

Genesis 7

Genesis 7:1 explains what is meant by the term " righteous in his generations" from Genesis 6:9.

Because Noah was faithful to serve God and to live by God's Word and because he had taught his family to do likewise; he and his family were saved from destruction.

Brethren, those who love a corporate church, leader or any other thing more than the love and obey the whole Word of God: will not be in the resurrection to spirit and eternal life life unless they sincerely repent.

If we obey the elder above obeying God and sin against the sanctity of the Sabbath, or sin in any other way; we are guilty of idolizing those whom we have obeyed in place of zealously keeping the whole Word of God. Those who commit this idolatry will be corrected and if still not sincerely repentant; they will be destroyed just like the wicked in Noah's day were destroyed. For it is written:

> **John 8:34** Jesus answered them, Verily, verily, I say unto you, Whosoever committeth sin is the servant of sin.

Judge all men and their words by the whole Word of God and then zealously live by every Word of God above the words of ANY man (1 Thess 5:21, Mat 7 and Mat 4:4). Even if you are the only one doing so on earth as was Noah and his family!

Genesis 7:1 And the LORD said unto Noah, Come thou and all thy house into the ark; **for thee have I seen righteous before me in this generation.**

Now it is revealed that each clean species would have seven males and seven females saved. Therefore the concept of clean and unclean must have been understood by Noah as it was understood by Abel in order to offer an acceptable sacrifice.

The Creator had taught the law of clean and unclean from the beginning.

7:2 Of every clean beast thou shalt take to thee by sevens, the male and his female: and of beasts that are not clean by two, the male and his female. **7:3** Of [clean] fowls also of the air by sevens, the male and the female; to keep seed alive upon the face of all the earth.

The clean animals by seven pairs represented being clean from all uncleanness and sin; and the unclean animals by only one pair of each species [necessary to save them physically to have their species remain on the earth] represented uncleanness and sin.

Seven days notice were given to Noah after the ark and his preaching of warning was completed.

7:4 For yet seven days, and I will cause it to rain upon the earth forty days and forty nights; and every living substance that I have made will I destroy from off the face of the earth.

Noah obeyed God as an example for us that we should also zealously live by every Word of God and teach our families to do likewise.

7:5 And Noah did according unto all that the LORD commanded him.

7:6 And Noah was six hundred years old when the flood of waters was upon the earth. **7:7** And Noah went in, and his sons, and his wife, and his sons' wives with him, into the ark, because of the waters of the flood. **7:8** Of clean beasts, and of beasts that are not clean, and of fowls, and of every thing that creepeth upon the earth, **7:9** There went in two and two unto Noah into the ark, the male and the female, as God had commanded Noah.

7:10 And it came to pass after seven days, that the waters of the flood were upon the earth. **7:11** In the six hundredth year of Noah's life, in the second month, the seventeenth day of the month, the same day were all the fountains of the great deep broken up, and the windows of heaven were opened.

The surface of the earth was quite different before this flood, with no high mountains.

Great earthquakes opened up the underground aquifers as the rain pelted done continually in a torrential deluge even more intense than the tropical downpours of today; and the waters swept over the nearly level land surface in great tidal surges and tsunami's.

7:12 And the rain was upon the earth forty days and forty nights.

The intense downpours and earthquakes began the same day that Noah and his family entered the ark.

7:13 In the selfsame day entered Noah, and Shem, and Ham, and Japheth, the sons of Noah, and Noah's wife, and the three wives of his sons with them, into the ark; **7:14** They, and every beast after his kind, and all the cattle after their kind, and every creeping thing that creepeth upon the earth after his kind, and every fowl after his kind, every bird of every sort. **7:15** And they went in unto Noah into the ark, two and two of all flesh, wherein is the breath of life. **7:16** And they that went in, went in male and female of all flesh, as God had commanded him: and the LORD shut him in.

Noah and his family entered the ark and the door was shut; as an instructional type that no one could pass over the sea of death who is not sincerely repentant and dedicated to enthusiastically live by every Word of God.

7:17 And the flood was forty days upon the earth; and the waters increased, and bare up the ark, and it was lift up above the earth.

7:18 And the waters prevailed, and were increased greatly upon the earth; and the ark went upon the face of the waters. **7:19** And the waters prevailed exceedingly upon the earth; and all the high hills, that were under the whole heaven, were covered.

The waters rose about 23 feet above the then existing earth. In that time the heights of land were far lower than today's modern mountains.

7:20 Fifteen cubits upward did the waters prevail; and the mountains were covered. **7:21** And all flesh died that moved upon the earth, both of fowl, and of cattle, and of beast, and of every creeping thing that creepeth upon the earth, and every man: **7:22 All in whose nostrils was the breath of life, of all that was in the dry land, died. 7:23** And every living substance was destroyed which was upon the face of the ground, both man, and cattle, and the creeping things, and the fowl of the heaven; and they were destroyed from the earth: and Noah only remained alive, and they that were with him in the ark.

7:24 And the waters prevailed upon the earth an hundred and fifty days.

The flood remained for 150 days, which was five months.

> Originally there were 12 thirty day months in a solar year. Early civilizations around the world used calendars with months of 30 days and years of 360 days. These calendars functioned well until sometime in the 8th century BC when suddenly it became necessary to change them. Then most civilizations around the world began to modify their calendars to allow for 5 extra days for the year and 6 fewer days for a lunar year of 12 full months; a modern lunar year is 354 days (12 months x 29.5 days).
>
> The number of days in a year change was marked by the second King of Rome, Numa Pompilius, and by his Jewish contemporary, King Hezekiah. Later other civilizations adopted the new 365 day year as well. These events are often linked with the shadow on the sundial going back 10 degrees in the days of Hezekiah around 700-750 BC.

Genesis 8

After 40 days and 40 nights God began to stop the rain and close up the fountains of waters; and the waters began to slowly recede over the next 110 days until the water level had fallen significantly.

Influencing the depth of the water, there would have been great earthquakes opening and later closing the deep aquifers of water inside the earth. Such massive violent earthquakes would have displaced water causing a great sloshing back and forth of billions of tons of water carrying rock and debris, which would have grooved the ground giving the appearance of ice ages and piling up huge numbers of bodies in various areas as we see in the fossil record today.

The ancient pre-flood civilizations would be buried under many feet of mud at the bottom of the sea today; the legend of a pre-flood one continent world may have some basis in fact.

Genesis 8:1 And God remembered Noah, and every living thing, and all the cattle that was with him in the ark: and God made a wind to pass over the earth, and the waters asswaged; **8:2** The fountains also of the deep and the windows of heaven were stopped, and the rain from heaven was restrained; **8:3** And the waters returned from off the earth continually: and after the end of the hundred and fifty days the waters were abated.

The Hebrew text says that the rain began on the 17th day of the second month and precisely five months later on the 17th day of the seventh month the waters had subsided enough for the ark to ground on a mountain height. [Note the Greek LXX translation specifies the 27th day of the month for each event].

This mountain may not even have existed pre-flood and could easily have been thrust up at the end of that cataclysm.

8:4 And the ark rested in the seventh month, on the seventeenth day of the month, upon the mountains of Ararat.

Three months later on the first day of the tenth month the tops of the mountains became visible as the water continued to recede. These were the mountain tops seen by Noah; huge mountains were also being upthrust around the earth but were not seen by Noah, being great distances away.

During this time some of the great canyons of the earth were formed, as upthrusts of land caused billions of acre feet of water to suddenly rush off the upthrust land; the water rushing downward to lower elevations gouging the soft water logged land like millions of high pressure hoses; just like during the creation week.

No, the Grand Canyon did not take millions of years to form; it took only months, as water ran off when the area was suddenly thrust upwards as God resurfaced the earth; thrusting up the land and causing vast quantities of water to run off at tremendous speed and pressure.

This present world with its high mountains, hills, valleys and plateaus was formed by God via this flood, and today's world is quite different from the pre-flood world. Doubtless that was planned out by God to divide people geographically instead of having all people live together on one continent.

8:5 And the waters decreased continually until the tenth month: in the tenth month, on the first day of the month, were the tops of the mountains seen.

Forty days after the barest surface of the land became visible in the waters, Noah sought to determine of there was enough dry land in the area to allow them to leave the ark: Therefore he sent out birds to find dry land.

The raven went daily from the ark to search for land until the waters had receded enough for it to find a place to live.

8:6 And it came to pass at the end of forty days, that Noah opened the window of the ark which he had made: **8:7** And he sent forth a raven, which went forth to and fro, until the waters were dried up from off the earth.

Noah also tried to find dry land with a dove.

8:8 Also he sent forth a dove from him, to see if the waters were abated from off the face of the ground; **8:9** But the dove found no rest for the sole of her foot, and she returned unto him into the ark, for the waters were on the face of the whole earth: then he put forth his hand, and took her, and pulled her in unto him into the ark.

Seven days later a dove was sent out again and that dove returned in the evening with an olive leaf. This itself was a sign from God for doves do not usually fly with leaves in their beaks. Both the dove and the olive tree are widely accepted symbols of peace and life; both spiritually in the Word of God and also physically in society.

8:10 And he stayed yet other seven days; and again he sent forth the dove out of the ark; **8:11** And the dove came in to him in the evening; and, lo, in her mouth was an olive leaf pluckt off: so Noah knew that the waters were abated from off the earth.

Seven days later, the dove had found a place to nest and did not return to Noah.

8:12 And he stayed yet other seven days; and sent forth the dove; which returned not again unto him any more.

Noah then opened up the ark on the first day of the first month of his 601st year of life.

8:13 And it came to pass in the six hundredth and first year, in the first month, the first day of the month, the waters were dried up from off the earth: and Noah removed the covering of the ark, and looked, and, behold, the face of the ground was dry.

On the 27th day of the second month God told Noah that he might leave the ark.

8:14 And in the second month, on the seven and twentieth day of the month, was the earth dried. **8:15** And God spake unto Noah, saying, **8:16** Go forth of the ark, thou, and thy wife, and thy sons, and thy sons' wives with thee. **8:17** Bring forth with thee every living thing that is with thee, of all flesh, both of fowl, and of cattle, and of every creeping thing that creepeth upon the earth; that they may breed abundantly in the earth, and be fruitful, and multiply upon the earth.

8:18 And Noah went forth, and his sons, and his wife, and his sons' wives with him: **8:19** Every beast, every creeping thing, and every fowl, and whatsoever creepeth upon the earth, after their kinds, went forth out of the ark.

The first thing Noah did was to offer a burnt offering in gratitude to God, this proves yet again that a sacrificial system was in place as well as the law of clean and unclean animals from the time of Adam's sin.

Brethren, it is so important to express appreciation to God and to be grateful for our calling and for the understanding that we have been given, for our blessings and even for our trials, which are making us into the people that God wants us to become.

Let us be intently zealous for our God to learn and to keep his Word faithfully, and let us be filled with rejoicing and gratitude for our Creator and our Righteous Father!

8:20 And Noah builded an altar unto the LORD; and took of every clean beast, and of every clean fowl, and offered burnt offerings on the altar.

Jesus Christ and God the Father accepted the offering; and a promise is made to humanity!

God removed some of the curse on the land making many areas very fertile; he promised to never again kill every living thing on the earth by water and he promised that the cycles of the seasons and the rotation of the earth will not be stopped as long as the earth exists.

8:21 And the LORD smelled a sweet savour [the burnt offering of gratitude]; and the LORD said in his heart, I will not again curse the ground any more for man's sake; for the imagination of man's heart is evil from his youth; neither will I again smite any more every thing living, as I have done. **8:22** While the earth remaineth, seedtime and harvest, and cold and heat, and summer and winter, and day and night shall not cease.

Genesis 9

The Implementing Creator who later gave up his God-hood to become flesh as Jesus Christ, again gave mankind dominance over the earth and its creatures

Genesis 9:1 And God blessed Noah and his sons, and said unto them, Be fruitful, and multiply, and replenish the earth. **9:2** And the fear of you and the dread of you shall be upon every beast of the earth, and upon every fowl of the air, upon all that moveth upon the earth, and upon all the fishes of the sea; into your hand are they delivered.

Only clean animals may be eaten and man is given power over the unclean animals to use them as he wills, as long as they are not eaten or their dead bodies used. This is so that man can learn to wisely care for and rule the creation.

9:3 Every moving thing that liveth shall be meat [subject to, judged by, ruled over by man] for you; even as the green herb have I given you all things.

This is not referring to all things as being fit to eat but to mankind being given sovereignty over all things (Lev 11 and Deu 14).

As we read in the law: We must never eat blood.

> **Deuteronomy 12:23** Only be sure that thou eat not the blood: for the blood is the life; and thou mayest not eat the life with the flesh.

Genesis 9:4 But flesh with the life thereof, which is the blood thereof, shall ye not eat.

God then commands that every man or beast that sheds the blood of a man, made in the image of God; must be killed. A responsibility is given to the rulers of men to execute this judgment and no individual should take the law into his own hands.

9:5 And surely your blood of your lives will I require; at the hand of every beast will I require it, and at the hand of man; at the hand of every man's brother will I require the life of man. **9:6** Whoso sheddeth man's blood, by man shall his blood be shed: for in the image of God made he man.

God then commands Noah and his sons to be fruitful and multiply. Consider the context that there were only eight souls left on the whole earth.

Conditions are quite different today and we need to exercise discretion and produce only the children that we can care for in a godly manner, to maintain a viable population without over populating the earth today.

9:7 And you, be ye fruitful, and multiply; bring forth abundantly in the earth, and multiply therein.

God then covenants with Noah, his descendants and all life on the earth; that God will never again destroy all life with a flood of waters.

9:8 And God spake unto Noah, and to his sons with him, saying, **9:9** And I, behold, I establish my covenant with you, and with your seed after you; **9:10** And with every living creature that is with you, of the fowl, of the cattle, and of every beast of the earth with you; from all that go out of the ark, to every beast of the earth. **9:11** And I will establish my covenant with you, neither shall all flesh be cut off any more by the waters of a flood; neither shall there any more be a flood to destroy the earth.

From then on God continues to bring rain on the earth in place of watering the earth by mist and dew, which rain began at the flood. The forming of rain drops in the atmosphere would now refract sunlight through the large droplets and produce the rainbow. Before this great flood there had been no rainbow because there was no rain drops, only mist [condensing dew overnight], which did not refract the light.

9:12 And God said, This is the token of the covenant which I make between me and you and every living creature that is with you, **for perpetual generations**: **9:13** I do **set my bow in the cloud**, and it shall be for a token of a covenant between me and the earth. **9:14** And it shall come to pass, when I bring a cloud over the earth, that the bow shall be seen in the cloud: **9:15** And I will remember my covenant, which is between me and you and every living creature of all flesh; and the waters shall no more become a flood to destroy all flesh. **9:16** And the bow shall be in the cloud; and I will look upon it, that I may remember the everlasting covenant between God and every living creature of all flesh that is upon the earth. **9:17** And God said unto Noah, This is the token of the covenant, which I have established between me and all flesh that is upon the earth.

Then Noah and his three sons and their wives went out from the ark with the animals; and all subsequent human life came from those eight persons, who were the descendants of Adam and Eve the parents of all humanity.

9:18 And the sons of Noah, that went forth of the ark, were Shem, and Ham, and Japheth: and Ham is the father of Canaan. **9:19** These are the three sons of Noah: and of them was the whole earth overspread.

A time came when Noah was drunken and lost his dignity as the father of his sons; therefore the law forbids drunkenness [any intoxication]; which can cause loss of control of ones thoughts and actions.

9:20 And Noah began to be an husbandman, and he planted a vineyard: **9:21** And he drank of the wine, and was drunken; and he was uncovered [naked] within his tent.

Noah's sons then respectfully covered him without willfully looking at his nakedness. Brethren, we should avoid intoxication with any substance and parents should NEVER deliberately expose themselves before their children or anyone outside of their own spouse.

9:22 And **Ham, the father of Canaan**, saw the nakedness of his father, and told his two brethren without. **9:23** And Shem and Japheth took a garment, and laid it upon both their shoulders, and went backward, and covered the nakedness of their father; and their faces were backward, and they saw not their father's nakedness.

Ham saw his father Noah naked and told his brothers who covered him.

9:24 And Noah awoke from his wine, and knew what his younger son [grandson H1121] had done unto him. **9:25** And he said, **Cursed be Canaan**; a servant of servants shall he be unto his brethren.

Note that this curse was on Canaan NOT Ham.

Noah then exalts Shem above Canaan [NOT above Ham], and prophecies that Canaan and his descendants [the Canaanites] will be the servants of the descendants of Shem [Israel].

This is about Israel the descendants of Shem dominating the Canaanites and has absolutely nothing to do with the other children of Ham as some falsely teach.

This does not say that black people should be the servants or slaves of white people as some racists claim, instead this is about the Canaanites who became profligately wicked and were used by God as a type of sin itself from the time of the exodus.

This was fulfilled in part when Israel [who was descended from Shem] was given the land of Canaan at the exodus.

9:26 And he said, Blessed be the LORD God of Shem [the father of Israel]; and Canaan shall be his [Israel's] servant.

In ancient times God led the twelve tribes of Israel out of Egypt and gave them the land of the Canaanites which we call Palestine today. Before they entered the promised land, God informed Israel through Moses [the whole book of Deuteronomy] that possession of the land was entirely dependent on the people continually living by every Word of God.

Some parts of the land were never fully controlled by the Israelites when they entered the land under Joshua. There is even the promise by God that some people would never be driven out if this was not accomplished by Joshua.

Later Israel's exclusive right to the land was lost through unbelief, and rejecting the theocratic rule of God and not keeping the law God gave them.

> Judges 2:2 describes God's message to sinning Israel. "you have not obeyed my voice, why have you done this?" The punishment is found in Judges 2:21, "I will not henceforth drive out from before them any of the nations which Joshua left when he died." And that specifically was the Gaza Strip, the area of Philistia and the Canaanites in Lebanon.
>
> The first verses of Judges 3 detail the peoples who would remain. "Now these are the nations which the Lord left, to prove Israel by them, even as many of Israel as had not known all the wars of Canaan. Namely, **the five lords of the Philistines, and all the**

Canaanites, and the Sidonians, and the Hivites that dwelt in **mount Lebanon, from mount Baalhermon** [Mount Hermon] **unto the entering in of Hamath**." This means that the native Canaanite people would remain in Lebanon and Gaza.

Others like the Hittites also remained in the land for a time. Heth the second son of Canaan was the father of the Hittites [later called Franks by the Romans]. The Hittites lived in Hebron (Gen 23:18-20) until most of whom were driven out of Canaan by Nebuchadnezzar and eventually migrated to Asia Minor founding an empire with the capital city of Troy.

After their defeat in the Trojan wars king Paris led them to what is now northern France where they founded a kingdom. Called the Franks by the Romans they named their capital after their king Paris.

Japheth is blessed with enlargement and multitudes of descendants, and Canaan will serve the descendants of Shem [ie the remaining Canaanites will serve a united Israel in the millennium].

The two brothers Shem and Japheth and their descendants are blessed, while a blessing on Ham is not mentioned. One son of Ham [Canaan] is delivered to be subject to the descendants of Shem [through Jacob, Israel] so that he might learn respect through service.

Mizraim a son of Ham became Egypt which is called one of the three greatest nations by God,.

> **Isaiah 19:24** In that day shall Israel be the third with Egypt and with Assyria, even a blessing in the midst of the land:

Ham's son Cush fathered the black people of central and southern Africa while Ham's other sons were given North Africa.

Genesis 9:27 God shall enlarge Japheth, and he shall dwell in the tents of [will be blessed like Shem] Shem; and Canaan shall be his [Shem's] servant.

9:28 And Noah lived after the flood three hundred and fifty years. **9:29** And all the days of Noah were nine hundred and fifty years: and he died.

Genesis 10

Genesis 10-11 is often called the Table of Nations because it lists the descendants of Noah who were scattered across the earth from Babel, founding the nations of today.

Before the flood the whole world was of one race, the race of Adam through Noah. Then the families of man were divided at Babel.

Shem, Ham and Japheth parented the main divisions of families; with their children also being divided into the seventy families [races] of man.

ALL races came from the same family of Adam through Noah separated from each other at Babel by Almighty God. Every human being of every race of man is the creation of God and has the exact same potential for eternal life as the children of God.

Do we not say that a red rose and a yellow rose are both roses and are both beautiful? Why then do many have that attitude over a flower that appears and is gone in a few days; and then despise the differences in mankind who are all the potential children of God?

Shame on those evil people who look down upon the children of God because of such differences made by God!

> **Colossians 3:11** Where there is neither Greek nor Jew, circumcision nor uncircumcision, Barbarian, Scythian, bond nor free: but Christ is all, and in all.

Genesis 10:1 Now these are the generations of the sons of Noah, Shem, Ham, and Japheth: and unto them were sons born after the flood.

Japheth is listed first since he is the firstborn of Noah, v 21. Japheth had seven sons.

The Descendants of Japheth

Genesis 10:2 The sons of Japheth;

Gomer, and Magog, and Madai, and Javan, and Tubal, and Meshech, and Tiras.

10:3 And the sons of Gomer;

Ashkenaz, and Riphath, and Togarmah.

10:4 And the sons of Javan;

Elishah, and Tarshish, Kittim, and Dodanim.

10:5 By these were the isles of the Gentiles divided in their lands; every one after his tongue, after their families, in their nations.

The Family of Gomer;

Ashkenaz: The modern Armenians

Togormah: Modern Georgia

Riphath: The Azeri people of modern Azerbaijan

The Family of Magog:

The peoples of modern central Asia

The Family of Madai:

Became the Medes of the Medo-Persian Empire and after the fall of that empire migrated into eastern Europe where they are known today as the Ukrainians and other closely related peoples.

The Family of Javan:

Elishah: Modern Greek Cyprus

Tarshish: Identified with Tartessus; Spain and Portugal

Kittim: Crete

Dodanim: The people of the Isle of Rhodes

The Family of Tubal:

Generally the Slavic peoples of the Balkans

The Family of Meshech:

Became modern Russia [Rosh]. **Moscow** (*Moskva*) was founded by King Mosokh son of Japheth (i.e. Meshech), and was named for him.

The Descendants of Ham

Genesis 10:6 And the sons of Ham; Cush, and Mizraim, and Phut, and Canaan.

10:7 And **the sons of Cush**;

Seba, and Havilah, and Sabtah, and Raamah, and Sabtechah: and the sons of Raamah; Sheba, and Dedan. [and Nimrod also]

10:8 And **Cush begat Nimrod**: he began to be a mighty one in the earth.

10:9 He was a mighty hunter before [in place of, or supplanting the LORD to lead men after himself] the LORD: wherefore it is said, Even as Nimrod the mighty hunter before the LORD.

10:10 And the beginning of his kingdom was Babel, and Erech, and Accad, and Calneh, in the land of Shinar.

An Inset regarding Asshur son of Shem

> **Genesis 10:11** Out of that land [Babel] went forth Asshur, and **builded Nineveh,** and the city **Rehoboth, and Calah**, **10:12** And **Resen** between Nineveh and Calah: the same is a great city.

The Family of Cush:

Seba, Havilah: Ethiopia and black Africa

Sabtah, Raamah and Sabtechah: Are the darker peoples of modern India

The Family of Mizraim [Hebrew Mizraim; Greek AEgyptos]

10:13 And Mizraim begat

Ludim, and Anamim, and Lehabim, and Naphtuhim,

10:14 And Pathrusim, and Casluhim, (out of whom came Philistim,) and Caphtorim.

> **As with Peleg no descendants of Phut are mentioned here,** probably meaning that Phut remained as one united family. Yet Phut had descendants because soldiers of Phut are mentioned as serving Tyre in Ezekiel 27:10.

Ludim: Their land was to the far west of Libya in Algeria, Tunisia, Morocco, North Africa along the Mediterranean Sea

Anamim: The Bible generally refers to the Egyptians as Mizraim, many ancient peoples referred to the Egyptians as "*Anami*"

Lehabim: Eastern Libya along the Egyptian border

Naphtuhim: Migrated from Memphis to South Egypt

Pathrusim: Lived at Pathros in Upper Egypt

Casluhim: Settled on the sea coast between Sinai and Ashkelon. They are the modern people of Gaza, the ancient Philistines. The people of Gaza are not the same people as the Palestinians.

Caphtorim: an Egyptian coastal locality in the vicinity of Pelusium

The Family of Canaan

Sidon remains Sidon of modern Lebanon

10:15 And **Canaan begat** Sidon [who founded today's Sidon, Lebanon] his first born, and Heth [the Hittites],

Genesis 10:16 And the Jebusite, and the Amorite, and the Girgasite,

10:17 And the Hivite, and the Arkite, and the Sinite,

10:18 And the Arvadite, and the Zemarite, and the Hamathite: and **afterward were the families of the Canaanites spread abroad.**

The Hittites [Franks]

Heth the second son of Canaan was the father of the Hittites [later called Franks by the Romans]. The Hittites lived in Hebron (Gen 23:18-20) which was given to Caleb of Judah, and were famous soldiers of Israel during and after the time of David [remember Uriah the mighty man of David?] until most of the Hittites were driven out of Canaan and migrated to Asia Minor, finally founding an empire with the capital city of Troy.

> WIKI: "The Trojan War was waged against the city of Troy by the Achaeans (Greeks) after Paris king of Troy took Helen from her husband Menelaus, king of Sparta."

After their empire was defeated and the Hittites [called Franks by the Romans] were expelled from Troy they migrated to northern Europe where they set up the empire of the Franks from which the word "France" is derived.

Although the Franks lived in northern France, today the whole nation of France is named after the Franks and the capital of France still bears the name of the Hittite king of Troy "Paris."

Getting ahead a little in the interests of identifying the French: after the fall of the Chaldean Empire at Babylon, many Mesopotamian people migrated to Southern Europe [where they were known as Gaul's], settling in the area we call southern France today.

Genesis 10:16 And the Jebusite, and the Amorite, and the Girgasite,

10:17 And the Hivite, and the Arkite, and the Sinite,

10:18 And the Arvadite, and the Zemarite, and the Hamathite: and **afterward were the families of the Canaanites spread abroad.**

After Israel entered the land of Canaan many Canaanites were destroyed and many others migrated from the area when the Assyrians who removed the ten tribes of Israel swept through Samaria and later Nebuhadnezzar swept through Judah.

10:19 And the border of the Canaanites was from Sidon, as thou comest to Gerar, unto Gaza; as thou goest, unto Sodom, and Gomorrah, and Admah, and Zeboim, even unto Lasha.

The families of Canaan formed the Canaanite tribes who lived from Egypt to Lebanon, bordered on the west by Gaza, Sidon and the sea, and including Sodom on the east.

10:20 These are the sons of Ham, after their families, after their tongues, in their countries, and in their nations.

The Descendants of Shem

Genesis 10:21 Unto Shem also, the father of all the children of Eber, the brother of Japheth the elder [his elder brother both being the sons of Noah], even to him were children born.

10:22 The children of Shem;

Elam, and Asshur, and Arphaxad, and Lud, and Aram.

Elam: Modern Poland

Asshur [Assyria]: Seventy years ago it was thought by some that Assyria descended from Abraham through Keturah. Since that time there has been an explosion of knowledge on ancient history and it is now understood that the Assyrians are actually descended from the Asshur son of Shem.

It was Asshur son of Shem who built Nineveh (Genesis 10:11) and founded the Assyrian peoples.

God later used the Assyrians to correct the Northern Ten Tribes of Israel c 721 B.C. and deport them from the Promised Land.

Remaining in the Promised Land was always CONDITIONAL on living by every Word of God.

> **Deuteronomy 30:15** See, I have set before thee this day life and good, and death and evil;
>
> **30:16** In that I command thee this day to love the LORD thy God, to walk in his ways, and to keep his commandments and his statutes and his judgments, that thou mayest live and multiply: and the LORD thy God shall bless thee in the land whither thou goest to possess it.
>
> **30:17** But if thine heart turn away, so that thou wilt not hear, but shalt be drawn away, and worship other gods, and serve them;
>
> **30:18** I denounce unto you this day, that ye shall surely perish, and that **ye shall not prolong your days upon the land,** whither thou passest over Jordan to go to possess it.

30:19 I call heaven and earth to record this day against you, that I have set before you life and death, blessing and cursing: therefore choose life, that both thou and thy seed may live:

30:20 That thou mayest love the LORD thy God, and that thou mayest obey his voice, and that thou mayest cleave unto him: for he is thy life, and the length of thy days: **that thou mayest dwell in the land** which the LORD sware unto thy fathers, to Abraham, to Isaac, and to Jacob, to give them.

Later the Assyrian Empire was supplanted by their brother people the Babylonians, and the Assyrians migrated northwest taking the Ten Tribes of Israel with them.

A Partial Listing of Assyrian tribes

Alemanni: Settled in Bavaria, Austria and Alsace

Boii: Settled in Bavaria

Quadi and Marcomani: settled in Bohemia and Moravia Czechoslovakia. At the close of WW 2 many went to Germany from the Sudetenland

Suabe: Settled in north Germany

Silesians: Settled in southwest Poland. After WW2 many migrated into Germany.

The Huns: were given Hungary [Hun-Land] by the Romans

The Ancient Assyrians today make up the modern nations of Germany, Austria and Hungary.

> **NOTE:** In the Middle Ages long after the Assyrians had migrated from the area, some Arab people were converted to the Eastern Orthodox Church.
>
> Although they had no connection with the Assyrian race, the Eastern Orthodox Church chose to call them Assyrian Christians based on their location in the heart of the ancient land of Assyria.
>
> Later some of them broke away to join Roman Catholicism and were called Chaldean Christians, again there is no racial connection to either the ancient Assyrians or Chaldeans

Lud: The Persians

Genesis 10:23 And **the children of Aram;** Uz, and Hul, and Gether, and Mash.

Aram: The Syrians

Arphaxad [Arpachshad]: Father of the Chaldeans; Arpachshad was the progenitor of Ura and Kesed, who founded the city of *Ur Kesdim* (Ur of the Chaldees) on the west bank of the Euphrates. After the fall of the Chaldean Empire many Chaldean people [later called Gaul's by the Romans] migrated to southern Europe settling in the area we call Italy and southern France today.

10:24 And **Arphaxad begat** Salah; and Salah begat Eber.

10:25 And **unto Eber were born two sons**: the name of one was Peleg; for in his days was the earth [the families were divided at Babel] divided;

[The descendants of Peleg are listed in Genesis 11] and his [Peleg's] brother's name was Joktan.

The Family of Joktan were various peoples of Mesopotamia

10:26 And **Joktan begat** Almodad, and Sheleph, and Hazarmaveth, and Jerah,

10:27 And Hadoram, and Uzal, and Diklah,

10:28 And Obal, and Abimael, and Sheba,

10:29 And Ophir, and Havilah, and Jobab: all these were the sons of Joktan.

10:30 And their dwelling was from Mesha, as thou goest unto Sephar a mount of the east.

10:31 These are the sons of Shem, after their families, after their tongues, in their lands, after their nations.

10:32 These are the families of the sons of Noah, after their generations, in their nations: and by these were the nations divided in the earth after the flood.

The Modern Palestinians

The children of Joktan took up residence in Mesopotamia where they lived under the Assyrian Empire.

Because of the sins of Solomon, God took the Ten Tribes of Israel away splitting the Ten Tribes of Israel away from the Kingdom of Judah.

Then over many years as the Ten Tribes sinned and apostatized from God into idolatry and much wickedness, refusing to repent after many warnings; God withdrew his protection from the Ten Tribes.

The Assyrian Empire then attacked and in a series of successive waves overcame Israel in c 721 B.C. and carried them away from off the land.

> **2 Kings 17:6** In the ninth year of Hoshea the king of Assyria took Samaria, and carried Israel away into Assyria, and placed them in Halah and in Habor by the river of Gozan, and in the cities of the Medes.
>
> **17:7** For so it was, that the children of Israel had sinned against the LORD their God, which had brought them up out of the land of Egypt, from under the hand of Pharaoh king of Egypt, and had feared other gods, **17:8** And walked in the statutes of the heathen, whom the LORD cast out from before the children of Israel, and of the kings of Israel, which they had made.

The king of Assyria then brought in people of Joktan from Mesopotamia to populate the land of Israel.

> **17:24** And the king of Assyria **brought men from Babylon, and from Cuthah, and from Ava, and from Hamath, and from Sepharvaim, and placed them in the cities of Samaria instead of the children of Israel:** and they possessed Samaria, and dwelt in the cities thereof.

Thus the area north of Jerusalem was populated by the Joktan peoples from Mesopotamia. The capital of the Ten Tribes was at Samaria and so the kingdom of the Ten Tribes of Israel was often called Samaria; and these new migrants were afterwards called Samaritans.

Fast forwarding to the eighth century, Islam swept through the region and most of these folks converted to Islam, leaving only a few with the original Samaritan religion.

Today those few holding to the Samaritan religion are still called Samaritans, but for political reasons the vast majority who are now Muslims or Catholics are called Palestinians.

The Families of Abraham

See also: Assyria

> **Genesis 11:18** And Peleg lived thirty years, and begat **Reu:**
>
> **11:19** And Peleg lived after he begat Reu two hundred and nine years, and begat sons and daughters.
>
> **11:20** And Reu lived two and thirty years, and begat **Serug**:
>
> **11:21** And Reu lived after he begat Serug two hundred and seven years, and begat sons and daughters.
>
> **11:22** And Serug lived thirty years, and begat **Nahor:**
>
> **11:23** And Serug lived after he begat Nahor two hundred years, and begat sons and daughters.
>
> **11:24** And Nahor lived nine and twenty years, and begat **Terah**:
>
> **11:25** And Nahor lived after he begat Terah an hundred and nineteen years, and begat sons and daughters.
>
> **11:26** And Terah lived seventy years, and begat **Abram, Nahor, and Haran.**
>
> **11:27** Now these are the generations of Terah: Terah begat Abram, Nahor, and Haran; and **Haran begat Lot.**
>
> **11:28** And Haran died before his father Terah in the land of his nativity, in Ur of the Chaldees.

Abram was a Chaldean of Ur

Ammon and Moab: Modern Jordan

After Abraham's nephew Lot had fled from the destruction of Sodom

> **Genesis 19:31** And the firstborn said unto the younger, Our father is old, and there is not a man in the earth to come in unto us after the manner of all the earth:
>
> **19:32** Come, let us make our father drink wine, and we will lie with him, that we may preserve seed of our father.

19:33 And they made their father drink wine that night: and the firstborn went in, and lay with her father; and he perceived not when she lay down, nor when she arose.

19:34 And it came to pass on the morrow, that the firstborn said unto the younger, Behold, I lay yesternight with my father: let us make him drink wine this night also; and go thou in, and lie with him, that we may preserve seed of our father.

19:35 And they made their father drink wine that night also: and the younger arose, and lay with him; and he perceived not when she lay down, nor when she arose.

19:36 Thus were both the daughters of Lot with child by their father.

19:37 And the first born bare a son, and called his name Moab: the same is the father of **the Moabites unto this day.**

19:38 And the younger, she also bare a son, and called his name Benammi: the same is the father of **the children of Ammon unto this day**.

The Arab Peoples

Genesis 11:30 But Sarai was barren; she had no child.

Abram and Sarai had longed for a child all of their lives and now that Sarai was old and well past child bearing, she sought a child by giving her maid to her husband.

In due time Hagar gave birth to a son Ishmael and began to despise Sarai and Sarai treated her very badly, but God gave Hagar a blessing for Ishmael.

Genesis 16:10 And the angel of the LORD said unto her, I will multiply thy seed exceedingly, that it shall not be numbered for multitude.

16:11 And the angel of the LORD said unto her, Behold, thou art with child and shalt bear a son, and shalt call his name Ishmael; because the LORD hath heard thy affliction.

16:12 And he will be a wild man; his hand will be against every man, and every man's hand against him; and he shall dwell in the presence of all his brethren [near to Israel].

Then God gave a child by his promise to Sarai.

Then filled with jealousy Sarai drove Hagar and Ishmael out.

> **Genesis 21:10** Wherefore she said unto Abraham, Cast out this bondwoman and her son: for the son of this bondwoman shall not be heir with my son, even with Isaac.
>
> **21:11** And the thing was very grievous in Abraham's sight because of his son.
>
> **21:12** And God said unto Abraham, Let it not be grievous in thy sight because of the lad, and because of thy bondwoman; in all that Sarah hath said unto thee, hearken unto her voice; for in Isaac shall thy seed be called.
>
> **21:13** And **also of the son of the bondwoman will I make a nation, because he is thy seed.**
>
> **21:14** And Abraham rose up early in the morning, and took bread, and a bottle of water, and gave it unto Hagar, putting it on her shoulder, and the child, and sent her away: and she departed, and wandered in the wilderness of Beersheba.
>
> **21:15** And the water was spent in the bottle, and she cast the child under one of the shrubs.
>
> **21:16** And she went, and sat her down over against him a good way off, as it were a bow shot: for she said, Let me not see the death of the child. And she sat over against him, and lift up her voice, and wept.
>
> **21:17** And God heard the voice of the lad; and the angel of God called to Hagar out of heaven, and said unto her, What aileth thee, Hagar? fear not; for God hath heard the voice of the lad where he is.
>
> **21:18** Arise, lift up the lad, and hold him in thine hand; for **I will make him a great nation.**
>
> **21:19** And God opened her eyes, and she saw a well of water; and she went, and filled the bottle with water, and gave the lad drink.

The Hagarenes

The Hagarenes are not of the family of Abraham, but being the children of Hagar are mentioned here.

After Hagar was driven out with Ishmael the son of Abraham, she remarried and had other sons. These other sons are called Hagarines to differentiate them from Ishmael the son of Abraham.

These descendants of Hagar dwelt with the descendants of Ishmael. The various sons of Hagar including Ishmael are the Arab peoples living today in the countries on the Arabian Peninsula.

Esau

Esau can be found in scripture under the names Esau, Edom, Mount Seir, Temen [the word Turkmen comes from Temen] and the various tribes of Esau notably the Amalekites.

> **Genesis 25:30** And Esau said to Jacob, Feed me, I pray thee, with that same red pottage; for I am faint: therefore was his name called **Edom.**
>
> **Genesis 36:8** Thus dwelt Esau in **mount Seir: Esau is Edom.**

Esau and Jacob were twin brothers. The story begins in:

> **Genesis 25:21** And Isaac intreated the LORD for his wife, because she was barren: and the LORD was intreated of him, and Rebekah his wife conceived.
>
> **25:22** And the children struggled together within her; and she said, If it be so, why am I thus? And she went to enquire of the LORD.
>
> **25:23** And the LORD said unto her, Two nations are in thy womb, and two manner of people shall be separated from thy bowels; and the one people shall be stronger than the other people; and the elder shall serve the younger.
>
> **25:24** And when her days to be delivered were fulfilled, behold, there were twins in her womb.

As the story continues Jacob takes advantage of Esau and buys from him a priceless birthright for a bowl of stew. This is an important lesson for us that we should value the birthright of eternal life very highly and not sell it for the temporary pleasures of the flesh.

Later Jacob steals the blessing reserved for the first born Esau by a deception, forcing him to flee for his life from an enraged Esau.

Then after many years in exile Jacob returns home to make peace with his brother. This part of the story ends as Esau chooses to live in Mount Seir and Jacob in Shechem.

> **Genesis 33:16** So Esau returned that day on his way unto Seir
>
> **33:17** And Jacob journeyed to Succoth, and built him an house, and made booths for his cattle: therefore the name of the place is called Succoth.

After Israel came out from Egypt, over the ensuing centuries Edom was overrun by Egypt, Babylon, Arabs, and Jordanians, and the people of Edom [Esau] migrated away from that place.

Esau migrated to central Asia where they founded the nation of Turkmenistan. Later in the eighth century A.D. Islam spread rapidly and certain of the tribes of Turkmens [from Temen; Esau], notably the Othmani and Amalekites joined in spreading the faith by war conquering the area now called Turkey and founding the Ottoman [Othmani] Empire.

Today the tribes of Esau constitute the modern nation of Turkey.

> **Genesis 36:9** And these are the generations of Esau the father of the Edomites in mount Seir:
>
> **36:10** These are the names of Esau's sons; **Eliphaz** the son of Adah the wife of Esau, **Reuel** the son of Bashemath the wife of Esau.
>
> **36:11** And **the sons of Eliphaz** were **Teman**, Omar, Zepho, and Gatam, and Kenaz.
>
> **36:12** And Timna was concubine to Eliphaz Esau's son; and she bare to Eliphaz **Amalek** [the Amalekites]: these were the sons of Adah Esau's wife.

Mount Seir was named for Seir, the Horite, whose offspring had inhabited the area (Genesis 14:6, 36:20) until the children of Esau (the Edomites) completely destroyed the Horites and took possession of the city (Deuteronomy 2:4-5, 12, 22).

From that time Seir has become synonymous with Esau who took possession of Seir and destroyed the Horites living there. (Genesis 32:3; 33:14, 16; 36:8; Joshua 24:4).

The main cities of Esau [Edom] were Seir and Petra until they were removed to the north into the area now called the Stan countries, particularly Turkmenistan. After they accepted Islam in the eighth century many of the Turkic tribes including the Othmani and Amalekites, swept into Turkey and established the Othmani [Ottoman] Empire.

The Ottoman Empire collapsed at the end of WW 1 and today Turkey is struggling with Egypt to gain back leadership of the Muslim world.

The identification of the various families of man is completed and we now go to the story of Babel and how these families were divided from one another at Babel.

Genesis 11

The Division at Babel

All the children of Noah and his three sons and their wives had one race and one language and were united as one people.

Genesis 11:1 And the whole earth was of one language, and of one speech.

They journeyed to the east and dwelt at Shinar in Mesopotamia and built a city there; then they proceeded to build a pyramid tower.

11:2 And it came to pass, as they journeyed from the east, that they found a plain in the land of Shinar; and they dwelt there. **11:3** And they said one to another, Go to, let us make brick, and burn them thoroughly. And they had brick for stone, and slime had they for morter.

Nimrod enticed the people to build this pyramid as a point to focus people on, so that they would not be scattered away from him. This pyramid was also for the purpose of observing the heavens and the worship of the heavenly bodies, astrology and sun worship.

Spiritually these heavenly bodies were symbols of spiritual realities with the sun representing Satan etc.

The ultimate evil power is not that of a physical dictatorship, but it is a dictatorship of the mind called false religion.

Men may be willing to resist a physical dictatorship, but few men will dare to face eternal punishment if they believe that some man has the power to cut them off from God and to inflict an eternal punishment on them.

When a person sincerely believes with all his heart that to disobey some other man will result in eternal punishment or the loss of an eternal reward; that person will do anything that he is told!

That is REAL POWER! That is the ultimate POWER! That belief places spiritual chains around the mind of the believer, far stronger than any mere physical chains or punishment ever could!

The claim that loyalty to men is the same as loyalty to God has enslaved humanity to the whims of other men and has separated many from God as they are deceived into thinking that the word of men is the same as loyalty to the Word of God. Since Nimrod popes and leaders of various religions, emperors and kings have falsely claimed to have power over the eternal fate of man.

This Nicolaitane governance system much hated by Jesus Christ (Rev 2) even exists in many of today's Ekklesia assemblies; where brethren do whatever their leader says instead of living by every Word of God.

11:4 And they said, Go to, let us build us a city and a tower, whose top may reach unto heaven; and let us make us a name, **lest we be scattered abroad** [divided] upon the face of the whole earth.

Then God looked on the people and decided that to prevent the same disastrous conditions that prevailed pre-flood, he would divide the families of man.

11:5 And the LORD came down to see the city and the tower [pyramid, ziggurat], which the children of men builded. **11:6** And the LORD said, Behold, the people is one, and they have all one language; and this they begin to do: and now nothing will be restrained from them, which they have imagined to do.

God then divided man by language and family [race].

11:7 Go to, let us go down, and there confound their language, that they may not understand one another's speech. **11:8** So the LORD scattered them abroad from thence upon the face of all the earth: and they left off to build the city.

11:9 Therefore is the name of it called Babel; [confusion, division] because the LORD did there confound the language of all the earth: and from thence did the LORD scatter them abroad upon the face of all the earth.

Moses now describes the ancestry of Abram

Genesis 11:10 These are the generations of Shem: Shem was an hundred years old, and begat Arphaxad two years after the flood: **11:11** And Shem lived after he begat Arphaxad five hundred years, and begat sons and daughters. **11:12** And Arphaxad lived five and thirty years, and begat Salah: **11:13** And Arphaxad lived after he begat Salah four hundred and three years, and begat sons and daughters. **11:14** And Salah lived thirty years, and begat Eber: **11:15** And Salah lived after he begat Eber four hundred and three years, and begat sons and daughters.

Abram was born approximately 392 years after the flood. The birth year of Abram can be determined with a little math.

> **Genesis 9:28** And Noah lived after the flood three hundred and fifty years.

Genesis 11:16 And Eber lived four and thirty years, and begat Peleg: **11:17** And Eber lived after he begat Peleg four hundred and thirty years, and begat sons and daughters. **11:18** And Peleg lived thirty years, and begat Reu: **11:19** And Peleg lived after he begat Reu two hundred and nine years, and begat sons and daughters. **11:20** And Reu lived two and thirty years, and begat Serug: **11:21** And Reu lived after he begat Serug two hundred and seven years, and begat sons and daughters.

11:22 And Serug lived thirty years, and begat Nahor: **11:23** And Serug lived after he begat Nahor two hundred years, and begat sons and daughters. **11:24** And Nahor lived nine and twenty years, and begat Terah: **11:25** And Nahor lived after he begat Terah an hundred and nineteen years, and begat sons and daughters.

11:26 And Terah lived seventy years, [Terah lived for 205 years] and begat Abram, Nahor, and Haran.

Terah's total age was 205 years, and to the casual reader of Genesis 11:26, Abram was born when Terah was 70 years of age, but in this case Abram was apparently placed first because of his spiritual legacy while the others may have been born before him.

The specific birth year of Abram can be found in Genesis 12:4 where Abram's age is recorded as being 75 years when his father Terah died at the age of 205 and Abram departed out of Haran. **By simply subtracting 75 from 205 we can date the birth of Abram in the 130th year of Terah.**

Genesis 11:27 Now **these are the generations of Terah:** Terah begat Abram, Nahor, and Haran; and **Haran begat Lot. 11:28** And **Haran died before his father Terah in the land of his nativity, in Ur** of the Chaldees.

Abram married his sister, and Nahor married his niece; which was still common from the necessity of the children of Adam to marry their kin.

This tradition continued in the royal families and nobles of Egypt. God gave instructions to Israel AFTER they came out of Egypt that his people should not marry any closer than cousins only.

11:29 And Abram and Nahor took them wives: the name of Abram's wife was Sarai; and the name of Nahor's wife, Milcah, the daughter of Haran, the father of Milcah, and the father of Iscah.

11:30 But Sarai was barren; she had no child.

Then Terah took his family from Ur to Haran.

11:31 And Terah took Abram his son, and Lot the son of Haran his son's son, and Sarai his daughter in law, his son Abram's wife; and they went forth with them from Ur of the Chaldees, to go into the land of Canaan; and they came unto Haran, and dwelt there. **11:32** And **the days of Terah were two hundred and five years: and Terah died in Haran.**

Genesis 12

Haran was the original destination of Terah and he died in Haran. Then the Being who later gave up his Godhood to be made flesh as Jesus Christ, called Abram from Haran to go to Canaan while the rest of the family remained at Haran.

Notice that the Eternal calls Abram and great promises are made, only IF he obeys and remained dedicated and faithful to live by every Word of God. The promise to Abram was physical blessings, and was also of salvation for all humanity through the Lamb of God through his line.

Abraham was an example of faithfulness to learn and to live by every Word of God as the father of the faithful.

We are also called and have a promise from God, IF we are faithful to live by every Word of God. The promise of entry into the spiritual Promised Land of eternal life is ABSOLUTELY CONDITIONAL on our living by every Word of God!

Genesis 12:1 Now the LORD had said unto Abram, Get thee out of thy country, and from thy kindred, and from thy father's house, unto a land that I will shew thee: **12:2** And I will make of thee a great nation, and I will bless thee, and **make thy name great; and thou shalt be a blessing: 12:3 And I will bless them that bless thee, and curse him that curseth thee: and in thee shall all families of the earth be blessed.**

Abram accepted, and believed [having FAITH that God was able to make good his promises and OBEYED, leaving Haran for Canaan.

12:4 So Abram departed, as the LORD had spoken unto him; and Lot went with him: and **Abram was seventy and five years old when he departed out of Haran. 12:5** And Abram took Sarai his wife, and Lot his brother's son, and all their substance that they had gathered, and the souls that they had gotten in Haran; and they went forth to go into the land of Canaan; and into the land of Canaan they came.

12:6 And Abram passed through the land unto the place of Sichem [Shechem] , unto the plain of Moreh. And the Canaanite was then in the land.

Abram journeyed around Canaan and the Eternal promised him that he through his descendants would be given every place that he traveled; Abram built altars to God at each longer resting place.

12:7 And the LORD appeared unto Abram, and said, Unto **thy seed will I give this land:** and **there builded he an altar unto the LORD**, who appeared unto him. **12:8** And he removed from thence unto a mountain on the east of Bethel, and pitched his tent, having Bethel on the west, and Hai on the east: and **there he builded an altar unto the LORD, and called upon the name of the LORD.**

Abram then went south into Egypt because of a famine in Canaan.

12:9 And Abram journeyed, going on still toward the south. **12:10** And there was a famine in the land: and Abram went down into Egypt to sojourn there; for the famine was grievous in the land.

Here Abram has a lapse of faith and tried to resolve an imagined fear in his own way. This is a powerful lesson for us, that in all our fears and trials, we should trust in our Great God for His deliverance and act according to the Word and Will of God, not trying to deliver ourselves on our own.

May all of God's people be full of faith and courage to stand unshakable on the solid foundation of the whole Word of God!

12:11 And it came to pass, when he was come near to enter into Egypt, that he said unto Sarai his wife, Behold now, I know that thou art a fair woman to look upon: **12:12** Therefore it shall come to pass, when the Egyptians shall see thee, that they shall say, This is his wife: and they will kill me, but they will save thee alive. **12:13** Say, I pray thee, thou art my sister: [she was his sister, the deception was in not revealing that she was also his wife] that it may be well with me for thy sake; and my soul shall live because of thee.

The law against bearing false witness refers to deceiving and is not limited to explicit outright lies. Deception through omission or out of context quotes or twisting the true meaning, is very common among the elders of today's Ekklesia. Remember the commandment is not only about outright lying, it is about any form of willful deception.

12:14 And it came to pass, that, when Abram was come into Egypt, the Egyptians beheld the woman that she was very fair. **12:15** The princes also of Pharaoh saw her, and commended her before Pharaoh: and the woman was taken into Pharaoh's house.

In Egypt, Pharaoh gave many gifts making Abram rich as he sought to gain the woman that Pharaoh desired.

12:16 And he entreated Abram well for her sake: and he had sheep, and oxen, and he asses, and menservants, and maidservants, and she asses, and camels.

Then the Eternal sent strong correction on Pharaoh and Egypt until they discovered that the cause was his desire for Sarai.

12:17 And the LORD plagued Pharaoh and his house with great plagues because of Sarai Abram's wife. **12:18** And Pharaoh [when he understood the cause of the plagues] called Abram and said, What is this that thou hast done unto me? why didst thou not tell me that she was thy wife?

Pharaoh gives Abram back his wife Sarai without having "known" her; Pharaoh was making ready for his marriage to Sarai and was delivered from this potential sin by God's correction. This is a lesson that sometimes we can be corrected BEFORE we sin, so as to save us from committing some sin.

12:19 Why saidst thou, She is my sister? so I might have taken her to me to wife: now therefore behold thy wife, take her, and go thy way. **12:20** And Pharaoh commanded his men concerning him: and they sent him away, and his wife, and all that he had.

Genesis 13

Lot traveled with Abram from Haran into Canaan and then into Egypt

Genesis 13:1 And Abram went up out of Egypt, he, and his wife, and all that he had, and Lot with him, into the south [Negev near Sodom].

Abram was rich and became richer from Pharaoh's gifts.

13:2 And Abram was very rich in cattle, in silver, and in gold.

Abram returns to Bethel [The House of God] and called on God; this may have been in repentance for his sin in Egypt.

13:3 And he went on his journeys from the south even to Bethel, unto the place where his tent had been at the beginning, between Bethel and Hai; **13:4** Unto the place of the altar, which he had make there at the first: and there Abram called on the name of the LORD.

By this time Abram and Lot had so many cattle and sheep that there was not enough grazing land.

13:5 And Lot also, which went with Abram, had flocks, and herds, and tents. **13:6** And the land was not able to bear them, that they might dwell together: for their substance was great, so that they could not dwell together.

The herdsmen began to fight over the grass and water.

13:7 And there was a strife between the herdmen of Abram's cattle and the herdmen of Lot's cattle: and the Canaanite and the Perizzite dwelled then in the land. **13:8** And Abram said unto Lot, Let there be no strife, I pray thee, between me and thee, and between my herdmen and thy herdmen; for we be brethren.

Abram then offers Lot whatever he wants and he will take the other half. Abram was meek before God and his nephew, trusting in God to work everything out. Contrast this with the today's spiritual Ekklesia.

13:9 Is not the whole land before thee? separate thyself, I pray thee, from me: if thou wilt take the left hand, then I will go to the right; or if thou depart to the right hand, then I will go to the left.

Lot chose the rich grasslands east of the Jordan River; which were later to become desert beginning with Sodom, because of the sins of the inhabitants.

13:10 And Lot lifted up his eyes, and beheld all the plain of Jordan, that it was well watered every where, before the LORD destroyed Sodom and Gomorrah, even as the garden of the LORD, like the land of Egypt, as thou comest unto Zoar. **13:11** Then Lot chose him all the plain of Jordan; and Lot journeyed east: and they separated themselves the one from the other.

Lot took the land east of Jordan and Abram was left with the land of the Canaanites west of Jordan. This was actually according to the Promise of God; because God had promised that the descendants of Abram would have the land of Canaan, fulfilling the curse of Noah on Canaan.

13:12 Abram dwelled in the land of Canaan, and Lot dwelled in the cities of the plain, and pitched his tent toward Sodom. **13:13** But the men of Sodom were wicked and sinners before the LORD exceedingly.

A lot of non Biblical speculation has been used to try to prove British Israel teachings; This has brought much discredit on British Israel doctrine because very many of the "proofs" used were actually false and have collapsed under modern investigation. As for me I am going to stand on the Word and promises of God.

Remembering that it is through Isaac that the promise would be fulfilled (Gen 17:21); highlighted below is a promise of God that has also been fulfilled.

13:14 And the LORD said unto Abram, after that Lot was separated from him, Lift up now thine eyes, and look from the place where thou art northward, and southward, and eastward, and westward: **13:15** For all the land which thou seest, to thee will I give it, and to thy seed [Isaac and his descendants] for ever. **13:16** And **I will make thy seed** [Isaac and his descendants] **as the dust of the earth: so that if a man can number the dust of the earth, then shall thy seed** [Isaac and his descendants] **also be numbered.**

Abram is then told to walk about and see the good land that God had given his descendants through Isaac and as if that were not enough, God gave him tens of millions of descendants through Ishmael and through Keturah and through many other wives and concubines.

The day will come when our Deliverer will come and resolve all of our differences and bring peace between the descendants of Abraham, and between all of humanity.

As we see the sorrow and slaughter of the past and of today; let us be zealous to learn and to keep the only way to peace; and let us long for the day that Christ will come to bring peace to the earth.

13:17 Arise, walk through the land in the length of it and in the breadth of it; for I will give it unto thee. **13:18** Then Abram removed his tent, and came and dwelt in the plain of Mamre, which is in Hebron, and built there an altar unto the LORD.

Genesis 14

It came about that there was war east of Jordan between certain kings

Genesis 14:1 And it came to pass in the days of **Amraphel** king of Shinar [Mesopotamia], **Arioch** king of Ellasar, **Chedorlaomer** king of Elam, and **Tidal** king of nations; **14:2** That these **made war with Bera king of Sodom, and with Birsha king of Gomorrah, Shinab king of Admah, and Shemeber king of Zeboiim, and the king of Bela, which is Zoar.**

The people southeast of Jordan served these other kings from Mesopotamia for twelve years and then decided to rebel in the thirteenth year.

14:3 All these were joined together in the vale of Siddim, which is the salt sea. **14:4** Twelve years they served Chedorlaomer, and in the thirteenth year they rebelled.

Then in the fourteenth year Chedorlaomer commanding the armies of the northeastern kings came to put down the rebellion and punish the rebels.

14:5 And in the fourteenth year came Chedorlaomer, and the kings that were with him, and smote the Rephaims in Ashteroth Karnaim, and the Zuzims in Ham, and the Emins in Shaveh Kiriathaim, **14:6** And the Horites in their mount Seir, unto Elparan, which is by the wilderness. **14:7** And they returned, and came to Enmishpat, which is Kadesh, and smote all the country of the Amalekites, and also the Amorites, that dwelt in Hazezontamar.

Sodom where Lot lived, also went out to fight and was defeated.

14:8 And there went out the king of Sodom, and the king of Gomorrah, and the king of Admah, and the king of Zeboiim, and the king of Bela (the same is Zoar;) and they joined battle with them in the vale of Siddim; **14:9** With Chedorlaomer the king of Elam, and with Tidal king of nations, and Amraphel king of Shinar, and Arioch king of Ellasar; four kings with five. **14:10** And the vale of Siddim was full of slimepits [deposits of pitch, asphalt, tar pits]; and the kings of Sodom and Gomorrah fled, and fell there; and they that remained fled to the mountain.

These armies of retribution took all the spoil including Lot and all his possessions.

14:11 And they took all the goods of Sodom and Gomorrah, and all their victuals, and went their way. **14:12** And they took Lot, Abram's brother's son, who dwelt in Sodom, and his goods, and departed.

Now this Abram was filled with concern for his nephew and went out to deliver his nephew.

14:13 And there came one that had escaped, and told Abram the Hebrew; for he dwelt in the plain of Mamre the Amorite, brother of Eshcol, and brother of Aner: and **these were confederate with Abram.**

Abram defeated these kings and chased them to the border of Damascus.

14:14 And when Abram heard that his brother was taken captive, he armed his trained servants, born in his own house, three hundred and eighteen, and pursued them unto Dan. **14:15** And he divided himself against them, he and his servants, by night, and smote them, and pursued them unto Hobah, which is on the left hand of Damascus. **14:16** And he brought back all the goods, and also brought again his brother Lot, and his goods, and the women also, and the people. **14:17** And the king of Sodom went out to meet him after his return from the slaughter of Chedorlaomer, and of the kings that were with him, at the valley of Shaveh, which is the king's dale.

Melchizedek

14:18 And Melchizedek king of Salem [the spirit High Priest of God the Father who later gave up his Godhood to be made flesh as Jesus Christ] brought forth bread and wine: and he was the priest of the most high God.

Melchizedek blessed Abram by God the Father, showing that Melchizedek was the High Priest and Intercessor between man and God the Father in heaven.

14:19 And he blessed him, and said, Blessed be Abram of the most high God, possessor of heaven and earth: **14:20** And blessed be the most high God, which hath delivered thine enemies into thy hand. And he [Abram] gave him tithes of all.

This is the first place that tithes are mentioned in the Bible, and here Abram gives this Melchizedek tithes of the spoil of battle; showing that while Israel is specifically commanded to tithe on agriculture [because they were an agricultural people] God the Father is entitled to a tithe of ALL, because he is ultimately the sustainer of ALL things. Who gave us the wisdom and skill to make war or to make clothes or cars? Tithing acknowledges God the Father as ALL in all; the fountain of all knowledge and wisdom!

14:21 And the king of Sodom said unto Abram, Give me the persons, and take the goods to thyself.

The king of Sodom asks only for the people to be returned and Abram gave everything back to him, for Abram went to battle to rescue the captives and not to take spoil to enrich himself. This is a powerful message for us that we are not to seek our own advantage at the expense of others; we are to seek the good of all.

14:22 And Abram said to the king of Sodom, I have lift up mine hand unto the LORD, the most high God, the possessor of heaven and earth, **14:23** That I will not take from a thread even to a shoelatchet, and that I will not take any thing that is thine, lest thou shouldest say, I have made Abram rich: **14:24** Save only that which the young men have eaten, and the portion of the men which went with me, Aner, Eshcol, and Mamre; let them take their portion.

Genesis 15

After the battle with the kings, Abram had a vision and received a promise from God

Genesis 15:1 After these things the word of the LORD came unto Abram in a vision, saying, Fear not, Abram: I am thy shield, and thy exceeding great reward.

Abram then asked God for a son; as his only heir then was his nephew Lot.

15:2 And Abram said, LORD God, what wilt thou give me, seeing I go childless, and the steward of my house is this Eliezer of Damascus? **15:3** And Abram said, Behold, to me thou hast given no seed: and, lo, one born in my house [Abram's brother's son Lot] is mine heir.

God promised Abram a multitude of his own descendants.

15:4 And, behold, the word of the LORD came unto him, saying, This [Lot] shall not be thine heir; but he that shall come forth out of thine own bowels shall be thine heir. **15:5** And he brought him forth abroad [outside the tent to see the stars], and said, **Look now toward heaven, and tell the stars, if thou be able to number them: and he said unto him, So shall thy seed be.**

15:6 And he believed in the LORD; and he [God] counted it [the belief; the faith of Abram was counted as righteousness because that belief was married to the works of faith] to him for righteousness.

Now the Elohim that became Jesus Christ reveals that he had caused Terah the Chaldean to leave Ur with his sons to bring them to Haran, so that Abram could be called from Haran to Canaan; to give Canaan to Abram for his descendants.

15:7 And he said unto him, **I am the LORD that brought thee out of Ur of the Chaldees, to give thee this land to inherit it.**

Abram then asked God for a sign and Abram is commanded to make a certain special offering; and Abram obeyed God.

15:8 And he said, LORD God, whereby shall I know that I shall inherit it? **15:9** And he said unto him, Take me an heifer of three years old, and a she goat of three years old, and a ram of three years old, and a turtledove, and a young pigeon. **15:10** And he took unto him all these, and divided [cut up] them in the midst, and laid each piece one against another: but the birds divided he [did not cut up but left whole] not. **15:11** And when the fowls [flesh eaters like crows, ravens and vultures] came down upon the carcases, Abram drove them away. [Abram had not burned the sacrifice]

God caused Abram to fall into a deep sleep and gave him a prophecy by a dream.

15:12 And when the sun was going down, a deep sleep fell upon Abram; and, lo, an horror of great darkness fell upon him.

In the prophetic dream God tells Abram that his descendants will wander without a land of their own for 400 years and will then be delivered by the power of God.

15:13 And he said unto Abram, Know of a surety that thy seed shall be a stranger in a land that is not their's [they will be wanderers in Canaan and then will be in Egypt for 400 years before they inherit the land], and shall serve them; and **they shall afflict them four hundred years;**

> The belief that the children of Israel were slaves in Egypt for 400 years is largely based upon these two verses.
>
> "And he said unto Abram, Know of a surety that **thy seed** shall be **a stranger in a land that is not theirs** [which includes all the time that they were wanderers in Palestine and lived in Egypt - from the birth of Isaac - before actually inheriting the land], and shall serve them; and they shall afflict them **four hundred years** ..." (Genesis 15:13). "And God spake on this wise, That **his seed** should sojourn in a strange land [a land that is not theirs, meant both Canaan

and Egypt]; and that they should bring them into bondage, and entreat them evil **four hundred years**" (Acts 7:6).

Here is the meaning; thy seed refers to the children of Abraham beginning with Isaac the son of promise, who would be wanderers having no land of their own for four hundred years beginning with the birth of Isaac.

Isaac was born when Abraham was one hundred years old; therefore the exodus and the Sinai Covenant would take place four hundred years after the birth of Isaac or five hundred years after the birth of Abraham!

Abraham was born in 2008 A.M. (c 1940 B.C.): therefore the Exodus was 500 years later in 2508 A.M. (c 1440 B.C.) with a margin of possible error of a few years.

God also tells Abram that Egypt would be judged and that Abram's descendants will be brought out with much spoil.

15:14 And also that nation, whom they shall serve, will I judge: and afterward shall they come out with great substance.

Abram is told that he will die, but that in their fourth generation after going into Egypt his descendants will return to inherit the land.

15:15 And thou shalt go to thy fathers in peace; thou shalt be buried in a good old age. **15:16** But in the fourth generation [after entering Egypt] they [the family of Abram] shall come hither again: for the iniquity of the Amorites is not yet full.

In the darkness of the night a great light passed over the altar and God made his promise that the land of Canaan would be given to the descendants of Abram through Isaac. Those who are of faith and submissive to live by every Word of God like Abraham was, are Abraham's spiritual seed and have God's promise of the inheritance of the spiritual Promised Land of eternal life: IF we are zealous to live by every Word of God.

15:17 And it came to pass, that, when the sun went down, and it was dark, behold a smoking furnace, and a burning lamp that passed between those pieces.

15:18 In the same day the LORD made a covenant with Abram, saying, **Unto thy seed have I given this land, from the river of Egypt [El Arish] unto the great river, the river Euphrates: 15:19 The Kenites, and the**

Kenizzites, and the Kadmonites, 15:20 And the Hittites, and the Perizzites, and the Rephaims, 15:21 And the Amorites, and the Canaanites, and the Girgashites, and the Jebusites [of Jerusalem].

Genesis 16

Sarai gives Abram her maid; in fact Abram was a rich man and already had many concubines (Gen 25:6); but the story of Sarai and Hagar was recorded as a special allegory for us today.

Hagar was a slave and was forced to do what she did, thereby Ishmael was the son of the slave as a type of being enslaved by sin and enslaved by the penalty of the law for sin. which penalty is death: While Sarai as a free and willing legal wife was an allegory of the bride of Christ who is freed from enslavement and bondage to sin and death.

> **Galatians 4:23** But he who was of the bondwoman was born after the flesh; but he of the freewoman was by promise [of God].

The Mosaic Covenant was a physical covenant with physical promises; its physical sacrifices could atone physically and maintain the physical Mosaic Covenant; but they could not free anyone from their sins to inherit any spiritual promises which is why the New Covenant of Jermiah 31:31 was needed.

Hagar the bond woman was an allegory of the Mosaic Covenant, while Sarai as the free woman, was an allegory of the New Covenant, in which the wages of our past sins if sincerely repented of have been paid by our Deliverer and we have been redeemed from bondage to sin and reconciled to God the Father in heaven.

> **Galatians 4:24** Which things are an allegory: for these are the two covenants; the one from the mount Sinai, which gendereth

to bondage, which is Agar. 4:25** For this Agar is mount Sinai in Arabia, and answereth to [physical] Jerusalem which now is [the Mosaic Covenant , and is in [spiritual bondage to sin] bondage with her children.

The promise to Sarai is an allegory of the New Covenant.

4:26 But [the heavenly Jerusalem of God the Father] Jerusalem which is above is free, which is the mother of us all. **4:27** For it is written, Rejoice, thou barren that bearest not; break forth and cry, thou that travailest not: for the desolate hath many more children than she which hath an husband.

Isaac was a child of God's promise and is an allegory of God's promises to the spiritually called out and redeemed from sin.

4:28 Now we, brethren, as Isaac was, are the children of promise.

Paul speaks of the Mosaic Covenant persecuting the spiritual New Covenant called out in his day. This is also fulfilled by the worldly persecuting the spiritually faithful in this society; and by the lax and lukewarm within today's Ekklesia persecuting their more zealous brethren.

4:29 But as then he that was born after the flesh persecuted him that was born after the Spirit, even so it is now.

Nevertheless the spiritually called out of the New Covenant who are faithful, are the true spiritual sons of Abraham.

4:30 Nevertheless what saith the scripture? Cast out the bondwoman and her son: for the son of the bondwoman shall not be heir with the son of the freewoman. **4:31** So then, brethren, we [the sincerely repentant and faithful] are not children of the bondwoman, but of the free.

Genesis 16:1 Now Sarai Abram's wife bare him no children: and she had an handmaid, an Egyptian, whose name was Hagar.

16:2 And Sarai said unto Abram, Behold now, the LORD hath restrained me from bearing: I pray thee, go in unto my maid; it may be that I may obtain children by her. And Abram hearkened to the voice of Sarai. **16:3** And Sarai Abram's wife took Hagar her maid the Egyptian, after Abram had dwelt ten years in the land of Canaan, and gave her to her husband Abram to be his wife.

Immediately after Hagar conceived, Hagar was filled with contempt for the barrenness of her mistress Sarai.

This sin was typical of the self-righteousness of those who become filled with pride in themselves and their own ways and reject any zeal to live by every Word of God. As Hagar was raised up above her mistress in her mind by her pride, so many have become proud and have exalted themselves above living by every Word of our Master to live by their own ways.

16:4 And he went in unto Hagar, and she conceived: and when she [Hagar] saw that she had conceived, [Hagar despised Sarai] her mistress was despised in her eyes.

Sarai then complains to her husband Abram about the attitude of Hagar.

16:5 And Sarai said unto Abram, My wrong be upon thee: I have given my maid into thy bosom; and **when she saw that she had conceived, I was despised in her eyes**: the LORD judge between me and thee.

Abram then gives Sarai his consent to treat Hagar as she pleased; and the harshness of Sarai for the sin of Hagar drove Hagar to flee from Sarai.

16:6 But Abram said unto Sarai, Behold, thy maid is in thine hand; do to her as it pleaseth thee. And when Sarai dealt hardly with her, she fled from her face.

Then Melchizedek [who later gave up his Godhood to become flesh as Jesus Christ] appears to Hagar and bids her to return and to submit to Sarai.

16:7 And the angel of the LORD found her by a fountain of water in the wilderness, by the fountain in the way to Shur. **16:8** And he said, Hagar, Sarai's maid, whence camest thou? and whither wilt thou go? And she said, I flee from the face of my mistress Sarai.

16:9 And the angel of the LORD said unto her, Return to thy mistress, and submit thyself under her hands.

Hagar also receives a physical promise and blessing from God.

16:10 And the angel of the LORD said unto her, I will multiply thy seed exceedingly, that it shall not be numbered for multitude. **16:11** And the angel of the LORD said unto her, Behold, thou art with child and shalt bear a son, and shalt call his name Ishmael; because the LORD hath heard thy affliction. **16:12** And he will be a wild man; his hand will be against every man, and every man's hand against him; and he shall dwell in the presence of all his brethren.

16:13 And she called the name of the LORD that spake unto her, **Thou God seest me**: for she said, Have I also here looked after him that seeth me? **16:14** Wherefore the well was called **Beerlahairoi**; behold, it is between Kadesh and Bered.

16:15 And Hagar bare Abram a son: and Abram called his son's name, which Hagar bare, Ishmael. **16:16** And Abram was fourscore and six years [86] old, when Hagar bare Ishmael to Abram.

Genesis 17

Thirteen years after the birth of Ishmael, God made a covenant with Abram

Genesis 17:1 And when Abram was ninety years old and nine, the LORD appeared to Abram, and said unto him, I am the Almighty God; walk before me, and be thou perfect. **17:2** And I will make my covenant between me and thee, and will multiply thee exceedingly.

The name of Abram is changed to Abraham; and he is promised millions of descendants: Abraham is now promised to become the father of many NATIONS!

17:3 And Abram fell on his face: and God talked with him, saying, **17:4** As for me, behold, my covenant is with thee, and **thou shalt be a father of many nations. 17:5** Neither shall thy name any more be called Abram, but **thy name shall be Abraham; for a father of many nations have I made thee. 17:6** And I will make thee exceeding fruitful, and I will make nations of thee, and kings shall come out of thee.

Then God covenants to be the God of Abraham and his descendants.

17:7 And I will establish my covenant between me and thee and thy seed after thee in their generations for an everlasting covenant, to be a God unto thee, and to thy seed after thee.

God promises to give Abraham the land of Canaan through Isaac.

17:8 And I will give unto thee, and to thy seed after thee, the land wherein thou art a stranger, all the land of Canaan, for an everlasting possession; and I will be their God.

There are two sides to any agreement and Abraham and his descendants are pledged to obey and live by every Word of God; and to circumcise all their males, as the sign of this covenant with God.

Physical circumcision is a type of the spiritual circumcision of the heart, which is a removal of the barrier between us and God through sincere repentance from all past sin and a dedicated commitment to live by every Word of God and to go and sin no more.

> **Jeremiah 4:4 Circumcise yourselves to the Lord, and take away the foreskins of your heart,** ye men of Judah and inhabitants of Jerusalem: lest my fury come forth like fire, and burn that none can quench it, because of the evil of your doings.

God's people are commanded by this covenant with God and again in the law given to Israel to circumcise all males on the eighth day of life, and that commandment is still binding as a physical lesson and reminding sign that we are to also become circumcised in heart.

In the millennium no uncircumcised person may enter the Ezekiel Temple [or the spiritual Family of] God.

> **Ezekiel 44:9** Thus saith the Lord God; No stranger, **uncircumcised in heart, nor uncircumcised in flesh**, shall enter into my sanctuary, of any stranger that is among the children of Israel.

Paul said that adults who are already circumcised in heart, need not go through the physical operation in this dispensation; but our children are not converted and circumcised in heart and we are still to obey the command regarding our children in the hope that they also may become circumcised in spirit.

Genesis 17:9 And God said unto Abraham, Thou shalt keep my covenant therefore, thou, and thy seed after thee in their generations. **17:10** This is my covenant, which ye shall keep, between me and you and thy seed after thee; Every man child among you shall be circumcised.

17:11 And ye shall circumcise the flesh of your foreskin; and it shall be a token of the covenant betwixt me and you. **17:12** And **he that is eight days old shall be circumcised among you, every man child in your generations, he that is born in the house, or bought with money of any**

stranger, which is not of thy seed. 17:13 He that is born in thy house, and he that is bought with thy money, must needs be circumcised: and **my covenant** [the sign of circumcision] **shall be in your flesh for an everlasting covenant.**

17:14 And **the uncircumcised man child whose flesh of his foreskin is not circumcised, that soul shall be cut off from his people; he hath broken my covenant.**

Sarai means "argumentative"; and her name was changed to Sarah, meaning "exalted" or "princess" when God exalted her from barrenness to become the mother of many nations and kings.

17:15 And God said unto Abraham, As for Sarai thy wife, thou shalt not call her name Sarai, but Sarah shall her name be. **17:16** And I will bless her, and give thee a son also of her: yea, I will bless her, and she shall be a mother of nations; kings of people shall be of her.

Abraham is quickly taught that nothing is impossible with God.

17:17 Then **Abraham fell upon his face, and laughed,** and said in his heart, Shall a child be born unto him that is an hundred years old? and shall Sarah, that is ninety years old, bear? **17:18** And Abraham said unto God, O that Ishmael might live before thee! **17:19** And God said, Sarah thy wife shall bear thee a son indeed; and thou shalt call his name Isaac [laughter]: and I will establish my covenant with him for an everlasting covenant, and with his seed after him.

Ishmael would be greatly blessed, but Isaac will be the inheritor of the promise to Abraham.

17:20 And as for Ishmael, I have heard thee: Behold, I have blessed him, and will make him fruitful, and will multiply him exceedingly; twelve princes shall he beget, and I will make him a great nation.

17:21 But **my covenant will I establish with Isaac**, which Sarah shall bear unto thee at this set time in the next year.

As soon as God left off speaking Abraham obeyed God and circumcised everyone in his household; and to this day the sons of Hagar and of Judah circumcise their male children.

17:22 And he left off talking with him, and God went up from Abraham.

17:23 And Abraham took Ishmael his son, and all that were born in his house, and all that were bought with his money, every male among the men of Abraham's house; and circumcised the flesh of their foreskin in the selfsame day, as God had said unto him. **17:24** And Abraham was ninety years old and nine, when he was circumcised in the flesh of his foreskin. **17:25** And Ishmael his son was thirteen years old, when he was circumcised in the flesh of his foreskin.

17:26 In the selfsame day was Abraham circumcised, and Ishmael his son. **17:27** And all the men of his house, born in the house, and bought with money of the stranger, were circumcised with him.

Genesis 18

Genesis 18:1 And the LORD appeared unto him [Abraham] in the plains of Mamre: and he sat in the tent door in the heat of the day;

Then the one who later became Jesus Christ came to visit Abraham with two others, and Abraham offered his hospitality; perhaps recognizing the man as the Melchizedek he knew.

18:2 And he lift up his eyes and looked, and, **lo, three men stood** by him: and when he saw them, he ran to meet them from the tent door, and bowed himself toward the ground, **18:3** And said, My LORD, if now I have found favour in thy sight, pass not away, I pray thee, from thy servant: **18:4** Let a little water, I pray you, be fetched, and wash your feet, and rest yourselves under the tree: **18:5** And I will fetch a morsel of bread, and comfort ye your hearts; after that ye shall pass on: for therefore are ye come to your servant. And they said, So do, as thou hast said.

18:6 And Abraham hastened into the tent unto Sarah, and said, Make ready quickly three measures of fine meal, knead it, and make cakes upon the hearth. **18:7** And Abraham ran unto the herd, and fetcht a calf tender and good, and gave it unto a young man; and he hasted to dress it.

Here I would like to point out to our Rabbinic friends that they did indeed eat milk and butter with their meat through their father Abraham; and the Eternal did likewise. Now the law was later to say that one might not simmer a kid in its own mother's milk which was a Canaanite fertility rite; this law has nothing to do with the eating of milk products and meat together.

18:8 And **he took butter, and milk, and the calf which he had dressed**, and set it before them; and he stood by them under the tree, and they did eat.

God then reiterates his promise to Abraham that Sarah will have a son saying that in the fulfillment of her time [pregnancy in 9 Roman months and ten days; or ten lunar months] she would bear a son.

18:9 And they said unto him, Where is Sarah thy wife? And he said, Behold, in the tent.

The natural child bearing years of Sarah had passed and God had allowed that to come so that the power of God could be revealed to them and to us; and that if we trust in God's promises and keep his Word physically and spiritually we will inherit all of his promises in his good time.

18:10 And he said, I will certainly return unto thee according to the time of life; and, lo, Sarah thy wife shall have a son. And Sarah heard it in the tent door, which was behind him. **18:11** Now Abraham and Sarah were old and well stricken in age; and it ceased to be with Sarah after the manner of women.

Then God knew what Sarah was thinking and asked right out; why she did not believe the promises of God.

18:12 Therefore Sarah laughed within herself, saying, After I am waxed old shall I have pleasure, my lord being old also? **18:13** And the LORD said unto Abraham, Wherefore did Sarah laugh, saying, Shall I of a surety bear a child, which am old?

18:14 Is any thing too hard for the LORD? At the time appointed I will return unto thee, according to the time of life, and Sarah shall have a son.

Sarah was afraid and ashamed and denied, but God also knows us and all our very thoughts.

18:15 Then Sarah denied, saying, I laughed not; for she was afraid. And he said, Nay; but thou didst laugh.

They then rose and took the way to Sodom, and Abraham went with them a short way to see them off.

18:16 And the men rose up from thence, and looked toward Sodom: and Abraham went with them to bring them on the way.

Abraham diligently taught his children to live by every Word of God just as we should also do, for it is the keepers of the whole Word of God who may enter the Promised Land of eternal life.

18:17 And the LORD said, Shall I hide from Abraham that thing which I do; **18:18** Seeing that Abraham shall surely become a great and mighty nation, and all the nations of the earth shall be blessed in him? **18:19** For I know him, that he will command his children and his household after him, and they shall keep the way of the LORD, to do justice and judgment; that the LORD may bring upon Abraham that which he hath spoken of him.

Melchizedek goes towards Sodom to see if it is as evil as the reports and he is prepared to destroy that city as an example for us; that all those who depart from the Word of God, if they remain unrepentant will likewise perish in the final lake of fire.

God made an object lesson out of those people, but they will be raised up in the main harvest and they will have their chance at eternal life.

God has this to say about Jerusalem which is a type of Judah, and spiritual Judah the later day Ekklesia. Our sins are greater than Sodom's sin for we are supposed to know better. Physical Judah had the Mosaic Covenant, and Spiritual Judah has the Holy Spirit of God; Sodom had neither.

The sin of Sodom was PRIDE which caused them to do as they pleased instead of living by every Word of God; and today's Ekklesia is also filled with PRIDE which has caused us to turn from any zeal to live by every Word of God to do as we decide for ourselves.

> **Ezekiel 16:48** As I live, saith the Lord God, Sodom thy sister hath not done, she nor her daughters, as thou hast done, thou and thy daughters.
>
> **16:49** Behold, this was the iniquity of thy sister Sodom, pride, fulness of bread, and abundance of idleness was in her and in her daughters, **neither did she strengthen the hand of the poor and needy. 16:50** And **they were haughty** [proud]**, and committed abomination** [all compromise with the Word of God is an abomination] **before me:** therefore I took them away as I saw good.

Genesis 18:20 And the LORD said, Because the cry [reports about] of Sodom and Gomorrah is great, and because their sin is very grievous;

18:21 I will go down now, and see whether they have done altogether according to the cry [reports about] of it, which is come unto me; and if not, I will know.

When these "men" told Abraham of their intention to destroy Sodom and then went towards Sodom, Abraham lingered and then drew near to them to ask about destroying the righteous with the wicked.

Surely Abraham was concerned about ANY possible righteous person in Sodom, but he must have also been very concerned about his nephew righteous Lot and Lot's family.

18:22 And the men turned their faces from thence, and went toward Sodom: but Abraham stood yet before the LORD.

Abraham begins by asking about fifty righteous being destroyed along with the wicked.

18:23 And Abraham drew near, and said, Wilt thou also destroy the righteous with the wicked? **18:24** Peradventure there be fifty righteous within the city: wilt thou also destroy and not spare the place for the fifty righteous that are therein? **18:25** That be far from thee to do after this manner, to slay the righteous with the wicked: and that the righteous should be as the wicked, that be far from thee: Shall not the Judge of all the earth do right? **18:26** And the LORD said, If I find in Sodom fifty righteous within the city, then I will spare all the place for their sakes.

Abraham then begins to bargain and keeps changing the figures.

18:27 And Abraham answered and said, Behold now, I have taken upon me to speak unto the LORD, which am but dust and ashes: **18:28** Peradventure there shall lack five of the fifty righteous: wilt thou destroy all the city for lack of five? And he said, If I find there forty and five, I will not destroy it. **18:29** And he spake unto him yet again, and said, Peradventure there shall be forty found there. And he said, I will not do it for forty's sake.

18:30 And he said unto him, Oh let not the LORD be angry, and I will speak: Peradventure there shall thirty be found there. And he said, I will not do it, if I find thirty there. **18:31** And he said, Behold now, I have taken upon me to speak unto the LORD: Peradventure there shall be twenty found there. And he said, I will not destroy it for twenty's sake. **18:32** And he said, Oh let not the LORD be angry, and I will speak yet but this once:

Peradventure ten shall be found there. And he said, I will not destroy it for ten's sake.

Melchizedek the God who later gave up his Godhood to become flesh as Jesus Christ, agrees to save the city if only ten are found righteous and then proceeds on his way.

18:33 And the LORD went his way, as soon as he had left communing with Abraham: and Abraham returned unto his place.

Abraham was bargaining for the entire city, that if even ten righteous persons were found there the WHOLE CITY would be spared. God did not find ten righteous men in Sodom and therefore removed the righteous out of the city before destroying the wicked.

Strangely the Ekklesia of today would declare that removing the faithful so that the wicked can be corrected is causing division in the church! They would accuse God of dividing their corporate church groups when it is they who have divided the people from GOD!

I will not lie to anyone, this work, by calling the brethren to a zeal for God and his Word and calling people to a sincere dedication to full spiritual unity with God; IS dividing the idolaters who exalt men and corporate entities above the Word of God from those faithful who stand unshakable on the solid foundation of the whole Word of God [which is the righteousness of God].

Those who are zealous to live by every Word of God are being separated out from lukewarm spiritually indolent Laodicea, so that the unrepentant of Laodicea [spiritual Sodom] might be corrected in tribulation.

The lesson is that; just as God delivered righteous Lot out of the city and Sodom was totally destroyed by fire from heaven; those who live by faith and by every Word of God will also be separated out from those who lack any zeal to learn and to live by every Word of God; before he corrects today's idolatrous Ekklesia in the affliction of great tribulation!

Genesis 19

Two angels came to Sodom to separate Lot and his family from the people of Sodom, and Lot was hospitable to them in the manner of a righteous man. Although Moses wrote that these two were angels, Lot may not have known that right off and may have just been hospitable to strangers.

Genesis 19:1 And there came two angels to Sodom at even; and Lot sat in the gate of Sodom: and Lot seeing them rose up to meet them; and he bowed himself with his face toward the ground; **19:2** And he said, Behold now, my lords, turn in, I pray you, into your servant's house, and tarry all night, and wash your feet, and ye shall rise up early, and go on your ways. And they said, Nay; but we will abide in the street all night. **19:3** And he pressed upon them greatly; and they turned in unto him, and entered into his house; and he made them a feast, and did bake unleavened bread, and they did eat.

Many men of Sodom then demanded sex from these two male guests of Lot.

19:4 But before they lay down, the men of the city, even the men of Sodom, compassed the house round, both old and young, all the people from every quarter: **19:5** And they called unto Lot, and said unto him, Where are the men which came in to thee this night? bring them out unto us, that we may know them.

Righteous Lot then loses his faith and does a very wicked and desperate thing by offering his two daughters to these men instead of crying out to God for deliverance.

19:6 And Lot went out at the door unto them, and shut the door after him, **19:7** And said, I pray you, brethren, do not so wickedly. **19:8** Behold now, I have two daughters which have not known man; let me, I pray you, bring them out unto you, and do ye to them as is good in your eyes: only unto these men do nothing; for therefore came they under the shadow of my roof.

Then the men of Sodom replied that Lot was a stranger who come to dwell among them, and that Lot took too much on himself to judge and resist them.

19:9 And they said, Stand back. And they said again, This one fellow [Lot] came in to sojourn, and he will needs be a judge: now will we deal worse with thee, than with them. And they pressed sore upon the man, even Lot, and came near to break the door.

The angels pulled Lot back inside and smote these sons of wickedness with blindness.

19:10 But the men put forth their hand, and pulled Lot into the house to them, and shut to the door. **19:11** And they smote the men that were at the door of the house with blindness, both small and great: so that they wearied themselves to find the door.

The angels confirming the reports of the wickedness of Sodom; told Lot to take his family and leave that city before it is destroyed.

19:12 And the men [angels] said unto Lot, Hast thou here any besides? son in law, and thy sons, and thy daughters, and whatsoever thou hast in the city, bring them out of this place: **19:13** For we will destroy this place, because the cry of them is waxen great before the face of the LORD; and **the LORD hath sent us to destroy it**.

Lot's married daughters and their families thought that Lot and his warnings to them to leave immediately were insane.

So it will be when God's two messengers warn the brethren to leave this land before our own correction. Most people even in the Ekklesia will think that these two servants of God are crazy and will not comply, instead they will stand on their own false prophetic traditions.

Only those who love and live by every Word of God and are quickly and sincerely repentant of their mistakes, the pillars who stand firmly on the whole Word of God: Will obey the word of God's servants and leave this land before its affliction.

The men of Sodom are analogous of our society today, and the family of Lot is analogous to the majority of today's Ekklesia; who are full of pride in their own ways and traditions and have no zeal to live by every Word of God.

19:14 And Lot went out, and spake unto his sons in law, which married his daughters, and said, Up, get you out of this place; for the LORD will destroy this city. But he seemed as one that mocked [his words seemed crazy to them] unto his sons in law.

Then in the morning the two messengers were urgent on Lot to separate from the wicked, so that they would be spared while the wicked were destroyed.

This work is an early warning message to prepare the brethren before the final warning of God's two witnesses; which will separate out the faithful pillars from the wicked proud, idolaters who stand on their own ways contrary to the whole Word of God.

Yes, God IS the author of division! God has called many out of this world dividing them from the worldly! God separates the faithful from the wicked, so that he may afflict the wicked and spare the faithful!

19:15 And when the morning arose, then the angels hastened Lot, saying, Arise, take thy wife, and thy two daughters, which are here; lest thou be consumed in the iniquity of the city.

When they delayed for packing, good byes etc the two messengers grabbed hold of them and forcefully brought them out of the company of wickedness.

19:16 And while he lingered, the men laid hold upon his hand, and upon the hand of his wife, and upon the hand of his two daughters; the LORD being merciful unto him: and they brought him forth, and set him without the city. **19:17** And it came to pass, when they had brought them forth abroad, that he said, Escape for thy life; look not behind thee, neither stay thou in all the plain; escape to the mountain, lest thou be consumed.

The two messengers were urgent that Lot and his family run for their lives as Jesus Christ has warned us in Matthew 24:15. This is an analogy that we are to run to separate ourselves from all wickedness.

Then Lot protested that the distance was too far and the angels showed a further mercy.

19:18 And Lot said unto them, Oh, not so, my LORD: **19:19** Behold now, thy servant hath found grace in thy sight, and thou hast magnified thy mercy, which thou hast shewed unto me in saving my life; and I cannot escape to the mountain, lest some evil take me, and I die: **19:20** Behold now, this city is near to flee unto, and it is a little one: Oh, let me escape thither, (is it not a little one?) and my soul shall live. **19:21** And he said unto him, See, I have accepted thee concerning this thing also, that I will not overthrow this city, for the which thou hast spoken. **19:22** Haste thee, escape thither; for I cannot do anything till thou be come thither. Therefore the name of the city was called Zoar.

Lot and his immediate family were taken out of Sodom in the early morning, and arrived in Zoar later in the day.

19:23 The sun was risen upon the earth when Lot entered into Zoar.

Then God destroyed Sodom and Gomorrah as an example to us, that he will destroy all those who are not zealous to live by EVERY WORD of GOD.

19:24 Then the LORD rained upon Sodom and upon Gomorrah brimstone and fire from the LORD out of heaven; **19:25** And he overthrew those cities, and all the plain, and all the inhabitants of the cities, and that which grew upon the ground.

Then Lot's wife disobeyed God's Word and looked back and was also destroyed. This is analogous of those who love this society and its sinful pleasures so much that they will long for it, and turn away from zeal for the Word of God.

19:26 But his wife looked back from behind him, and she became a pillar of salt.

Abraham was at Shechem and looked out over nearly a hundred miles to see the smoke ascending into the heavens; just as the destruction of all those who refuse to separate themselves from the wickedness of rejecting zeal to live by every Word of God will be seen by all.

19:27 And Abraham gat up early in the morning to the place where he stood before the LORD: **19:28** And he looked toward Sodom and Gomorrah, and toward all the land of the plain, and beheld, and, lo, the smoke of the country went up as the smoke of a furnace.

Here Moses informs us that even righteous Lot was resistant to separate himself from the wicked and was virtually dragged out and saved; because of Abraham!

19:29 And it came to pass, when God destroyed the cities of the plain, that God remembered Abraham, and sent Lot out of the midst of the overthrow, when he overthrew the cities in the which Lot dwelt.

Lot, apparently afraid that Zoar would also be destroyed went up to hide in the mountains instead of remaining in the city of Zoar.

19:30 And Lot went up out of Zoar, and dwelt in the mountain, and his two daughters with him; for he feared to dwell in Zoar: and he dwelt in a cave, he and his two daughters.

Here Lot's two daughters lacked faith and tried to do what they thought was right in their circumstances, instead of relying on the Word of God.

Instead of discussing the matter with their father who would have inquired of God they decided to use deception to attain their purpose; this an indication that they knew that their father Lot would object.

We lack full information and the wisdom of God and so our own ways are foolish compared to God's Word. When we blindly stand on our own human traditions instead of on the Word of God, we are truly spiritually blind! We are just as blind and foolish as these well meaning young ladies.

19:31 And the firstborn said unto the younger, Our father is old, and there is not a man in the earth to come in unto us after the manner of all the earth: **19:32** Come, let us make our father drink wine, and we will lie with him, that we may preserve seed of our father.

This illustrates the evils of drunkenness during which we can lose control of ourselves and become susceptible to things that we would regard as unthinkable when sober. The spiritual essence of the command to not be drunk is that we are never to give control of a sound mind over to anyone or any substance.

This refers to being drunk with alcohol and drugs, and it also refers to being made drunk with sin and pride in ourselves and our group; so that we exalt them above the Word of God as is done in the majority of today's spiritual Ekklesia.

Compromising with the whole Word of God and turning away from God to our own ways is spiritual fornication with false religion and false teachings. To fornicate is to become ONE with these things and to separate ourselves from God.

> **Revelation 17:2** With whom the kings of the earth have committed fornication, and the inhabitants of the earth have been made drunk with the wine of her fornication.

Genesis 19:33 And they made their father drink wine that night: and the firstborn went in, and lay with her father; and he perceived not when she lay down, nor when she arose. **19:34** And it came to pass on the morrow, that the firstborn said unto the younger, Behold, I lay yesternight with my father: let us make him drink wine this night also; and go thou in, and lie with him, that we may preserve seed of our father. **19:35** And they made their father drink wine that night also: and the younger arose, and lay with him; and he perceived not when she lay down, nor when she arose.

19:36 Thus were both the daughters of Lot with child by their father. **19:37** And the first born bare a son, and **called his name Moab: the same is the father of the Moabites unto this day. 19:38** And the younger, she also bare a son, and **called his name Benammi: the same is the father of the children of Ammon unto this day.**

The descendants of these two boys are the indigenous people of Jordan today. Jordanians are not the descendants of Ishmael and they are not Arabs; they are the family of Abraham through his nephew Lot.

Genesis 20

Abraham travels around Canaan as God had instructed him

Genesis 20:1 And Abraham journeyed from thence toward the south country, and dwelled between Kadesh and Shur, and sojourned in Gerar.

Abraham then repeats the mistake that he made in Egypt and fails to trust in God.

20:2 And Abraham said of Sarah his wife, She is my sister: and Abimelech king of Gerar sent, and took Sarah.

God then warns Abimelech in a dream, to save him from the sin of adultery. Yes, God does work in dreams and visions, and sometimes uses a still small voice.

Of course we must test what we receive according to the whole Word of God as Peter did. Peter rightly rejected the idea that the dream was allowing the eating of unclean animals and God had to open Peter's mind and reveal the true meaning before Peter understood that God was really saying that all sincerely repentant men are acceptable to God, and that his dream was not about eating clean and unclean animals.

If a dream, vision or voice is not consistent with the whole Word of God; it is to be rejected.

Now Abimelech and his family were afflicted by God because of Sarah, and Abimelech had been seeking an answer as to why the plague had come upon them; at which point God comes to him in a dream in answer to his prayer.

20:3 But God came to Abimelech in a dream by night, and said to him, Behold, thou art but a dead man, for the woman which thou hast taken; for she is a man's wife. **20:4** But Abimelech had not come near her: and he said, LORD, wilt thou slay also a righteous nation? **20:5** Said he not unto me, She is my sister? and she, even she herself said, He is my brother: in the integrity of my heart and innocency of my hands have I done this.

20:6 And God said unto him in a dream, Yea, I know that thou didst this in the integrity of thy heart; for I also withheld thee from sinning against me: therefore suffered I thee not to touch her. 20:7 Now therefore restore the man his wife; for **he is a prophet**, and he shall pray for thee, and thou shalt live: and if thou restore her not, know thou that thou shalt surely die, thou, and all that are thine.

Abimelech was very afraid and demanded an explanation from Abraham.

20:8 Therefore Abimelech rose early in the morning, and called all his servants, and told all these things in their ears: and the men were sore afraid. **20:9** Then Abimelech called Abraham, and said unto him, What hast thou done unto us? and what have I offended thee, that thou hast brought on me and on my kingdom a great sin? thou hast done deeds unto me that ought not to be done. **20:10** And Abimelech said unto Abraham, What sawest thou, that thou hast done this thing?

Abraham responds by telling Abimelech of his fears.

Brethren, there are times in our lives when we all face fears; that is the time to RUN to our Mighty Fortress of Strength and to Trust in the promises and deliverance of our High Tower and Refuge: The God who parted the sea!

Let us not lean to our own ways, which are like a rotten walking stick which when we lean on breaks under us causing us to fall.

20:11 And Abraham said, Because I thought, Surely the fear of God is not in this place; and they will slay me for my wife's sake. **20:12** And yet indeed she is my sister; she is the daughter of my father, but not the daughter of my mother; and she became my wife. **20:13** And it came to pass, when God caused me to wander from my father's house, that I said unto her, This is thy kindness which thou shalt shew unto me; at every place whither we shall come, say of me, He is my brother.

God delivered Abimelech, Abraham and Sarah because the deception of Abimelech by Abraham could have killed Abimelech, defiled Sarah, and confused the parentage of Isaac.

Trust in God and passionately keep his Word, and our Mighty Deliverer will save us; and if he chooses not to save us physically in this life we will be with him in our next conscious moment!

Abimelech then restores Sarah to Abraham and gives him great wealth because of his fear of God; for surely Abraham deserved punishment and not gifts.

20:14 And Abimelech took sheep, and oxen, and menservants, and womenservants, and gave them unto Abraham, and restored him Sarah his wife. **20:15** And Abimelech said, Behold, my land is before thee: dwell where it pleaseth thee. **20:16** And unto Sarah he said, Behold, I have given thy brother a thousand pieces of silver: behold, he is to thee a covering of the eyes, unto all that are with thee, and with all other: thus she was reproved.

Now it is revealed that God had sent some kind of disease on Abimelech and his family [seemingly involving reproduction] before appearing to him in a dream to reveal the reason for the plague.

20:17 So Abraham prayed unto God: and **God healed Abimelech, and his wife, and his maidservants; and they bare children. 20:18 For the LORD had fast closed up all the wombs of the house of Abimelech,** because of Sarah Abraham's wife.

Genesis 21

God is ABLE to fulfill ALL his promises! If at any time he does not, it is because many of his promises are CONDITIONAL on our sincere repentance and on our passion for learning and keeping his Word! God's promises are also subject to God's own good timing, or to the timing that has been aforetime appointed, such as the date of the coming of Messiah the Christ!

Genesis 21:1 And the LORD visited Sarah as he had said, and the LORD did unto Sarah as he had spoken. **21:2** For Sarah conceived, and bare Abraham a son in his old age, at the set time of which God had spoken to him.

Isaac meaning "laughter" was a perpetual reminder to Abraham and Sarah of their lack of faith when the promise of Isaac was given. This name "Laughter" is also indicative of the great joy of Abraham and Sarah at the birth of a son in their old age.

21:3 And Abraham called the name of his son that was born unto him, whom Sarah bare to him, Isaac. **21:4** And Abraham **circumcised his son Isaac being eight days old, as God had commanded him.**

We are to likewise obey this command of God to circumcise our sons on the eighth day. This circumcision on the Eighth Day is a prophecy of the Eighth Day Feast; when ALL humanity will be circumcised in heart and will go forth sensitive and subject to the whole Word of God for all eternity.

21:5 And Abraham was an hundred years old, when his son Isaac was born unto him.

Sarah then exclaimed that she will now laugh for joy! and that others who hear of her joy will also smile and laugh for joy with her.

21:6 And Sarah said, God hath made me to laugh [God has given her joy with the gift of a son.] **, so that all that hear will laugh with me. 21:7** And she said, Who would have said unto Abraham, that Sarah should have given children suck? for **I have born him a son in his old age.**

Abraham made a feast of rejoicing for Isaac when he was about four years old; and Hagar again mocked Sarah because of her son Ishmael who was the first born.

21:8 And the child grew, and was weaned: and Abraham made a great feast the same day that Isaac was weaned. 21:9 And Sarah saw the son of Hagar the Egyptian, which she had born unto Abraham, mocking.

Sarah then demanded of Abraham that he should cast away the son of the bondwoman so that the son of bondage should not be heir with the free born son of promise. Ishmael being an allegory of the Mosaic Covenant which brought no spiritual inheritance, for the Mosaic Covenant could not inherit spiritual things and its members will not inherit spiritual promises until they are called into a New Covenant (Jer 31, Hebrews).

21:10 Wherefore she said unto Abraham, Cast out this bondwoman and her son: for the son of this bondwoman shall not be heir with my son, even with Isaac.

> **Galatians 4:22** For it is written, that Abraham had two sons, the one by a bondmaid, the other by a freewoman. **4:23** But he who was of the bondwoman was born after the flesh [An allegory of the Mosaic Covenant which had no promise of spiritual inheritance]; but he of the freewoman was by promise [An allegory of the promise of a spiritual inheritance in a New Covenant].
>
> **4:24** Which things are an allegory: for these are the two covenants; the one from the mount Sinai [The Mosaic Covenant], which gendereth to bondage [Bondage to death is the penalty of sin, since the blood of animals only reconciled them to the Mosaic Covenant and could not bring them into the spiritual New Covenant with its

spiritual promises.], which is Agar. **4:25** For this Agar is mount Sinai [the bond servant Hagar is a picture of the physical Mosaic Covenant] in Arabia, and answereth to [physical earthly] Jerusalem which now is, and is in bondage with her children.

4:26 But Jerusalem which is above is free [The heavenly Jerusalem represents the spiritual New Covenant of promise, Jeremiah 31 pictured by Isaac, and faithfulness to God in sincere repentance, having the sacrifice of Christ applied to us and committing to go and sin no more; which then reconciles us to God spiritually and frees the sincerely repentant from bondage to death which is the wages of sin], which is the mother of us all.

All physical scriptural things are instructions in spiritual principles and the story if Abraham and Isaac is **an allegory of God the Father and Jesus Christ**.

Abraham loved his first born and was grieved to send Ishmael away; and Ishmael has been grieved at the supposed loss of his birthright as the first born son ever since. God then told Abraham that this was from him, for Isaac was the son of promise [representing the New Covenant of promise] and not Ishmael.

Genesis 21:11 And the thing was very grievous in Abraham's sight because of his son. **21:12** And God said unto Abraham, Let it not be grievous in thy sight because of the lad, and because of thy bondwoman; in all that Sarah hath said unto thee, hearken unto her voice; for **in Isaac shall thy seed be called.**

God then gave Ishmael to be a nation because of Abraham his father.

21:13 And also of the son of the bondwoman will I make a nation, because he is thy seed.

Then Abraham obeyed and sent Ishmael and Hagar away.

21:14 And Abraham rose up early in the morning, and took bread, and a bottle of water, and gave it unto Hagar, putting it on her shoulder, and the child, and sent her away: and she departed, and wandered in the wilderness of Beersheba. **21:15** And the water was spent in the bottle, and she cast the child under one of the shrubs [for shade].

Ishmael a young man of about 17 cried for water, dying of thirst, and Hagar could not bear it and went a little way off to weep herself. Imagine yourself in these circumstances, these are real people suffering real distress. The Word of God is not some dry history; it is about real people and real lessons for life.

God saved Hagar and Ishmael to KEEP HIS PROMISE to Abraham; that Ishmael would become a great nation!

Almighty God keeps his promises! His faithful trust and depend on HIM; and do not lean to their own ways!

21:16 And she went, and sat her down over against him a good way off, as it were a bow shot: for she said, Let me not see the death of the child. And she sat over against him, and lift up her voice, and wept. **21:17** And God heard the voice of the lad; and the angel of God called to Hagar out of heaven, and said unto her, What aileth thee, Hagar? fear not; for God hath heard the voice of the lad where he is.

God then delivers Hagar and Ishmael.

21:18 Arise, lift up the lad, and hold him in thine hand; for I will make him a great nation. **21:19** And God opened her eyes, and she saw a well of water; and she went, and filled the bottle with water, and gave the lad drink.

21:20 And God was with the lad; and he grew, and dwelt in the wilderness, and became an archer. **21:21** And he dwelt in the wilderness of Paran: and his mother took him a wife out of the land of Egypt.

The founding of Beer Sheba

Abimelech's servants take a well that Abraham 's servants had dug in Abimelech's territory; causing a dispute between Abraham and Abimelech. At that time the area belonged to the Philistines and Abraham's servants had dug a well on Abimelech's land.

Abraham makes a covenant with Abimelech to settle the dispute with him.

Abimelech knew about the God of all creation through the example of Abraham. He knew that Abraham's God was the one who had healed his wife and maidservants so that they would bear him children. Abimelech knew that Abraham's God was with him in all that he did.

When it came to a dispute over land and a well (in that part of the world a very important thing since it was a dry land), all Abimelech needed was for Abraham to swear by his God that he was telling the truth and did actually dig the well he claimed and that there would be peace between Abraham and Abimelech's descendants from then on.

Payment for the land was made by Abraham, the oath solemnly confirmed by the gift of 7 ewe lambs, and that settled everything.

21:22 And it came to pass at that time, that Abimelech and Phichol the chief captain of his host spake unto Abraham, saying, God is with thee in all that thou doest: **21:23** Now therefore swear unto me here by God that thou wilt not deal falsely with me, nor with my son, nor with my son's son: but according to the kindness that I have done unto thee, thou shalt do unto me, and to the land wherein thou hast sojourned. **21:24** And Abraham said, I will swear.

21:25 And Abraham reproved Abimelech because of a well of water, which Abimelech's servants had violently taken away. **21:26** And Abimelech said, I wot not who hath done this thing; neither didst thou tell me, neither yet heard I of it, but to day.

See how these men resolved the problem instead of fighting. Abraham proved the well was his, and Abimelech proved he owned the land; so they agreed that Abraham would buy that land with cattle and sheep; and Beer Sheba became the property of Abraham and through him the property of Isaac.

21:27 And Abraham took sheep and oxen, and gave them unto Abimelech; and both of them made a covenant.

Abraham then sets seven ewe's as a seven fold oath that his servants had dug the well and that the well was his. When Abimelech accepted these seven ewe's he accepted that Abraham had indeed dug the well.

21:28 And Abraham set seven ewe lambs of the flock by themselves. **21:29** And Abimelech said unto Abraham, What mean these seven ewe lambs which thou hast set by themselves? **21:30** And he said, For **these seven ewe lambs shalt thou take of my hand**, that they may be a witness unto me, that I have digged this well.

21:31 Wherefore he called that place Beersheba [Beer-sheba = "well of the sevenfold oath"]; because there they sware both of them.

Abimelech then returned from the strife back to his royal city of the Philistines.

21:32 Thus they made a covenant at Beersheba: then Abimelech rose up, and Phichol the chief captain of his host, and they returned into the land of the Philistines. **21:33** And Abraham planted a grove [trees] in Beersheba, and called there on the name of the LORD, the everlasting God. **21:34** And Abraham sojourned in the Philistines' land many days.

Genesis 22

Knowing the mind of God, one could easily think that the following event happened around Passover. In any case this is a profound allegory about the Passover and is one key to understanding the Passover.

God tests Abraham concerning Isaac.

When Abraham trusted God and did not withhold his only son, his beloved son of promise; God provided a lamb. This test is an allegory of how God the Father gave his only begotten son to die as the Lamb of God for the sins of the world.

Genesis 22:1 And it came to pass after these things, that God did tempt Abraham, and said unto him, Abraham: and he said, Behold, here I am.

22:2 And he said, **Take now thy son, thine only son Isaac, whom thou lovest**, and get thee into the land of Moriah [the threshing floor at the top of the Temple Mount; which had as yet no Temple.]; and **offer him there for a burnt offering** upon one of the mountains which I will tell thee of.

God had promised Abraham that Isaac would be the father of many nations and millions of people; Abraham believed the promise of God and yet was ready to give his son of promise, believing that God would somehow still find a way to keep his promise to him.

After many years and much developing of faith and learning on the way, Abraham was ready for the final test which would make him the spiritual father of all those who are faithful to God. This is the kind of total dedication to obeying the whole word of God that is expected of every faithful called out pillar of God!

Abraham was willing to give his beloved son of promise, the most precious thing he possessed; because he believed, trusted and obeyed God! And most of us will not give up a visit to a restaurant on the Sabbath to obey and please God! Oh, how far we have fallen from the faith and loving obedience of Abraham!

Moses takes two servants and Isaac with him and begins his journey to the Mount. The journey must have been filled with confusion of mind as Abraham struggled with the apparent contradiction between the promise and the command; and filled with tears over what he was commanded to do.

The poor man must have been in agony of spirit, because he had already lost his beloved Ishmael and now Isaac was apparently being taken to please God; yet he trusted God and obeyed his Word! Think about this when you are tried in your own life; be faithful to the whole Word of God, and he will make a way for you.

22:3 And Abraham rose up early in the morning, and saddled his ass, and took two of his young men with him, and Isaac his son, and clave the wood for the burnt offering, and rose up, and went unto the place of which God had told him.

On the third day Abraham left his servants and went to the Mount with Isaac.

22:4 Then on the third day Abraham lifted up his eyes, and saw the place afar off. **22:5** And Abraham said unto his young men, Abide ye here with the ass; and I and the lad will go yonder and worship, and come again to you. **22:6** And Abraham took the wood of the burnt offering, and laid it upon Isaac his son; and he took the fire in his hand, and a knife; and they went both of them together.

Abraham said to Isaac: "God will provide a lamb my son"; this being a prophecy, that God the Father would provide HIS son as the Lamb of God, to be sacrificed for our sins in our place.

22:7 And Isaac spake unto Abraham his father, and said, My father: and he said, Here am I, my son. And he said, Behold the fire and the wood: but where is the lamb for a burnt offering? **22:8** And Abraham said, **My son, God will provide himself a lamb for a burnt of**fering: so they went both of them together.

Abraham obeyed God and Isaac also obeyed God, permitting himself to be bound and laid upon the wood. This was an analogy that God the Father would not withhold his ONLY begotten son and would sacrifice him for OUR sins; and that his son Jesus Christ would allow himself as the Creator of humanity, to be sacrificed to save mankind!

Brethren, God has given us such a gift; how can we not be zealous to follow Abraham's example of obedience and be passionately zealous to learn and to live by every Word of God?

22:9 And they came to the place which God had told him of; and Abraham built an altar there, and laid the wood in order, and bound Isaac his son, and laid him on the altar upon the wood.

As Abraham was about to obey God and kill his son of promise to please God; the LORD called out to him and stayed his hand.

22:10 And Abraham stretched forth his hand, and took the knife to slay his son. **22:11** And the angel of the LORD called unto him out of heaven, and said, Abraham, Abraham: and he said, Here am I. **22:12** And he said, Lay not thine hand upon the lad, neither do thou any thing unto him: **for now I know that thou fearest God, seeing thou hast not withheld thy son, thine only son from me.**

Abraham did not withhold even his beloved son of promise, and the overwhelming majority of today's Ekklesia will not even refrain from doing their own thing on Sabbath and polluting it.

Consider the comparison of zeal for God and the lack of love and zeal for God in the Ekklesia today. No wonder we make Jesus Christ SICK to his stomach, so that he will vomit out those who are lukewarm for God's Word; expelling them out of his body and out of his mouth (Rev 3:16).

For the faithful and passionately zealous to learn, to teach and to live by every Word of God: God has provided his Lamb, Jesus Christ; and God will apply that perfect sacrifice to all who come to him in sincere repentance, committing to go and SIN NO MORE!

22:13 And Abraham lifted up his eyes, and looked, and behold behind him a ram caught in a thicket by his horns: and Abraham went and took the ram, and offered him up for a burnt offering in the stead of his son.

Jehovahjireh: "The Eternal has provided".

22:14 And Abraham called the name of that place Jehovahjireh: as it is said to this day [the day that Moses wrote this], In the mount of the LORD [the Trmple Mount at Jebus, Jerusalem] it shall be seen.

After the sacrifice of the ram God again calls out to Abraham from heaven.

22:15 And the angel of the LORD called unto Abraham out of heaven the second time,

Abraham is blessed for his faithful obedience to the whole Word of God even to giving up his most precious and beloved possession, and we cannot even give up our false traditions in which we take so much pleasure! For shame!

22:16 And said, By myself have I sworn, saith the LORD, for because thou hast done this thing, and hast not withheld thy son, thine only son: **22:17** That in blessing I will bless thee, and in multiplying I will multiply thy seed as the stars of the heaven, and as the sand which is upon the sea shore; and thy seed shall possess the gate of his enemies; **22:18** And in thy seed shall all the nations of the earth be blessed; because thou hast obeyed my voice.

Here God promises that all nations would be blessed through Abraham's seed ISAAC and not of his other sons. It is obvious that this refers to a birthright promise which would be handed on to Isaac's descendants and not to the descendants of Abraham's other sons.

All physical scriptural things are instructions in spiritual principles and the story if Abraham and Isaac is **an allegory of God the Father and Jesus Christ**. Paul explains in Galatians that the promise of being a physical blessing on all nations which was given to Isaac, was an allegory of **a spiritual blessing on all nations** through Jesus Christ the son of God the Father.

22:19 So Abraham returned unto his young men, and they rose up and went together to Beersheba; and Abraham dwelt at Beersheba.

Then Abraham heard that his brother Nahor who had remained at Haran had also had children and an extended family. This news causes Abraham to send his servant there to seek a wife for Isaac out of Isaac's cousins in Haran.

22:20 And it came to pass after these things, that it was told Abraham, saying, Behold, Milcah, she hath also born children unto thy brother Nahor; **22:21** Huz his firstborn, and Buz his brother, and Kemuel the father of Aram, **22:22** And Chesed, and Hazo, and Pildash, and Jidlaph, and Bethuel. **22:23** And Bethuel begat Rebekah: these eight Milcah did bear to Nahor, Abraham's brother. **22:24** And his concubine, whose name was Reumah, she bare also Tebah, and Gaham, and Thahash, and Maachah.

Genesis 23

The death of Sarah

Genesis 23:1 And Sarah was an hundred and seven and twenty years old: these were the years of the life of Sarah. **23:2** And Sarah died in Kirjatharba; the same is **Hebron** in the land of Canaan: and Abraham came to mourn for Sarah, and to weep for her.

Abraham buys Machpelah

23:3 And Abraham stood up from before his dead, and spake unto the sons of Heth, saying, **23:4** I am a stranger and a sojourner with you: give me a possession of a buryingplace with you, that I may bury my dead out of my sight. **23:5** And the children of Heth answered Abraham, saying unto him, **23:6** Hear us, my lord: thou art a mighty prince among us: in the choice of our sepulchres bury thy dead; none of us shall withhold from thee his sepulchre, but that thou mayest bury thy dead.

Abraham humbles himself before the people of the land and asks only to buy a burying place in Hebron.

23:7 And Abraham stood up, and bowed himself to the people of the land, even to the children of Heth. **23:8** And he communed with them, saying, If it be your mind that I should bury my dead out of my sight; hear me, and intreat for me to Ephron the son of Zohar, **23:9** That he may give me the cave of Machpelah, which he hath, which is in the end of his field; for as much money as it is worth he shall give it me for a possession of a buryingplace amongst you.

Because Abraham was known to be a just and honorable man and his example was righteous in the Word of God before all his neighbours; God had caused even the unconverted to respect him.

23:10 And Ephron dwelt among the children of Heth: and Ephron the Hittite answered Abraham in the audience of the children of Heth, even of all that went in at the gate of his city, saying, **23:11** Nay, my lord, hear me: the field give I thee, and the cave that is therein, I give it thee; in the presence of the sons of my people give I it thee: bury thy dead.

Abraham insists on paying for the land.

23:12 And Abraham bowed down himself before the people of the land. **23:13** And he spake unto Ephron in the audience of the people of the land, saying, But if thou wilt give it, I pray thee, hear me: I will give thee money for the field; take it of me, and I will bury my dead there. **23:14** And Ephron answered Abraham, saying unto him, **23:15** My lord, hearken unto me: the land is worth four hundred shekels of silver; what is that betwixt me and thee? bury therefore thy dead. **23:16** And Abraham hearkened unto Ephron; and Abraham weighed to Ephron the silver, which he had named in the audience of the sons of Heth, four hundred shekels of silver, current money with the merchant.

So Abraham bought the field in Hebron as a burying place for his family, and to this day the cave of Machpelah is venerated as the tomb of the immediate family of Abraham.

23:17 And the field of Ephron which was in Machpelah, which was before Mamre, the field, and the cave which was therein, and all the trees that were in the field, that were in all the borders round about, were made sure **23:18** Unto Abraham for a possession in the presence of the children of Heth [the Hittites who were later driven out of Palestine during the time of Nebuchadnezzar] before all that went in at the gate of his city.

23:19 And after this, Abraham buried Sarah his wife in the cave of the field of Machpelah before Mamre: the same is Hebron in the land of Canaan. **23:20** And the field, and the cave that is therein, were made sure unto Abraham for a possession of a buryingplace **by the sons of Heth** [the Hittites].

Genesis 24

A Bride for Isaac

This chapter is about the faithfulness and power of God to keep his promises to his faithful; and about the faithfulness of God's true people to keep God's Word and trust in him.

Abraham trusted God and acted on that trust, as does his servant as did Isaac.

Isaac waited on God and did not take a wife from the Canaanites but took a wife from his own people; which was an allegory of Jesus Christ coming to take the converted and faithful as his bride.

There is also great faith on the part of Rebecca who was willing to leave her home and travel a great distance to take a husband, Rebecca and her marriage to Isaac being analogous of the faithful converted bride of Christ which will be resurrected to the marriage of the Lamb.

Genesis 24:1 And Abraham was old, and well stricken in age: and the LORD had blessed Abraham in all things.

Abraham bound his servant with an oath against his descendants if he failed to provide a wife for Isaac out of his brother Nahor's family.

24:2 And Abraham said unto his eldest servant of his house, that ruled over all that he had, Put, I pray thee, thy hand under my thigh:

Abraham and his descendants are types of the spiritually called out, while the Canaanites were to become type of sin. For a faithful person to knowingly marry an unconverted person, is to bind good and evil together as ONE flesh; and is a physical type of spiritually becoming one with sin.

We are not to tolerate any sin among our assemblies, or within ourselves personally!

24:3 And I will make thee swear by the LORD, the God of heaven, and the God of the earth, that thou shalt not take a wife unto my son of the daughters of the Canaanites, among whom I dwell: **24:4** But thou shalt go **unto my country** [Haran in Syria]**, and to my kindred** [the family of Abraham's brother Nahor]**, and take a wife unto my son Isaac.**

The servant then asks a relevant question to which Abraham replies that Isaac must NOT return to dwell in Syria for God has commanded them to dwell in Canaan.

24:5 And the servant said unto him, Peradventure the woman will not be willing to follow me unto this land: must I needs bring thy son again unto the land from whence thou camest? **24:6** And Abraham said unto him, Beware thou that thou bring not my son thither again.

Abraham encourages his servant that God will provide a wife for Isaac. Again Abraham trusts and relies on the promises of God that Isaac would be the father of millions!

24:7 The LORD God of heaven, which took me from my father's house, and from the land of my kindred, and which spake unto me, and that sware unto me, saying, Unto thy seed will I give this land; he shall send his angel before thee, and thou shalt take a wife unto my son from thence. **24:8** And if the woman will not be willing to follow thee, then thou shalt be clear from this my oath: only bring not my son thither again.

The servant then swore by all his descendants to Abraham; that he would obey all the words of Abraham.

24:9 And the servant put his hand under the thigh of Abraham his master, and sware to him concerning that matter.

This servant was given whatever he required for his journey, and left for Haran of Syria the city of Nahor. The word "Mesopotamia" might confuse some people into thinking that this servant was going to Ur; but "Mesopotamia" means the land between the rivers and goes right up through Syria and into modern Turkey.

24:10 And the servant took ten camels of the camels of his master, and departed; for all the goods of his master were in his hand: and he arose, and went to Mesopotamia, unto the city of Nahor.

At the approach to Haran [modern Harran] the city of Nahor, Abraham's servant rested his camels and sought water. He asked God to give him directions that he might quickly find the house of Nahor.

24:11 And he made his camels to kneel down without the city by a well of water at the time of the evening, even the time that women go out to draw water.

Abraham's servant did not dare to make his own choice but asks for a sign directly from God identifying God's choice for Isaac. We see in this that Abraham had taught his servants to trust in God like he did. This woman was not courted by Isaac, but came from a far country and was chosen for him directly by God.

24:12 And he said O LORD God of my master Abraham, I pray thee, send me good speed this day, and shew kindness unto my master Abraham. **24:13** Behold, I stand here by the well of water; and the daughters of the men of the city come out to draw water: **24:14** And let it come to pass, that the damsel to whom I shall say, Let down thy pitcher, I pray thee, that I may drink; and she shall say, Drink, and I will give thy camels drink also: let the same be she that thou hast appointed for thy servant Isaac; and thereby shall I know that thou hast shewed kindness unto my master.

And immediately Rebecca appeared and fulfilled the requested sign, being the daughter of Bethuel and granddaughter of Nahor the brother of Abraham.

24:15 And it came to pass, before he had done speaking, that, behold, Rebekah came out, who was born to Bethuel, son of Milcah, the wife of Nahor, Abraham's brother, with her pitcher upon her shoulder. **24:16** And the damsel was very fair to look upon, a virgin, neither had any man known her: and she went down to the well, and filled her pitcher, and came up.

24:17 And the servant ran to meet her, and said, Let me, I pray thee, drink a little water of thy pitcher. **24:18** And she said, Drink, my lord: and she hasted, and let down her pitcher upon her hand, and gave him drink. **24:19** And when she had done giving him drink, she said, I will draw water for thy camels also, until they have done drinking. **24:20** And she hasted, and emptied her pitcher into the trough, and ran again unto the well to draw water, and drew for all his camels.

24:21 And the man wondering at her held his peace, to wit [to see if she was the one] whether the LORD had made his journey prosperous or not.

Abraham's servant then asked the maid about her family, and when he had found that she was of Abraham's brother Nahor's family and that she was hospitable, he thanked God for he knew that she was God's choice for Isaac.

24:22 And it came to pass, as the camels had done drinking, that the man took a golden earring of half a shekel weight, and two bracelets for her hands of ten shekels weight of gold;

Abraham's servant now nearly convinced, but taking great care, gives her gold bracelets for drawing the water [a very large gift] and asks her about a lodging place to test her further. Rebecca offers him the hospitality of her father's house without Abraham's servant even identifying himself or his mission.

24:23 And said, Whose daughter art thou? tell me, I pray thee: is there room in thy father's house for us to lodge in? **24:24** And she said unto him, I am the daughter of Bethuel the son of Milcah, which she bare unto Nahor. **24:25** She said moreover unto him, We have both straw and provender enough, and room to lodge in.

Abraham's servant being a man of faith, then thanked God for his mercies in aiding his mission.

24:26 And the man bowed down his head, and worshipped the LORD. **24:27** And he said, Blessed be the LORD God of my master Abraham, who hath not left destitute my master of his mercy and his truth: I being in the way, the LORD led me to the house of my master's brethren.

24:28 And the damsel ran, and told them of her mother's house these things.

24:29 And Rebekah had a brother, and his name was Laban [the same Laban who Jacob later ran to.]: and Laban ran out unto the man, unto the well. **24:30** And it came to pass, when he saw the earring and bracelets upon his sister's hands, and when he heard the words of Rebekah his sister, saying, Thus spake the man unto me; that he came unto the man; and, behold, he stood by the camels at the well.

Laban prepared a place for Abraham's servant straight away upon hearing from Rebecca; not yet knowing the servant's mission.

24:31 And he said, Come in, thou blessed of the LORD; wherefore standest thou without? for I have prepared the house, and room for the camels.

24:32 And the man came into the house: and he [Laban] ungirded his camels, and gave straw and provender for the camels, and water to wash his feet, and the men's feet that were with him. **24:33** And there was set meat before him to eat: but he [Abraham's servant] said, I will not eat, until I have told mine errand. And he said, Speak on.

Abraham relates the story of his mission.

24:34 And he said, I am Abraham's servant. **24:35** And the LORD hath blessed my master greatly; and he is become great: and he hath given him flocks, and herds, and silver, and gold, and menservants, and maidservants, and camels, and asses. **24:36** And Sarah my master's wife bare a son to my master when she was old: and unto him hath he given all that he hath. **24:37** And my master made me swear, saying, Thou shalt not take a wife to my son of the daughters of the Canaanites, in whose land I dwell: **24:38** But thou shalt go unto my father's house, and to my kindred, and take a wife unto my son.

24:39 And I said unto my master, Peradventure the woman will not follow me. **24:40** And he said unto me, The LORD, before whom I walk, will send his angel with thee, and prosper thy way; and thou shalt take a wife for my son of my kindred, and of my father's house: **24:41** Then shalt thou be clear from this my oath, when thou comest to my kindred; and if they give not thee one, thou shalt be clear from my oath.

24:42 And I came this day unto the well, and said, O LORD God of my master Abraham, if now thou do prosper my way which I go: **24:43** Behold, I stand by the well of water; and it shall come to pass, that when the virgin cometh forth to draw water, and I say to her, Give me, I pray thee, a little water of thy pitcher to drink; **24:44** And she say to me, Both drink thou, and I will also draw for thy camels: let the same be the woman whom the LORD hath appointed out for my master's son.

24:45 And before I had done speaking in mine heart, behold, Rebekah came forth with her pitcher on her shoulder; and she went down unto the well, and drew water: and I said unto her, Let me drink, I pray thee. **24:46** And she made haste, and let down her pitcher from her shoulder, and said,

Drink, and I will give thy camels drink also: so I drank, and she made the camels drink also.

24:47 And I asked her, and said, Whose daughter art thou? And she said, the daughter of Bethuel, Nahor's son, whom Milcah bare unto him: and I put the earring upon her face, and the bracelets upon her hands. **24:48** And I bowed down my head, and worshipped the LORD, and blessed the LORD God of my master Abraham, which had led me in the right way to take my master's brother's daughter unto his son.

Abraham's servant is so excited he asks for an immediate answer even before eating!

24:49 And now if ye will deal kindly and truly with my master, tell me: and if not, tell me; that I may turn to the right hand, or to the left.

Bethuel the father of Laban and Rebecca, and Laban himself; accept the Word of God.

24:50 Then Laban and [Laban's father] Bethuel answered and said, The thing proceedeth from the LORD: we cannot speak unto thee bad or good. **24:51** Behold, Rebekah is before thee, take her, and go, and let her be thy master's son's wife, as the LORD hath spoken.

The servant of Abraham then thanked God and gave gifts to Rebecca and her family as the custom was.

24:52 And it came to pass, that, when Abraham's servant heard their words, he worshipped the LORD, bowing himself to the earth. **24:53** And the servant brought forth jewels of silver, and jewels of gold, and raiment, and gave them to Rebekah: he gave also to her brother and to her mother precious things.

They feasted through the night rejoicing together and then Abraham's servant was urgent to leave and return with Isaac's wife. Then Laban wanted them to delay for ten days, but the servant refused because he was on a mission for Abraham and for God to bring to Isaac the mother of many nations.

24:54 And they did eat and drink, he and the men that were with him, and tarried all night; and they rose up in the morning, and he said, Send me away unto my master. **24:55** And her brother and her mother said, Let the damsel abide with us a few days, at the least ten; after that she shall go. **24:56** And he said unto them, Hinder me not, seeing the LORD hath prospered my way; send me away that I may go to my master.

They then asked the maid, and she was willing to go quickly.

24:57 And they said, **We will call the damsel, and enquire at her mouth. 24:58 And they called Rebekah, and said unto her, Wilt thou go with this man? And she said, I will go. 24:59** And they sent away Rebekah their sister, and her nurse, and Abraham's servant, and his men.

The blessing of Rebekah was according to the blessings of God upon Abraham and Isaac.

24:60 And they blessed Rebekah, and said unto her, **Thou art our sister, be thou the mother of thousands of millions, and let thy seed possess the gate of those which hate them**.

24:61 And Rebekah arose, and her damsels [maids and servants, her family being well off], and they rode upon the camels, and followed the man: and the servant took Rebekah, and went his way.

24:62 And Isaac came from the way of the well Lahairoi; for he dwelt in the south country. **24:63** And Isaac went out to meditate in the field at the eventide: and he lifted up his eyes, and saw, and, behold, the camels were coming. **24:64** And Rebekah lifted up her eyes, and when she saw Isaac, she lighted off the camel.

Immediately upon seeing Isaac, she acknowledging that was no longer a single woman, she covered her head [hair] with a veil as was the custom of a married wife in public. See our article on women covering the hair during worship (1 Corinthians 11).

24:65 For she had said unto the servant, What man is this that walketh in the field to meet us? And the servant had said, It is my master: therefore she took a vail, and covered herself.

24:66 And the servant told Isaac all things that he had done.

24:67 And Isaac brought her into his mother Sarah's tent, and took Rebekah, and she became his wife; and he loved her: and Isaac was comforted after his mother's death.

Genesis 25

Keturah means *perfumed* or *incense* (SH 6989), The word *qetorah* (SH 6988, from 6989), found only in Deuteronomy 33:10, also means *smoke of sacrifice* or *incense*.

The children of Keturah

Genesis 25:1 Then again Abraham took a wife, and her name was Keturah.

25:2 And she bare him Zimran, and Jokshan, and Medan and Midian [This Midian was and is the Bedouins, from which the father in law of Moses came.], and Ishbak, and Shuah [Also called Shuach]

Shuah the sixth and last of Keturah's sons has a name meaning variously wealth (BDB) or dell, sink, incline (Strong: SHD 7744). He was the progenitor of the Shuhites, the most notable of whom was **Bildad, son of Shuach, and one of Job's 'comforters'** (Job 2:11). This dates Job as about the time of Jacob.

The second son of Keturah by Abraham, Jokshan, had two sons Sheba and Dedan. Dedan is recorded as being the progenitor of the Asshurim, the Letushim and the Leummim (Gen. 25:3) the three Baltic Lettish nations of today.

Confusion can arise with several of these names. For instance: although the term Asshurim here is related to *Asshur* (SHD 804), it refers to a completely different people from the Assyrians (also 804), who were descendants of Asshur son of Shem. Similarly, Sheba was the name given generations earlier to one of thirteen sons of Joktan, son of Eber (from whom the *Hebrews* are named).

25:3 And **Jokshan** begat Sheba, and Dedan. And the sons of **Dedan** were Asshurim , and Letushim, [The Lettish people; modern Estonia, Latvia and Lithuania. **Letushim** (SHD 3912) means *hammered* or *oppressed* (Strong's), directly related to a word (3913) meaning *to sharpen, hammer, whet* (BDB),] and Leummim [(SHD 3817) means *peoples* or *communities*, from a root word meaning *to gather*.

25:4 And the **sons of Midian**; [Not the Medes, but the Midianites; the Bedouin]]Ephah, and Epher, and Hanoch, and Abidah, and Eldaah. All these were the children of Keturah. (Also 1 Ch 1:33).

Abraham sent these sons to the east with many gifts, but the inheritance of Canaan was for Isaac.

25:5 And Abraham gave all that he had unto Isaac. **25:6** But unto the sons of [of Keturah and the concubines who are not named] the concubines, which Abraham had, Abraham gave gifts, and sent them away from Isaac his son, while he yet lived, eastward, unto the east country.

They were sent away because God had promised the land of Canaan to Isaac.

Abraham dies at 175 years old.

25:7 And these are the days of the years of Abraham's life which he lived, an hundred threescore and fifteen years. **25:8** Then Abraham gave up the ghost, and died in a good old age, an old man, and full of years; and was gathered to his people.

Abraham was buried with his beloved Sarah.

25:9 And his sons Isaac and Ishmael buried him in the cave of Machpelah, in the field of Ephron the son of Zohar the Hittite, which is before Mamre; **25:10** The field which Abraham purchased of the sons of Heth: there was Abraham buried, and Sarah his wife.

25:11 And it came to pass after the death of Abraham, that God blessed his son Isaac; and Isaac dwelt by the well Lahairoi [The well where the Lord met with Hagar (Genesis 16:7-14)].

The Family of Ishmael

Ishmael fathered twelve princes.

25:12 Now these are the generations of Ishmael, Abraham's son, whom Hagar the Egyptian, Sarah's handmaid, bare unto Abraham: **25:13** And these are the names of the sons of Ishmael, by their names, according to their generations: the firstborn of Ishmael, Nebajoth; and Kedar, and Adbeel, and Mibsam, **25:14** And Mishma, and Dumah, and Massa, **25:15** Hadar, and Tema, Jetur, Naphish, and Kedemah: **25:16** These are the sons of Ishmael, and these are their names, by their towns, and by their castles; twelve princes according to their nations.

Ishmael died at 137 years old, and his sons dwelt in Arabia.

25:17 And these are the years of the life of Ishmael, an hundred and thirty and seven years: and he gave up the ghost and died; and was gathered unto his people. **25:18** And they dwelt from Havilah unto Shur, that is before Egypt, as thou goest toward Assyria: and he died in the presence of all his brethren.

The family of Isaac

25:19 And these are the generations of Isaac, Abraham's son: Abraham begat Isaac: **25:20** And Isaac was forty years old when he took Rebekah to wife, the [granddaughter of Nahor the brother of Abraham] daughter of Bethuel the Syrian of Padanaram, the sister to Laban the Syrian.

Rebecca was barren and God gave her twins in answer to the prayers of Isaac.

These twins from God were to be an allegory of those who sought the birthright and blessings of God with enthusiastic zeal; and those who were lukewarm, uncaring and who think little of God's promises; instead exalting their own ways and wants above the Word of God.

25:21 And Isaac intreated the LORD for his wife, because she was barren: and the LORD was intreated of him, and Rebekah his wife conceived.

God reveals to Rebecca what is taking place within her. Remember that this pregnancy was from God and this is a God given allegory about the difference between the lukewarm [Laodicea] and the zealous.

25:22 And the children struggled together within her; and she said, If it be so, why am I thus? And she went to enquire of the LORD. **25:23** And the LORD said unto her, Two nations are in thy womb, and two manner of people shall be separated from thy bowels; and the one people shall be stronger than the other people; and the elder shall serve the younger.

25:24 And when her days to be delivered were fulfilled, behold, there were twins in her womb. **25:25** And the first came out red, all over like an hairy garment; and they called his name Esau.

Isaac was 60 when his first children were born to the barren Rebecca.

This was a miracle from God to teach us to seek to have a deep, deep, desire for the birthright and blessings of our calling to God; and to hold our calling as the most precious thing in all our lives, so that we are exuberantly passionate to learn and live by every Word of God and overcome all sin, to receive the birthright of our calling which is eternal life!

Esau was rightfully the first born and had the right and the blessings of the first born; but he held this is small esteem, so that he was willing to give them up for relief from any small adversity. But Jacob reached out for, sought for and fought for the birthright and the blessings physically.

This is a spiritual lesson that only those who are HOT for, who value and who delight in the birthright of their calling to become like God the Father, those who work day and night to internalize the whole Word of God and with passion learn it, to keep it and to internalize it: will receive the blessings and the promised birthright of our spiritual calling: Which is the spiritual Promised Land of eternal life!

Yes, Jacob took Esau's birthright and his blessing by subterfuge and deceit and that was wrong! Yet if Esau had valued his birthright and blessings he would have been zealous to protect them always and could not have been tricked into giving them up

The deceit of Jacob is the subplot, the main plot is that we are to VALUE and hold PRECIOUS our spiritual calling and birthright as the Son's of God the Father. We are to be faithful and full of love and passion to live by every Word of God and to internalize the very nature of God; so that we might attain to the birthright of our calling and enter the Promised Land of eternal life!

25:26 And after that came his brother out, and his hand took hold on Esau's heel; and his name was called Jacob: and Isaac was threescore years old when she bare them.

25:27 And the boys grew: and Esau was a cunning hunter, a man of the field; and Jacob was a plain man, dwelling in tents. **25:28** And Isaac loved Esau, because he did eat of his venison: but Rebekah loved Jacob.

Esau undervalues his birthright and sells it for a pot of stew to ease his hunger. He could have gone and taken something from the family kitchen, but he wanted that stew and would give anything for it. That is like most brethren today; they want their own ways and they do not value the birthright of their calling, and they are not faithful to the Word of God that they were called to.

25:29 And Jacob sod pottage: and Esau came from the field, and he was faint: **25:30** And Esau said to Jacob, Feed me, I pray thee, with that same red pottage; for I am faint: therefore was his name called Edom.

25:31 And Jacob said, Sell me this day thy birthright.

25:32 And Esau said, Behold, I am at the point to die: and what profit shall this birthright do to me? **25:33** And Jacob said, Swear to me this day; and he sware unto him: and he sold his birthright unto Jacob. **25:34** Then Jacob gave Esau bread and pottage of lentiles; and he did eat and drink, and rose up, and went his way: **thus Esau despised his birthright**.

Will you despise the birthright of your calling by polluting the Sabbath or idolizing the contrary to scripture Rabbinic Calendar? Will you despise the birthright of your calling to turn and blindly obey without question some mere mortal man; contrary to the whole Word of God? Then just like Esau lost his physical birthright because he did not value it; you will lose the birthright of your spiritual calling!

Genesis 26

Isaac goes to the friend of his father Abraham, Abimelech the king of the Philistines. Since Abraham had died by this time, Abimelech would also be very old, or is this man the son of Abimelech with the same name?

Genesis 26:1 And there was a famine in the land, beside the first famine that was in the days of Abraham. And Isaac went unto Abimelech king of the Philistines unto Gerar.

The God Being who later became flesh as became Jesus Christ, instructed Isaac to remain in Gerar and not to go into Egypt, and Isaac obeyed God.

26:2 And the LORD appeared unto him, and said, Go not down into Egypt; dwell in the land which I shall tell thee of: **26:3** Sojourn in this land, and I will be with thee, and will bless thee; for unto thee, and unto thy seed, I will give all these countries, and I will perform the oath which I sware unto Abraham thy father; **26:4** And I will make thy seed to multiply as the stars of heaven, and will give unto thy seed all these countries; and in thy seed shall all the nations of the earth be blessed; **26:5** Because that Abraham obeyed my voice, and kept my charge, my commandments, my statutes, and my laws. **26:6** And Isaac dwelt in Gerar:

Then Isaac made the same mistake that his father Abraham had made. No doubt Abraham or Isaac's mother must have told him of these things, yet Isaac also made the same mistake, possibly with the same king or his son.

26:7 And the men of the place asked him of his wife; and he said, She is my sister: for he feared to say, She is my wife; lest, said he, the men of the place should kill me for Rebekah; because she was fair to look upon.

Nevertheless Abimelech and the people of Gerar left Rebecca alone; until one day Abimelech saw Isaac and Rebecca in an affectionate act.

26:8 And it came to pass, when he had been there a long time, that Abimelech king of the Philistines looked out at a window, and saw, and, behold, Isaac was sporting with Rebekah his wife.

Abimelech then confronts Isaac because of the danger Isaac had brought to his people, because some man might have innocently fancied Rebecca.

26:9 And Abimelech called Isaac, and said, Behold, of a surety she is thy wife; and how saidst thou, She is my sister? And Isaac said unto him, Because I said, Lest I die for her. **26:10** And Abimelech said, What is this thou hast done unto us? one of the people might lightly have lien with thy wife, and thou shouldest have brought guiltiness upon us.

Abimelech then warned all of his people to stay away from Rebecca.

26:11 And Abimelech charged all his people, saying, He that toucheth this man or his wife shall surely be put to death.

God blessed Isaac mightily with a hundredfold increase that year.

26:12 Then Isaac sowed in that land, and received in the same year an hundredfold: and the LORD blessed him. **26:13** And the man waxed great, and went forward, and grew until he became very great:

The Philistines began to envy and to fear Isaac; and some began to try and drive him away by filling in some of his wells which had been dug by Isaac's father Abraham.

26:14 For he had possession of flocks, and possession of herds, and great store of servants: and the Philistines envied him. **26:15** For all the wells which his father's servants had digged in the days of Abraham his father, the Philistines had stopped them, and filled them with earth.

Then because strife was rising, Abimelech asked Isaac to leave them.

26:16 And Abimelech said unto Isaac, Go from us; for thou art much mightier than we. **26:17** And Isaac departed thence, and pitched his tent in the valley of Gerar, and dwelt there.

Isaac left Gerar and its immediate outskirts, going out into the countryside where he opened the wells of his father Abraham in the land of the kingdom of Gerar and the inhabitants of the land strove with his servants.

26:18 And Isaac digged again the wells of water, which they had digged in the days of Abraham his father; for the Philistines had stopped them after the death of Abraham: and he called their names after the names by which his father had called them. **26:19** And Isaac's servants digged in the valley, and found there a well of springing water. **26:20** And the herdmen of Gerar did strive with Isaac's herdmen, saying, The water is ours: and he called the name of the well Esek; because they strove with him.

Isaac did not fight but moved on a bit and opened up another well of his father Abraham from which he also retreated from the same kind of strife.

26:21 And they digged another well, and strove for that also: and he called the name of it Sitnah.

Again Isaac moved further away and opened another well of his father Abraham and this time peace prevailed.

26:22 And he removed from thence, and digged another well; and for that they strove not: and he called the name of it Rehoboth; and he said, For now the LORD hath made room for us, and we shall be fruitful in the land.

God calls Isaac in a dream in Beer-Sheba and pronounces him to be the heir to the promises God had given Abraham.

26:23 And he went up from thence to Beersheba.

26:24 And the LORD appeared unto him the same night, and said, I am the God of Abraham thy father: fear not, for I am with thee, and will bless thee, and multiply thy seed for my servant Abraham's sake. **26:25** And he builded an altar there, and called upon the name of the LORD, and pitched his tent there: and there Isaac's servants digged a well.

Isaac makes a peace treaty with Abimelech.

26:26 Then Abimelech went to him from Gerar, and Ahuzzath one of his friends, and Phichol the chief captain of his army. **26:27** And Isaac said unto them, Wherefore come ye to me, seeing ye hate me, and have sent me away from you? **26:28** And they said, We saw certainly that the LORD was with thee: and we said, Let there be now an oath betwixt us, even betwixt us and thee, and let us make a covenant with thee; **26:29** That thou wilt do us no hurt, as we have not touched thee, and as we have done unto thee nothing but good, and have sent thee away in peace: thou art now the blessed of the LORD.

26:30 And he made them a feast, and they did eat and drink. **26:31** And they rose up betimes in the morning, and sware one to another: and Isaac sent them away, and they departed from him in peace.

That day Isaac's diggers found water while digging out the well of Abraham at Beer Sheba.

26:32 And it came to pass the same day, that Isaac's servants came, and told him concerning the well [of Abraham] which they had digged, and said unto him, We have found water. **26:33** And he called it Shebah: therefore the name of the city is Beersheba unto this day.

Beer Sheva; well of the seven fold oath, or well of seven [ewe's], a well dug by Abraham, and so named because he and Abimelech here entered into a compact (Gen. 21:31), long before Isaac came there to dig out the wells of his father Abraham.

Isaac's son Esau took him wives of the Canaanites; Judith and Bashemath both Hittites, which grieved Isaac and Rebecca, his parents.

But the birthright and the blessings were to be Jacob's as God had promised Rebecca when she was pregnant.

26:34 And Esau was forty years old when he took to wife Judith the daughter of Beeri the Hittite, and Bashemath the daughter of Elon the Hittite: **26:35** Which were a grief of mind unto Isaac and to Rebekah.

Genesis 27

When Jacob was yet in his mother's womb God prophesied that Jacob would excel over his brother Esau. Now Rebecca loved Jacob more than Esau and one can only imagine how much the prophecy motivated her actions of favoritism in helping Jacob defraud his brother.

Yet the event of the selling of the birthright contained no deceit and Esau clearly did not value his birthright, but later the taking of the blessing was by obvious deceit and the blessings were for all practical purposes stolen by Jacob.

In both cases the overall lesson is that Esau did not value either his blessing or his birthright while Jacob valued the blessings and birthright striving to gain them.

As a young man Jacob acted to obtain the birthright by deceit and through his own ways; which was and is a great sin. It is a great sin for us to seek to obtain God's promises of eternal life and a kingdom by our own ways and not by patiently living by every Word of God.

We obtain the birthright of our calling; by our merciful calling from God and by our diligently seeking to please and to become like God: NOT by grasping for it in our own way as Jacob did.

We have been called by God's mercy and we are to diligently value and seek to learn and to keep the whole Word of God, so that we might receive the promises which are given to those who please and obey God.

> **Romans 9:10** "And not only this; but when Rebecca also had conceived by one, even by our father Isaac; **9:11** (For the children being not yet born, neither having done any good or evil, that the purpose of God according to election might stand, not of works, but of him that calleth;) **9:12** It was said unto her, The elder shall serve the younger.
>
> **9:13** As it is written, Jacob have I loved, but Esau have I hated. **9:14** What shall we say then? *Is there* unrighteousness with God? God forbid. **9:15** For he saith to Moses, I will have mercy on whom I will have mercy, and I will have compassion on whom I will have compassion. So then *it is* not of him that willeth, nor of him that runneth, but of God that sheweth mercy.

Each of the called out brethren has been called to a birthright promise of eternal life and many blessings, IF we remain the faithful sons of God; but if we seek our own ways and not the will of God our Father we will become spiritual bastards and lose our birthright just as Esau lost his birthright and blessing.

> **Hebrews 12:8** But if ye be without chastisement [refuse the correction and teaching of God], whereof all [children] are partakers, then are ye bastards, and not sons.

Now this Jacob was called and given the birthright promise and blessings from the womb, yet he did not trust in God and tried to seize them from his brother by his own ways: Yet over his life Jacob learned his lesson and repented of this sin and turned to serve the Eternal and reconcile with Esau.

In our own lives many of us who have been called to the birthright and blessings of eternal life in the spiritual Promised Land of God also make the same mistake and rush off to seek the birthright and blessing of our calling by doing what we think is right, and failing to seek out and do what God commands is right.

Isaac near death prepares to give his blessing to Esau.

Genesis 27:1 And it came to pass, that when Isaac was old, and his eyes were dim, so that he could not see, he called **Esau his eldest son**, and said unto him, My son: and he said unto him, Behold, here am I. **27:2** And he said, Behold now, I am old, I know not the day of my death: **27:3** Now therefore take, I pray thee, thy weapons, thy quiver and thy bow, and go out to the field, and take me some venison; **27:4** And make me savoury meat, such as I love, and bring it to me, that I may eat; that my soul may bless thee before I die.

Rebecca hears Isaac and tells Jacob to obey her in deceiving her husband. This was a conspiracy against Esau initiated by Rebecca. Jacob sinned by obeying his mother and deceiving his father; we also sin when we obey anyone contrary to God our Father in heaven.

27:5 And Rebekah heard when Isaac spake to Esau his son. And Esau went to the field to hunt for venison, and to bring it. **27:6** And Rebekah spake unto Jacob her son, saying, Behold, I heard thy father speak unto Esau thy brother, saying, **27:7** Bring me venison, and make me savoury meat, that I may eat, and bless thee before the LORD before my death. **27:8** Now therefore, my son, obey my voice according to that which I command thee. **27:9** Go now to the flock, and fetch me from thence two good kids of the goats; and I will make them savoury meat for thy father, such as he loveth: **27:10** And thou shalt bring it to thy father, that he may eat, and that he may bless thee before his death.

Jacob is quick to join the conspiracy to deceive his father and steal the blessing from his brother Esau.

27:11 And Jacob said to Rebekah his mother, Behold, Esau my brother is a hairy man, and I am a smooth man:

Jacob fears that the deception will be found out and he will be cursed and not blessed. In this he knows that the deed is worthy of a curse and not a blessing; yet he is willing if not eager to be convinced by his mother to go ahead with the wicked deed. Even so, many in today's Ekklesia are often all too eager to obey men who deceive us with promises of blessings for obeying them contrary to the Word and Will of God.

27:12 My father peradventure will feel me, and I shall seem to him as a deceiver; and I shall bring a curse upon me, and not a blessing.

Rebecca believing the Promise of God and trying to fulfill it by her own methods asked that any curse be upon her and not on Jacob.

27:13 And his mother said unto him, Upon me be thy curse, my son: only obey my voice, and go fetch me them.

Then the conspiracy was decided and began. Rebecca made Isaac's favorite food and dressed Jacob up in Esau's clothing and covered him with hairy skins.

27:14 And he went, and fetched, and brought them to his mother: and his mother made savoury meat, such as his father loved. **27:15** And Rebekah took goodly raiment of her eldest son Esau, which were with her in the house, and put them upon Jacob her younger son: **27:16** And she put the skins of the kids of the goats upon his hands, and upon the smooth of his neck: **27:17** And she gave the savoury meat and the bread, which she had prepared, into the hand of her son Jacob.

Jacob then goes to his father with deception and even invokes God to his father.

27:18 And he came unto his father, and said, My father: and he said, Here am I; who art thou, my son? **27:19** And Jacob said unto his father, I am Esau thy first born; I have done according as thou badest me: arise, I pray thee, sit and eat of my venison, that thy soul may bless me. **27:20** And Isaac said unto his son, How is it that thou hast found it so quickly, my son? And he said, Because the LORD thy God brought it to me.

Isaac has his doubts and asks to feel Esau who had a hairy body while Jacob was smooth skinned.

27:21 And Isaac said unto Jacob, Come near, I pray thee, that I may feel thee, my son, whether thou be my very son Esau or not. **27:22** And Jacob went near unto Isaac his father; and he felt him, and said, The voice is Jacob's voice, but the hands are the hands of Esau. **27:23** And he discerned him not, because his hands were hairy, as his brother Esau's hands: so he blessed him.

Jacob lies to his father

At this point I must say that we cannot deceive our Father in heaven to steal any blessings from him! He KNOWS whether we are faithful to him and if we are zealous to please him; or if we are lying to him and doing our own ways instead of living by every Word of God,

27:24 And he said, Art thou my very son Esau? And he said, I am.

Isaac eats the venison [young goat or deer are of the same family and very much alike]

27:25 And he said, Bring it near to me, and I will eat of my son's venison, that my soul may bless thee. And he brought it near to him, and he did eat: and he brought him wine and he drank.

27:26 And his father Isaac said unto him, Come near now, and kiss me, my son. **27:27** And he came near, and kissed him: and he smelled the smell of his raiment,

The blessing that Jacob stole

. . . and blessed him, and said, See, the smell of my son is as the smell of a field which the LORD hath blessed: **27:28** Therefore God give thee of the [good watered land] dew of heaven, and the fatness of the earth, and plenty of corn [grain] and wine: **27:29 Let people serve thee, and nations bow down to thee: be lord over thy brethren**, and let **thy mother's sons bow down to thee** [we should not assume that Rebecca remained barren after the twins were born]: cursed be every one that curseth thee, and blessed be he that blesseth thee.

As Jacob left, Esau comes into the room with his savory meat. What a shock this must have been to Isaac and to Esau, for this was outright theft from his brother and was a betrayal of the trust of his father.

27:30 And it came to pass, as soon as Isaac had made an end of blessing Jacob, and Jacob was yet scarce gone out from the presence of Isaac his father, that Esau his brother came in from his hunting. **27:31** And he also had made savoury meat, and brought it unto his father, and said unto his father, Let my father arise, and eat of his son's venison, that thy soul may bless me. **27:32** And Isaac his father said unto him, Who art thou? And he said, I am thy son, thy firstborn Esau.

Isaac shook with rage at this theft of his son's blessings. Almighty God is also extremely angry with us for our rejection of any zeal to live by his Word while being zealous to follow men into sin like Jacob followed his mother.

27:33 And Isaac trembled very exceedingly, and said, Who? where is he that hath taken venison, and brought it me, and I have eaten of all before thou camest, and have blessed him? yea, and he shall be blessed.

Esau was also outraged at this betrayal by his brother.

27:34 And when Esau heard the words of his father, he cried with a great and exceeding bitter cry, and said unto his father, Bless me, even me also, O my father.

Isaac responds to Esau's request

27:35 And he said, Thy brother came with subtilty, and hath taken away thy blessing.

Then Esau cries out, and asks for a blessing also.

27:36 And he said, Is not he rightly named Jacob? for he hath supplanted me these two times: he took away my birthright; and, behold, now he hath taken away my blessing. And he said, Hast thou not reserved a blessing for me?

Isaac laments that he has given all to Jacob.

27:37 And Isaac answered and said unto Esau, Behold, I have made him thy lord, and all his brethren have I given to him for servants; and with corn and wine have I sustained him: and what shall I do now unto thee, my son?

Esau wept

27:38 And Esau said unto his father, Hast thou but one blessing, my father? bless me, even me also, O my father. And Esau lifted up his voice, and wept.

Isaac then blesses Esau also, with deliverance from Jacob so that he might be a nation on his own part.

27:39 And Isaac his father answered and said unto him, Behold, **thy dwelling shall be the fatness of the earth, and of the dew of heaven from above; 27:40 And by thy sword shalt thou live, and shalt serve thy brother; and it shall come to pass when thou shalt have the dominion, that thou shalt break his yoke from off thy neck.**

Esau decided to wait for the imminent death of Isaac and to then kill his brother so that he might retain the physical birthright and the physical blessing when Jacob was dead.

27:41 And Esau hated Jacob because of the blessing wherewith his father blessed him: and Esau said in his heart, The days of mourning [the death of] for my father are at hand; then will I slay my brother Jacob.

Esau's word's were overheard and told to Rebecca who warns Jacob to flee.

27:42 And these words of Esau her elder son were told to Rebekah: and she sent and called Jacob her younger son, and said unto him, Behold, thy brother Esau, as touching thee, doth comfort himself, purposing to kill thee.

27:43 Now therefore, my son, obey my voice; arise, flee thou **to Laban my brother to Haran**; **27:44** And tarry with him a few days, until thy brother's fury turn away; **27:45** Until thy brother's anger turn away from thee, and he forget that which thou hast done to him: then I will send, and fetch thee from thence: why should I be deprived also of you both in one day?

Rebecca devises a stratagem to entice Isaac to send Jacob away. She tells him that Jacob should marry in the family and not into the Canaanites as Esau had done. So Isaac allows Jacob to depart to Haran.

27:46 And Rebekah said to Isaac, I am weary of my life because of the daughters of Heth: if Jacob take a wife of the daughters of Heth, such as these which are of the daughters of the land, what good shall my life do me?

This entire episode is about brothers fighting over the physical birthright and physical blessing instead of waiting on God to work things out.

This is a lesson for us that we cannot achieve the spiritual birthright of our calling by our own methods. We must repent of our own ways and go forward to sin no more, becoming zealous to please God.

Did Isaac delight in this quarreling between his sons? I dare say NO! Does God our Father in heaven take delight in our seeking his blessings by doing our own ways and not by fulfilling his Word? I dare say NO!

God cannot be deceived and his eyes are not dim that he cannot see! Our Father in heaven knows what we do to each other in our strife to have the chief seats; he knows that most leaders seek the chief seats by whatever means and are not zealous to learn and to live by every Word of God the Father.

Right now the church of God is no better than Jacob and Esau fighting over the chief seats, and not being zealous to please and live by every Word of God our Father in heaven!

The story is not yet over and BOTH Jacob and Esau will eventually learn their lesson and repent before God and before each other! Jacob repents of his wickedness and Esau repents of his laxity and hatred!

Even so it will be that in the end of things the vast majority of the truly called out will also learn to reject their own ways for a true passionate exuberant zeal to live by EVERY WORD of GOD our Father!

Brethren, when we mourn over all the evils within these organizations: Remember also that we are all unfinished products in the Master Potter's hands; and that the day will come when we learn our lessons like Jacob and Esau did!

God speed that day!

Genesis 28

Isaac then sends Jacob to Haran to take a wife from among his cousins there, as Rebecca had insisted.

Genesis 28:1 And Isaac called Jacob, and blessed him, and charged him, and said unto him, Thou shalt not take a wife of the daughters of Canaan. **28:2** Arise, go to Padanaram, to the house of Bethuel thy mother's father; and **take thee a wife from thence of the daughers of Laban thy mother's brother**.

In spite of everything Isaac again is inspired to bless Jacob again and to confer upon him the promises made to Abraham; this because of the prophecies made by God to Abraham.

28:3 And God Almighty bless thee, and make thee fruitful, and multiply thee, that thou mayest be a multitude of people; **28:4** And give thee the blessing of Abraham, to thee, and to thy seed with thee; that thou mayest inherit the land wherein thou art a stranger, which God gave unto Abraham. **28:5** And Isaac sent away Jacob: and he went to Padanaram unto Laban, son of Bethuel the Syrian, the brother of Rebekah, Jacob's and Esau's mother.

Esau then took wives of the children of Ishmael Abraham's son, to seek to please his father Isaac.

28:6 When Esau saw that Isaac had blessed Jacob, and sent him away to Padanaram, to take him a wife from thence; and that as he blessed him he gave him a charge, saying, Thou shalt not take a wife of the daughers of Canaan; **28:7** And that Jacob obeyed his father and his mother, and was gone to Padanaram; **28:8 And Esau seeing that the daughters of Canaan pleased not Isaac his father; 28:9 Then went Esau unto Ishmael, and took unto the wives which he had Mahalath the daughter of Ishmael Abraham's son, the sister of Nebajoth, to be his wife.**

Jacob journeys to Haran

28:10 And Jacob went out from Beersheba, and went toward Haran.

28:11 And he lighted upon a certain place, and tarried there all night, because the sun was set; and he took of the stones of that place, and put them for his pillows, and lay down in that place to sleep.

At that time Jacob must have been filled with fear for his life over his theft of the blessing from his brother Esau, he must also have been very lonely and more than a little discouraged in spite of his father's blessings. Here he was, forced to flee from the very land he had been promised by his father's blessing.

Then God appears to him in a dream and blesses him; this because God has faith that Jacob will learn his lesson and repent of his evil deeds.

Before, Jacob had believed his parents concerning the prophecy and sought to fulfill it by his own methods. This speaks to the Ekklesia today, many of whom seek to gain eternal life through man devised methods and try to obtain the blessings by following idols of men, instead of through zeal to live by every Word of God.

Suddenly the God who later gave up his God-hood to be made flesh as Jesus Christ appeared to Jacob personally and blessed him according to what his parents had told him. This must have been an incredible shock for Jacob to hear the voice of God and God's blessings for himself!

God then began to work with Jacob humbling him and teaching him that his own ways bring sorrow and it is God's ways that are righteous. That ONLY through the zealous keeping of the whole Word of God both physically and spiritually, can we be blessed and inherit the birthright of eternal life.

During the years after he fled from Esau God worked with Jacob to humble him. Jacob went to Laban as a wicked self-centered man; and he left the house of Laban having been humbled and taught to live by every Word of God and not to live by his own methods.

28:12 And he dreamed, and behold a ladder set up on the earth, and the top of it reached to heaven: and behold the angels of God ascending and descending on it. **28:13** And, behold, the LORD stood above it, and said, I am the LORD God of Abraham thy father, and the God of Isaac: **the land whereon thou liest, to thee will I give it, and to thy seed; 28:14 And thy seed shall be as the dust of the earth, and thou shalt spread abroad to the west, and to the east, and to the north, and to the south: and in thee and in thy seed shall all the families of the earth be blessed. 28:15 And, behold, I am with thee, and will keep thee in all places whither thou goest, and will bring thee again into this land; for I will not leave thee, until I have done that which I have spoken to thee of.**

Jacob awoke deeply moved at the appearance of God to him and God's blessings, and he set up a stone and anointed it with oil; which stone is figurative of the Rock of our Salvation, even Jesus Christ, the Chief Cornerstone of Salvation!

Let me add here that some have taught that this stone was brought by Jeremiah and is the Stone of Scone today. That is totally false, and that error has brought great damage to the understanding of the latter day identity of Israel.

Jeremiah would never have supported any such idolatry; we know this because God permitted the staff of serpents to be destroyed and even the Ark of the Covenant to be lost; even the Temple was destroyed TWICE.

These things were merely symbols of a far greater spiritual reality and we are to focus on that spiritual reality and not exalt the physical symbols. Focusing on the physical symbols and not on the spiritual reality is IDOLATRY! A sin that Jeremiah would have [and did] condemned to the utmost.

28:16 And Jacob awaked out of his sleep, and he said, Surely the LORD is in this place; and I knew it not. **28:17** And he was afraid, and said, How dreadful is this place! this is none other but the house of God, and this is the gate of heaven. **28:18** And Jacob rose up early in the morning, and took the stone that he had put for his pillows, and set it up for a pillar, and poured oil upon the top of it.

Jacob called the place Beth-El meaning the house of God.

28:19 And he called the name of that place Bethel: but the name of that city was called Luz at the first.

Jacob then vowed that he would give a tenth of all his increase to God, if God would fulfill his promises. The tithe is in acknowledgement of ALL the blessings of God upon his people, an acknowledgement that the Eternal is God and the Creator and Great Provider of all things.

28:20 And Jacob vowed a vow, saying, If God will be with me, and will keep me in this way that I go, and will give me bread to eat, and raiment to put on, **28:21** So that I come again to my father's house in peace; then shall the LORD be my God: **28:22** And this stone, which I have set for a pillar, shall be God's house: and of all that thou shalt give me **I will surely give the tenth unto thee.**

Genesis 29

Jacob finds his family in Haran

Genesis 29:1 Then Jacob went on his journey, and came into the land of the people of the east. **29:2** And he looked, and behold a well in the field, and, lo, there were three flocks of sheep lying by it; for out of that well they watered the flocks: and a great stone was upon the well's mouth. **29:3** And thither were all the flocks gathered: and they rolled the stone from the well's mouth, and watered the sheep, and put the stone again upon the well's mouth in his place.

Jacob meets Rachel

29:4 And Jacob said unto them, My brethren, whence be ye? And they said, Of Haran are we. **29:5** And he said unto them, Know ye Laban the son of Nahor? And they said, We know him. **29:6** And he said unto them, Is he well? And they said, He is well: and, behold, Rachel his daughter cometh with the sheep.

The herdsmen were waiting for the flocks to come to remove the well cover stone so that the sheep could be watered.

29:7 And he said, Lo, it is yet high day, neither is it time that the cattle should be gathered together: water ye the sheep, and go and feed them. **29:8** And they said, We cannot, until all the flocks be gathered together, and till they roll the stone from the well's mouth; then we water the sheep.

Jacob seeing Rachel was struck with her and fell in love at first sight; he jumped up to roll away the stone and water her flock.

29:9 And while he yet spake with them, Rachel came with her father's sheep; for she kept them. **29:10** And it came to pass, when Jacob saw Rachel the daughter of Laban his mother's brother, and the sheep of Laban his mother's brother, that Jacob went near, and rolled the stone from the well's mouth, and watered the flock of Laban his mother's brother.

Jacob ran to Rachel and kissed her, probably on the hand, cheek or neck as was the custom of greeting a relative. It is from this custom that Paul tells us to greet our brethren with a "holy kiss" (1 Thess 5:26, 1 Cor 16:20, 2 Cor 13:12, Romans 16:16).

29:11 And Jacob kissed Rachel, and lifted up his voice, and wept.

29:12 And Jacob told Rachel that he was her father's brother [near kinsman], and that **he was Rebekah's son:** and she ran and told her father.

Laban receives Jacob with joy

29:13 And it came to pass, when Laban heard the tidings of Jacob his sister's son, that he ran to meet him, and **embraced him, and kissed him**, and brought him to his house. And he told Laban all these things. **29:14** And Laban said to him, Surely thou art my bone and my flesh. And he abode with him the space of a month.

Laban proposes to pay Jacob for any help he gives and Jacob asks for Rachel and not for money.

29:15 And Laban said unto Jacob, Because thou art my brother [kinsman], shouldest thou therefore serve me for nought? tell me, what shall thy wages be? **29:16** And Laban had two daughters: the name of the elder was Leah, and the name of the younger was Rachel.

The first stage of the humbling of Jacob was when he was forced to flee before his bother.

Jacob would now be taught through Laban to serve the Eternal and not to seek to exalt himself by his own ways; a lesson that most of us still need to learn!

Jacob offers to serve for seven years for Rachel and Laban accepts. This begins the trial of patience and the intermediate stage of the humbling of Jacob.

29:17 Leah was tender eyed; but Rachel was beautiful and well favoured. **29:18** And Jacob loved Rachel; and said, I will serve thee seven years for Rachel thy younger daughter. **29:19** And Laban said, It is better that I give her to thee, than that I should give her to another man: abide with me.

Jacob fulfilled his service for Rachel.

29:20 And Jacob served seven years for Rachel; and they seemed unto him but a few days, for the love he had to her. **29:21** And Jacob said unto Laban, Give me my wife, for my days are fulfilled, that I may go in unto her. **29:22** And Laban gathered together all the men of the place, and made a feast.

Jacob was caused to drink wine and then in the darkness Leah was brought to him instead of Rachel. By this time Laban would have remembered his sister Rebecca being taken away to Isaac and probably feared that his daughter Rachel would also to be taken far away.

29:23 And it came to pass in the evening, that he took Leah his daughter, and brought her to him; and he went in unto her. **29:24** And Laban gave unto his daughter Leah Zilpah his maid for an handmaid. **29:25** And it came to pass, that in the morning, behold, it was Leah: and he said to Laban, What is this thou hast done unto me? did not I serve with thee for Rachel? wherefore then hast thou beguiled me? **29:26** And Laban said, It must not be so done in our country, to give the younger before the firstborn.

Then Jacob serves seven more years for Rachel; for a total of fourteen years service to Laban. Oh, how much he loved that lady and how long God humbled him through Laban for his wicked deeds of deception and theft from his brother.

29:27 Fulfil her week, and we will give thee this [Rachel] also for the service which thou shalt serve with me yet seven other years. **29:28** And Jacob did so, and fulfilled her week: and he gave him Rachel his daughter to wife also. **29:29** And Laban gave to Rachel his daughter Bilhah his handmaid to be her maid. **29:30** And he went in also unto Rachel, and he loved also Rachel more than Leah, and served with him yet seven other years.

So Jacob served Laban for twenty-one years

29:31 And when the LORD saw that Leah was hated, he opened her womb: but Rachel was barren. **29:32** And Leah conceived, and bare a son, and she called his name Reuben: for she said, Surely the LORD hath looked upon my affliction; now therefore my husband will love me.

God then gave Leah a child and this consoled Leah and may have caused Jacob to appreciate her more as the mother of his firstborn.

29:33 And she conceived again, and bare a son; and said, Because the LORD hath heard I was hated, he hath therefore given me this son also: and she called his name Simeon. **29:34** And she conceived again, and bare a son; and said, Now this time will my husband be joined unto me, because I have born him three sons: therefore was his name called Levi. **29:35** And she conceived again, and bare a son: and she said, Now will I praise the LORD: therefore she called his name Judah; and left bearing.

Leah had four sons: Reuben, Simeon, Levi and Judah; all brothers by the same parents.

Genesis 30

Rachel, jealous of her sister Leah, then insists that Jacob take her maid to bear children for her. This is almost a duplicate of the story of Sarai and Hagar with Abraham. Rachel had never known Sarai but would likely have heard the story.

Genesis 30:1 And when Rachel saw that she bare Jacob no children, Rachel envied her sister; and said unto Jacob, Give me children, or else I die. **30:2** And Jacob's anger was kindled against Rachel: and he said, Am I in God's stead, who hath withheld from thee the fruit of the womb? **30:3** And she said, Behold my maid Bilhah, go in unto her; and she shall bear upon my knees, that I may also have children by her. **30:4** And she gave him Bilhah her handmaid to wife: and Jacob went in unto her.

When Bilhah had produced a son Rachel called the boy's name Dan "God has Judged."

30:5 And Bilhah conceived, and bare Jacob a son. **30:6** And Rachel said, God hath judged me, and hath also heard my voice, and hath given me a son: therefore called she his name Dan. **30:7** And Bilhah Rachel's maid conceived again, and bare Jacob a second son.

Rachel called the second child of Bilhah, Naphtali; meaning "wrestling." At this point the contention in the family of Jacob is obvious and God sees that the jealousy between sisters is aroused by competing for the affections of the same husband. Ultimately this leads to the commandment not to marry sisters during their lifetime.

30:8 And Rachel said, With great wrestlings have I wrestled with my sister, and I have prevailed: and she called his name Naphtali.

Then Leah decided to follow the example of her sister Rachel and insisted that Jacob also take her maid Zilpah. When Zilpah bears a son; Leah is full of joy that through Zilpah she may have many more sons and names Zilpah's firstborn Gad "a Troop or company of many."

30:9 When Leah saw that she had left bearing, she took Zilpah her maid, and gave her Jacob to wife. **30:10** And Zilpah Leah's maid bare Jacob a son. **30:11** And Leah said, A troop cometh: and she called his name Gad.

A second son is born to Leah by her maid Zilpah and she calls his name Asher meaning "happiness."

30:12 And Zilpah Leah's maid bare Jacob a second son. **30:13** And Leah said, Happy am I, for the daughters will call me blessed: and she called his name Asher.

Reuben discovered some mandrakes in a field and Rachel desired some of them from Leah Reuben's mother.

30:14 And Reuben went in the days of wheat harvest, and found mandrakes in the field, and brought them unto his mother Leah. Then Rachel said to Leah, Give me, I pray thee, of thy son's mandrakes.

Leah shows her jealousy of Rachel and refuses to give any mandrakes to her sister. Rachel then offers Leah her turn with Jacob in exchange for some mandrakes. Here we begin to see some of the issues with polygamy and the contentious jealousies and unhappiness that can rage within a polygamous family. It was certainly possible that Jacob preferred his favorite Rachel and that he had been neglecting his duty to Leah v 15. This would have been the root of God's command at Sinai that all wives must be treated equally.

30:15 And she said unto her, **Is it a small matter that thou hast taken my husband?** and wouldest thou take away my son's mandrakes also? And Rachel said, Therefore he shall lie with thee to night for thy son's mandrakes.

Leah then went to Jacob and demanded sex of him, openly telling him that she had bought his services for that day from Rachel.

30:16 And Jacob came out of the field in the evening, and Leah went out to meet him, and said, Thou must come in unto me; for surely I have hired thee with my son's mandrakes. And he lay with her that night.

God heard the prayer of Leah and she conceived a fifth son.

30:17 And God hearkened unto Leah, and she conceived, and bare Jacob the fifth son.

The child was named Issachar meaning "my reward" for purchasing the services of her husband for that day.

30:18 And Leah said, God hath given me my hire, because I have given my maiden to my husband: and she called his name Issachar.

Leah then bore a sixth son and called his name Zebulun "a habitation."

30:19 And Leah conceived again, and bare Jacob the sixth son. **30:20** And Leah said, God hath endued me with a good dowry; now will my husband dwell with me, because I have born him six sons: and she called his name Zebulun.

Of Jacob's daughters (others are noted in Gen 46:15), only Dinah, meaning "vindicated," is mentioned by name.

30:21 And afterwards she bare a daughter, and called her name Dinah.

After Leah has borne six sons God opened the womb of the barren Rachel and she named her firstborn sin Joseph "increase" because she has finally become a mother and is beginning to increase.

30:22 And God remembered Rachel, and God hearkened to her, and opened her womb. **30:23** And she conceived, and bare a son; and said, God hath taken away my reproach: **30:24** And she called his name Joseph; and said, The LORD shall add to me another son.

Joseph the firstborn of Jacob's favorite beloved Rachel becomes the favorite of Jacob, later the birthright of the firstborn would be removed from Reuben for sin and given to the firstborn of the intended first wife.

Jacob then seeks to return home to Canaan and Laban finding much increase and blessing in his services begs him to stay and asks Jacob what wages he wants.

30:25 And it came to pass, when Rachel had born Joseph, that Jacob said unto Laban, Send me away, that I may go unto mine own place, and to my country. **30:26** Give me my wives and my children, for whom I have served thee, and let me go: for thou knowest my service which I have done thee.

30:27 And Laban said unto him, I pray thee, if I have found favour in thine eyes, tarry: for I have learned by experience that the LORD hath blessed me for thy sake. **30:28** And he said, Appoint me thy wages, and I will give it.

30:29 And he [Jacob] said unto him, Thou knowest how I have served thee, and how thy cattle was with me.

Jacob replies that he must think about caring for his own family and no longer about enriching Laban.

30:30 For it was little which thou hadst before I came, and it is now increased unto a multitude; and the LORD hath blessed thee since my coming: and now when shall I provide for mine own house also?

Jacob then demands the wages of all the streaked, spotted and speckled cattle and sheep of Laban.

30:31 And he said, What shall I give thee? And Jacob said, Thou shalt not give me any thing: if thou wilt do this thing for me, I will again feed and keep thy flock. **30:32** I will pass through all thy flock to day, removing from thence all the speckled and spotted cattle [lesser cattle; goats and sheep, see v33], and all the brown [discolored] cattle [sheep are often called cattle as in lessor cattle, this refers to brown (discolored) sheep not cows] among the sheep, and the spotted and speckled among the goats: and of such shall be my hire.

30:33 So shall my righteousness answer for me in time to come, when it shall come for my hire before thy face: every one that is not **speckled and spotted among the goats, and brown** [discolored] **among the sheep,** that shall be counted stolen with me.

NOTE: The word cattle throughout this story refers to "lessor cattle," as in sheep and goats; not to bulls and cows.

30:34 And Laban said, Behold, I would it might be according to thy word.

30:35 And he removed that day the he goats that were ringstraked [streaked] and spotted, and all the she goats that were speckled and spotted, and every one that had some white [were mottled] in it, and all the brown [discolored] among the sheep, and gave them into the hand of his sons. **30:36** And he set three days' journey betwixt himself and Jacob: and Jacob fed the rest of Laban's flocks.

Then Jacob cheats Laban by stripping some of the bark from sticks [especially hazel and chestnut] and placing them in the water so that tannin is leached into the water from the sticks. Regular drinking of this tannin water resulted in a discoloring of the coats of the developing lambs and kids in the womb. This was clearly wrong on Jacob's part and Laban was well within his rights to change the deal when he caught Jacob cheating.

30:37 And Jacob took him rods of green poplar, and of the hazel and chesnut tree; and pilled white strakes [Peeled strips of the bark off the sticks so that tannin could leach into the drinking water.] in them, and made the white appear which was in the rods. **30:38** And he set the rods which he had pilled before the flocks **in the gutters in the watering troughs** when the flocks came to drink, that they should conceive when they came to drink. **30:39** And the flocks conceived before the rods, and brought forth cattle [lessor cattle; sheep and goats] ringstraked [discolored, streaked], speckled, and spotted.

Jacob separated out the discolored lambs of the sheep and goats into flocks of his own; and he had brought only the strongest of Laban's flocks to drink the tannin water of his stripped sticks so that the lambs of the strongest might be his.

30:40 And Jacob did separate the lambs, and set the faces of the flocks toward the ringstraked [striped peeled sticks] , and all the brown [discolored] in the flock of Laban; and he put his own flocks by themselves, and put them not unto Laban's cattle.

30:41 And it came to pass, whensoever the stronger cattle did conceive, that Jacob laid the rods before the eyes of the cattle in the gutters, that they might conceive among the rods. **30:42** But when the cattle were feeble, he put them not in: so the feebler were Laban's, and the stronger Jacob's. **30:43** And the man increased exceedingly, and had much cattle, and maidservants, and menservants, and camels, and asses.

Jacob increased by trickery and fraud against his benefactor who was also his uncle and father in law, just as he had taken his brother Esau's birthright and blessing.

Laban caught Jacob cheating him many times and there was constant friction between them. It took Jacob a long time to learn his lesson to be honest and trust in the Eternal, and God kept Jacob with Laban until Jacob had finally learned his lesson through being repeatedly caught by Laban.

Genesis 31

Jacob departs from Laban with his possessions.

Jacob had taken much from Laban and he overheard Laban's sons complaining about him. Jacob also noticed that Laban was getting more and more unhappy with him. Then God intervened to tell Jacob that it was time to return home.

Genesis 31:1 And he heard the words of Laban's sons, saying, Jacob hath taken away all that was our father's; and of that which was our father's hath he gotten all this glory. **31:2** And Jacob beheld the countenance of Laban, and, behold, it was not toward him as before. **31:3** And the LORD said unto Jacob, Return unto the land of thy fathers, and to thy kindred; and I will be with thee.

Jacob then communed with his wives in the fields.

31:4 And Jacob sent and called Rachel and Leah to the field unto his flock, **31:5** And said unto them, I see your father's countenance, that it is not toward me as before; but the God of my father hath been with me.

Now we have things revealed that were not covered previously in detail.

31:6 And ye know that with all my power I have served your father. **31:7** And your father hath deceived me, and **changed my wages ten times;** but God suffered him not to hurt me.

It is now said that Laban agreed that the speckled should be Jacob's wages and when many were born speckled Laban changed Jacob's wages to the streaked ones and so on.

31:8 If he said thus, The speckled shall be thy wages; then all the cattle bare speckled: and if he said thus, The ringstraked [streaked] shall be thy hire; then bare all the cattle ringstraked. **31:9** Thus God hath taken away the cattle [lesser cattle; ie goats and sheep] of your father, and given them to me.

Jacob tells his wives of his dream and how the angel of God promised him that the kids and lambs would be his.

31:10 And it came to pass at the time that the cattle conceived, that I lifted up mine eyes, and saw in a dream, and, behold, the **rams which leaped upon the** [ewes, lessor cattle] **cattle** were ringstraked, speckled, and grisled.

31:11 And the angel of God spake unto me in a dream, saying, Jacob: And I said, Here am I. **31:12** And he said, Lift up now thine eyes, and see, all the rams which leap upon the cattle are ringstraked, speckled, and grisled: for I have seen all that Laban doeth unto thee. **31:13** I am the God of Bethel, where thou anointedst the pillar, and where thou vowedst a vow unto me: now arise, get thee out from this land, and return unto the land of thy kindred.

Then Jacob's wives with whom he had consulted, agreed to go with him.

31:14 And Rachel and Leah answered and said unto him, Is there yet any portion or inheritance for us in our father's house? **31:15** Are we not counted of him strangers? for he hath sold us, and hath quite devoured also our money. **31:16** For all the riches which God hath taken from our father, that is ours, and our children's: now then, whatsoever God hath said unto thee, do.

31:17 Then Jacob rose up, and set his sons and his wives upon camels; **31:18** And he carried away all his [lessor or small cattle ie sheep and goats] cattle [flocks of sheep and herds of goats], and all his goods which he had gotten, the cattle of his getting, which he had gotten in Padanaram, for to go to Isaac his father in the land of Canaan.

Rachel steals the idol of her father; whether this was for its value, or in spite, or because she thought it a god is not revealed.

31:19 And Laban went to shear his sheep: and Rachel had stolen the images that were her father's.

Jacob slipped away in secret.

31:20 And Jacob stole away unawares to Laban the Syrian, in that he told him not that he fled. **31:21** So he fled with all that he had; and he rose up, and passed over the river, and set his face toward the mount Gilead.

After three days Laban pursues Jacob.

31:22 And it was told Laban on the third day that Jacob was fled. **31:23** And he took his brethren with him, and pursued after him seven days' journey; and they overtook him in the mount Gilead.

God warns Laban to be careful with Jacob.

31:24 And God came to Laban the Syrian in a dream by night, and said unto him, Take heed that thou **speak not to Jacob either good or bad.**

31:25 Then Laban overtook Jacob. Now Jacob had pitched his tent in the mount: and Laban with his brethren pitched in the mount of Gilead.

Laban then seeks an opportunity to say good bye to his children and to Jacob.

31:26 And Laban said to Jacob, What hast thou done, that thou hast stolen away unawares to me, and carried away my daughters, as captives taken with the sword? **31:27** Wherefore didst thou flee away secretly, and steal away from me; and didst not tell me, that I might have sent thee away with mirth, and with songs, with tabret, and with harp? **31:28** And hast not suffered me to kiss my sons and my daughters? thou hast now done foolishly in so doing.

Laban then informs Jacob about the warning from God and insists that he intends no hurt to Jacob.

31:29 It is in the power of my hand to do you hurt: but the God of your father spake unto me yesternight, saying, Take thou heed that thou speak not to Jacob either good or bad.

Laban then makes it clear that he wants his idol back.

31:30 And now, though thou wouldest needs be gone, because thou sore longedst after thy father's house, yet **wherefore hast thou stolen my gods?**

Jacob says that he left secretly because he was afraid of being prevented, and that he knows nothing of Laban's idol.

31:31 And Jacob answered and said to Laban, Because I was afraid: for I said, Peradventure thou wouldest take by force thy daughters from me. **31:32** With whomsoever thou findest thy gods, let him not live: before our brethren discern thou [take what you think is yours] what is thine with me, and take it to thee. For Jacob knew not that Rachel had stolen them.

Laban searches but does not find what Rachel has hidden.

31:33 And Laban went into Jacob's tent, and into Leah's tent, and into the two maidservants' tents; but he found them not. Then went he out of Leah's tent, and entered into Rachel's tent. **31:34** Now Rachel had taken the images, and put them in the camel's furniture [saddle], and sat upon them. And Laban searched all the tent, but found them not. **31:35** And she said to her father, Let it not displease my lord that I cannot rise up before thee; for the custom of women is upon me. And he searched but found not the images.

Jacob is angry with Laban, not knowing the deceit of Rachel, and remonstrates with him.

31:36 And Jacob was wroth, and chode with Laban: and Jacob answered and said to Laban, What is my trespass? what is my sin, that thou hast so hotly pursued after me? **31:37** Whereas thou hast searched all my stuff, what hast thou found of all thy household stuff? set it here before my brethren and thy brethren, that they may judge betwixt us both.

31:38 This twenty years have I been with thee; thy ewes and thy she goats have not cast their young, and the rams of thy flock have I not eaten. **31:39** That which was torn of beasts I brought not unto thee; I bare the loss of it; of my hand didst thou require it, whether stolen by day, or stolen by night. **31:40** Thus I was; in the day the drought consumed me, and the frost by night; and my sleep departed from mine eyes.

31:41 Thus have I been twenty years in thy house; I served thee fourteen years for thy two daughters, and six years for thy cattle [sheep and goats]: and thou hast changed my wages ten times. **31:42** Except the God of my father, the God of Abraham, and the fear of Isaac, had been with me, surely thou hadst sent me away now empty. God hath seen mine affliction and the labour of my hands, and rebuked thee yesternight.

Laban answers Jacob saying that his family is also Laban's family and he has no evil intent towards them.

31:43 And Laban answered and said unto Jacob, These daughters are my daughters, and these children are my children, and these cattle are my cattle, and all that thou seest is mine: and what can I do this day unto these my daughters, or unto their children which they have born?

Laban makes a covenant with Jacob before God.

31:44 Now therefore come thou, let us make a covenant, I and thou; and let it be for a witness between me and thee.

They set up a heap of stones as their border marker.

31:45 And Jacob took a stone, and set it up for a pillar. **31:46** And Jacob said unto his brethren, Gather stones; and they took stones, and made an heap: and they did eat there upon the heap. **31:47** And Laban called it Jegarsahadutha: but Jacob called it Galeed. **31:48** And Laban said, This heap is a witness between me and thee this day. Therefore was the name of it called Galeed; **31:49** And Mizpah; for he said, The LORD watch between me and thee, when we are absent one from another.

Laban demands that Jacob take no other wives or afflict his daughters in Canaan; then Laban pledges that he will not pass beyond the pillar and stones to come unto Jacob in anger.

31:50 If **thou shalt afflict my daughters, or if thou shalt take other wives beside my daughters**, no man is with us; see, God is witness betwixt me and thee. **31:51** And Laban said to Jacob, Behold this heap, and behold this pillar, which I have cast betwixt me and thee: **31:52** This heap be witness, and this pillar be witness, that **I will not pass over this heap to thee, and that thou shalt not pass over this heap and this pillar unto me, for harm.**

31:53 The God of Abraham, and the God of Nahor, the God of their father, judge betwixt us. And Jacob sware by the fear of his father Isaac.

31:54 Then Jacob offered sacrifice upon the mount, and called his brethren [the people with Laban to eat with his own family] to eat bread: and they did eat bread, and tarried all night in the mount.

In the morning Laban said his good byes and went back to his home.

31:55 And early in the morning Laban rose up, and kissed his sons and his daughters, and blessed them: and Laban departed, and returned unto his place.

Jacob had left his family and his brother Esau, fleeing alone and penniless from the just wrath of his brother, after he had bought the birthright and stolen the blessing from his brother Esau.

As a young man Jacob must have heard of God's prophecy regarding himself from his mother and had sought its fulfillment by his own worldly dishonest ways, instead of obeying the Word of God and waiting on God to bless him in God's own way and time.

Today the spiritually called out mainly rely on their own ways and traditions, instead of learning and living by every Word of God. Just like Jacob we are trying to achieve eternal life in the spiritual Promised Land by our own ways, by doing what we think is right and following our own false traditions; instead of trusting and faithfully keeping the whole Word of God.

Yet after more than 20 years Jacob had been humbled and been made rich through many trials, and it is through many trials that the spiritually called out are humbled and made spiritually rich.

Most of today's spiritual Israel is now about to go into a grave trial that will humble us and teach us to exalt the whole Word of God above all else.

Just as Jacob learned during his trials, I am quite certain that most of us will also be humbled and learn; and that we will become rich with the spiritual gold tried in the fire of affliction.

Genesis 32

Certain angels from God meet Jacob on his journey

Genesis 32:1 And Jacob went on his way, and the angels of God met him. **32:2** And when Jacob saw them, he said, This is God's host: and he called the name of that place Mahanaim.

Jacob sends messengers to his brother Esau: this time he calls Esau his lord and calls himself the servant of Esau. Jacob has grown up and learned many lessons over his twenty years with Laban!

Brethren, we are all unfinished products who still have much to learn to become truly godly people; let us examine and correct ourselves so that we might spiritually grow to become ever more like God our Father in heaven and like the Son, by zealously keeping the whole Word of God.

32:3 And Jacob sent messengers before him to Esau his brother unto the land of Seir, the country of Edom. **32:4** And he commanded them, saying, Thus shall ye speak unto my lord Esau; Thy servant Jacob saith thus, I have sojourned with Laban, and stayed there until now: **32:5** And I have oxen, and asses, flocks, and menservants, and womenservants: and I have sent to tell my lord, that I may find grace in thy sight.

The messengers returned to Jacob and told him that Esau was coming with 400 men. Now Esau went forth to greet and welcome Jacob, but Jacob because of his guilt was terrified and took steps to save at least half of his family.

32:6 And the messengers returned to Jacob, saying, We came to thy brother Esau, and also he cometh to meet thee, and four hundred men with him. **32:7** Then Jacob was greatly afraid and distressed: and he divided the people that was with him, and the flocks, and herds, and the camels, into two bands; **32:8** And said, If Esau come to the one company, and smite it, then the other company which is left shall escape.

After doing what he could physically, Jacob then calls out to God in real sincere repentance as he remembers his guilt against his brother. Jacob at last was humbled and understood his true personal wickedness and need for God. Jacob deeply repented and began to rely on the eternal instead of living by his own ways.

Jacob finally learned that he could not inherit the birthright or the blessings by doing his own ways, and that only by being zealously faithful to God and God's Word would he be saved and inherit the promises.

Brethren, we also need to learn this lesson to exalt the Eternal and live by his Word, above our own leaders and our own ways. God's promises are conditional on our faithfulness to do his will and to live by every Word of God.

32:9 And Jacob said, O God of my father Abraham, and God of my father Isaac, the LORD which saidst unto me, Return unto thy country, and to thy kindred, and I will deal well with thee: **32:10 I am not worthy of the least of all the mercies, and of all the truth, which thou hast shewed unto thy servant**; for with my staff I passed over this Jordan; and now I am become two bands. **32:11** Deliver me, I pray thee, from the hand of my brother, from the hand of Esau: for I fear him, lest he will come and smite me, and the mother with the children. **32:12** And thou saidst, I will surely do thee good, and make thy seed as the sand of the sea, which cannot be numbered for multitude.

Jacob then sends presents of peace and repentance ahead of him to Esau; as is fitting for a godly person. Physically Jacob repented and gave gifts to his brother who he had sinned against.

Spiritually we are to likewise humble ourselves before God against who we have sinned and sincerely repent; and we must then give God the gift of faithful loving obedience to our Awesome Father and his Son.

32:13 And he lodged there that same night; and took of that which came to his hand a present for Esau his brother; **32:14** Two hundred she goats, and twenty he goats, two hundred ewes, and twenty rams, **32:15** Thirty milch camels with their colts, forty kine, and ten bulls, twenty she asses, and ten foals.

32:16 And he delivered them into the hand of his servants, every drove [flock] by themselves; and said unto his servants, Pass over before me, and put a space betwixt drove and drove.

Jacob had separated each gift so that they reached Esau one after the other and not all together.

Spiritually this represents the continual giving of the gift of our passionate love and wholehearted faithful lifelong [eternal] keeping of the Word of God.

32:17 And he commanded the foremost, saying, When Esau my brother meeteth thee, and asketh thee, saying, Whose art thou? and whither goest thou? and whose are these before thee? **32:18** Then thou shalt say, They be thy servant Jacob's; it is a present sent unto my lord Esau: and, behold, also he is behind us. **32:19** And so commanded he the second, and the third, and all that followed the droves, saying, On this manner shall ye speak unto Esau, when ye find him.

As the heart of Esau was melted by the display of humility and generous love form Jacob; so we will become acceptable to God our Father through our sincere repentance, the application of the Passover sacrifice of the Lamb of God, and by our personal loving gift of continual HOT ZEAL for all God's Will and Word to learn them and to keep them.

Brethren, God has given us more that we could ever even begin to repay; all He asks is that we return his love by doing what he has recorded in his Word for our own good.

32:20 And say ye moreover, Behold, thy servant Jacob is behind us. For he said, I will appease him with the present that goeth before me, and afterward I will see his face; peradventure he will accept of me. **32:21** So went the present over before him: and himself lodged that night in the company.

Jacob then sent his most precious possessions ahead of himself, and in doing this Jacob trusted in the mercy of God to motivate reconciliation with his brother Esau.

32:22 And he rose up that night, and took his two wives [Rachel and Leah], and his two womenservants [Bilhah and Zilpah], and his eleven sons, and passed over the ford Jabbok. **32:23** And he took them, and sent them over the brook, and sent over that he had

When Jacob was alone in the night an angel came to him and wrestled with him.

32:24 And Jacob was left alone; and there wrestled a man with him until the breaking of the day. **32:25** And when he saw that he prevailed not against him, he touched the hollow of his thigh; and the hollow of Jacob's thigh was out of joint, as he wrestled with him. **32:26** And he said, Let me go, for the day breaketh. And he said, I will not let thee go, except thou bless me.

Just as Jacob would not let go; we are never to let go of our zeal for the whole Word of God for therein lies a great blessing! IF we are faithful to cleave to every Word of God with all our hearts and minds and with all the strength that a merciful God gives us; then we shall inherit the birthright and promises of our calling!

32:27 And he said unto him, What is thy name? And he said, Jacob.

The name "Jacob" means usurper or supplanter and refers to the evil nature of Jacob when he trusted in himself and his own ways before he learned to be faithful to God. The word "Israel" means to be strong with God; as in trusting and obedient to, and so having power [influence] with.

32:28 And he said, Thy name shall be called no more Jacob, but Israel: for as a prince hast thou power [persevered] with God and with men, and hast prevailed.

No man ever prevails OVER God; instead we prevail over evil with God's help

The word "power" is not best translation. Best translation is "as a prince you have persevered [and not given up]". Jacob was no quitter.

> ### See Strong's numbers.
>
> **Genesis 32:28** And he said **559 8799**, Thy name **8034** shall be called **559 8735** no more Jacob **3290**, but Israel **3478**: for as a prince hast thou power [properly persevered] **8280 8804** with God **430** and with men **582**, and hast prevailed **3201 8799**.(Israel: that is, A prince of God)

The meaning is that by persevering and cleaving to God and not letting go of God [never quitting] he has prevailed; and received a blessing.

This is an allegory that we are to persevere in the pursuit of godliness and cleave to God and never let go of God; so that WITH God's help we can prevail against Satan and sin like true prince of God, and so receive God's blessing.

The life of Jacob is a marvelous example of God's ability to perform his will and mold us into the vessels he wants us to be.

This man Jacob left his home a selfish usurper, liar and thief and returned home a humble godly man: Having learned perseverance through his dedicated love for Rachel, and through that perseverance he learned humility, and through humility he learned godliness.

God provided the lessons and Jacob persevered and would not give up. Then on his return to his own land God met with Jacob and tested him one last time to see if he was a quitter or if he would remain in his new found commitment to godliness.

Jacob sought the name of the angel [messenger], who refused to reveal his name; he was likely the Elohim who later became Jesus Christ.

32:29 And Jacob asked him, and said, Tell me, I pray thee, thy name. And he said, Wherefore is it that thou dost ask after my name? And he blessed him there. **32:30** And Jacob called the name of the place Peniel: for **I have seen God face to face**, and my life is preserved.

Jacob limped as he journeyed in the morning.

32:31 And as he passed over Penuel the sun rose upon him, and he halted [limped] upon his thigh.

32:32 Therefore the children of Israel eat not of the sinew which shrank, which is upon the hollow of the thigh, unto this day: because he touched the hollow of Jacob's thigh in the sinew that shrank.

Genesis 33

Jacob divided his family according to their mothers as Esau approaches

Genesis 33:1 And Jacob lifted up his eyes, and looked, and, behold, Esau came, and with him four hundred men. And he divided the children unto Leah, and unto Rachel, and unto the two handmaids. **33:2** And he put the handmaids and their children foremost, and Leah and her children after, and Rachel and Joseph hindermost.

Jacob came before Esau and bowed seven times in a mark of the greatest respect and submission. So too, we are to totally submit to and respect our heavenly Father and his Son.

33:3 And he passed over before them, and bowed himself to the ground seven times, until he came near to his brother.

Esau forgave and accepted Jacob and welcomed him with joy!

When we have acquired the humility and the sincerely repentant attitude of Jacob; when we have turned from our own ways to faithfully obey God our Father and do HIS will: Then we will be accepted by our merciful Father and welcomed into his spiritual family with great joy!

33:4 And Esau ran to meet him, and embraced him, and fell on his neck, and kissed him: and they wept.

Jacob presented his family to Esau.

33:5 And he lifted up his eyes, and saw the women and the children; and said, Who are those with thee? And he said, The children which God hath graciously given thy servant. **33:6** Then the handmaidens came near, they and their children, and they bowed themselves. **33:7** And Leah also with her children came near, and bowed themselves: and after came Joseph near and Rachel, and they bowed themselves.

Then Esau gave back to Jacob his gifts, but Jacob insisted and so Esau took them. Even so, if we give to our Father in heaven the spiritual gift of faithful service, HE will bless us beyond our present comprehension.

33:8 And he said, What meanest thou by all this drove which I met? And he said, These are to find grace in the sight of my lord. **33:9** And Esau said, I have enough, my brother; keep that thou hast unto thyself.

33:10 And Jacob said, Nay, I pray thee, if now I have found grace in thy sight, then receive my present at my hand: for therefore I have seen thy face, as though I had seen the face of God, and thou wast pleased with me. **33:11** Take, I pray thee, my blessing that is brought to thee; because God hath dealt graciously with me, and because I have enough. And he urged him, and he took it.

Esau then wanted Jacob to rush home to see the family, and Jacob needed to go slowly for the sake of the young in the flocks. This lambing seems to put the time as early spring.

33:12 And he said, Let us take our journey, and let us go, and I will go before thee. **33:13** And he said unto him, My lord knoweth that the children are tender, and the flocks and herds with young are with me: and if men should overdrive them one day, all the flock will die. **33:14** Let my lord, I pray thee, pass over before his servant: and I will lead on softly, according as the cattle that goeth before me and the children be able to endure, until I come unto my lord unto Seir.

Esau offers help but it is not needed and Esau returns home.

33:15 And Esau said, Let me now leave with thee some of the folk that are with me. And he said, What needeth it? let me find grace in the sight of my lord. **33:16** So Esau returned that day on his way unto Seir.

33:17 And Jacob journeyed to Succoth, and built him an house, and made booths for his cattle: therefore the name of the place is called Succoth.

Shalem [safety] probably the village of Salim some 2 miles east of Jacob's well at Succoth. A place with abundant water.

33:18 And Jacob came to Shalem, a city of Shechem, which is in the land of Canaan, when he came from Padanaram; and pitched his tent before the city.

33:19 And he bought a parcel of a field, where he had spread his tent, at the hand of the children of Hamor, Shechem's father, for an hundred pieces of money. **33:20** And he erected there an altar, and called it EleloheIsrael ["God, the God of Israel"].

Genesis 34

The tragedy of Dinah who is the only one of the daughters of Jacob mentioned by name

Genesis 34:1 And Dinah the daughter of Leah, which she bare unto Jacob, went out to see the daughters of the land.

Shechem saw Dinah and loved her and took her without the proper approvals of her father and mother.

Our children are to keep the age old and honorable custom of seeking parental approval for marriage, for this is one of the Ten Commandments: Honor thy father and thy mother and marriage is one of the most important decisions that we can make.

34:2 And when Shechem the son of Hamor the Hivite, prince of the country, saw her, he took her, and lay with her, and defiled her. **34:3** And his soul clave unto Dinah the daughter of Jacob, and he loved the damsel, and spake kindly unto the damsel. **34:4** And Shechem spake unto his father Hamor, saying, Get me this damsel to wife.

Shechem wanted to marry Dinah and his father sent emissaries to Jacob for that purpose. Jacob waited for his sons to come so as to have a family discussion of the matter for Shechem was a Canaanite. At the same time it should be noted that Jacob's sons married Canaanite women (Gen 38:2).

34:5 And Jacob heard that he had defiled Dinah his daughter: now his sons were with his cattle in the field: and Jacob held his peace until they were come.

34:6 And Hamor the father of Shechem went out unto Jacob to commune with him. **34:7** And the sons of Jacob came out of the field when they heard it: and the men were grieved, and they were very wroth, because he had wrought folly in Israel in lying with Jacob's daughter: which thing ought not to be done.

Hamor did his best to arrange a marriage between Dinah and Shechem and he sought to unite his clan with Jacob's clan through marriages.

34:8 And Hamor communed with them, saying, The soul of my son Shechem longeth for your daughter: I pray you give her him to wife. **34:9** And make ye marriages with us, and give your daughters unto us, and take our daughters unto you. **34:10** And ye shall dwell with us: and the land shall be before you; dwell and trade ye therein, and get you possessions therein. **34:11** And Shechem said unto her father and unto her brethren, Let me find grace in your eyes, and what ye shall say unto me I will give. **34:12** Ask me never so much dowry and gift, and I will give according as ye shall say unto me: but give me the damsel to wife.

Then the sons of Jacob agreed to blend their family with the family of Hamor and then demanded that Shechem be circumcised. They offered to agree to marry into the family of Hamor to become one family with them, if all his family were circumcised. This was a great demand but the union of families was a major enticement to Hamor for Jacob was very rich.

At this point we must ask ourselves: What is the value of being circumcised or baptized for the wrong reasons; for some personal reason and not as a real commitment to live by every Word of God?

I must also point out that circumcision means nothing if the person does not keep the whole Word of God. Baptism also means absolutely NOTHING; if we are not zealous to fulfill our baptismal commitment and passionately live by every Word of God.

Do not rely on lies saying I am circumcised or I am baptized therefore I am godly; which is a lie! We will never have it made it made and we must continually WORK HARD to be counted worthy to receive the birthright of our calling.

Philippians 3:11 If by any means I might attain unto the resurrection of the dead. **3:12** Not as though I had already attained, either were already perfect: but I follow after, if that I may apprehend that for which also I am apprehended of Christ Jesus.

3:13 Brethren, I count not myself to have apprehended: but this one thing I do, forgetting those things which are behind, and reaching forth unto those things which are before, **3:14** I press toward the mark for the prize of the high calling of God in Christ Jesus.

Genesis 34:13 And the sons of Jacob answered Shechem and Hamor his father deceitfully, and said, because he had defiled Dinah their sister: **34:14** And they said unto them, We cannot do this thing, to give our sister to one that is uncircumcised; for that were a reproach unto us: **34:15** But in this will we consent unto you: If ye will be as we be, **that every male of you be circumcised**; **34:16** Then will we give our daughters [plural] unto you, and **we will take your daughters to us, and we will dwell with you, and we will become one people. 34:17** But if ye will not hearken unto us, to be circumcised; then will we take our daughter, and we will be gone.

Shechem had himself circumcised with alacrity to gain the hand of his beloved. This act had nothing to do with conversion and was to gain a bride.

34:18 And their words pleased Hamor, and Shechem Hamor's son. **34:19** And the young man deferred not to do the thing, because he had delight in Jacob's daughter: and he was more honourable than all the house of his father.

Then king Hamor and his son the prince Shechem, encouraged all the men of that city to be circumcised with reports of how rich they would become. This was a false conversion and was only agreeing to circumcision for monetary gain.

34:20 And Hamor and Shechem his son came unto the gate of their city, and communed with the men of their city, saying, **34:21** These men are peaceable with us; therefore let them dwell in the land, and trade therein; for the land, behold, it is large enough for them; let us **take their daughters** to us for wives, and let us give them our daughters. **34:22** Only herein will the men consent unto us for to dwell with us, to be one people, if every male among us be circumcised, as they are circumcised. **34:23 Shall not their cattle and their substance and every beast of their's be our's? only let us consent unto them, and they will dwell with us.**

Then were all the men of the city circumcised because of the word of Jacob and his sons.

34:24 And unto Hamor and unto Shechem his son hearkened all that went out of the gate of his city; and every male was circumcised, all that went out of the gate of his city.

Then when the men were still not recovered, Simeon and Levi crept into the city and killed all the males.

34:25 And it came to pass on the third day, when they were sore, that two of the sons of Jacob, Simeon and Levi, Dinah's brethren, took each man his sword, and came upon the city boldly, and slew all the males. **34:26** And they slew Hamor and Shechem his son with the edge of the sword, and took Dinah out of Shechem's house, and went out.

Then all of Jacob's sons seeing the deed done, came and spoiled the city.

34:27 The sons of Jacob came upon the slain, and spoiled the city, because they had defiled their sister. **34:28** They took their sheep, and their oxen, and their asses, and that which was in the city, and that which was in the field, **34:29** And all their wealth, and all their little ones, and their wives took they captive, and spoiled even all that was in the house.

Then Jacob rebuked them for he feared that all the Canaanites would turn on him for vengeance.

34:30 And Jacob said to Simeon and Levi, Ye have troubled me to make me to stink among the inhabitants of the land, among the Canaanites and the Perizzites: and I being few in number, they shall gather themselves together against me, and slay me; and I shall be destroyed, I and my house.

They justified themselves before their father.

34:31 And they said, Should he deal with our sister as with an harlot?

This is a false claim since Shechem was not treating her as a harlot but was deeply desiring to marry her and the deal had been made. There is much left unsaid here like the desires of the maid.

This was a horrible situation and it appears that the incident was recorded to illustrate the cruelty of Simeon and Levi.

Genesis 35

The Elohim who later became Jesus Christ then appeared to Jacob and called his family to put away all strange gods and go to Beth-El [the House of God] to appear before him. It is therefore self evident that the sons of Jacob did have false gods among them, perhaps idols taken from the family of Hamor and kept by them.

Brethren, it is time that we also put away our strange gods; the idols of men, corporate entities, past false traditions, physical wealth, social club man pleasing and ANYTHING that comes between us and our zeal for the whole Word of our Mighty One!

Genesis 35:1 And God said unto Jacob, Arise, go up to Bethel, and dwell there: and make there an altar unto God, that appeared unto thee when thou fleddest from the face of Esau thy brother. **35:2** Then Jacob said unto his household, and to all that were with him, Put away the strange gods that are among you, and be clean, and change your garments: **35:3** And let us arise, and go up to Bethel; and I will make there an altar unto God, who answered me in the day of my distress, and was with me in the way which I went. **35:4** And they gave unto Jacob all the strange gods which were in their hand, and all their earrings which were in their ears; and Jacob hid them under the oak which was by Shechem.

God caused the Canaanites to fear Jacob and his family for their deed against Hamor and Shechem and their city; so that instead of seeking vengeance the Canaanites shook with fear.

35:5 And they journeyed: and the terror of God was upon the cities that were round about them, and they did not pursue after the sons of Jacob.

35:6 So Jacob came to Luz, which is in the land of Canaan, that is, Bethel, he and all the people that were with him. **35:7** And he built there an altar, and called the place Elbethel: because there God appeared unto him, when he fled from the face of his brother. **35:8** But Deborah Rebekah's nurse died, and she was buried beneath Bethel under an oak: and the name of it was called Allonbachuth [the Oak of weeping].

In the short recall inset of Genesis 35:9-10, it is repeated that God had changed Jacob's name to Israel, at Bethel, at the time that God appeared to him as he journeyed from Laban; and now God appeared to Jacob [Israel] again in the same place.

35:9 And God appeared unto Jacob again, when he came out of Padanaram, and blessed him. **35:10** And God said unto him, Thy name is Jacob: thy name shall not be called any more Jacob, but Israel shall be thy name: and he called his name Israel.

God appeared to Jacob again after Deborah Rebekah's nurse died and repeated his promises to Israel [Jacob].

35:11 And God said unto him, **I am God Almighty: be fruitful and multiply; a nation and a company of nations shall be of thee, and kings shall come out of thy loins; 35:12 And the land which I gave Abraham and Isaac, to thee I will give it, and to thy seed after thee will I give the land. 35:13** And God went up from him in the place where he talked with him.

Then Jacob set up a pillar stone just as he had done many years before when he was leaving his father's house, and poured wine and oil upon it.

35:14 And Jacob set up a pillar in the place where he talked with him, even a pillar of stone: and he poured a drink offering thereon, and he poured oil thereon. **35:15** And Jacob [Israel] called the name of the place where God spake with him, Bethel.

Then Rachel had a second son in her old age, dying in childbirth.

35:16 And they journeyed from Bethel; and there was but a little way to come to Ephrath: and Rachel travailed, and she had hard labour. **35:17**

And it came to pass, when she was in hard labour, that the midwife said unto her, Fear not; thou shalt have this son also.

35:18 And it came to pass, as her soul was in departing, (for she died) that she called his name Benoni [son of sorrows]: but his father called him Benjamin [son of my right hand].

35:19 And Rachel died, and was buried in the way to Ephrath, which is Bethlehem. **35:20** And Jacob set a pillar upon her grave: that is the pillar of Rachel's grave unto this day [the day that this was written]. **35:21** And Israel journeyed, and spread his tent beyond the tower of Edar.

Reuben defiles himself with his father's concubine. Reuben would lose the birthright of the first born which was taken from him and given to Joseph for this sin.

35:22 And it came to pass, when Israel dwelt in that land, that **Reuben went and lay with Bilhah his father's concubine: and Israel heard it.**

Now the sons of Jacob were twelve:

35:23 The sons of **Leah; Reuben, Jacob's firstborn, and Simeon, and Levi, and Judah, and Issachar, and Zebulun:**

35:24 The sons of **Rachel; Joseph, and Benjamin:**

35:25 And the sons of **Bilhah**, Rachel's handmaid; **Dan, and Naphtali:**

35:26 And the sons of **Zilpah**, Leah's handmaid: **Gad, and Asher**: these are the sons of Jacob, which were born to him in Padanaram.

Jacob came to his father Isaac who died at 180 years old.

35:27 And Jacob came unto Isaac his father unto Mamre, unto the city of Arbah, which is Hebron, where Abraham and Isaac sojourned. **35:28** And the days of Isaac were an hundred and fourscore years. **35:29** And Isaac gave up the ghost, and died, and was gathered unto his people, being old and full of days: and his sons Esau and Jacob buried him.

Genesis 36

Details concerning the offspring of Esau who lived in the south east of Palestine and how Mount Seir came to be called Edom

Eventually after many generations many of the descendants of Esau left Palestine and migrated into Turkistan in central Asia. Later when Islam swept through the region the Othmani Turks [Esau's descendants in Turkmenistan] migrated to modern day Turkey where they formed the Ottoman [Othmani, Uthmani, Osmani] Empire. Here is a short overview of the migration into Turkey by the Osmani from their own historians.

Genesis 36:1 Now these are the generations of Esau, who is Edom.

36:2 Esau took his wives of the daughters of Canaan; Adah the daughter of Elon the Hittite, and Aholibamah the daughter of Anah the daughter of Zibeon the Hivite; **36:3** And Bashemath Ishmael's daughter, sister of Nebajoth.

The sons of Esau

36:4 And Adah bare to Esau **Eliphaz**; and Bashemath bare **Reuel**; **36:5** And Aholibamah bare **Jeush, and Jaalam, and Korah**: these are the sons of Esau, which were born unto him in the land of Canaan.

36:6 And Esau took his wives, and his sons, and his daughters, and all the persons of his house, and his cattle, and all his beasts, and all his substance, which he had got in the land of Canaan; and went into the country from the face of his brother Jacob. **36:7** For their riches were more than that they might dwell together; and the land wherein they were strangers could not bear them because of their cattle.

A key to understanding prophecy and Job

Scripturally the term Mount Seir, or Edom, always applies to the sons of after Esau migrated there; previous to Esau, Mount Seir belonged to the Horites.

Mount Seir was named for Seir the Horite, whose offspring had inhabited the area (Genesis 14:6, 36:20) until the children of Esau (the Edomites) completely destroyed or integrated the Horites and took possession of the city (Deuteronomy 2:4-5, 12, 22).

From that time Seir has become synonymous with Esau who took possession of Seir and destroyed or assimilated the Horites living there. (Genesis 32:3; 33:14, 16; 36:8; Joshua 24:4).

36:8 Thus dwelt Esau in mount Seir: Esau is Edom.

36:9 And these are the generations of Esau the father of the Edomites in mount Seir: **36:10** These are the names of Esau's sons; **Eliphaz** the son of Adah the wife of Esau, Reuel the son of Bashemath the wife of Esau.

A few words about Eliphaz [also called duke Timnah, v 40]: One of the leaders [dukes] [princes] of Esau was Eliphaz.

The biblical account of Job records an interesting detail. One of Job's friends is mentioned in **Job 2:11** Now when Job's three friends heard of all this evil that was come upon him, they came every one from his own place; **Eliphaz** [also called duke Timnah, v 40]: **the Temanite**—This Eliphaz was the son [mentioned first, indicating he was the first born] of Esau! Who dwelled in Temen [the southeast, ie a village of Mount Seir] and named his land and his son Temen after himself.

Eliphaz [Timnah] was the firstborn son of Esau; and Shuach, the sixth and last of Keturah's sons was the father of Bildad. The lives of both of Job's friends dating Job to the era of the sons of Esau.

The first indication of the date of Job is Shuah in Genesis 25:2. [Also called Shuach, this sixth and **last of Keturah's sons** has a name meaning *wealth* (Strong: SHD 7744). He was the progenitor of the Shuhites, the most notable of whom was **Bildad, son of Shuach**, and one of Job's 'comforters' (Job 2:11).

In our careful study of Genesis we have now found two proofs that Job was real and not simply an instructive story and dated his life to the period of Esau's children.

36:11 And **the sons of Eliphaz** [Timnah] were Teman [named after his father Timnah (Eliphaz)], Omar, Zepho, and Gatam, and Kenaz.

Amalek was the grandson of Esau and was a vicious people, famous for cutting off arms and legs and many other tortures. They became the enemy of Israel who fought with Israel from the time they sought to enter Canaan until Saul and David largely defeated them. These were the people about which Saul sinned by leaving their animals alive (1 Sam 15).

36:12 And Timna was concubine to **Eliphaz** Esau's son; and she bare to Eliphaz **Amalek**: these were the sons of Adah Esau's wife.

36:13 And these are **the sons of Reuel; Nahath, and Zerah, Shammah, and Mizzah**: these were the sons of Bashemath Esau's wife.

36:14 And these were the sons of Aholibamah, the daughter of Anah the daughter of Zibeon, Esau's wife: and she bare to Esau **Jeush, and Jaalam, and Korah.**

The names of these son's of Esau are repeated for emphasis and can be traced to modern times.

36:15 These were dukes of the sons of Esau: the sons of Eliphaz the firstborn son of Esau; duke Teman, duke Omar, duke Zepho, duke Kenaz, **36:16** Duke Korah, duke Gatam, and duke Amalek: these are the dukes that came of Eliphaz in the land of Edom; these were the sons of Adah. **36:17** And these are the sons of Reuel Esau's son; duke Nahath, duke Zerah, duke Shammah, duke Mizzah: these are the dukes that came of Reuel in the land of Edom; these are the sons of Bashemath Esau's wife. **36:18** And these are the sons of Aholibamah Esau's wife; duke Jeush, duke Jaalam, duke Korah: these were the dukes that came of Aholibamah the daughter of Anah, Esau's wife.

36:19 These are the sons of Esau, who is Edom, and these are their dukes.

Seir was the father of the Horites and the city of Mount Seir, long before Esau.

The first mention of the Horites was when they were defeated in Abraham's time by a coalition of Eastern kings led by Chedorlaomer of Elam. These kings had come through the Horite territory to subdue a rebellion by a coalition of other 'kings' of peoples in Sodom and the surrounding area whom they had ruled for twelve years, who were living near the Salt Sea (the Dead Sea) and Sodom and Gomorrah (Genesis 14:1-12).

The **Horites** were among the people rescued by Abraham when he rescued Lot. **Their country was called Mount Seir after their father Seir** and was a hill top village near to Sodom in the south.

Later, according to Genesis 36, the Horites co-existed and inter-married with the family of Esau, grandson of Abraham through Isaac (Genesis 25:21-25). They were eventually integrated and brought under the rule of the descendants of Esau, Esau then becoming known as Edom.

These are the dukes [princes, rulers] **of the Horites**

36:20 These are the **sons of Seir the Horite**, who inhabited the land; Lotan, and Shobal, and Zibeon, and Anah, **36:21** And Dishon, and Ezer, and Dishan: these are the dukes of the Horites, the children of Seir in the land of Edom. **36:22** And the children of Lotan were Hori and Hemam; and Lotan's sister was Timna.

The family of Shobal.

36:23 And the children of Shobal were these; Alvan, and Manahath, and Ebal, Shepho, and Onam.

The family of Zibeon.

36:24 And these are the children of Zibeon; both Ajah, and Anah: this was that Anah that found the mules in the wilderness, as he fed the asses of Zibeon his father. **36:25** And the children of Anah were these; Dishon, and Aholibamah the daughter of Anah.

The family of Dishon

36:26 And these are the children of Dishon; Hemdan, and Eshban, and Ithran, and Cheran.

The family of Ezer

36:27 The children of Ezer are these; Bilhan, and Zaavan, and Akan.

The family of Dishan

36:28 The children of Dishan are these; Uz, and Aran.

36:29 These are the dukes that came of the Horites; duke Lotan, duke Shobal, duke Zibeon, duke Anah, **36:30** Duke Dishon, duke Ezer, duke Dishan: these are the dukes that came of Hori, among their dukes in the land of Seir.

Abraham rescued these Horites and they lived in Mount Seir near Sodom. Later Abraham's grandson Esau went to live with his family in the south by Mount Seir and intermarried and became mixed with the Horites as one people.

Hence Esau gained the name of Mount Seir, added to his own name. Esau had a certain darkness or copperness of skin and that earned him the appellation Edom meaning red. This attribute would have been reduced by intermarriage of the family of Esau with the Horites.

The kings of Esau in Edom, before Saul reigned in Israel

36:31 And these are **the kings that reigned in the land of Edom, before there reigned any king over the children of Israel. 36:32** And Bela the son of Beor reigned in Edom: and the name of his city was Dinhabah.

36:33 And Bela died, and Jobab the son of Zerah of Bozrah reigned in his stead. **36:34** And Jobab died, and Husham of the land of Temani reigned in his stead.

36:35 And Husham died, and Hadad the son of Bedad, who smote Midian in the field of Moab, reigned in his stead: and the name of his city was Avith. **36:36** And Hadad died, and Samlah of Masrekah reigned in his stead.

36:37 And Samlah died, and Saul of Rehoboth by the river reigned in his stead. **36:38** And Saul died, and Baalhanan the son of Achbor reigned in his stead.

36:39 And Baalhanan the son of Achbor died, and Hadar reigned in his stead: and the name of his city was Pau; and his wife's name was Mehetabel, the daughter of Matred, the daughter of Mezahab.

Again the sons of Esau were

36:40 And these are the names of the dukes that came of Esau, according to their families, after their places, by their names; **duke Timnah** [Eliphaz is not named here but the firstborn who was Eliphaz, is named as Timnah] **, duke Alvah, duke Jetheth, 36:41 Duke Aholibamah, duke Elah, duke Pinon, 36:42 Duke Kenaz, duke Teman, duke Mibzar, 36:43 Duke Magdiel, duke Iram:** these be the dukes of Edom, according to their habitations in the land of their possession: he is Esau the father of the Edomites.

Genesis 37

Jacob had favorites with his children, and Joseph was molded unwittingly by his father into a spoiled selfish Papa's boy who earned the hatred of his brothers

This is also a story about how all things work together for good in the hands of God.

First, Joseph was imprisoned wrongfully and humbled for seven years, transforming him from a spoiled child into a man of character fit to rule a kingdom. While his imprisonment was wrongful it was necessary for his character development.

That is the key lesson of Job; that God performs his will for his greater purposes even though sometimes it may appear to us that we suffer wrongly.

The reason why the "righteous" suffer, is to prune them, build them and perfect them; so that they become MORE righteous and bear much fruit, John 15.

This whole situation in which Joseph appears to suffer wrongfully and then Israel suffers wrongfully as slaves in Egypt, and then God himself hardens Pharaoh's heart so that he could afflict Egypt; was to establish the lesson and allegory for us about the slavery of sin.

The lesson of Egypt is intended to teach us about God's deliverance of physical Israel from Egypt, as a lesson for us about God's deliverance from bondage to Satan, sin and death, and the need to faithfully live by every Word of God. It is also a lesson that God is the Master Potter who uses his tools as he sees fit, to form us into the beings he desires.

As you read these things please consider this lesson on the greatness and incredible wisdom of God, and how God works things out to fulfill his own purposes in spite of the failings and desires of men.

The story of Joseph begins with his reporting on his brothers to his father Israel [Jacob]. This tattling added to the natural animosity against him for being his father's favorite and Papa's boy.

This family rivalry goes back to Laban and his substituting Leah for Jacob's beloved Rachel. Rachel had only two sons and after her death Jacob loved her first born Joseph, just as he had loved Rachel.

This playing of favorites among his sons brought about a deep family rivalry which God used to fulfill his prophecy to Abraham that his family would go down into Egypt.

Genesis 37:1 And Jacob dwelt in the land wherein his father was a stranger, in the land of Canaan. **37:2** These are the generations of Jacob.

Joseph, being seventeen years old, was feeding the flock with his brethren; and the lad was with the sons of Bilhah, and with the sons of Zilpah, his father's wives: and Joseph brought unto his father a bad report about them.

Then Israel [Jacob] made Joseph a multi colored coat in a time when dyes and colors were rare and expensive; and did not honor his other sons in this way, playing favorites.

37:3 Now Israel loved Joseph more than all his children, because he was the son of his old age: and he made him a coat of many colours.

This favoritism by Israel for Joseph above his other sons, produced a natural strife in the family and a strong upset between Joseph and his brothers.

37:4 And when his brethren saw that their father loved him more than all his brethren, they hated him, and could not speak peaceably unto him.

Then Joseph had a dream that he was exalted above his whole family and Joseph did not keep his mouth shut about it; which of course added to the anger of his brothers.

37:5 And Joseph dreamed a dream, and he told it his brethren: and they hated him yet the more.

When told the dream the brothers and parents well understood its meaning.

37:6 And he said unto them, Hear, I pray you, this dream which I have dreamed: **37:7** For, behold, we were binding sheaves in the field, and, lo, my sheaf arose, and also stood upright; and, behold, your sheaves stood round about, and made obeisance to my sheaf.

37:8 And his brethren said to him, Shalt thou indeed reign over us? or shalt thou indeed have dominion over us? And they hated him yet the more for his dreams, and for his words.

Joseph had a second dream with the same meaning as the first and did not have the good sense to keep his mouth shut.

37:9 And he dreamed yet another dream, and told it his brethren, and said, Behold, I have dreamed a dream more; and, behold, the sun and the moon and the eleven stars made obeisance to me.

37:10 And he told it to his father, and to his brethren: and his father rebuked him, and said unto him, What is this dream that thou hast dreamed? Shall I and thy mother and thy brethren indeed come to bow down ourselves to thee to the earth? **37:11** And his brethren envied him; but his father observed [thought about the dream] the saying.

37:12 And his brethren went to feed their father's flock in Shechem.

Israel sent Joseph to get news about his sons and flocks.

37:13 And Israel said unto Joseph, Do not thy brethren feed the flock in Shechem? come, and I will send thee unto them. And he said to him, Here am I. **37:14** And he said to him, Go, I pray thee, see whether it be well with thy brethren, and well with the flocks; and bring me word again. So he sent him out of the vale of Hebron, and he came to Shechem. **37:15** And a certain man found him, and, behold, he was wandering in the field: and the man asked him, saying, What seekest thou? **37:16** And he said, I seek my brethren: tell me, I pray thee, where they feed their flocks. **37:17** And the man said, They are departed hence; for I heard them say, Let us go to Dothan. And Joseph went after his brethren, and found them in Dothan.

The son's of Israel then decided to do away with this arrogant little Papa's boy who had vexed them so.

37:18 And when they saw him afar off, even before he came near unto them, they conspired against him to slay him. **37:19** And they said one to another, Behold, this dreamer cometh. **37:20** Come now therefore, and let us slay him, and cast him into some pit, and we will say, Some evil beast hath devoured him: and we shall see what will become of his dreams.

Then Reuben the first born, insisted that they only teach Joseph a lesson and not kill him.

37:21 And Reuben heard it, and he delivered him out of their hands; and said, Let us not kill him.

Reuben counselled them to cast Joseph into a pit, so that Reuben might secretly return later and save Joseph. In doing this he showed promise as a good man; yet his adultery with his father's concubine was evil and this instability of character was later mentioned in the prophecy about the future of Reuben.

37:22 And Reuben said unto them, Shed no blood, but cast him into this pit that is in the wilderness, and lay no hand upon him; that he might rid him out of their hands, to deliver him to his father again.

When Joseph came to visit them they took off his coat which they hated as the symbol of their father's favoritism and cast Joseph into a pit [perhaps a dry well].

37:23 And it came to pass, when Joseph was come unto his brethren, that they stript Joseph out of his coat, his coat of many colours that was on him; **37:24** And they took him, and cast him into a pit: and the pit was empty, there was no water in it.

Then Judah suggested that they sell their brother Joseph as a slave to be taken to Egypt. In this Judah sought profit but he also sought to save the lad's life and to deliver them from the wrath of their father if Joseph should escape and relate the story to Israel.

37:25 And they sat down to eat bread: and they lifted up their eyes and looked, and, behold, a company of Ishmeelites came from Gilead with their camels bearing spicery and balm and myrrh, going to carry it down to Egypt. **37:26** And Judah said unto his brethren, What profit is it if we slay our brother, and conceal his blood? **37:27** Come, and let us sell him to the Ishmeelites, and let not our hand be upon him; for he is our brother and our flesh. And his brethren were content.

Joseph was sold for twenty pieces of silver and was taken to Egypt.

37:28 Then there passed by Midianites merchantmen; and they drew and lifted up Joseph out of the pit, and sold Joseph to the Ishmeelites for twenty pieces of silver: and they brought Joseph into Egypt.

When Reuben returned he was greatly vexed that his brother Joseph was gone, and concerned for his father Israel.

37:29 And Reuben returned unto the pit; and, behold, Joseph was not in the pit; and he rent his clothes. **37:30** And he returned unto his brethren, and said, The child is not; and I, whither shall I go?

The brothers then decided to claim that Joseph was dead.

37:31 And they took Joseph's coat, and killed a kid of the goats, and dipped the coat in the blood; **37:32** And they sent the coat of many colours, and they brought it to their father; and said, This have we found: know now whether it be thy son's coat or no. **37:33** And he knew it, and said, It is my son's coat; an evil beast hath devoured him; Joseph is without doubt rent in pieces.

Jacob was devastated because his son, his firstborn son by his beloved deceased Rachel, was thought dead.

37:34 And Jacob rent his clothes, and put sackcloth upon his loins, and mourned for his son many days.

Here Jacob is said to have daughters in the plural as well as sons.

37:35 And all his sons and **all his daughters** rose up to comfort him; but he refused to be comforted; and he said, For I will go down into the grave unto my son mourning. Thus his father wept for him.

In Egypt Joseph was sold to a senior official in the court of the king.

37:36 And the Midianites sold him into Egypt unto Potiphar, an officer of Pharaoh's, and captain of the guard.

Genesis 38

Judah marries a Canaanite

Genesis 38:1 And it came to pass at that time, that Judah went down from his brethren, and turned in to a certain **Adullamite, whose name was Hirah. 38:2** And Judah saw there a daughter of a certain Canaanite, whose name was **Shuah**; and he took her, and went in unto her. **38:3** And she conceived, and bare a son; and he called his name **Er. 38:4** And she conceived again, and bare a son; and she called his name **Onan. 38:5** And she yet again conceived, and bare a son; and called his name **Shelah**: and he was at Chezib, when she bare him.

Judah has three sons by Shuah; Er, Onan and Shelah.

Judah then gave his son Er; Tamar to wife; but Er was a wicked man and God killed him.

38:6 And Judah took a wife for Er his firstborn, whose name was Tamar. **38:7** And Er, Judah's firstborn, was wicked in the sight of the LORD; and the LORD slew him.

Then Judah called on Onan to raise up a son for his dead brother in Liverate Marriage.

38:8 And Judah said unto Onan, Go in unto thy brother's wife, and marry her, and raise up seed to thy brother.

Onan knowing that any child would be considered his brother's and not his, obeyed his father and took her, but withdrew at the last minute in a form of birth control, spilling his seed on the ground to avoid impregnating her. He had taken Tamar under false pretenses and defrauded her and his brother of a son.

Taking ones brother's wife is forbidden except for the purpose of raising up a son for the childless dead. Therefore the Elohim who later gave up his God-hood to be made flesh as Jesus Christ, killed this man for his sin against his brother and his brother's wife.

38:9 And Onan knew that the seed should not be his; and it came to pass, when he went in unto his brother's wife, that he spilled it on the ground, lest that he should give seed to his brother. **38:10** And the thing which he did displeased the LORD: wherefore he slew him also.

Then Judah fearing for the life of his remaining son Shelah, kept Tamer as a widow refusing to give her his last son as her husband.

38:11 Then said Judah to Tamar his daughter in law, Remain a widow at thy father's house, till Shelah my son be grown: for he said, Lest peradventure he die also, as his brethren did. And Tamar went and dwelt in her father's house.

Over time Judah's wife Shuah died and Judah sought comfort and visited his friend.

38:12 And in process of time the daughter of Shuah Judah's wife died; and Judah was comforted, and went up unto his sheepshearers to Timnath, he and his friend **Hirah the Adullamite.**

Tamar was told and she went to meet Judah because Judah's son was older and able to marry her and give her a son and he was not given to her.

38:13 And it was told Tamar, saying, Behold thy father in law goeth up to Timnath [Timnah of Esau of Genesis 36] to shear his sheep. **38:14** And she put her widow's garments off from her, and covered her with a vail, and wrapped herself, and sat in an open place, which is by the way to Timnath; for **she saw that Shelah was grown, and she was not given unto him to wife**.

Judah seeks consolation because of the death of his wife and not recognizing her, takes Tamar for a harlot. She demands a token of his pledge until lambing time, when she should receive a kid as her gift.

NOTE: In those days it was the custom for a married woman to cover her hair but not her face. It was the custom of a whore to cover her face so as to hide her identity since the penalty for harlotry was severe.

38:15 When Judah saw her, he thought her to be an harlot; because she had covered her face. **38:16** And he turned unto her by the way, and said, Go to, I pray thee, let me come in unto thee; (for he knew not that she was his daughter in law.) And she said, What wilt thou give me, that thou mayest come in unto me? **38:17** And he said, I will send thee a kid from the flock. And she said, Wilt thou give me a pledge, till thou send it? **38:18** And he said, What pledge shall I give thee? And she said, Thy signet, and thy bracelets, and thy staff that is in thine hand. And he gave it her, and came in unto her, and she conceived by him.

Tamar was no real professional harlot and did what she did for the sake of a child by the family of Judah. She returned home and had no other.

38:19 And she arose, and went away, and laid by her vail from her, and put on the garments of her widowhood.

Judah sought to pay his pledge but the woman was not found.

38:20 And Judah sent the kid by the hand of his friend the Adullamite, to receive his pledge from the woman's hand: but he found her not. **38:21** Then he asked the men of that place, saying, Where is the harlot, that was openly by the way side? And they said, There was no harlot in this place. **38:22** And he returned to Judah, and said, I cannot find her; and also the men of the place said, that there was no harlot in this place. **38:23** And Judah said, Let her take it to her, lest we be shamed: behold, I sent this kid, and thou hast not found her.

Judah is told three months later that Tamar was pregnant and said that she should be brought to him to be burned in the fire for being a harlot. So we see that Tamar took a considerable risk and did this neither for money nor for lust.

38:24 And it came to pass about three months after, that it was told Judah, saying, Tamar thy daughter in law hath played the harlot; and also, behold, she is with child by whoredom. And Judah said, Bring her forth, and let her be burnt.

Tamar then gives her evidence, the tokens left to her by Judah.

38:25 When she was brought forth, she sent to her father in law, saying, By the man, whose these are, am I with child: and she said, Discern, I pray thee, whose are these, the signet, and bracelets, and staff.

Judah acknowledged her and his sin in withholding his son from her, and he kept himself from her from that time, having produced a son for his dead firstborn son Er.

38:26 And Judah acknowledged them, and said, She hath been more righteous than I; because that I gave her not to Shelah my son. And he knew her again no more.

Just like Jacob and Esau were twins, the second being born before the first; so Tamar also had twins, the second being born before the first.

38:27 And it came to pass in the time of her travail, that, behold, twins were in her womb. **38:28** And it came to pass, when she travailed, that the one put out his hand: and the midwife took and bound upon his hand a scarlet thread, saying, This came out first.

38:29 And it came to pass, as he drew back his hand, that, behold, his brother came out: and she said, How hast thou broken forth? this breach be upon thee: therefore his name was called Pharez. **38:30** And afterward came out his brother, that had the scarlet thread upon his hand: and his name was called Zarah.

Genesis 39

Potiphar bought Joseph to be a servant and Joseph prospered

Genesis 39:1 And Joseph was brought down to Egypt; and Potiphar, an officer of Pharaoh, captain of the guard, an Egyptian, bought him of the hands of the Ishmeelites, which had brought him down thither. **39:2** And the LORD was with Joseph, and he was a prosperous man; and he was in the house of his master the Egyptian.

God blessed Joseph greatly and Potiphar was impressed with Joseph and made him lord of all his household.

39:3 And his master saw that the LORD was with him, and that the LORD made all that he did to prosper in his hand. **39:4** And **Joseph found grace in his sight, and he served him: and he made him overseer over his house, and all that he had he put into his hand. 39:5** And it came to pass from the time that he had made him overseer in his house, and over all that he had, that the LORD blessed the Egyptian's house for Joseph's sake; and the blessing of the LORD was upon all that he had in the house, and in the field.

Potiphar gave everything he had into the hand of Joseph.

39:6 And he left all that he had in Joseph's hand; and he knew not ought he had, save the bread which he did eat. And Joseph was a goodly person, and well favoured.

Then Potiphar's wife, enticed by the power that Joseph had and by his youth, desired him. Of course this was a temptation from Satan which God allowed to test Joseph; just like God allows Satan to tempt us today to test us and to build our character to make us stronger.

Remember how Pharaoh desired Sarai and was saved by God, and how Abimelech desired her and was saved by God. The men of those days including Joseph knew that to take another's wife was a great sin against God. Even the wickedness of the Canaanites had not yet come to the fullness that would climax in the time of Moses. Joseph knew that this would be a sin against GOD and therefore he rejected her.

Physical adultery is an allegory of spiritual adultery; which is to follow any man or organization contrary to following the whole Word of God the Father (Mat 4:4) and of our espoused Husband Jesus Christ; who is the LOGOS the Word of God.

We have all been tempted by spiritual adultery which is the idolizing of men or allowing anything at all to come between us and God. Some have rejected committing spiritual adultery against Christ, just like Joseph rejected Potiphar's wife, while the vast majority in today's Ekklesia are guilty of this sin and idolize men or some corporate organization.

Joseph defended himself and responded to the temptation by saying that his master had given all things in his house to Joseph, and therefore to commit adultery against him would betray that trust and would be a great wickedness.

Brethren, OUR Master Jesus Christ has promised to give us and HAS given us more than Potiphar ever gave to Joseph! For our espoused Husband Jesus Christ has bought us at the cost of his very life! Why then are we not faithful to OUR Master like Joseph was faithful to Potiphar? Why do we follow men blindly, unquestioningly and thoughtlessly; instead of proving all things as to their consistency with the will of our LORD? (1 Thess 5:21).

The vast majority of those in today's Ekklesia idolize either a dead man, or a present leader, corporate entity, elder, or circle of friends; exalting them above the Word of God in our lives! There is still time to sincerely repent of our spiritual adultery. Let us turn to our Master quickly lest we reap the reward of a spiritual adulterer and idolater. Let us reject the temptation of adultery just as Joseph did!

39:7 And it came to pass after these things, that his master's wife cast her eyes upon Joseph; and she said, Lie with me. **39:8** But he refused, and said unto his master's wife, Behold, my master wotteth not what is with me in the house, and he hath committed all that he hath to my hand; **39:9** There is none greater in this house than I; neither hath he kept back any thing from me but thee, because thou art his wife: **how then can I do this great wickedness**, and **sin against God?**

Joseph resisted the temptation daily just as we should also continually resist spiritual adultery through each and every day; always remaining passionately faithful to live by every Word of God our Father and our espoused Husband Jesus Christ. Resist the temptation to commit just a little sin; resist the LIE that Christ is love and will wink at a little willful sin.

It is because Christ is love and hates the sin that harms us; that he will never wink at ANY unrepentant sin.

39:10 And it came to pass, as she spake to Joseph day by day, that he hearkened not unto her, to lie by her, or to be with her.

This was not a matter of a shy young boy being timid: This went on day after day for a long time until she finally caught him alone, and even then he fled from this sin out of respect for God and for his master.

How much respect do we have for our spiritual Master who bought us with his very life when we commit adultery against him by following men instead of living by every Word of God?

39:11 And it came to pass about this time, that Joseph went into the house to do his business; and there was none of the men of the house there within. **39:12** And she caught him by his garment, saying, Lie with me: and he left his garment in her hand, and fled, and got him out.

A woman scorned: Satan is very angry when we scorn his temptations! Yes there is a price to be paid for our rejection of spiritual adultery, we will cast us out of their assemblies [synagogues] because of our zeal to live by every Word of God. They will consider us a bad example because we are faithful to God and do not idolize their false traditions and human leaders.

Yet in the end, if we are willing to pay the price like Joseph, after we have fully learned humility and patience and faithfulness to the righteousness of the whole Word of God; we will be delivered to life eternal if we faint not.

39:13 And it came to pass, when she saw that he had left his garment in her hand, and was fled forth, **39:14** That she called unto the men of her house, and spake unto them, saying, See, he hath brought in an Hebrew unto us to mock us; he came in unto me to lie with me, and I cried with a loud voice: **39:15** And it came to pass, when he heard that I lifted up my voice and cried, that he left his garment with me, and fled, and got him out. **39:16** And she laid up his garment by her, until his lord came home. **39:17** And she spake unto him according to these words, saying, The Hebrew servant, which thou hast brought unto us, came in unto me to mock me: **39:18** And it came to pass, as I lifted up my voice and cried, that he left his garment with me, and fled out.

The woman's husband believed her lie and cast Joseph into prison, this was allowed by God so that Joseph might be perfected through trials.

Often trials come, not because we have done something wrong, but because we have done something right! God allows this to further prune and mold us into the ultimate product that God seeks to make of us; to perfect us and make us fit for eternal life as faithful loyal kings and priests of God. That is the lesson of the book of Job.

> **Acts 14:22** Confirming the souls of the disciples, and exhorting them to continue in the faith, and **that we must through much tribulation enter into the kingdom of God**.

Genesis 39:19 And it came to pass, when his master heard the words of his wife, which she spake unto him, saying, After this manner did thy servant to me; that his wrath was kindled. **39:20** And Joseph's master took him, and put him into the prison, a place where the king's prisoners were bound: and he was there in the prison.

God caused Joseph to find favor for his faithfulness even in prison, and Joseph became the assistant governor of the prison. At the time Joseph would not have seen this as training to rule Egypt, but it was; and ruling Egypt was a training to rule in some high office in the soon coming Kingdom of God!

Our trials and temptations are to test us and to build us up into the people which God has in mind for us to become; to prepare us for the office that God has in mind for us; if we overcome and faint not.

39:21 But the LORD was with Joseph, and shewed him mercy, and gave him favour in the sight of the keeper of the prison. **39:22** And **the keeper of the prison committed to Joseph's hand all the prisoners that were in**

the prison; and whatsoever they did there, he was the doer of it. **39:23** The keeper of the prison looked not to any thing that was under his hand; because the LORD was with him, and that which he did, the LORD made it to prosper.

Genesis 40

Pharaoh's butler and baker offend him

Genesis 40:1 And it came to pass after these things, that the butler of the king of Egypt and his baker had offended their lord the king of Egypt. **40:2** And Pharaoh was wroth against two of his officers, against the chief of the butlers, and against the chief of the bakers. **40:3** And he put them in ward in the house of the captain of the guard, into the prison, the place where Joseph was bound. **40:4** And the captain of the guard charged Joseph with them, and he served them: and they continued a season in ward.

After a time in prison they each dreamed a dream on the same night.

40:5 And they dreamed a dream both of them, each man his dream in one night, each man according to the interpretation of his dream, the butler and the baker of the king of Egypt, which were bound in the prison.

40:6 And Joseph came in unto them in the morning, and looked upon them, and, behold, they were sad. **40:7** And he asked Pharaoh's officers [the butler and the baker] that were with him in the ward of his lord's house, saying, Wherefore look ye so sadly to day? **40:8** And they said unto him, We have dreamed a dream, and there is no interpreter of it.

Here we have a key to interpreting dreams: Far too often we try to interpret a dream according to our own preconceived notions; when the only correct understanding comes from the God who inspired the dream.

When we have a vivid dream that does not go away; the correct thing to do is to test the dream to determine whether it is consistent with the Word of God and to pray and to ask God for the meaning: We should never assume for ourselves what the dream might mean.

And Joseph said unto them, **Do not interpretations belong to God?** tell me them, I pray you.

The butler's dream

40:9 And the chief butler told his dream to Joseph, and said to him, In my dream, behold, a vine was before me; **40:10** And in the vine were three branches: and it was as though it budded, and her blossoms shot forth; and the clusters thereof brought forth ripe grapes: **40:11** And Pharaoh's cup was in my hand: and I took the grapes, and pressed them into Pharaoh's cup, and I gave the cup into Pharaoh's hand.

The interpretation that God gave to Joseph: Note that the proof of a dream or vision is in its fulfillment.

40:12 And Joseph said unto him, This is the interpretation of it: The three branches are three days: **40:13** Yet within three days shall Pharaoh lift up thine head, and restore thee unto thy place: and thou shalt deliver Pharaoh's cup into his hand, after the former manner when thou wast his butler.

Joseph asks that he be remembered before Pharaoh.

40:14 But think on me when it shall be well with thee, and shew kindness, I pray thee, unto me, and make mention of me unto Pharaoh, and bring me out of this house: **40:15** For indeed I was stolen away out of the land of the Hebrews: and here also have I done nothing that they should put me into the dungeon.

The baker's dream

40:16 When the chief baker saw that the interpretation was good, he said unto Joseph, I also was in my dream, and, behold, I had three white baskets on my head: **40:17** And in the uppermost basket there was of all manner of bakemeats for Pharaoh; and the birds did eat them out of the basket upon my head.

The interpretation that God gave to Joseph

40:18 And Joseph answered and said, This is the interpretation thereof: The three baskets are three days: **40:19** Yet within three days shall Pharaoh lift up thy head from off thee, and shall hang thee on a tree; and the birds shall eat thy flesh from off thee.

In three days time both dreams were fulfilled precisely according to the understanding that God had given to Joseph.

40:20 And it came to pass the third day, which was Pharaoh's birthday, that he made a feast unto all his servants: and he lifted up the head of the chief butler and of the chief baker among his servants. **40:21** And he restored the chief butler unto his butlership again; and he gave the cup into Pharaoh's hand: **40:22** But he hanged the chief baker: as Joseph had interpreted to them.

The butler perhaps fearing to speak to Pharaoh, did not mention Joseph to him.

Joseph must have been waiting, hoping, for word; this too was a test to see how Joseph would react when his hopes were deferred. Hope deferred is a most bitter sorrow, and God wanted to know if Joseph would turn away from God in his trials, or could Joseph be counted on to be loyal to the Word of God regardless of the trials he suffered.

Brethren, do we fall to temptation because we lose patience when things seem to be going badly, do we give up and turn from the Word of God in our sorrows and trials? Or do we stand fast in passionate, faithful, loving, Christ-like zeal to live by every Word of God; no matter what the physical consequences, just like Joseph did?

When we face a temptation to commit a sin that is desirable to us [like the great sin of patronizing a restaurant or hiring a catered a meal on the Sabbath], do we flee that temptation like Joseph did? Even though it means the loss of everything we have? Or do we give in to the temptation to take the easy way instead of diligently studying and keeping the whole Word of God?

Do we fear being driven out of the assemblies of the ungodly: Do we fear men and love men more than we fear and love God and sinfully conform to their wicked ways; instead of fearing to offend our Mighty One?

When we face prolonged sorrows and trials, and our hopes of deliverance are delayed: Do we give way to despair and lose our zeal for our God and his Word; or do we stand strong to keep the whole Word of God just like Joseph did?

40:23 Yet did not the chief butler remember Joseph, but forgat him.

Genesis 41

Two years after the baker died, Pharaoh himself had a dream and then the butler finally remembered Joseph

Genesis 41:1 And it came to pass **at the end of two full years**, that Pharaoh dreamed: and, behold, he stood by the river. **41:2** And, behold, there came up out of the river seven well favoured kine and fatfleshed; and they fed in a meadow. **41:3** And, behold, seven other kine came up after them out of the river, ill favoured and leanfleshed; and stood by the other kine upon the brink of the river. **41:4** And the ill favoured and leanfleshed kine did eat up the seven well favoured and fat kine. So Pharaoh awoke.

Pharaoh's dream was reinforced by a second dream.

41:5 And he slept and dreamed the second time: and, behold, seven ears of corn [grain] came up upon one stalk, rank and good. **41:6** And, behold, seven thin ears and blasted with the east wind sprung up after them. **41:7** And the seven thin ears devoured the seven rank and full ears. And Pharaoh awoke, and, behold, it was a dream.

None of the wise men could interpret the two dreams by the wisdom of men, because dreams and visions from God cannot be interpreted by the wisdom of man; they can only be interpreted by the wisdom from God, who gives understanding to those who obey him.

Even godly men cannot interpret dreams and visions, unless the understanding is given to them directly by God; for many ancient prophets desired to understand many things and understanding was withheld from them (Dan 12).

If we sin willfully, or if we reject any part of God's Word to cling to our preconceived notions;, or if we compromise with any part of the Word of God; we are cut off from God and cut off from understanding the things of God; as is the case in most of today's spiritual Ekklesia. They will not forsake their spiritual adultery and idolatry of men and the false traditions of men to be faithful to the Word of God; therefore there is no godly wisdom among them.

To correctly interpret a dream or vision from God; **we MUST ask God for the correct understanding, rather then jump to our own conclusions**.

41:8 And it came to pass in the morning that his spirit was troubled; and he sent and called for all the magicians of Egypt, and all the wise men thereof: and Pharaoh told them his dream; but there was none that could interpret them unto Pharaoh.

Then the butler remembered Joseph as a true man of God and recommended that Pharaoh send for him.

41:9 Then spake the chief butler unto Pharaoh, saying, I do remember my faults this day: **41:10** Pharaoh was wroth with his servants, and put me in ward in the captain of the guard's house, both me and the chief baker: **41:11** And we dreamed a dream in one night, I and he; we dreamed each man according to the interpretation of his dream. **41:12** And there was there with us a young man, an Hebrew, servant to the captain of the guard; and we told him, and he interpreted to us our dreams; to each man according to his dream he did interpret. **41:13** And it came to pass, as he interpreted to us, so it was; me he restored unto mine office, and him he hanged.

Pharaoh sends for the man of God to interpret his two dreams.

41:14 Then Pharaoh sent and called Joseph, and they brought him hastily out of the dungeon: and he shaved himself [cleaned himself up from the prison], and changed his raiment, and came in unto Pharaoh.

Joseph then tells Pharaoh that it is God who gives the understanding.

41:15 And Pharaoh said unto Joseph, I have dreamed a dream, and there is none that can interpret it: and I have heard say of thee, that thou canst understand a dream to interpret it. **41:16** And Joseph answered Pharaoh, saying, **It is not in me: God shall give Pharaoh an answer of peace** [peace of mind from the dreams].

Pharaoh then relates his two dreams.

41:17 And Pharaoh said unto Joseph, In my dream, behold, I stood upon the bank of the river: **41:18** And, behold, there came up out of the river seven kine, fatfleshed and well favoured; and they fed in a meadow: **41:19** And, behold, seven other kine came up after them, poor and very ill favoured and leanfleshed, such as I never saw in all the land of Egypt for badness: **41:20** And the lean and the ill favoured kine did eat up the first seven fat kine: **41:21** And when they had eaten them up, it could not be known that they had eaten them; but they were still ill favoured, as at the beginning. So I awoke.

41:22 And I saw in my dream, and, behold, seven ears came up in one stalk, full and good: **41:23** And, behold, seven ears, withered, thin, and blasted with the east wind, sprung up after them: **41:24** And the thin ears devoured the seven good ears: and I told this unto the magicians; but there was none that could declare it to me.

Joseph then gives God's explanation of the two dreams; revealing that they both mean the same thing. The two dreams meaning a double emphasis, the second confirming the first and confirming that the thing is sure.

41:25 And Joseph said unto Pharaoh, The dream of Pharaoh is one: God hath shewed Pharaoh what he is about to do. **41:26** The seven good kine are seven years; and the seven good ears are seven years: the dream is one. **41:27** And the seven thin and ill favoured kine that came up after them are seven years; and the seven empty ears blasted with the east wind shall be seven years of famine.

God gives the interpretation of the two dreams because Joseph sought the understanding from God and it was God's will to exalt Joseph in Pharaoh's sight.

41:28 This is the thing which I have spoken unto Pharaoh: What God is about to do he sheweth unto Pharaoh. **41:29** Behold, there come **seven years of great plenty** throughout all the land of Egypt: **41:30** And there shall arise after them **seven years of famine**; and all the plenty shall be forgotten in the land of Egypt; and the famine shall consume the land; **41:31** And the plenty shall not be known in the land by reason of that famine following; for it shall be very grievous.

The two dreams are to emphasize that the matter is well established by God, for by two or three witnesses all things are established.

41:32 And for that the dream was doubled unto Pharaoh twice; it is because the thing is established by God, and God will shortly bring it to pass.

Then Joseph give this wise advice, based on the interpretation that God had given.

Even so we should become wise in spiritual matters by looking to learn and to keep every Word of God. For God gives his Spirit and spiritual understanding; ONLY to those who obey his Word (Acts 5:32)

41:33 Now therefore let Pharaoh look out a man discreet and wise, and set him over the land of Egypt. **41:34** Let Pharaoh do this, and let him appoint officers over the land, and take up the fifth part of the land of Egypt in the seven plenteous years. **41:35** And let them gather all the food of those good years that come, and lay up corn under the hand of Pharaoh, and let them keep food in the cities. **41:36** And that food shall be for store to the land against the seven years of famine, which shall be in the land of Egypt; that the land perish not through the famine.

41:37 And the thing was good in the eyes of Pharaoh, and in the eyes of all his servants.

Because Joseph was a man of God, filled with the wisdom of God, Pharaoh chose Joseph to fulfill the vital task of preserving the nation. Consider that God could have prevented any famine and blessed Egypt for a hundred or a thousand years of he had wanted to.

Therefore this famine was to bring the family of Israel into Egypt, to keep the prophecy of God regarding Israel in Egypt and to reunite that family and fulfill the two dreams of Joseph, causing his brothers and parents to exalt him according to the very dream that Almighty God had previously given to Joseph!

In that case God allowed the family of Joseph to understand his dreams - in spite of their attitudes - for God's own purpose. The bottom line is that understanding of dreams from God comes from God who reveals the meaning as he wills.

God perfects his people through the experiences that he ordains they experience in their lives, and God fulfills his purposes in ways often mysterious to men, but he always keeps his Word.

Just as Joseph was prepared by experiences of trials, to become a great man in Egypt and to save his family along with the Egyptians; when we endure some trial, sometimes even for doing good; it is because God is teaching us very important things which will prepare us for the marvelous future that God has in mind for us!

41:38 And Pharaoh said unto his servants, Can we find such a one as this is, a man in whom the Spirit of God is? **41:39** And Pharaoh said unto Joseph, Forasmuch as God hath shewed thee all this, there is none so discreet and wise as thou art: **41:40** Thou shalt be over my house, and according unto thy word shall all my people be ruled: only in the throne will I be greater than thou.

God caused Pharaoh to exalt Joseph over Egypt because of his faithful enduring loyalty to God. Even so we will be exalted if we also endure faithfully and if we zealously live by every Word of God: And if we endure faithfully we will rise with a resurrected Joseph to rule the earth with our King of kings, Jesus Christ.

Just as Joseph was made the second ruler in all of Egypt; we have the opportunity to be made second rulers under Jesus Christ in the land of our spiritual inheritance: If we passionately love God and his whole Word, to exalt the whole Word of God above all else in our lives!

41:41 And Pharaoh said unto Joseph, See, I have set thee over all the land of Egypt. **41:42** And Pharaoh took off his ring from his hand, and put it upon Joseph's hand, and arrayed him in vestures of fine linen, and put a gold chain about his neck; **41:43** And he made him to ride in the second chariot which he had; and they cried before him, Bow the knee: and he made him ruler over all the land of Egypt.

We have the potential to fulfill the birthright of our calling; which is to receive the gift of eternal life to rule the nations; not like bullies as the wicked do, but teaching all peoples the righteousness of God and his Word, in service to God and to humanity.

41:44 And Pharaoh said unto Joseph, I am Pharaoh, and **without thee shall no man lift up his hand or foot in all the land of Egypt**. **41:45** And Pharaoh called Joseph's name Zaphnathpaaneah ["the man to whom mysteries are revealed"]; and he gave him to wife Asenath the daughter of Potipherah priest of On. And Joseph went out over all the land of Egypt.

At the age of thirty and after much sorrow Joseph became the second ruler in all of Egypt.

41:46 And Joseph was thirty years old when he stood before Pharaoh king of Egypt. And Joseph went out from the presence of Pharaoh, and went throughout all the land of Egypt.

Joseph fulfilled his own advice and with the warning given by God, saved the plenty of the seven good years to survive the little of the seven years of famine.

41:47 And in the seven plenteous years the earth brought forth by handfuls. **41:48** And he gathered up all the food of the seven years, which were in the land of Egypt, and laid up the food in the cities: the food of the field, which was round about every city, laid he up in the same. **41:49** And Joseph gathered corn [grain] as the sand of the sea, very much, until he left numbering; for it was without number.

Later Joseph was to replace Reuben as the firstborn of Jacob, because of Reuben's sin (Gen 35:22). Joseph was to be accounted the firstborn, for he was the firstborn of Rachel the intended first wife.

According to the custom of inheritance, the firstborn was to receive a double portion and along with that came the responsibility of caring for his elderly parents and helping his brethren.

Therefore Joseph inherited a double portion in Israel; each of his two son's having his own portion in Israel, Then Levi was given no inheritance in Israel; keeping the inheriting tribes at 12; for the inheritance of Levi was in the Eternal to be the servants of the Eternal to teach righteousness to all Israel.

41:50 And unto Joseph were born two sons before the years of famine came, which Asenath the daughter of Potipherah priest of On bare unto him. **41:51** And Joseph called the name of the firstborn **Manasseh: For God, said he, hath made me forget all my toil, and all** [the trials of] **my father's house. 41:52** And the name of the second called he **Ephraim: For God hath caused me to be fruitful in the land of my affliction.** **41:53** And the seven years of plenteousness, that was in the land of Egypt, were ended.

This famine covered all Egypt including Canaan which was controlled by Egypt at that time.

41:54 And the seven years of dearth began to come, according as Joseph had said: and the dearth was in all lands; but in all the land of Egypt there was bread. **41:55** And when all the land of Egypt was famished, the people cried to Pharaoh for bread: and Pharaoh said unto all the Egyptians, Go unto Joseph; what he saith to you, do. **41:56** And the famine was over all the face of the earth: and Joseph opened all the storehouses, and sold unto the Egyptians; and the famine waxed sore in the land of Egypt. **41:57** And all countries came into Egypt to Joseph for to buy corn [grain food] ; because that the famine was so sore in all lands.

Genesis 42

The next few chapters, are a narrative of the reconciliation of Joseph and his family and give an idea of how God will work out all things in the end

Ultimately all humanity will be humbled learning what God intends to teach each of us, and most will be brought to sincere repentance before God.

Almost every person in due time will be reconciled to God the Father and to each other to go forward is true peace with God and humanity for eternity, represented by the Feast of the Eighth Day!

May God speed the day that we will all sit together as brothers, united with God and with each other!

The Eighth Day! Oh Happy Day! Oh Day of Great Joy! Shout For Joy at the Excellence of our Mighty God!

The family of Jacob united through learning and sincere repentance!

Israel [Jacob] hears that there is food in Egypt and sends his sons to buy. Yet Jacob holds back his only remaining son by Rachel, Benjamin; for fear that he might lose both of Rachel's sons. Jacob's love at first sight of Rachel was a deep, abiding and passionate love; like our love for our espoused Husband Jesus Christ should be!

Genesis 42:1 Now when Jacob saw that there was corn [grain] in Egypt, Jacob said unto his sons, Why do ye look one upon another? **42:2** And he said, Behold, I have heard that there is corn in Egypt: get you down thither, and buy for us from thence; that we may live, and not die. **42:3** And Joseph's ten brethren went down to buy corn in Egypt. **42:4** But Benjamin, Joseph's brother, Jacob sent not with his brethren; for he said, Lest peradventure mischief befall him.

The first dream (Gen 37:5) of the young man Joseph was fulfilled when his brothers bowed down before him to seek his approval to buy grain and save themselves alive because of the famine. When something is of God; we can be assured that God will fulfill his Word.

42:5 And the sons of Israel came to buy corn [grain] among those that came: for the famine was in the land of Canaan. **42:6** And Joseph was the governor over the land, and he it was that sold to all the people of the land: and Joseph's brethren came, and bowed down themselves before him with their faces to the earth.

Joseph hid his identity from his brothers, and discomfited them because of their early hatred of him; intending to make them understand the great evil that they had done.

42:7 And Joseph saw his brethren, and he knew them, but made himself strange unto them, and spake roughly unto them; and he said unto them, Whence come ye? And they said, From the land of Canaan to buy food. **42:8** And Joseph knew his brethren, but they knew not him. **42:9** And Joseph remembered the dreams which he dreamed of them, and said unto them, Ye are spies; to see the nakedness of the land ye are come.

They give their reason for coming to Egypt, identifying themselves to Joseph who they did not recognize.

42:10 And they said unto him, Nay, my lord, but to buy food are thy servants come. **42:11** We are all one man's sons; we are true men, thy servants are no spies. **42:12** And he said unto them, Nay, but to see the nakedness of the land ye are come. **42:13** And they said, Thy servants are twelve brethren, the sons of one man in the land of Canaan; and, behold, the youngest is this day with our father, and one is not.

Joseph then demands to see Benjamin for his heart yearns for his brother the son of Rachel his own mother, and he seeks to test his brothers to see if their hatred of him has abated and if they have changed in their evil thoughts towards him.

42:14 And Joseph said unto them, That is it that I spake unto you, saying, Ye are spies: **42:15** Hereby ye shall be proved: By the life of Pharaoh ye shall not go forth hence, except your youngest brother come hither. **42:16** Send one of you, and let him fetch your brother, and ye shall be kept in prison, that your words may be proved, whether there be any truth in you: or else by the life of Pharaoh surely ye are spies. **42:17** And he put them all together into ward three days.

After three days in prison he allows his brothers to return home with food and keeps Simeon as hostage until they could return with Benjamin.

42:18 And Joseph said unto them the third day, This do, and live; for I fear God: **42:19** If ye be true men, let one of your brethren be bound in the house of your prison: go ye, carry corn for the famine of your houses: **42:20** But bring your youngest brother unto me; so shall your words be verified, and ye shall not die. And they did so.

In their own distress the brothers remember the anguish that they had caused Joseph.

42:21 And they said one to another, We are verily guilty concerning our brother, in that we saw the anguish of his soul, when he besought us, and we would not hear; therefore is this distress come upon us. **42:22** And Reuben answered them, saying, Spake I not unto you, saying, Do not sin against the child; and ye would not hear? therefore, behold, also his blood is required. **42:23** And they knew not that Joseph understood them; for he spake unto them by an interpreter.

Joseph wept at the anguish of his brothers, and also wept for joy that they acknowledged their guilt and were repenting. Simeon was taken hostage and Joseph commanded that with the sacks of grain every man's money be restored to him.

42:24 And he turned himself about from them, and wept; and returned to them again, and communed with them, and took from them Simeon, and bound him before their eyes. **42:25** Then Joseph commanded to fill their sacks with corn, and to restore every man's money into his sack, and to give them provision for the way: and thus did he unto them.

The money was placed at the top of the grain in the sacks and the brothers quickly discovered what had been done.

42:26 And they laded their asses with the corn, and departed thence. **42:27** And as one of them opened his sack to give his ass provender in the inn, he espied his money; for, behold, it was in his sack's mouth.

Then they were terrified thinking that this was done to create an incident and an excuse to arrest them also, but it was done because Joseph loved his father and his brothers.

42:28 And he said unto his brethren, My money is restored; and, lo, it is even in my sack: and their heart failed them, and they were afraid, saying one to another, What is this that God hath done unto us?

Then they returned home and reported these things to their father.

42:29 And they came unto Jacob their father unto the land of Canaan, and told him all that befell unto them; saying, **42:30** The man, who is the lord of the land, spake roughly to us, and took us for spies of the country. **42:31** And we said unto him, We are true men; we are no spies: **42:32** We be twelve brethren, sons of our father; one is not, and the youngest is this day with our father in the land of Canaan.

42:33 And the man, the lord of the country, said unto us, Hereby shall I know that ye are true men; leave one of your brethren here with me, and take food for the famine of your households, and be gone: **42:34** And bring your youngest brother unto me: then shall I know that ye are no spies, but that ye are true men: so will I deliver you your brother, and ye shall traffick in the land. **42:35** And it came to pass as they emptied their sacks, that, behold, every man's bundle of money was in his sack: and when both they and their father saw the bundles of money, they were afraid.

Joseph had demanded that Benjamin come to Egypt to be seen by Joseph as his price for releasing Sineon. Jacob grieved for his sons and the brothers beheld the anguish of their father, and were deeply convicted of their sins.

42:36 And Jacob their father said unto them, Me have ye bereaved of my children: Joseph is not, and Simeon is not, and ye will take Benjamin away: all these things are against me.

Reuben guarantees Benjamin's life with the lives of his own two sons.

42:37 And Reuben spake unto his father, saying, Slay my two sons, if I bring him not to thee: deliver him into my hand, and I will bring him to thee again.

Jacob says no, but finally runs out of food and is forced by the severity of the famine to send to Egypt for more grain.

42:38 And he said, My son [Benjamin] shall not go down with you; for his brother is dead, and he is left alone: if mischief befall him by the way in the which ye go, then shall ye bring down my gray hairs with sorrow to the grave.

Genesis 43

Then after they had eaten up all the grain from Egypt Jacob sent them back for more.

Genesis 43:1 And the famine was sore in the land. **43:2** And it came to pass, when they had eaten up the corn which they had brought out of Egypt, their father said unto them, Go again, buy us a little food.

All this time Simeon remained in prison, and now Judah reminds Jacob that they are required to take Benjamin back with them.

43:3 And Judah spake unto him, saying, The man did solemnly protest unto us, saying, Ye shall not see my face, except your brother be with you. **43:4** If thou wilt send our brother with us, we will go down and buy thee food: **43:5** But if thou wilt not send him, we will not go down: for the man said unto us, Ye shall not see my face, except your brother be with you.

Jacob complains

43:6 And Israel said, Wherefore dealt ye so ill with me, as to tell the man whether ye had yet a brother? **43:7** And they said, The man asked us straitly of our state, and of our kindred, saying, Is your father yet alive? have ye another brother? and we told him according to the tenor of these words: could we certainly know that he would say, Bring your brother down?

Judah gives himself a surety for Benjamin like Reuben had done. Now, they were guaranteeing the security of Benjamin, when before they had sold his brother Joseph. Over these years they had matured, seeing the anguish of their father day by day and year by year. They realized the enormity of what they had done, and were humbled to deep repentance.

43:8 And Judah said unto Israel his father, Send the lad with me, and we will arise and go; that we may live, and not die, both we, and thou, and also our little ones. **43:9** I will be surety for him; of my hand shalt thou require him: if I bring him not unto thee, and set him before thee, then let me bear the blame for ever: **43:10** For except we had lingered, surely now we had returned this second time.

Jacob finally says to go down and take Benjamin with them and what presents that they might have.

43:11 And their father Israel said unto them, If it must be so now, do this; take of the best fruits in the land in your vessels, and carry down the man a present, a little balm, and a little honey, spices, and myrrh, nuts, and almonds: **43:12** And take double money in your hand; and the money that was brought again in the mouth of your sacks, carry it again in your hand; peradventure it was an oversight: **43:13** Take also your brother, and arise, go again unto the man: **43:14** And God Almighty give you mercy before the man, that he may send away your other brother, and Benjamin. If I be bereaved of my children, I am bereaved.

When Joseph saw Benjamin his heart burned for his brother the son of his mother, and he called them all to a feast.

43:15 And the men took that present, and they took double money in their hand and Benjamin; and rose up, and went down to Egypt, and stood before Joseph. **43:16** And when Joseph saw Benjamin with them, he said to the ruler [he commanded his butler] of his house, Bring these men home, and slay, and make ready; for these men shall dine with me at noon. **43:17** And the man did as Joseph bade; and the man brought the men into Joseph's house.

The brothers remembered what they had done in selling Joseph and feared that some evil would now come upon them.

43:18 And the men were afraid, because they were brought into Joseph's house; and they said, Because of the money that was returned in our sacks at the first time are we brought in; that he may seek occasion against us, and fall upon us, and take us for bondmen, and our asses.

Then they spoke to the house steward and he reassured them.

43:19 And they came near to the steward of Joseph's house, and they communed with him at the door of the house, **43:20** And said, O sir, we came indeed down at the first time to buy food: **43:21** And it came to pass, when we came to the inn, that we opened our sacks, and, behold, every man's money was in the mouth of his sack, our money in full weight: and we have brought it again in our hand. **43:22** And other money have we brought down in our hands to buy food: we cannot tell who put our money in our sacks. **43:23** And he said, **Peace be to you, fear not: your God, and the God of your father, hath given you treasure in your sacks: I had your money** [and gave it back to you at my Master's command]. And he brought Simeon out unto them.

They washed and prepared themselves for the royal table.

43:24 And the man brought the men into Joseph's house, and gave them water, and they washed their feet; and he gave their asses provender. **43:25** And they made ready the present against [for] Joseph came at noon: for they heard that they should eat bread there.

They bowed before Joseph this time also [fulfilling Joseph's dream of Genesis 37:5] and gave him a present.

43:26 And when Joseph came home, they brought him the present which was in their hand into the house, and bowed themselves to him to the earth.

Joseph asks about their [his] father

43:27 And he asked them of their welfare, and said, Is your father well, the old man of whom ye spake? Is he yet alive? **43:28** And they answered, Thy servant our father is in good health, he is yet alive. And they bowed down their heads, and made obeisance.

Joseph saw Benjamin his mother's son and blessed him; Then losing his composure he went to a side chamber to weep.

43:29 And he lifted up his eyes, and saw his brother Benjamin, his mother's son, and said, Is this your younger brother, of whom ye spake unto me? And he said, God be gracious unto thee, my son. **43:30** And Joseph made haste; for his bowels did yearn upon his brother: and he sought where to weep; and he entered into his chamber, and wept there.

After washing, Joseph came out and commanded the luncheon feast prepared for his brothers to be served.

43:31 And he washed his face, and went out, and refrained himself, and said, Set on bread.

Three tables were set: one for Joseph; one for his brothers; and one for the Egyptians.

43:32 And they set on for him by himself, and for them by themselves, and for the Egyptians, which did eat with him, by themselves: because the Egyptians might not eat bread with the Hebrews; for that is an abomination unto the Egyptians.

Joseph had his brothers sit down in order of birth and they were amazed that he would know that.

43:33 And they sat before him, the firstborn according to his birthright, and the youngest according to his youth: and the men marvelled one at another.

Joseph had plates of food sent to each brother and five times as much to Benjamin his brother the beloved son of his beloved mother, Rachael.

43:34 And he took and sent messes unto them from before him: but Benjamin's mess was five times so much as any of their's. And they drank, and were merry with him.

Genesis 44

When we are born we know nothing and must learn and grow; the same thing is true spiritually. When we are first converted we know very little and we must learn and grow over a lifetime.

The fact is, physical or spiritual maturity is not the province of children. We must learn and grow for many years before we become physically or spiritually mature.

The story of Joseph and his brothers is a story of the learning and maturing of Joseph and his brothers from basic carnality to a level of spiritual maturity, and is an instructional lesson that each one of us needs to also grow in spiritual maturity over our lifetimes.

Joseph's story has very much to do with the need of every person to continually examine ourselves and to root out all error; replacing all error and sin with the truth, the Word of God and internalizing the very nature of God within ourselves, which nature is truth and love.

Joseph then arranges events so that his brothers would have to bring his father to Egypt the next time they came.

Genesis 44:1 And he commanded the steward of his house, saying, Fill the men's sacks with food, as much as they can carry, and put every man's money in his sack's mouth. **44:2** And put my cup, the silver cup, in the sack's mouth of the youngest, and his corn money. And he did according to the word that Joseph had spoken. **44:3** As soon as the morning was light, the men were sent away, they and their asses.

Joseph sends his servants to chase after his brothers and arrest them.

44:4 And when they were gone out of the city, and not yet far off, Joseph said unto his steward, Up, follow after the men; and when thou dost overtake them, say unto them, Wherefore have ye rewarded evil for good? **44:5** Is not this it in which my lord drinketh, and whereby indeed he divineth? ye have done evil in so doing. **44:6** And he overtook them, and he spake unto them these same words.

The brothers are convinced of their own innocence and make a rash promise.

44:7 And they said unto him, Wherefore saith my lord these words? God forbid that thy servants should do according to this thing: **44:8** Behold, the money, which we found in our sacks' mouths, we brought again unto thee out of the land of Canaan: how then should we steal out of thy lord's house silver or gold? **44:9 With whomsoever of thy servants it be found, both let him die, and we also will be my lord's bondmen.**

Joseph agreed to their words that the guilty should become his servant, but allowed that the innocent were blameless.

44:10 And he said, Now also let it be according unto your words: he with whom it is found shall be my servant; and ye shall be blameless. **44:11** Then they speedily took down every man his sack to the ground, and opened every man his sack.

The cup was found with Benjamin

44:12 And he searched, and began at the eldest, and left at the youngest: and the cup was found in Benjamin's sack.

The brothers were devastated for they had guaranteed the safety of Benjamin to their father who they had bereaved of Joseph.

They now began to really understand and to sincerely repent of the sins of their youth. Imagine the deep anguish of sorrow they must have had over what they had done to Joseph and their father.

44:13 Then they rent their clothes, and laded every man his ass, and returned to the city.

Judah and his brothers presented themselves to Joseph.

44:14 And Judah and his brethren came to Joseph's house; for he was yet there: and they fell before him on the ground. **44:15** And Joseph said unto them, What deed is this that ye have done? wot ye not that such a man as I can certainly divine [know secret things]?

Judah then alluded to their own guilt in selling Joseph to be a slave, and owned that they should justly become servants also.

44:16 And Judah said, What shall we say unto my lord? what shall we speak? or how shall we clear ourselves? God hath found out the iniquity of thy servants: behold, **we are my lord's servants, both we, and he also with whom the cup is found.**

Joseph ruled that only the guilty, as was supposed; should be punished.

44:17 And he said, God forbid that I should do so: but the man in whose hand the cup is found, he shall be my servant; and as for you, get you up in peace unto your father.\

Judah then pleads for Benjamin and his father Jacob, fulfilling his promise as guarantor of Benjamin.

44:18 Then Judah came near unto him, and said, Oh my lord, let thy servant, I pray thee, speak a word in my lord's ears, and let not thine anger burn against thy servant: for thou art even as Pharaoh. **44:19** My lord asked his servants, saying, Have ye a father, or a brother? **44:20** And we said unto my lord, We have a father, an old man, and a child of his old age, a little one; and his brother is dead, and he alone is left of his mother, and his father loveth him. **44:21** And thou saidst unto thy servants, Bring him down unto me, that I may set mine eyes upon him. **44:22** And we said unto my lord, The lad cannot leave his father: for if he should leave his father, his father would die. **44:23** And thou saidst unto thy servants, Except your youngest brother come down with you, ye shall see my face no more.

44:24 And it came to pass when we came up unto thy servant my father, we told him the words of my lord. **44:25** And our father said, Go again, and buy us a little food. **44:26** And we said, We cannot go down: if our youngest brother be with us, then will we go down: for we may not see the man's face, except our youngest brother be with us. **44:27** And thy servant my father said unto us, Ye know that my wife bare me two sons: **44:28** And the one went out from me, and I said, Surely he is torn in pieces; and I saw him not since: **44:29** And if ye take this also from me, and mischief befall him, ye shall bring down my gray hairs with sorrow to the grave.

44:30 Now therefore when I come to thy servant my father, and the lad be not with us; seeing that his life is bound up in the lad's life; **44:31** It shall come to pass, when he seeth that the lad is not with us, that he will die: and thy servants shall bring down the gray hairs of thy servant our father with sorrow to the grave. **44:32** For thy servant [Judah] became surety for the lad unto my father, saying, If I bring him not unto thee, then I shall bear the blame to my father for ever.

Judah offers himself for Benjamin: an act of love towards Benjamin and towards Jacob his father. This was a complete turnabout from the anger and hatred that they had had for Joseph at the first. The nature of Joseph had been completely changed by his experiences, and so had the nature of his brothers.

And so our own natures and the natures of all humanity will be completely changed by the end of God's plan for humanity.

44:33 Now therefore, I pray thee, let thy servant abide instead of the lad a bondman to my lord; and let the lad go up with his brethren. **44:34** For how shall I go up to my father, and the lad be not with me? lest peradventure I see the evil that shall come on my father.

Genesis 45

Joseph makes himself known to his brothers after he was sure they had all learned through experience; and the bitterness of the past vanished away in the joy of reconciliation.

Genesis 45:1 Then Joseph could not refrain himself before all them that stood by him; and he cried, Cause every man to go out from me. And there stood no man with him, while Joseph made himself known unto his brethren. **45:2** And he wept aloud: and the Egyptians and the house of Pharaoh heard.

Who could not weep emotionally in such circumstances? Shall we all not weep for joy in the day that we are reconciled to God our Father in Heaven with all our brethren? Truly God our Father is the giver of all good gifts, and it is his choice gift to reconcile as many as possible to himself, so that we may also ultimately be reconciled with one another and all the sorrows of the past can fade away.

> **Revelation 21:3** And I heard a great voice out of heaven saying, Behold, the tabernacle of God is with men, and he will dwell with them, and they shall be his people, and God himself shall be with them, and be their God. **21:4** And **God shall wipe away all tears from their eyes; and there shall be no more death, neither sorrow, nor crying, neither shall there be any more pain: for the former things are passed away.**

Genesis 45:3 And Joseph said unto his brethren, I am Joseph; doth my father yet live? And his brethren could not answer him; for they were troubled [disturbed that he might want revenge] at his presence. **45:4** And Joseph said unto his brethren, Come near to me, I pray you. And they came near. And he said, I am Joseph your brother, whom ye sold into Egypt.

Joseph comforts and consoles them, explaining that he was sent ahead so that they might be saved. Now how did Joseph know that? He had come to understand this as he matured spiritually, and in doing so he came to forgive his brothers. Spiritual understanding and love of God is the ultimate key to forgiveness and reconciliation.

Indeed God fulfills all his purposes and is able to keep all his promises.

45:5 Now therefore be not grieved, nor angry with yourselves, that ye sold me hither: for God did send me before you to preserve life. **45:6** For these two years hath the famine been in the land: and yet there are five years, in the which there shall neither be earing nor harvest. **45:7** And God sent me before you to preserve you a posterity in the earth, and to save your lives by a great deliverance. **45:8** So now it was not you that sent me hither, but God: and he hath made me a father to Pharaoh, and lord of all his house, and a ruler throughout all the land of Egypt.

Joseph then sends for his father to tell him that he [Joseph] lives and asks his father Jacob to come down to him in Egypt. Truly Jacob must have been stunned at the news and after getting past the shock would have made haste to see his beloved son.

45:9 Haste ye, and go up to my father, and say unto him, Thus saith thy son Joseph, God hath made me lord of all Egypt: come down unto me, tarry not: **45:10** And thou shalt dwell in the land of Goshen, and thou shalt be near unto me, thou, and thy children, and thy children's children, and thy flocks, and thy herds, and all that thou hast: **45:11** And there will I nourish thee; for yet there are five years of famine; lest thou, and thy household, and all that thou hast, come to poverty.

They wept for overwhelming love, happiness and and joy at their reconciliation. Truly they learned a lesson about family that shines as an example for us today; that despite the trials we may have along the way; in the end the promises of God will all be fulfilled.

45:12 And, behold, your eyes see, and the eyes of my brother Benjamin, that it is my mouth that speaketh unto you. **45:13** And ye shall tell my father of all my glory in Egypt, and of all that ye have seen; and ye shall haste and bring down my father hither. **45:14** And he fell upon his brother Benjamin's neck, and wept; and Benjamin wept upon his neck. **45:15** Moreover he kissed all his brethren, and wept upon them: and after that his brethren talked with him.

Pharaoh heard of the matter and gave a parcel of choice land to Jacob.

45:16 And the fame thereof was heard in Pharaoh's house, saying, Joseph's brethren are come: and it pleased Pharaoh well, and his servants.

Pharaoh sent Egyptian wagons to fetch their father and all their families back to safety in Egypt.

45:17 And Pharaoh said unto Joseph, Say unto thy brethren, This do ye; lade your beasts, and go, get you unto the land of Canaan; **45:18** And take your father and your households, and come unto me: and I will give you the good of the land of Egypt, and ye shall eat the fat of the land. **45:19** Now thou art commanded, this do ye; take you wagons out of the land of Egypt for your little ones, and for your wives, and bring your father, and come. **45:20** Also regard not your stuff; for the good of all the land of Egypt is your's.

45:21 And the children of Israel did so: and Joseph gave them wagons, according to the commandment of Pharaoh, and gave them provision for the way. **45:22** To all of them he gave each man changes of raiment; but to Benjamin he gave three hundred pieces of silver, and five changes of raiment.

45:23 And to his father he sent after this manner; ten asses laden with the good things of Egypt, and ten she asses laden with corn [grain] and bread and meat for his father by the way. **45:24** So he sent his brethren away, and they departed: and he said unto them, See that ye fall not out by the way.

45:25 And they went up out of Egypt, and came into the land of Canaan unto Jacob their father, **45:26** And told him, saying, Joseph is yet alive, and he is governor over all the land of Egypt. And Jacob's heart fainted, for he believed them not.

45:27 And they told him all the words of Joseph, which he had said unto them: and when he saw the wagons which Joseph had sent to carry him, the spirit of Jacob their father revived: **45:28** And Israel said, It is enough; Joseph my son is yet alive: I will go and see him before I die.

We who have been called ahead of time to follow Christ in living by every Word of God will some day also see our beloved children, parents, brothers and sisters, our dear friends and brethren from whom we have been separated by our love of God; also turn to our Great God and we shall all be reconciled to God and to each other!

The plan of God is for the ultimate reconciliation of all humanity: First with him as our Father and we as his children; at peace with God our Father and with each other for all eternity; and then being at one with God we will all also be at one with each other!

On that day, who will not weep for joy at the awesomeness of our God and all his mighty deeds?

Genesis 46

God speaks to Israel [Jacob] in Beer-Sheba

Genesis 46:1 And Israel took his journey with all that he had, and came to Beersheba, and offered sacrifices unto the God of his father Isaac. **46:2** And God spake unto Israel in the visions of the night, and said, Jacob, Jacob. And he said, Here am I.

God encourages Israel to go down to Egypt to see Joseph and repeats the promises he had made to Abraham to make of his descendants a great nation.

46:3 And he said, I am God, the God of thy father: fear not to go down into Egypt; for I will there make of thee a great nation: **46:4** I will go down with thee into Egypt; and I will also surely bring thee up again: and Joseph shall put his hand upon thine eyes.

Jacob then goes down to Egypt with his whole extended family, including his daughters here in the plural indicating other daughters besides Dinah.

46:5 And Jacob rose up from Beersheba: and the sons of Israel carried Jacob their father, and their little ones, and their wives, in the wagons which Pharaoh had sent to carry him. **46:6** And they took their cattle, and their goods, which they had gotten in the land of Canaan, and came into Egypt, Jacob, and all his seed with him: **46:7** His sons, and his sons' sons with him, his daughters, and his sons' daughters, and all his seed brought he with him into Egypt.

Moses then names the sons of Israel [Jacob] and their sons as well. The sons of Israel are the fathers of the tribes, and the sons of their sons are the fathers of the clans within the tribes.

46:8 And these are the names of the children of Israel, which came into Egypt, Jacob and his sons:

The sons of Leah

. . . **Reuben, Jacob's firstborn. 46:9** And the sons of Reuben; Hanoch, and Phallu, and Hezron, and Carmi.

46:10 And **the sons of Simeon;** Jemuel, and Jamin, and Ohad, and Jachin, and Zohar, and Shaul the son of a Canaanitish woman.

46:11 And **the sons of Levi;** Gershon, Kohath, and Merari become the heads of the Levitical clans.

46:12 And **the sons of Judah;** Er, and Onan, and **Shelah, and Pharez, and Zarah:** but Er and Onan died in the land of Canaan. And **the sons of Pharez were Hezron and Hamul.**

46:13 And **the sons of Issachar;** Tola, and Phuvah, and Job, and Shimron.

46:14 And **the sons of Zebulun;** Sered, and Elon, and Jahleel.

46:15 These be the sons of Leah, which she bare unto Jacob in Padanaram, with his daughter Dinah: all the souls of his sons and his daughters were thirty and three.

The sons of Zilpah

46:16 And **the sons of Gad;** Ziphion, and Haggi, Shuni, and Ezbon, Eri, and Arodi, and Areli.

46:17 And the **sons of Asher;** Jimnah, and Ishuah, and Isui, and Beriah, and **Serah their sister**: and the sons of Beriah; Heber, and Malchiel.

46:18 These are the sons of Zilpah, whom Laban gave to Leah his daughter, and these she bare unto Jacob, even sixteen souls. [sons and grandsons, and one named granddaughter; Serah]

The sons of Rachel.

46:19 The sons of Rachel Jacob's wife; Joseph, and Benjamin. **46:20 And unto Joseph in the land of Egypt were born Manasseh and Ephraim**, which Asenath the daughter of Potipherah priest of On bare unto him.

46:21 And **the sons of Benjamin were Belah, and Becher, and Ashbel, Gera, and Naaman, Ehi, and Rosh, Muppim, and Huppim, and Ard.**

46:22 These are the sons of Rachel, which were born to Jacob: all the souls were fourteen.

The sons of Bilhah.

46:23 And **the sons of Dan**; Hushim.

46:24 And **the sons of Naphtali**; Jahzeel, and Guni, and Jezer, and Shillem.

46:25 These are the sons of Bilhah, which Laban gave unto Rachel his daughter, and she bare these unto Jacob: all the souls were seven.

66 male persons of Israel went into Egypt; plus their wives and female children. Jacob plus Joseph and his two sons, plus all the other males of Jacob totaled 70 males.

46:26 All the souls that came with Jacob into Egypt, which came out of his loins, besides Jacob's sons' wives, all the souls were threescore and six; **46:27** And the sons of Joseph, which were born him in Egypt, were two souls: all the souls of the house of Jacob, which came into Egypt, were threescore and ten.

Judah led the way to Goshen

46:28 And he sent Judah before him unto Joseph, to direct his face unto Goshen; and they came into the land of Goshen.

Joseph goes by chariot to meet his father Jacob.

46:29 And Joseph made ready his chariot, and went up to meet Israel his father, to Goshen, and presented himself unto him; and he fell on his neck, and wept on his neck a good while.

Jacob feels completed and satisfied that his greatest desire has been fulfilled.

46:30 And Israel said unto Joseph, Now let me die, since I have seen thy face, because thou art yet alive.

Joseph instructs his family to be sure to tell Pharaoh that they are shepherds so that they will be given a space to themselves and not mixed with the Egyptians.

46:31 And Joseph said unto his brethren, and unto his father's house, I will go up, and shew Pharaoh, and say unto him, My brethren, and my father's house, which were in the land of Canaan, are come unto me; **46:32** And the men are shepherds, for their trade hath been to feed cattle; and they have brought their flocks, and their herds, and all that they have.

46:33 And it shall come to pass, when Pharaoh shall call you, and shall say, What is your occupation? **46:34** That ye shall say, Thy servants' trade hath been about cattle from our youth even until now, both we, and also our fathers: that ye may dwell in the land of Goshen; for every shepherd is an abomination unto the Egyptians.

Genesis 47

Genesis 47:1 Then Joseph came and told Pharaoh, and said, My father and my brethren, and their flocks, and their herds, and all that they have, are come out of the land of Canaan; and, behold, they are in the land of Goshen.

Joseph presents five of his brothers to Pharaoh

47:2 And he took some of his brethren, even five men, and presented them unto Pharaoh. **47:3** And Pharaoh said unto his brethren, What is your occupation? And they said unto Pharaoh, Thy servants are shepherds, both we, and also our fathers. **47:4** They said morever unto Pharaoh, For to sojourn in the land are we come; for thy servants have no pasture for their flocks; for the famine is sore in the land of Canaan: now therefore, we pray thee, let thy servants dwell in the land of Goshen.

Pharaoh gives them Goshen and also places them in charge of his own flocks and herds.

47:5 And Pharaoh spake unto Joseph, saying, Thy father and thy brethren are come unto thee: **47:6** The land of Egypt is before thee; in the best of the land make thy father and brethren to dwell; in the land of Goshen let them dwell: and if thou knowest any men of activity among them, then make them rulers over my cattle.

Pharaoh meets Israel [Jacob] Joseph's father

47:7 And Joseph brought in Jacob his father, and set him before Pharaoh: and Jacob blessed Pharaoh. **47:8** And Pharaoh said unto Jacob, How old art thou? **47:9** And Jacob said unto Pharaoh, The days of the years of my pilgrimage are **an hundred and thirty years**: few and evil have the days of the years of my life been, and have not attained unto the days of the years of the life of my fathers in the days of their pilgrimage. **47:10** And Jacob blessed Pharaoh, and went out from before Pharaoh.

47:11 And Joseph placed his father and his brethren, and gave them a possession in the land of Egypt, in the best of the land, **in the land of Rameses** [The land of Goshen was renamed Ramses some 200 years later.], as Pharaoh had commanded.

Goshen is here identified as the land of Ramses. Ramses I, did not rule for another 200 years [1290-1292 B.C.] and this name was later changed from Goshen to Ramses to update the location of the land of Goshen. This change of name from Goshen [aka Avaris] to Ramses has caused much confusion about the date of the Exodus.

Then Joseph rations out grain for them in Goshen.

47:12 And Joseph nourished his father, and his brethren, and all his father's household, with bread, according to their families.

The situation in Egypt

The food in Egypt was exhausted but Joseph had gathered food by order of Pharaoh for seven years. Joseph sold the grain until there was no money left in Egypt to buy food, because Pharaoh now had all the money in the land.

47:13 And there was no bread in all the land; for the famine was very sore, so that the land of Egypt and all the land of Canaan fainted by reason of the famine. **47:14** And Joseph gathered up **all the money that was found in the land of Egypt, and in the land of Canaan, for the corn** [grain] **which they bought**: and Joseph brought the money into Pharaoh's house.

Joseph then asks the people for their greater and lesser cattle [greater cattle being cows and lesser cattle being their flocks of sheep and herds of goats] in exchange for food in place of money.

47:15 And when money failed in the land of Egypt, and in the land of Canaan, all the Egyptians came unto Joseph, and said, Give us bread: for why should we die in thy presence? for the money faileth. **47:16** And

Joseph said, Give your cattle; and I will give you for your cattle, if money fail.

In the space of one year they had sold all their farm animals for food.

47:17 And they brought their cattle unto Joseph: and Joseph gave them bread in exchange for horses, and for the flocks, and for the cattle of the herds, and for the asses: and he fed them with bread for all their cattle for that year.

Then the people of Egypt sold themselves and their land for food, and so Pharaoh became the owner and feudal lord of all Egypt, its land and its people.

47:18 When that year was ended, they came unto him the second year, and said unto him, We will not hide it from my lord, how that our money is spent; my lord also hath our herds of cattle; there is not ought left in the sight of my lord, but our bodies, and our lands: **47:19** Wherefore shall we die before thine eyes, both we and our land? buy us and our land for bread, and we and our land will be servants unto Pharaoh: and give us seed, that we may live, and not die, that the land be not desolate.

47:20 And Joseph bought all the land of Egypt for Pharaoh; for the Egyptians sold every man his field, because the famine prevailed over them: so the land became Pharaoh's. **47:21** And as for the people, he removed them to cities from one end of the borders of Egypt even to the other end thereof.

The priests were fed by Pharaoh

47:22 Only the land of the priests bought he not; for the priests had a portion assigned them of Pharaoh, and did eat their portion which Pharaoh gave them: wherefore they sold not their lands.

After the years of famine Joseph sets up a share cropping system with 20% of the crop going to Pharaoh.

47:23 Then Joseph said unto the people, Behold, I have bought you this day and your land for Pharaoh: lo, here is seed for you, and ye shall sow the land. **47:24** And it shall come to pass in the increase, that ye shall give the fifth part unto Pharaoh, and four parts shall be your own, for seed of the field, and for your food, and for them of your households, and for food for your little ones. **47:25** And they said, Thou hast saved our lives: let us find grace in the sight of my lord, and we will be Pharaoh's servants.

47:26 And Joseph made it a law over the land of Egypt unto this day [the day this was written by Moses], that Pharaoh should have the fifth part, except the land of the priests only, which became not Pharaoh's.

This system of 20% belonging to Pharaoh except for the priests portion, continued after the famine into at least the days of Moses. Meanwhile Israel prospered for thirty years until Joseph had passed away and his righteous deeds were forgotten. Then a new Pharaoh come to the throne of Egypt

47:27 And Israel dwelt in the land of Egypt, in the country of Goshen; and they had possessions therein, and grew, and multiplied exceedingly. **47:28 And Jacob lived in the land of Egypt seventeen years: so the whole age of Jacob was an hundred forty and seven years.**

47:29 And the time drew nigh that Israel must die: and he called his son Joseph, and said unto him, If now I have found grace in thy sight, put, I pray thee, thy hand under my thigh [Joseph was asked to put his hand on his father's genitals to sware by all his progeny that he will bury Jacob in Machpelah], and deal kindly and truly with me; bury me not, I pray thee, in Egypt: **47:30** But **I will lie with my fathers, and thou shalt carry me out of Egypt, and bury me in their buryingplace.** And he said, I will do as thou hast said.

47:31 And he said, Swear unto me. And he sware unto him. And Israel bowed himself upon the bed's head.

Genesis 48

Joseph brought his two sons for his father's blessing

Genesis 48:1 And it came to pass after these things, that one told Joseph, Behold, thy father is sick: and he took with him his two sons, Manasseh and Ephraim. **48:2** And one told Jacob, and said, Behold, thy son Joseph cometh unto thee: and Israel strengthened himself, and sat upon the bed.

Israel [Jacob] told Joseph that God had talked to him and promised him a multitude of descendants. This promise to Abraham of a great multitude of descendants was an allegory of the fact that God the Father will be the Father of a vast multitude of repentant humanity when the plan of God is completed.

Abraham as the father of the faithful was a type of God the Father, who is the true and ultimate Father of all those who love him as their Father, and keep his Word in loving zeal.

The promise to Abraham was dual: a physical land with physical descendants and a spiritual promised land and spiritual descendants of faithfulness to God, because Abraham was faithful to God.

> **Galatians 3:6** Even as Abraham believed God, and it was accounted to him for righteousness. **3:7** Know ye therefore that they which are of faith, the same are the children of Abraham.

Galatians 3:29 And if ye be Christ's, then are ye Abraham's seed, and heirs according to the [spiritual aspect of the] promise.

Just as Abraham learned and grew in faith through the things that he experienced, We must also learn the same kind of faith in God.

If we do the works of Abraham in faithfully living by every Word of God through an Abrahamic faith in the Word of God; then we are the spiritual children of Abraham and the spiritual children of God the Father, just like Abraham was a child of God the Father.

Faith and the Works of Faith

> **James 2:14** What doth it profit, my brethren, though a man say he hath faith, and have not works? Can faith save him? **2:5** If a brother or sister be naked, and destitute of daily food, **2:16** and one of you say unto them, Depart in peace, be ye warmed and filled; notwithstanding ye give them not those things which are needful to the body, what doth it profit?
>
> **2:17** Even so **faith, if it hath not works, is dead, being alone. 2:18** Yea, a man may say, You hast faith, and I have works. **Show me thy faith without thy works, and I will show thee my faith by my works. 2:19** Thou believest that there is one God; thou doest well: the devils also believe, and tremble [Yet the demons will not obey God's Word, therefore their belief brings them nothing but the sure knowledge of their coming judgment.]. **2:20** But wilt thou know, O vain man, that **faith without works is dead**?
>
> **2:21** Was not Abraham our father justified [by his deeds] by works when he [obeyed God] had offered Isaac his son upon the altar? **2:22** Seest thou how faith wrought [worked with] with his works and by works was faith made perfect? **2:23** And the scripture was fulfilled which saith, Abraham believed God, and it was imputed unto him for righteousness: and he was called the Friend of God.
>
> **2:24** Ye see then how that by works a man is justified, and not by faith only. **2:25** Likewise also was not Rehab the harlot justified by works, when she had received the messengers, and had sent them out another way? **2:26** For **as the body without the spirit is dead, so faith without works is dead.**

Yes, there is a spirit in our body. It is a spirit of man, a spirit in man, and without the body man's spirit cannot function; it cannot think, it is not conscious; it must be plugged into the body to function.

The spirit must be plugged into the body to function; and faith must be plugged into works. Faith cannot stand on its own. If we have faith, if we believe God, we will do what God says which is our works of faith.

We cannot do what God says if we do not believe [have faith that his Word is true] Him, anymore than the spirit can live without the body. These things are inseparable: Godly faith is inseparable from the works of faith. If we have faith and no works, our faith is meaningless, it is a waste of time.

Believing without acting on that belief is a waste of time; it won't get us anywhere.

Genesis 48:3 And Jacob said unto Joseph, God Almighty appeared unto me at Luz in the land of Canaan, and blessed me, **48:4** And said unto me, Behold, I will make thee fruitful, and multiply thee, and I will make of thee a multitude of people; and will give this land to thy seed after thee for an everlasting possession.

Jacob takes Joseph as his firstborn over Reuben and adopts the two sons of Joseph conferring physical blessings on them.

These physical blessings have now been partially fulfilled, but will be fulfilled in their fullness in the Millennial Kingdom of God.

Soon the spiritual blessings upon the spiritually faithful will also be fulfilled when all those who love God and passionately live by every Word of God internalizing the very nature of God are resurrected and changed to spirit.

48:5 And now thy two sons, Ephraim and Manasseh, which were born unto thee in the land of Egypt before I came unto thee into Egypt, are mine; as Reuben and Simeon, they shall be mine.

The following is a statement that Joseph would have a double portion, replacing Reuben as the first born with the blessing of the first born; the double portion consisting of two tribes in Israel.

48:6 And thy [descendants] issue, which thou begettest after [by them] them, shall be thine, and shall be called after the name of their brethren in their inheritance.

Jacob tells Joseph that his mother Rachel is buried near Bethlehem.

48:7 And as for me, when I came from Padan, Rachel died by me in the land of Canaan in the way, when yet there was but a little way to come unto Ephrath: and I buried her there in the way of Ephrath; **the same is Bethlehem**.

Jacob calls Joseph's sons to bless them.

48:8 And Israel beheld Joseph's sons, and said, Who are these? **48:9** And Joseph said unto his father, They are my sons, whom God hath given me in this place. And he said, Bring them, I pray thee, unto me, and I will bless them.

Jacob embraces Joseph's sons and rejoices over seeing Joseph and his sons.

48:10 Now the eyes of Israel were dim for age, so that he could not see. And he brought them near unto him; and he kissed them, and embraced them. **48:11** And Israel said unto Joseph, I had not thought to see thy face: and, lo, God hath shewed me also thy seed. **48:12** And Joseph brought them out from between his knees [from Jacob's embrace], and he bowed himself with his face to the earth.

Joseph then set his sons for the blessing, with the elder to the right hand of Jacob.

48:13 And Joseph took them both, Ephraim in his [Joseph's] right hand **toward Israel's left hand**, and Manasseh in his

[Joseph's] left hand toward Israel's right hand, and brought them near unto him.

Jacob then crosses his arms to lay his right hand on Ephraim.

48:14 And Israel stretched out his right hand, and laid it upon Ephraim's head, who was the younger, and his left hand upon Manasseh's head, guiding his hands wittingly; for Manasseh was the firstborn.

Jacob first blesses Joseph, which blessing would fall on BOTH of Joseph's sons.

The blessing on BOTH Ephraim and Manasseh was that the name Israel would be upon these two men and all their descendants and that they would have a multitude of descendants; this blessing meant that these two tribes would be foremost in Israel and all prophecies made concerning Israel apply primarily to Ephraim and Manasseh [the modern British and American founding peoples].

Jacob thus conferred the birthright of the first born on Ephraim and Manasseh.

48:15 And he blessed Joseph, and said, God, before whom my fathers Abraham and Isaac did walk, the God which fed me all my life long unto this day, **48:16** The Angel which redeemed me from all evil, bless the lads; and **let my name be named on them, and the name of my fathers Abraham and Isaac; and let them grow into a multitude in the midst of the earth.**

Then Joseph saw that his father's right hand was on the second born and corrected his father.

48:17 And when Joseph saw that his father laid his right hand upon the head of Ephraim, it displeased him: and he held up his father's hand, to remove it from Ephraim's head unto Manasseh's head. **48:18** And Joseph said unto his father, Not so, my father: for this is the firstborn; put thy right hand upon his head.

Jacob informed Joseph that the second born Ephraim, was to be greater than his brother Manasseh. Jacob prophesies that Ephraim will become a multitude of nations while Manasseh shall be one great nation.

Regardless of the contentious claims concerning the migrations of nations; Ephraim has fulfilled this prophecy as the Anglo Saxon company of nations; and Manasseh has fulfilled the prophecy to become the greatest, most powerful and richest nation in world history the United States of America.

We have been blessed not because we are a great people; but because God is a great God who has fulfilled his promises to Abraham, Isaac, Jacob and Moses.

Today we are now about to fall into great tribulation because of our departure from the Word of God and the overspreading of our many abominations which have flooded the whole world with our wickedness.

America and the British company of nations will soon be corrected and they will then exalt their God. Even so today's Ekklesia will also be corrected for their idolatry and many sins in great affliction, but in the end most will overcome and exalt the Eternal with all their hearts!

48:19 And his father refused, and said, I know it, my son, I know it: **he also shall become a people, and he also shall be great**: but truly his younger brother **shall be greater than he, and his seed shall become a multitude of nations.**

48:20 And he blessed them that day, saying, In thee shall Israel bless, saying, God make thee as Ephraim and as Manasseh: and he set Ephraim before Manasseh.

Jacob is ready to die and has given a double portion of the birthright to Joseph the first born of his beloved Rachel.

48:21 And Israel said unto Joseph, Behold, I die: but God shall be with you, and bring you again unto the land of your fathers. **48:22** Moreover I have given to thee one portion above thy brethren, which I took out of the hand of the Amorite with my sword and with my bow.

Genesis 49

Jacob is inspired to prophesy about his son's descendants in the last days. We are living in the close of the last days before the coming of Christ today.

Genesis 49:1 And Jacob called unto his sons, and said, Gather yourselves together, that I may tell you that which shall befall you in the last days. **49:2** Gather yourselves together, and hear, ye sons of Jacob; and hearken unto Israel your father.

Reuben

49:3 Reuben, thou art my firstborn, my might, and the beginning of my strength, **the excellency of dignity, and the excellency of power**: **49:4** Unstable as water, **thou shalt not excel** [not to have a nation of your own]; because thou wentest up to thy father's bed; then defiledst thou it: he went up to my couch.

Reuben would be cultured and strong, but unstable and would not excel [have no independent nation of his own]. Losing the double portion of the first born and having no nation for his own is his punishment for his defilement of his father's concubine.

The tribe of Reuben became a part of the people migrating with the Germanic tribes of Assyria after the fall of the Assyrian Empire. Reuben later separated from other Normans [North Men] and settled in Normandy in northern France.

The term Norman means North Men and is a general term for those tribes of Israel who migrated north into Scandinavia; some of them remaining in Scandinavia and others sweeping out into Britain and Normandy

Normandy takes its name from the invaders from the north collectively called Vikings or North Men; who menaced large parts of Europe towards the end of the first millennium in two phases (790–930, then 980–1030). Medieval Latin documents referred to them as Nortmanni, which means "men of the North". This name provides the etymological basis for the modern words "Norman" and "Normandy."

There is absolutely no doubt that Reuben migrated into northern France [Normandy], but to say that they dominate and control France today, defies the prophecy for Reuben.

Even to say that Reuben remained in France in large numbers is a mere supposition since so many hundreds of thousands of people migrated to Louisiana and Quebec in the new world from France in the 17 and 1800's.

Many of them migrated from France to Canada and became the Quebecois; others migrated to New Orleans and Louisiana, and later some were expelled from Eastern Canada by the British, also ending up in the US where they are called Cajuns and Acadians.

While Lower Louisiana had been settled by Normandy French colonists since the late 17th century, the Cajuns trace their roots to the influx of Acadian settlers after the Great Expulsion from their homeland in Maritime Canada, during the French and British hostilities prior to the Seven Years' War (1756 to 1763), In the USA those deported by Britain to Louisiana are called Cajuns [French les Acadiens] or Accadians.

Reuben makes up a substantial part of the populations of the United States and Canada with some possibly remaining in Normandy France.

Simeon and Levi

49:5 Simeon and Levi are brethren; instruments of cruelty are in their habitations. **49:6** O my soul, come not thou into their secret; unto their assembly, mine honour, be not thou united: for in their anger they slew a man, and in their selfwill they digged down a wall. **49:7** Cursed be their anger, for it was fierce; and their wrath, for it was cruel: **I will divide them in Jacob, and scatter them in Israel.**

Simeon and Levi were not to have nations of their own either, they would be scattered in the other tribes lest being united, their cruelty would bring them to dishonor. Levi became divided amongst all the tribes of Israel as the tribe of God; while Simeon has been mainly associated with the Scots.

Judah

49:8 Judah, thou art he whom thy brethren shall praise: thy hand shall be in the neck of thine enemies; thy father's children shall bow down before thee. **49:9** Judah is a lion's whelp: from the prey, my son, thou art gone up: he stooped down, he couched as a lion, and as an old lion; who shall rouse him up?

Judah would ultimately be praised for his royal strength. The scepter [Royal line] in Israel would belong to Judah, which shows that the choice of Saul as Israel's first king was prophesied to fail nearly a thousand years before he was crowned. See "The Dynasty of David" article.

49:10 The sceptre shall not depart from Judah, nor a lawgiver from between his feet [born to him and his descendants, this is to be fulfilled by the resurrected David] until Shiloh [Messiah] come; and unto him shall the gathering of the people be [the people being gathered to Judah implies that many Jews will still live in Judea when Christ comes]. **49:11** [A prophecy of Messiah born into Judah] Binding his foal unto the vine, and his ass's colt unto the choice vine; he washed his garments in wine, and his clothes in the blood of grapes [speaking prophetically of the sacrifice of the Lamb of God; wine being a metaphor for blood]: **49:12** His eyes shall be red with wine, and his teeth white with milk [Messiah shall be as perfect and pure as the white of milk].

Zebulun

49:13 Zebulun shall **dwell at the haven of the sea; and he shall be for an haven of ships; and his border shall be unto Zidon.**

Zebulun is the modern Netherlands.

Issachar

49:14 Issachar is a strong ass couching down between two burdens: **49:15** And he saw that rest was good, and the land that it was pleasant; and bowed his shoulder to bear, and became a servant unto tribute.

Dan

49:16 Dan shall judge his people, as one of the tribes of Israel. **49:17** Dan shall be a serpent by the way, an adder in the path, that biteth the horse heels, so that his rider shall fall backward. **49:18** I have waited for thy salvation, O LORD.

Dan would have a nation of his own but will be given to intrigue and shall be a burden to his fellow tribal nations.

Gad

49:19 Gad, a troop shall overcome him [during the tribulation]: but he shall overcome at the last [Gad will overcome and also sincerely repent when Messiah comes].

Asher

49:20 Out of **Asher** his bread shall be fat, and he shall yield royal dainties.

Asher will be rich.

Naphtali

49:21 Naphtali is a hind let loose: he giveth goodly words.

In the millennium Naphtali will be graceful in his words like the freely running deer, and full of courteous language, diplomacy and the wisdom of men. Naphtali will have a long sea coast and has settled in Sweden and Norway.

Joseph

49:22 Joseph is a fruitful bough, even a fruitful bough by a well [a well watered plant which grows strong]; whose branches run over the wall: **49:23** The archers have sorely grieved him, and shot at him, and hated him: **49:24** But his [Britain and America are to be militarily strong by the blessing of the power of God supporting them.] bow abode in strength, and the arms of his hands were **made strong by the hands of the mighty God of Jacob;** (from thence [God] is [Messiah] the shepherd, the stone of Israel:)

49:25 [Joseph will be made strong] Even by the God of thy father, who shall help thee; and by the Almighty, who shall bless thee with blessings of heaven above, blessings of the deep that lieth under, blessings of the breasts, and of the womb: **49:26 The blessings of thy father have prevailed above the blessings of my progenitors unto the utmost bound of the everlasting hills: they shall be on the head of Joseph, and on the crown of the head of him that was separate from his brethren.**

The blessings of Joseph apply to BOTH Ephraim [the British peoples] and Manasseh [the founding peoples of America].

Benjamin

49:27 Benjamin shall ravin as a wolf: in the morning he shall devour the prey, and at night he shall divide the spoil.

Benjamin would be a warrior people accompanying Judah and he will be closely linked to Judah forever (Gen 43:9).

49:28 All these are the twelve tribes of Israel: and this is it that their father spake unto them, and blessed them; every one according to his blessing he blessed them.

Jacob then charged his son's to take him to Canaan and bury him at Machpelah when they left Egypt.

49:29 And he charged them, and said unto them, I am to be gathered unto my people: bury me with my fathers in the cave that is in the field of Ephron the Hittite, **49:30** In the cave that is in the field of Machpelah, which is before Mamre, in the land of Canaan, which Abraham bought with the field of Ephron the Hittite for a possession of a buryingplace. **49:31** There they buried Abraham and Sarah his wife; there they buried Isaac and Rebekah his wife; and there I buried Leah. **49:32** The purchase of the field and of the cave that is therein was from the children of Heth.

Israel dies

49:33 And when Jacob had made an end of commanding his sons, he gathered up his feet into the bed, and yielded up the ghost, and was gathered unto his people.

The Ten Tribes Removed From the Line of David

In Genesis we are told that Jacob was renamed Israel by God.

Genesis 32:28 And he said, Thy name shall be called no more Jacob, but **Israel**: for as a prince hast thou power with God and with men, and hast prevailed.

Later we learn that Israel [Jacob] had twelve sons, and each was to grow to become a tribe. Then when they were in Egypt God gave a double portion, which is the right of the first born to Joseph, and his two sons Ephraim and Manasseh would each become full tribes in Israel; and Levi was called out of Israel to become the tribe of God, or the priesthood tribe.

When Israel entered the Promised Land the nation consisted of one priesthood tribe and twelve tribes, each with its own area, only one of which was Judah or the Jews.

Then during the days of Solomon because of his sins in exalting idols God told Solomon that he would break the bounds of brotherhood between the ten tribes of Israel and Judah/Benjamin, removing the northern ten tribes of Israel from the kingdom of Judah and Benjamin and the Davidic royal line.

From the death of Solomon the ten tribes would be estranged from the line of David until Messiah the Christ comes with a resurrected David and restores the ten tribes to David.

Ezekiel 37:21 And say unto them, Thus saith the Lord God; Behold, I will take the children of Israel from among the heathen, whither they be gone, and will gather them on every side, and bring them into their own land:

37:22 And I will make them one nation in the land upon the mountains of Israel; and one king shall be king to them all: and they shall be no more two nations, neither shall they be divided into two kingdoms any more at all.

37:23 Neither shall they defile themselves any more with their idols, nor with their detestable things, nor with any of their transgressions: but I will save them out of all their dwellingplaces, wherein they have sinned, and will cleanse them: so shall they be my people, and I will be their God.

37:24 And **David my servant shall be king over them**; and they all shall have one shepherd: they shall also walk in my judgments, and observe my statutes, and do them.

37:25 And they shall dwell in the land that I have given unto Jacob my servant, wherein your fathers have dwelt; and they shall dwell therein, even they, and their children, and their children's children for ever: and my servant David shall be their prince for ever.

1 Kings 11:9 And the LORD was angry with Solomon, because his heart was turned from the LORD God of Israel, which had appeared unto him twice,

11:10 And had commanded him concerning this thing, that he should not go after other gods: but he kept not that which the LORD commanded.

11:11 Wherefore the LORD said unto Solomon, Forasmuch as this is done of thee, and thou hast not kept my covenant and my statutes, which I have commanded thee, I will surely rend the kingdom from thee, and will give it to thy servant.

11:12 Notwithstanding in thy days I will not do it for David thy father's sake: but I will rend it out of the hand of thy son.

11:13 Howbeit I will not rend away all the kingdom; but will give one tribe to thy son for David my servant's sake, and for Jerusalem's sake which I have chosen.

Then after Solomon had died, God rent the ten tribes of Israel from the kingdom of Judah in this manner:

1 Kings 12:3 That they sent and called him. And Jeroboam and all the congregation of Israel came, and spake unto Rehoboam, saying,

12:4 Thy father made our yoke grievous: now therefore make thou the grievous service of thy father, and his heavy yoke which he put upon us, lighter, and we will serve thee.

12:5 And he said unto them, Depart yet for three days, then come again to me. And the people departed.

12:6 And king Rehoboam consulted with the old men, that stood before Solomon his father while he yet lived, and said, How do ye advise that I may answer this people?

12:7 And they spake unto him, saying, If thou wilt be a servant unto this people this day, and wilt serve them, and answer them, and speak good words to them, then they will be thy servants for ever.

12:8 But he forsook the counsel of the old men, which they had given him, and consulted with the young men that were grown up with him, and which stood before him: **12:9** And he said unto them, What counsel give ye that we may answer this people, who have spoken to me, saying, Make the yoke which thy father did put upon us lighter?

12:10 And the young men that were grown up with him spake unto him, saying, Thus shalt thou speak unto this people that spake unto thee, saying, Thy father made our yoke heavy, but make thou it lighter unto us; thus shalt thou say unto them, My little finger shall be thicker than my father's loins.

12:11 And now whereas my father did lade you with a heavy yoke, I will add to your yoke: my father hath chastised you with whips, but I will chastise you with scorpions.

12:12 So Jeroboam and all the people came to Rehoboam the third day, as the king had appointed, saying, Come to me again the third day.

12:13 And the king answered the people roughly, and forsook the old men's counsel that they gave him; **12:14** And spake to them after the counsel of the young men, saying, My father made your yoke heavy, and I will add to your yoke: my father also chastised you with whips, but I will chastise you with scorpions [many tailed whips].

12:15 Wherefore the king hearkened not unto the people; for the cause was from the LORD, that he might perform his saying, which the LORD spake by Ahijah the Shilonite unto Jeroboam the son of Nebat.

12:16 So when all Israel saw that the king hearkened not unto them, the people answered the king, saying, What portion have we in David? neither have we inheritance in the son of Jesse: to your tents, O Israel: now see to thine own house, David. So Israel departed unto their tents.

Then the ten tribes of Israel were separated from the tribes of Judah and Benjamin, with Benjamin remaining with Judah because their land bordered on Judah and surrounded Jerusalem.

From here the Bible is full of the rivalries and wars between Judah and Israel.

The Kingdom of Israel immediately began to fall into idolatry as Jeroboam set up idols in the land for fear that Israel would rebel against him when they went up to Jerusalem to keep the annual Festivals of God.

1 Kings 12:26 And Jeroboam said in his heart, Now shall the kingdom return to the house of David:

12:27 If this people go up to do sacrifice in the house of the LORD at Jerusalem, then shall the heart of this people turn again unto their lord, even unto Rehoboam king of Judah, and they shall kill me, and go again to Rehoboam king of Judah.

12:28 Whereupon the king took counsel, and made two calves of gold, and said unto them, It is too much for you to go up to Jerusalem: behold thy gods, O Israel, which brought thee up out of the land of Egypt.

12:29 And he set the one in Bethel, and the other put he in Dan. **12:30** And this thing became a sin: for the people went to worship before the one, even unto Dan.

12:31 And he made an house of high places, and made priests of the lowest of the people, which were not of the sons of Levi.

12:32 And Jeroboam ordained a feast in the eighth month, on the fifteenth day of the month, like unto the feast that is in Judah, and he offered upon the altar. So did he in Bethel, sacrificing unto the calves that he had made: and he placed in Bethel the priests of the high places which he had made.

From that time onward God repeatedly sent his prophets over many years to warn Israel to repent until finally God removed his blessings and allowed waves of Assyrians to sweep into Israel, finally culminating in the fall of the capitol Samaria c721 B.C. and the removal of the ten tribes.

Some in Israel repented at the preaching of the prophets, and especially when Judah had good kings some migrated to Judea where they were assimilated into Judah, but Israel as a whole did not turn from their wicked ways.

2 Kings 17:6 In the ninth year of Hoshea the king of Assyria took Samaria, and carried Israel away into Assyria, and placed them in Halah and in Habor by the river of Gozan, and in the cities of the Medes.

17:7 For so it was, that the children of Israel had sinned against the LORD their God, which had brought them up out of the land of Egypt, from under the hand of Pharaoh king of Egypt, and had feared other gods,

17:8 And walked in the statutes of the heathen, whom the LORD cast out from before the children of Israel, and of the kings of Israel, which they had made.

These ten tribes of Israel then migrated with the Assyrians into North-Western Europe.

The Tribes of Israel Today

To understand where they migrated to, and where the so called "lost" ten tribes may be found today it is important to see what Bible prophecy says about the tribes of Israel for the latter days and then to look at the history and migrations of these nations.

The Bible prophecies that most of the tribes of Israel would be independent nations and several would become more than one latter day nation.

These prophecies are only partially fulfilled at this time due to the sins of the nations. They will be realized in their fullness in the millennial Kingdom of God.

At that time the tribes of Israel will continue and prosper in their various prophesied locations while a core population of each tribe of Israel will be brought back to the physical Promised Land and the division between Israel and Judah will be healed

Deuteronomy 33

Moses before his death blessed the tribes and prophesied from God about their latter days when they shall become many independent nations on this earth. These prophecies have been fulfilled only in part today and will be fulfilled in its fullness during the millennium.

Deuteronomy 33:1 And **this is the blessing, wherewith Moses the man of God blessed the children of Israel before his death.**

33:2 And he said, The LORD came from Sinai, and rose up from Seir unto them; he shined forth from mount Paran, and he came with ten thousands of saints: from his right hand went a fiery law for them.

33:3 Yea, he loved the people; all his saints are in thy hand: and they sat down at thy feet; every one shall receive of thy words.

33:4 Moses commanded us a law, even the inheritance of the congregation of Jacob [Israel].

33:5 And he [God] was king in **Jeshurun**, when the heads of the people and the tribes of Israel were gathered together.

> **Jeshurun** (Hebrew: יְשֻׁרוּן), in the Hebrew Bible, is a poetic name for Israel, derived from a root word meaning upright, just or straight. Jeshurun appears four times in the Hebrew Bible — three times in Deuteronomy and once in Isaiah. It can mean the people of Israel (Deut. 32:15; 33:26), the Land of Israel (Deut. 33:5;), or the Patriarch Jacob (whom an Angel renamed Israel in Genesis 32:29):

From this point I am going to add the Prophetic Blessings of Jacob in Genesis 49, to the Prophetic Blessings of Moses in Deuteronomy 33 for a fuller picture of each tribe in the latter days.

Reuben

Deuteronomy 33:6 Let Reuben live, and not die; and let not his men be few.

Genesis 49:3 Reuben, thou art my firstborn, my might, and the beginning of my strength, the excellency of dignity, and the excellency of power: **49:4** Unstable as water, thou shalt not excel; because thou wentest up to thy father's bed; then defiledst thou it: he went up to my couch.

Reuben would not become an independent nation in his own right in the latter days because of instability.

The tribe of Reuben became a part of the people migrating with the Germanic tribes of Assyria after the fall of the Assyrian Empire. Known as Normans [North Men] **Reuben settled in Normandy in northern France.**

There is absolutely no doubt that Reuben migrated into northern France, but to say that they dominate and control France today, defies the prophecy for Reuben.

Even to say that Reuben remained in France in large numbers is a mere supposition since so many hundreds of thousands of people migrated to Louisiana and Quebec in the new world from France in the 17 and 1800's.

Most of them migrated from France to Canada and became the Quebecois, others migrated to New Orleans and Louisiana, and later some were expelled from Eastern Canada by the British also ending up in the US where they are called Cajuns and Acadians.

The term Norman means North Men and is a general term for those tribes of Israel who migrated north into Scandinavia; some of them remaining in Scandinavia and others sweeping out into Britain and Normandy

Normandy takes its name from the invaders from the north collectively called Vikings or North Men; who menaced large parts of Europe towards the end of the first millennium in two phases (790–930, then 980–1030). Medieval Latin documents referred to them as Nortmanni, which means "men of the North". This name provides the etymological basis for the modern words "Norman" and "Normandy",

Most Louisianans and French Canadians originate from Normandy and they came from what is now called Upper Normandy, Lower Normandy and the Channel Islands.

Judah

Deuteronomy 33:7 And this is the blessing of Judah: and he said, Hear, LORD, the voice of Judah, and bring him unto his people: let his hands be sufficient for him; and be thou an help to him from his enemies.

Genesis 49:8 Judah, thou art he whom thy brethren shall praise: thy hand shall be in the neck of thine enemies; thy father's children shall bow down before thee. **49:9** Judah is a lion's whelp: from the prey, my son, thou art gone up: he stooped down, he couched as a lion, and as an old lion; who shall rouse him up?

49:10 The sceptre shall not depart from Judah, nor a lawgiver from between his feet, until Shiloh [Christ] come; and unto him shall the gathering of the people be. **49:11** Binding his foal unto the vine, and his ass's colt unto the choice vine; he washed his garments in wine, and his clothes in the blood of grapes: **49:12** His eyes shall be red with wine, and his teeth white with milk.

Judah is to be blessed with leadership skills and would be a self sufficient people and will ultimately be respected by the nations. Messiah the Christ will come to Judah at Jerusalem first.

Today the Jews are scattered worldwide but about half of them occupy the present Jewish State in Palestine.

Levi

Levi was chosen to be the priests of God, yet many of them would strive with God and did rebel against God. Levi would have no nation of his own and would be scattered throughout the other twelve tribes of Israel.

Deuteronomy 33:8 And of Levi he said, Let thy Thummim and thy Urim be with thy holy one, whom thou didst prove at Massah, and with whom thou didst strive at the waters of Meribah;

Yet many [the sons of Zadok] will serve in the Ezekiel Temple; because of the godly loyalty of their forefather Zadok.

Ezekiel 44:15 But the priests the Levites, the sons of **Zadok**, that kept the charge of my sanctuary when the children of Israel went astray from me, they shall come near to me to minister unto me, and they shall stand before me to offer unto me the fat and the blood, saith the Lord God:

Deuteronomy 33:9 Who said unto his father and to his mother, I have not seen him; neither did he acknowledge his brethren, nor knew his own children: for **they have observed thy word, and kept thy covenant.**

In the millennium Levi via the descendants of Zadok shall yet serve God to teach the people righteousness.

33:10 They **shall teach Jacob thy judgments, and Israel thy law:** they shall put incense [representing the prayers of the faithful] before thee, and whole burnt sacrifice [representing wholehearted service to God] upon thine altar.

A blessing for the faithful of Levi during the millennium

They shall prosper serving God in his millennial Temple and no enemy shall touch them.

33:11 Bless, LORD, his substance, and accept the work of his hands; smite through the loins of them that rise against him, and of them that hate him, that they rise not again.

Simeon

Levi and Simeon were men of temper and were not to become independent nations and would be divided [scattered] in all the tribes of Israel

Genesis 49:5 Simeon and Levi are brethren; instruments of cruelty are in their habitations. **49:6** O my soul, come not thou into their secret; unto their assembly, mine honour, be not thou united: for in their anger they slew a man, and in their selfwill they digged down a wall. **49:7** Cursed be their anger, for it was fierce; and their wrath, for it was cruel: I will divide them in Jacob, and scatter them in Israel.

Today Levi is scattered mainly in Judah, while Simeon is generally thought to be the Simonii [Welsh] living in Wales

Benjamin

Benjamin was a war like people shedding much blood in Israel during the period of the Judges. Benjamin would remain attached to Judah and would not be considered to be one of the Ten Tribes of Israel but part of Judah, later - in the millennium - settling down and enjoying the riches of his inheritance, dwelling in a safe place.

Deuteronomy 33:12 And of Benjamin he said, **The beloved of the LORD shall dwell in safety by him**; and the Lord shall cover [defend] him all the day long, and he shall dwell between his shoulders.

Genesis 49:27 Benjamin shall ravin as a wolf: in the morning he shall devour the prey, and at night he shall divide the spoil

Joseph

[Ephraim (The British Peoples) and Manasseh (the founding American peoples)]

Joseph replaced Reuben as the first born and was granted a double portion to become many nations.

NOTE: In Deuteronomy 33:17 thousands and ten thousands are mistranslation

The term used "thousands" for Manasseh actually means an innumerable multitude.

The term "ten thousands" for Ephraim, more properly means a myriad or large number.

Deuteronomy 33:17 His [Joseph's; BOTH Ephraim and Manasseh] glory is like the firstling of his bullock, and his horns are like the horns of unicorns [properly; strong bulls]: with them he shall push the people together to the ends of the earth: and they are the ten thousands [properly; multitudes] of Ephraim, and they are the thousands [properly; innumerable multitudes] of Manasseh.

Deuteronomy 33:13 And of Joseph he said, Blessed of the LORD be his land, for the precious things of heaven, for the dew, and for the deep that coucheth beneath,

33:14 And for the precious fruits brought forth by the sun, and for the precious things put forth by the moon, **33:15** And for the chief things of the ancient mountains, and for the precious things of the lasting hills,

33:16 And for the precious things of the earth and fulness thereof, and for the good will of him that dwelt in the bush: let the blessing come upon the head of Joseph, and upon the top of the head of him that was separated from his brethren.

33:17 His glory is like the firstling of his bullock, and his horns are like the horns of unicorns: with them he shall push the people together to the ends of the earth: and they are the ten thousands [properly multitudes] of **Ephraim,** and they are the thousands [properly innumerable multitudes] of **Manasseh.**

[The Anglo Saxon British and Americans] shall be warlike and fight many wars, and God will bless them with mighty blessing of good things.

Genesis 49:22 Joseph is a fruitful bough, even a fruitful bough by a well; whose branches run over the wall: **49:23** [They will have many enemies and much war, but will be blessed by God with great strength over their enemies] The archers have sorely grieved him, and shot at him, and hated him: **49:24** But his bow abode in strength, and the arms of his hands were **made strong by the hands of the mighty God of Jacob;**

49:25 Even by the God of thy father [Abraham], who shall help thee; and by the Almighty, who shall bless thee with blessings of heaven above, blessings of the deep that lieth under, blessings of the breasts, and of the womb:

49:26 The blessings of thy father have prevailed above the blessings of my progenitors unto the utmost bound of the everlasting hills: they shall be on the head of Joseph, and on the crown of the head of him that was separate from his brethren.

Zebulun

Zebulun is to dwell by the sea and be a large port for ships like Zidon.

<u>This link is a good source for the history of the Dutch people</u>

Deuteronomy 33:18 And of Zebulun he said, Rejoice, Zebulun, in thy going out; and, Issachar, in thy tents.

33:19 They shall call the people unto the mountain [In the millennium they shall turn to God and call the nations to go up to the mountain of the Lord]; there they shall offer sacrifices of righteousness: for they shall suck of the abundance of the seas, and of treasures hid in the sand.

Genesis 49:13 Zebulun shall dwell at the haven of the sea; and he shall be for an haven of ships; and his border [the greatness of his port shall be like Zidon] shall be unto [like] Zidon.

The tribe of Zebulun are the [Frisians-Daci-Belgae] today called the Netherlands or Dutch people and their great ports are Amsterdam and Rotterdam.

Issachar

Genesis 49:14 Issachar is a strong ass couching down between two burdens: **49:15** And he saw that rest was good, and the land that it was pleasant; and bowed his shoulder to bear, and became a servant unto tribute.

Issachar is the Suomi; Finland; the official name of Finland is Suomi Finland

Gad

Deuteronomy 33:20 And of Gad he said, Blessed be he that enlargeth Gad: he dwelleth as a lion, and teareth the arm with the crown of the head.

33:21 And he provided the first part for himself, because there, in a portion of the lawgiver, was he seated; and he came with the heads of the people, he executed the justice of the LORD, and his judgments with Israel.

Genesis 49:19 Gad, a troop shall overcome him [in the tribulation]: but he shall overcome at the last [Gad will overcome and sincerely repent when Messiah comes].

Gad shall be overcome but will overcome in the end, and in the millennium Gad is to be a people wise in the Word of God teaching and enforcing godly justice.

Dan

Deuteronomy 33:22 And of Dan he said, Dan is a lion's whelp: he shall leap from Bashan.

Genesis 49:16 Dan shall judge his people, as one of the tribes of Israel. Dan shall be a serpent by the way, an adder in the path, that biteth the horse heels, so that his rider shall fall backward.

Dan shall leap from Bashan [the Golan], he shall have his own nation and he will vex his brothers. This speaking of the Irish [Dan] fight with the British [Ephraim].

The Patriarch Dan was born from the handmaid of Rachel, Bilhah. Rachel was in envy of her sister Leah and she wanted so badly to bear a child for Jacob, that she gave him her handmaid to bear a son. That son was Dan and when he was born she said, "God hath judged me, and hath also heard my voice, and hath given me a son: therefore she called his name Dan." (Gen 30:6). The meaning of the word "Dan" is "Judge" (Strong's #1777 "judge").

When Israel took possession of the promised land, the tribe of Dan was allotted its tribal inheritance in the South Western area on the Mediterranean Sea, and included the busy port of Joppa, next to modern Tel-Aviv (Joshua 19:40-48).

Many Danes later left the land sailing from Joppa in ships while others migrated northwards to Laish, and called the city Dan, after their father, see Judges 18.

The northern city Laish, renamed Dan, by the tribe of Dan, was about thirty miles inland from the ancient busy port of Tyre.

Dan was divided into two halves as an early migration by ship to Ireland was later followed by a second migration with their Assyrian [Germanic] captors from Laish [Dan] ending up in Denmark.

Ephraim [The British] has tried to dominate the western Irish half tribe of Dan which in return has vexed Ephraim, while the eastern Danish half tribe has been a peaceable nation.

Naphtali

In the millennium Naphtali is to be known for wise words.

Deuteronomy 33:23 And of Naphtali he said, O Naphtali, satisfied with favour, and full with the blessing of the LORD: possess thou the west and the south [properly the sea or a long sea coast (settling in Norway and Sweden) Strong's H3220].

Genesis 49:21 Naphtali is a hind let loose [a swift and agile warrior]: he giveth goodly words.

Naphtali the Sved-Daci-Ephtalites - Naphtalites Sweden and Norway

Asher

Asher would be strong all his days, and would be wealthy and have access to oil.

Deuteronomy 33:24 And of Asher he said, Let Asher be blessed with children; let him be acceptable to his brethren, and let him dip his foot in oil. **33:25** Thy shoes shall be iron and brass; and as thy days, so shall thy strength be.

Genesis 49:20 Out of Asher his bread shall be fat, and he shall yield royal dainties.

Asher probably the Belgae: Belgium-Luxembourg.

All Israel and their nations will be blessed of the Eternal in the Kingdom of God.

Brethren, these prophecies are only in part for now, and are to be fulfilled in the Kingdom of God when all Israel repents and turns to the Eternal with a whole heart.

Jeshurun (Hebrew: יְשֻׁרוּן), in the Hebrew Bible, is a poetic name for Israel, derived from a root word meaning upright, just or straight. Jeshurun appears four times in the Hebrew Bible — three times in Deuteronomy and once in Isaiah. It can mean the people of Israel (Deut. 32:15; 33:26), the Land of Israel (Deut. 33:5;), or the Patriarch Jacob (whom an Angel renamed Israel in Genesis 32:29):

Deuteronomy 33:26 There is none like unto the God of Jeshurun, who rideth upon the heaven in thy help, and in his excellency on the sky.

33:27 The eternal God is thy refuge, and underneath are the everlasting arms: and he shall thrust out the enemy from before thee; and shall say, Destroy them.

33:28 Israel then shall dwell in safety alone: the fountain of Jacob shall be upon a land of corn and wine; also his heavens shall drop down dew.

33:29 Happy art thou, O Israel: who is like unto thee, O people saved by the LORD, the shield of thy help, and who is the

sword of thy excellency! and thine enemies shall be found liars unto thee; and thou shalt tread upon their high places.

Possession of the Promised Land

When Israel was about to enter the Promised Land, Moses wrote his fifth book called Deuteronomy.

In that book Moses recounted the history of Israel from their departure out of Egypt and warned the people from God that their possession of the Land was absolutely CONDITIONAL on them faithfully living by EVERY WORD of God.

Deuteronomy 4:1 Now therefore **hearken, O Israel, unto the statutes and unto the judgments, which I teach you, for to do them, that ye may live, and go in and possess the land which the LORD God of your fathers giveth you.**

4:2 Ye shall not add unto the word which I command you, neither shall ye diminish ought from it, that ye may keep the commandments of the LORD your God which I command you.

4:3 Your eyes have seen what the LORD did because of Baalpeor: for all the men that followed Baalpeor, **the LORD thy God hath destroyed them from among you.**

The history of Israel from the time they left Egypt until this day is a demonstration that God cares for those who faithfully follow him to live by His Word; and that God will strongly rebuke those who depart from the

Word of God to do as they please and to follow anyone other than God and God's Word; which is the sin of idolatry.

Historically God removed the Ten Tribes of Israel from off their land when they would not stop their wickedness and idolatries.

Later Judah was also removed from the land by God through the hand of the Babylonians and again later by the Romans, for their pride and sins. If we are full of sin today, God will again correct us! For Almighty God is consistent.

Look at Judah in Palestine today and you will find a secular state where 80% of the Jews are not religious; and the about 20% who are religious follow their own traditions. It is the same in Britain and America who profess godliness as we fill our lands with wickedness.

Today Britain, America and the Jewish State are overspread with wickedness against the Word of God and we close our eyes to what God did to our forefathers for these same sins and we think that we can continue to be blessed and remain on the land without any correction from God.

The other nations of the Ten Tribes of Israel are no better. We have been given the fairest portions of the earth and have been blessed above all people in all of history, being given riches unimaginable to people of a few centuries ago and these blessings have filled us with pride and the false assumption that we are a righteous people as we fill our lands with the sins of our forefathers.

It is beyond any argument that today's British peoples, America, the Dutch, Scandinavia and the Jewish state are full of Sabbath breaking, cheating, corruption and stealing; lying, adultery, fornication and homosexuality, followers of the occult and overwhelming idolatry [placing things between us and God].

Yes all of the other nations on earth are just as bad, yet we are the ones who have received God's blessings; we are the ones who are supposed to be an example of righteousness for the earth.

We have utterly failed to do so, therefore Almighty God will withdraw his blessings and his protection and God will make us an example of what happens when men defy God.

Without God's blessings we shall surely fall, after which the turn of the other nations will come; until all humanity is humbled and ready to accept the coming of Messiah the Christ to save us and to rule all nations in godly righteousness.

Genesis 50

Jacob died and Joseph wept

Genesis 50:1 And Joseph fell upon his father's face, and wept upon him, and kissed him. **50:2** And Joseph commanded his servants the physicians to embalm his father: and the physicians embalmed Israel.

The Egyptians also mourned for Jacob for 70 days.

50:3 And forty days were fulfilled for him; for so are fulfilled the days of those which are embalmed: and the **Egyptians mourned for him threescore and ten days**.

Then Joseph asked Pharaoh's consent to take his father Jacob to Canaan to bury Jacob in the tomb of his fathers.

50:4 And when the days of his mourning were past, Joseph spake unto the house of Pharaoh, saying, If now I have found grace in your eyes, speak, I pray you, in the ears of Pharaoh, saying, **50:5** My father made me swear, saying, Lo, I die: in my grave which I have digged for me in the land of Canaan, there shalt thou bury me. Now therefore let me go up, I pray thee, and bury my father, and I will come again.

Pharaoh said go, and the house of Jacob except for the youngest children, went up to Canaan to mourn and to bury their father Joseph in the tomb of his father at Machpelah.

50:6 And Pharaoh said, Go up, and bury thy father, according as he made thee swear. **50:7** And Joseph went up to bury his father: and with him went up all the servants of Pharaoh, the elders of his house, and all the elders of the land of Egypt, **50:8** And all the house of Joseph, and his brethren, and his father's house: only their little ones, and their flocks, and their herds, they left in the land of Goshen. **50:9** And there went up with him [an honor guard of Egyptian] both chariots and horsemen: and it was a very great company.

50:10 And they came to the threshingfloor of Atad, which is beyond Jordan, and there they mourned with a great and very sore lamentation: and he made a mourning for his father seven days. **50:11** And when the inhabitants of the land, the Canaanites, saw the mourning in the floor of Atad, they said, This is a grievous mourning to the Egyptians: wherefore the name of it was called Abelmizraim, [mourning of Egypt] which is beyond Jordan.

Then Jacob was buried by his family with his fathers in Machpelah.

50:12 And his sons did unto him according as he commanded them: **50:13** For his sons carried him into the land of Canaan, and buried him in the cave of the field of Machpelah, which Abraham bought with the field for a possession of a buryingplace of Ephron the Hittite, before Mamre.

Joseph and the family of Jacob return to Egypt.

50:14 And Joseph returned into Egypt, he, and his brethren, and all that went up with him to bury his father, after he had buried his father.

After the death of Jacob the brothers again feared that Joseph would become vengeful and appealed to him for mercy.

50:15 And when Joseph's brethren saw that their father was dead, they said, Joseph will peradventure hate us, and will certainly requite us all the evil which we did unto him.

50:16 And they sent a messenger unto Joseph, saying, Thy father did command before he died, saying, **50:17** So shall ye say unto Joseph, Forgive, I pray thee now, the trespass of thy brethren, and their sin; for they did unto thee evil: and now, we pray thee, forgive the trespass of the servants of the God of thy father. And Joseph wept when they spake unto him.

50:18 And his brethren also went and fell down before his face; and they said, Behold, we be thy servants.

Joseph consoled his brothers and promised mercy to them.

50:19 And Joseph said unto them, Fear not: for am I in the place of God? **50:20** But as for you, ye thought evil against me; but God meant it unto good, to bring to pass, as it is this day, to save much people alive. **50:21** Now therefore fear ye not: I will nourish you, and your little ones. And he comforted them, and spake kindly unto them.

Joseph died at 110 years old, with his children and their children around him.

50:22 And Joseph dwelt in Egypt, he, and his father's house: and Joseph lived an hundred and ten years. **50:23** And Joseph saw Ephraim's children of the third generation: the children also of Machir the son of Manasseh were brought up upon Joseph's knees.

Then Joseph made his brothers and family to swear to take his bones with them when they returned to Canaan.

50:24 And Joseph said unto his brethren, I die: and God will surely visit you, and bring you out of this land unto the land which he sware to Abraham, to Isaac, and to Jacob. **50:25** And Joseph took an oath of the children of Israel, saying, God will surely visit you, and ye shall carry up my bones from hence.

50:26 So Joseph died, being an hundred and ten years old: and they embalmed him, and he was put in a coffin in Egypt.

This concludes the First Book of Moses called Genesis, which covers the period from creation to the death of Joseph. This history was written for our instruction and example, and I commented on many of the events and their spiritual meaning and application during this study.

Right now the Ekklesia is at a point where the majority of the leaders and elders are attacking their zealous faithful to God brethren, just like the brothers attacked Joseph. In a way the story of Joseph is being repeated in the assemblies today.

Brethren, this was recorded to teach us spiritual lessons. Today God is molding both the persecuted and the persecutors into the beings he wants them to be. Some like Joseph need a different kind of molding then their brethren and are being separated out, as Joseph was separated out, to a different kind of training.

Dear Brethren, the sorrow of the present circumstances will pass; and we will all be brought into a full unity with God our Father, and with our brothers; just as Joseph was reconciled with his brothers and reunited with his father Jacob.

Let us be as forgiving as Joseph was when we are offended by our brethren, for the sake of our zeal for the Eternal and his Word; knowing full well that our brothers sincerely believe that they are right and are doing God a service.

Therefore do not let a root of bitterness grow up inside us, but pray that every person will learn as he ought to, and that all humanity will be reconciled to God the Father, and let us be merciful as Jesus and Stephen both prayed: "Forgive them Father, for they know not what they do."

In due time if we faint not, we will all learn our lessons from God our Father, and will become the kind of children of God that we ought to be. Then when we are all reconciled to God our Father in heaven we shall also be reconciled with one another.

Exodus

Prophecies of the Exodus

Biblical Chronology From Creation to the Exodus

Adam became the father of Seth at 130. (Genesis 5:3) 0 + 130 = 130

Seth became the father of Enosh at 105. (Genesis 5:6) 130 + 105 = 235

Enosh became the father of Kenan at 90. (Genesis 5:9) 235 + 90 = 325

Cainan became the father of Mahalalel at 70. (Genesis 5:12) 325 + 70 = 395

Mahalalel became the father of Jared at 65. (Genesis 5:15) 395 + 65 = 460

Jared became the father of Enoch at 162. (Genesis 5:18) 460 + 162 = 622

Enoch became the father of Methuselah at 65. (Genesis 5:21) 622 + 65 = 687

Methuselah became the father of Lamech at 187. (Genesis 5:25) 687 + 187 = 874

Lamech became the father of Noah at 182. (Genesis 5:28) 874 + 182 = 1056

The Flood started when Noah was 600. (Genesis 7:6) 1056 + 600 = 1656

From creation to the beginning of the flood: 1656 A.M. 2294 B.C.

NOTE: There are a number of errors in Bishop Ushers A.D. - B.C. system and **the B.C dates are given only as a general reference, and are not accurate.** The Biblical "Era of Man" end of the year 6,000 is late 2o22 A.D. by the erroneous Bishop Usher chronology.

From the Flood to the Exodus

Shem was born 97 years (1559 A.M. 2391 B.C.) before the flood when Noah was 503 years old; since Shem's son Arphaxad was born when Shem was one hundred years old, two years after the flood and the flood itself took a full year.

Genesis 11:10 These are the generations of Shem: Shem was an hundred years old, and begat Arphaxad two years after the flood: **Arphaxad was born two years after the flood began 1656 + 2 = 1658 A.M. (2290 B.C.)**

11:12 And Arphaxad lived five and thirty years, and begat Salah 1658 + 35 = 1693

11:14 And Salah lived thirty years, and begat Eber: 1693 + 30 = 1723

Genesis 11:16 And Eber lived four and thirty years, and begat Peleg:

1722 + 34 = 1757

Genesis 11:18 And Peleg lived thirty years, and begat **Reu** 1757 + 30 = 1787

11:20 And Reu lived two and thirty years, and begat **Serug**: 1787 + 32 = 1819

11:22 And Serug lived thirty years, and begat **Nahor**: 1819 + 30 = 1849

11:24 And Nahor lived nine and twenty years, and begat **Terah**: 1849 + 29 = 1878

The Birth Date of Abram

11:26 And Terah lived seventy years, and begat **Abram, Nahor, and Haran.**

Terah's total age was 205 years, and to the casual reader of Genesis 11:26, Abram was born when Terah was 70 years of age, but in this case Abram was apparently placed first because of his spiritual legacy while the others may have been born before him.

The specific birth year of Abram can be found in Genesis 12:4 where Abram's age is recorded as being 75 years when his father Terah died at the age of 205 and Abram departed out of Haran. **By simply subtracting 75 from 205 we can date the birth of Abram in the 130th year of Terah.**

Genesis 12:4 So Abram departed, as the Lord had spoken unto him; and Lot went with him: and **Abram was seventy and five years old when he departed out of Haran.**

Genesis 11:31 And Terah took Abram his son, and Lot the son of Haran his son's son, and Sarai his daughter in law, his son Abram's wife; and they went forth with them from Ur of the Chaldees, to go into the land of Canaan; **and they came unto Haran, and dwelt there. 11:32 And the days of Terah were two hundred and five years: and Terah died in Haran.**

Terah's birth in 1878 up to the birth of Abram in Terah's 130 year is 2008.

Abram was born: 2008 A.M. (c 1940 B.C.)

21:5 And Abraham was **an hundred years old, when his son Isaac was born unto him.**

Abraham was 100 when **Isaac was born** in 2108 A.M. (1840 B.C.)

25:26 And after that came his brother out, and his hand took hold on Esau's heel; and his name was called Jacob: and **Isaac was threescore years old when she bare them.**

Isaac was sixty when **Jacob was born** in 2168 A.M. (1780 B.C.)

47:28 And **Jacob lived in the land of Egypt seventeen years: so the whole age of Jacob was an hundred forty and seven years.**

A lifespan of 147 years minus 17 years in Egypt, means that Jacob was 130 years old when he went into Egypt.

2168 A.M. + 130 = 2298 A.M. (c 1650 B.C.) since the creation of Adam, when Jacob went down to Egypt with all his family.

NOTE: There are a number of errors in Bishop Ushers A.D. - B.C. system and the B.C dates are given only as a general reference, and are not accurate.

The 430 Years Prophecy

God called Abram in Ur at the age of 70, promising him that if he left to follow God to a new land he would be greatly blessed. The family then went to Haran where Terah died being 205 years old and Abram was 75 years old; after which Abram journeyed from Haran to Canaan at the age of 75.

The 430 years prophecy refers to 430 years after the PROMISE was made to Abraham in Ur when he was 70 years old; 30 years BEFORE the birth of Isaac!

"Now the sojourning of the children of Israel, who dwelt in Egypt, was **four hundred and thirty years**. And it came to pass at the end of the four hundred and thirty years, even the selfsame day it came to pass, that all the hosts of the LORD went out from the land of Egypt" (Exodus 12:40-41).

Here the word "sojourning" gives an impression that they sojourned or lived in Egypt for 430 years; when in fact the word sojourning refers to the wanderings of Abram and his descendants from the time of God's promise to Abram in Ur when Abram was seventy years old; which calling and promise caused Abram to leave Ur when he was 70 and then to leave Haran when the promise was repeated five years later, to become a wanderer [through faith in the promise] until they became the covenant nation at Sinai.

This refers to God's PROMISE to Abraham in Ur, and not to the Genesis 15 promise made in Canaan concerning Isaac; God's PROMISE to the seventy year old Abram in Ur was made 430 years before the Covenant at Sinai and the promise was repeated five years later in Haran.

Shaul (Saul, Paul) a highly respected scholar of the Pharisees who is speaking concerning a dating on which there was absolutely no controversy in his day; wrote of the PROMISE of God being made to the seventy year old Abram in Ur 430 years BEFORE the Sinai Covenant.

The promise made by God to Abram in the land in Genesis 15, was only a repeating of the previous PROMISE in Ur when the wanderings based on faith in the promise began 30 years BEFORE the birth of Isaac.

This does not mean that the children of Israel dwelt in Egypt for 430 years.

Paul explains that the 430 years extends from the time of God's PROMISE to Abram until the children of Israel left Egypt. "And this I say, that the covenant, that was confirmed before [at Sinai] of God in Christ, the law, which was four hundred and thirty years after [after the PROMISE was made to the seventy year old Abram in Ur and later repeated in Haran and then repeated again in Palestine before the birth of Isaac], cannot disannul, **that it should make the promise of none effect**" (Galatians 3:17).

That is, the Sinai Covenant cannot disannul the PROMISE made to Abram in Haran 430 years BEFORE the Sinai Covenant.

Genesis 11:31 And Terah took Abram his son, and Lot the son of Haran his son's son, and Sarai his daughter in law, his son Abram's wife; and they went forth with them from Ur of the Chaldees, to go into the land of Canaan; and they came unto Haran, and dwelt there. **11:32** And **the days of Terah were two hundred and five years: and Terah died in Haran.**

The 430 years prophecy of Exodus 12:40-41 is a reference to Israel inheriting the promise and becoming a nation at Sinai; 430 years AFTER the PROMISE was made to Abram in Ur!

Meanwhile the 400 years prophecy was that from the birth of Isaac 400 years remained to the exodus and the covenant at Sinai.

The descendants of Abram exited Egypt as a great nation 400 years after the birth of Isaac and 500 years after the birth of Abram in the 130th year of Terah; and precisely 430 years after the promise was given to the seventy year old Abraham in Ur.

God brought Israel out of Egypt and fulfilled his promise exactly 430 years after it was first given in Ur; and four hundred years after the birth of Isaac.

The 400 Years Prophecy

The belief that the children of Israel were slaves in Egypt for 400 years is largely based upon these two verses.

"And he said unto Abram, Know of a surety that **thy seed** shall be **a stranger in a land that is not theirs** [This includes not only Egypt but all of the time that they were wanderers in Palestine from the birth of Isaac; before actually inheriting the land.], and shall serve them; and they shall afflict them **four hundred years** ..." (Genesis 15:13). "And God spake on this wise, That **his seed** should sojourn in a strange land [a land that is not theirs, not necessarily Egypt]; and that they should bring them into bondage, and entreat them evil **four hundred years**" (Acts 7:6).

Here is the meaning; thy seed refers to the children of Abram beginning with Isaac the son of promise, who would be wanderers having no land of their own for four hundred years beginning with the birth of Isaac.

Isaac was born when Abraham was one hundred years old; therefore the exodus and the Sinai Covenant would take place four hundred years after the birth of Isaac or five hundred years after the birth of Abraham!

Abraham was born in 2008 A.M. (c 1940 B.C.): therefore the Exodus was 500 years later in 2508 A.M. (c 1440 B.C.) with a margin of possible error of a few years.

The Fourth Generation Prophecy

Genesis 15:14 And also that nation, whom they shall serve, will I judge [BOTH Egypt and the nations of Canaan were judged by God]: and afterward shall they come out with great substance. **15:15** And thou [Abraham] shalt go to thy fathers in peace; thou shalt be buried in a good old age. **15:16** But **in the fourth generation they** [the descendants of Abraham through Isaac and Jacob] **shall come hither again**: for the iniquity of the Amorites is not yet full.

Levi was one of Jacob's 12 sons and went down to Egypt with Jacob. We see from Genesis 46:8-11 that Kohath, the son of Levi and grandfather of Moses, was already born when Jacob and his family entered Egypt. Kohath lived to be 133, and his son Amram lived to be 137 (Exodus 6:18-20).

Born 80 years before the exodus from Egypt, Moses was the son of Amram, the son of Kohath, the son of Levi (1 Chronicles 6:1-3).

Moses was thus the fourth generation of those who had entered Egypt:

1. Levi;
2. Kohath;
3. Amram;
4. Moses.

The exodus was very definitely not in early 1200 B.C. as some suppose.

Now Moses was eighty years old at the time of the exodus, so counting back 80 years from 1440 B.C. comes to the approximate birth date of Moses in 1520 B.C.

Exodus 7:7 And Moses was fourscore **years** old, and **Aaron** fourscore and **three years** old, when they spake unto Pharaoh.

Notice that Aaron was three years older than Moses.

Israel went down into Egypt in 1650 B.C. and came out in 1440 B.C. meaning that their total time in Egypt was 210 years.

The Temple

In 1 Kings 6:1 we are told that Solomon began building the temple in the 480th year after the exodus: 960 B.C.

In Acts 13 Paul gives a longer period but Paul is giving a general historical overview and uses the word "about" obviously approximating and not being concerned with specific dates in his address, therefore the 1 Kings date is the accurate date.

1 Kings 6:1 And it came to pass in the **four hundred and eightieth year after the children of Israel were come out of the land of Egypt, in the fourth year of Solomon's reign** over Israel, in the month Zif, which is the second month, that he began to build the house of the Lord.

The conventional date for the beginning of the Temple construction is 960-970 B.C. The Biblical Chronology would put the Exodus in about 1440 B.C. and the start of construction of the Temple 480 years later in 960 B.C.

Solomon's Temple took 7 years to build 1 Kings 6:38 being completed in c 953 B.C.

Exodus 1

Moses in Egypt

The account of the exodus begins with the final climax of affliction in the book of Exodus, which covers the history of Israel leaving Egypt and then the journey to Mount Sinai and their marriage to the God who later gave up his God-hood to be made flesh as Jesus Christ.

Of course God could have prevented all this distress and just moved Pharaoh to let Israel go, instead God himself hardened Pharaoh so that all these things could happen.

WHY? Because this was to be an instructional allegory about bondage to sin for the called out of spiritual Egypt.

In this history, bondage in Egypt was a type of bondage and enslavement to the god of this word, Satan. This history is an allegory about a people being called out of bondage to sin in this world's evil societies; while Canaan was an example and type of sin itself.

The exodus is an allegory about the great love of God for his called out bride, calling her out of bondage to the freedom of the righteousness of the whole Word of God.

It is about the fact that we cannot deliver ourselves an we can only delivered from the wages of our sins by the Passover sacrifice of the Lamb, the Son of God.

> **1 Corinthians 10:11** Now **all these things happened unto them for examples: and they are written for our admonition,** upon whom the ends of the world are come.

Exodus begins with Israel in Egypt and how they came to be in bondage, then the history of Moses, his education and preparation, and then God's deliverance of Israel from bondage.

The names of the males of Jacob who entered Egypt; which, added to Jacob himself, Joseph and his two sons totaled 70 male persons.

Exodus 1:1 Now these are the names of the children of Israel, which came into Egypt; every man and his household came with Jacob. **1:2** Reuben, Simeon, Levi, and Judah, **1:3** Issachar, Zebulun, and Benjamin, **1:4** Dan, and Naphtali, Gad, and Asher. **1:5** And all the souls that came out of the loins of Jacob were seventy souls [males, plus their females]: for Joseph was in Egypt already. **1:6** And Joseph died, and all his brethren, and all that generation.

Israel was fruitful and multiplied until the whole generation that had entered Goshen [renamed Ramses about 200 years later] passed on, after which a new ruler came to the throne and found the strength of Israel to be a problem that needed to be dealt with.

1:7 And the children of Israel were fruitful, and increased abundantly, and multiplied, and waxed exceeding mighty; and the land was filled with them.

Pharaoh's initial purpose was to drive Israel out of Egypt, for he was afraid of Israel.

1:8 Now there arose up a new king over Egypt, which knew not Joseph. **1:9** And he said unto his people, **Behold, the people of the children of Israel are more and mightier than we: 1:10 Come on, let us deal wisely with them; lest they multiply, and it come to pass, that, when there falleth out any war, they join also** unto our enemies, and fight against us, and so get them up out of the land.

Israel was then tasked with heavy burdens. This was like a special tax on Israel to be paid by their labor, instead of the money we are taxed with today.

1:11 Therefore they did set over them taskmasters to afflict them with their burdens. And they built for Pharaoh treasure [fortified] cities, **Pithom and Raamses**.

> **Ramses:** From this statement some conclude that the pharaoh of the Exodus was Ramses. Here the name Ramses is confusing because the Hebrews built vast storage facilities at Avaris which was renamed Ramses by Ramses I about 200 years later.
>
> Later scripture copyists updated the name of Avaris to Ramses in place of the older Goshen or Avaris, after Ramses 1 changed the name some 200 years later.
>
> Because of the word "Ramses," some have mistakenly concluded that the pharaoh Ramses I or II had built the city with Hebrew workers and misdated the exodus by about 200 years.
>
> **Wiki: Avaris (/ˈævərɪs/; Egyptian**, Budge notation: *Hut-waret*, Greek: Αὔαρις, *Auaris* was located at modern Tell el-Dab'a in the northeastern region of the Nile Delta [Goshen].
>
> Avaris was built and occupied from about 1783: Jacob went to Egypt 1651 B.C. and later Israel was made to build up enormous storehouses for pharaoh at Avaris and Pithom.
>
> Later the city was re-occupied by various pharaohs including the famous Seti and finally Ramses I (1292–1290 BC) renamed the city after himself.
>
> This confusion has caused many to misdate the Exodus from its proper date of c 1441 B.C. to around 1221 B.C.

Israel continued to multiply and increase

1:12 But the more they afflicted them, the more they multiplied and grew.

The Egyptians feared Israel and were vexed that Israel was growing greater than the Egyptians in their own land. Therefore they increased their exaction's from Israel.

The families of Israel still had their homes in their villages and their pastures, flocks and herds but were required to pay a very heavy burden in the form of labor tax.

And they were grieved because of the children of Israel. **1:13** And the Egyptians made the children of Israel to serve with rigour: **1:14** And they made their lives bitter with hard bondage, in morter, and in brick, and in all manner of service in the field: all their service, wherein they made them serve, was with rigour.

Then Pharaoh thought to limit the growth of Israel by killing their new born sons

1:15 And the king of Egypt spake to the Hebrew midwives, of which the name of the one was Shiphrah, and the name of the other Puah: **1:16** And he said, When ye do the office of a midwife to the Hebrew women, and see them upon the stools; if it be a son, then ye shall kill him: but if it be a daughter, then she shall live.

The midwives refused to obey the orders of the king, as **we should also refuse to obey unlawful orders** from our leaders.

That includes refusing the biblically unlawful instructions of those claiming to be leaders and elders in the Ekklesia, who want us to turn away from a zeal to live by every Word of God to serve them and their false teachings instead.

1:17 But the midwives feared God, and did not as the king of Egypt commanded them, but saved the men children alive.

The midwives give their defense to Pharaoh and **GOD delivered them out of the hand of the king because they obeyed GOD and not the physical rulers.**

1:18 And the king of Egypt called for the midwives, and said unto them, Why have ye done this thing, and have saved the men children alive? **1:19** And the midwives said unto Pharaoh, Because the Hebrew women are not as the Egyptian women; for they are lively, and are delivered ere the midwives come in unto them. **1:20 Therefore God dealt well with the midwives**: and the people multiplied, and waxed very mighty.

God delivers those who love and obey him, more than they love men.

1:21 And it came to pass, **because the midwives feared God**, that he made them houses.

God made the houses of the midwives (families) famous in Israel because they obeyed God and not the king. God will also make famous all people who chose to live by every Word of God, despite what any person may demand.

Aaron was born and three years later Moses was born after Pharaoh had then commanded that every son be cast into the river.

1:22 And Pharaoh charged all his people, saying, Every son that is born ye shall cast into the river, and every daughter ye shall save alive.

Exodus 2

Then a descendant of Levi called Moses [Hebrew Moshe] was born and when he was three months old he was placed in a basket and cast into the Nile.

This is now specifically about Moses, his parents had married and Aaron [Hebrew Aharon] had been born three years before Moses.

Exodus 2:1 And there went a man of the house of Levi, and took to wife a daughter of Levi. **2:2** And the woman conceived, and bare a son: and when she saw him that he was a goodly child, she hid him three months. **2:3** And when she could not longer hide him, she took for him an ark of bulrushes, and daubed it with slime and with pitch [tar], and put the child therein; and she laid it in the flags by the river's brink.

Notice that she placed him in the river as pharaoh had commanded, but not to drown as Pharaoh had intended.

Little Miriam was sent to watch the child for her parents

2:4 And his sister stood afar off, to wit what would be done to him.

The basket was seen by a daughter of Pharaoh [most probably Hatshupset] and brought to her.

2:5 And the daughter of Pharaoh came down to wash herself at the river; and her maidens walked along by the river's side; and when she saw the ark among the flags, she sent her maid to fetch it. **2:6** And when she had opened it, she saw the child: and, behold, the babe wept. And she had compassion on him, and said, This is one of the Hebrews' children.

Miriam then approached Pharaoh's daughter and suggested that a woman be brought to nurse the hungry child and Pharaoh's daughter agreed to the suggestion because the hungry weeping child aroused her sympathies.

2:7 Then said his sister to Pharaoh's daughter, Shall I go and call to thee a nurse of the Hebrew women, that she may nurse the child for thee? **2:8** And Pharaoh's daughter said to her, Go. And the maid went and called the child's mother.

The wonders of God for those who love and serve him! Moses' own sister Miriam went and the child's own mother was paid wages to raise the child!

2:9 And Pharaoh's daughter said unto her, Take this child away, and nurse it for me, and I will give thee thy wages. And the women took the child, and nursed it.

When the child was older his mother brought him to Pharaoh's daughter and he was raised as her son, a prince of the Egyptians; and taught all the facets of human leadership in the court of Pharaoh.

The name Moses means "one drawn [called] out" and was an apt name, for Moses was to be called out by God.

2:10 And the child grew, and she brought him unto Pharaoh's daughter, and he became her son. And she called his name Moses [drawn or called out]: and she said, Because I drew him out of the water.

Moses grows up in Egypt

When this Moses was fully learned in the education of the court of Pharaoh and had served Pharaoh to about forty years of age; he visited his brethren.

Now we begin to get into some really interesting Egyptian history.

This woman, pharaoh's daughter, moved by a baby's cries in 1521 B.C., was the daughter of the absolute monarch who would be a queen herself one day.

Hatshepsut (meaning *Foremost of Noble Ladies)* was the elder of two daughters born to Thutmose I and his queen, Ahmes.

The death of Thutmose I, is dated as around [circa] 1508 B.C.

After her father Thutmose I died, her half brother Thutmose II reigned as pharaoh c 1508 - 1504 B.C. Thutmose II married the lawful daughter of pharaoh, his half sister Hatshepsut, to legitimize his reign and she became his queen.

Then upon the untimely death of Thutmose II in 1504 B.C. she became regent and co-ruler of Egypt with her husband's child by a concubine, Thutmose III

Thutmose II had had a son [Thutmose III] by a priestess of Amun-Ra, who was destined to become pharaoh of Egypt and the priests and priestesses of Amun-Ra did not miss the opportunity to train the future pharaoh as a priest of Amun-Ra.

A few words about the religion of Amun-Ra

Amon was "the secret one" visible as Ra the sun god and was often called Amun-Ra. Thutmose I exalted the worship of "the hidden one" [Lucifer, Satan] and his symbol of the sun in Egypt. Thutmose III wrote the Book of the Dead which is the Satanic Bible and the backbone of the occult and Lucifer/Satan worship including today's Masonry, the Illuminati, Skull and Bones and many others.

Dating Moses

Hatshepsut reigned as co-pharaoh while her husband's son Thutmose III grew up in the temple of Amun, the secret god [Lucifer, Satan] whose manifestation was the sun god Ra; and when Thutmose III became a child pharaoh, Hatshepsut remained as co-ruler until her death c 1482 B.C., thereupon Thutmose III became sole pharaoh of Egypt.

The Memphis sources date Hatshepsut's rule with Thutmose III as 1504 - 1482.

In c 1521 B.C. pharaoh's daughter Hatshepsut whose birth date is not recorded in any known source, found the infant Moses crying on the river Nile; long before she would be Queen of Egypt, and throughout her life her only son was the adopted Moses.

In scripture much water is often used as a symbol of the general mass of people and this beginning for Moses was an allegory from God that Moses had been "Called Out" from among the people to lead Israel out of Egypt.

Moses was nursed and certainly taught by his true mother and must have been aware of the prophecy to Abraham that God would call Israel out of Egypt at a certain time. Moses was also beloved of his adoptive mother Hatshepsut, and given the best education that a potential future pharaoh of Egypt could be given.

> **Acts 7:20** In which time Moses was born, and was exceeding fair, and nourished up in his father's house three months: **7:21** And when he was cast out, Pharaoh's daughter took him up, and nourished him for her own son.
>
> **7:22** And Moses was learned in all the wisdom of the Egyptians, and was mighty in words and in deeds.

Remember that Hatshepsut took Moses for her own son in c 1521 B.C. and did not herself begin to reign until at least 1508 B.C. [with Thutmose II] and then she reigned as regent for Thutmose III from 1504 B.C. when Moses was about 20 years old.

Conventional Dates of the death of Thutmose III very from 1450 to 1426 B.C. but we know from biblical chronology that he died in c 1441 B.C.

> All the dates for the Eighteenth Dynasty are open to dispute because of uncertainty about the circumstances surrounding the recording of a **Heliacal Rise of Sothis** in the reign of **Amenhotep I**.
>
> A papyrus from Amenhotep I's reign records this astronomical observation which, theoretically, could be used to correlate the Egyptian chronology with the modern calendar; however, to do this the **latitude** where the observation was taken must also be known.
>
> This document has no note of the place of observation, but it is ASSUMED that it was taken in either a Delta city such as Memphis or Heliopolis, or in Thebes. These two latitudes give dates twenty years apart, the High and Low chronologies, respectively.
>
> This observation could very easily have been in another location and these assumed possible dates could easily be off by several years. These historical chronologies are competing assumptions and the biblical chronology is about midway between the two assumptions I

chose to go with the biblical chronology of the exodus and death of Thutmose III in 1441 B.C.

It is interesting to note that the firstborn son and heir to the throne of Thutmose III, Amenemhat, predeceased Thutmose III: Which would fulfill the Word of God:.

> **Exodus 4:22-23** And thou shalt say unto Pharaoh, Thus saith the Lord, Israel is my son, even my firstborn: And I say unto thee, Let my son go, that he may serve me: and if thou refuse to let him go, behold, **I will slay thy son, even thy firstborn**.
>
> **Exodus 11:5** And all the **firstborn** in the land of Egypt shall die, from the first born of Pharaoh that sitteth upon his throne, even unto the **firstborn** of the maidservant that is behind the mill; and all the **firstborn** of beasts.

For the first 22 years c 1504 - 1482 B.C. Hatshepsut ruled as the regent co-ruler with the child Thutmose III who became full pharaoh in 1482 after the death of Hatshepsut.

At the age of 40 or about c 1481 B.C. [just as Thutmose III was beginning to assert himself] Moses fled Egypt having taken the decision to serve God rather than the gods of Egypt.

Consider the dynamic of this relationship

Hatshepsut took Moses for her own son in c 1521 B.C. and Moses was raised in all the wisdom of Egypt. That wisdom would have included their religion and Moses would have been raised by the Egyptians to worship Amun-Ra!

Yet God was working with Moses and opened his mind to spiritual things and Moses who could have been pharaoh rejected Amun-Ra for the Eternal and left his adoptive mother of 40 years Queen Hatshepsut, for his birth mother and for his birth people!

Meanwhile Thutmose III, who could easily have been twenty years younger than Moses, was also raised in all the wisdom of Egypt and its religion of Amun-Ra.

When this Moses was fully learned in the education of the court of Pharaoh and was about forty years of age; he visited his brethren.

Exodus 2:11 And it came to pass in those days, when Moses was grown, that **he went out unto his brethren**, and looked on their burdens: and he spied an Egyptian smiting an Hebrew, one of his brethren.

The heart of Moses was moved for justice for his brethren and he slew an Egyptian bully: Yet he hid the Egyptian and tried to hide the deed.

2:12 And he looked this way and that way, and when he saw that there was no man, he slew the Egyptian, and hid him in the sand.

The very next day Moses tries to provide justice to two Israelites, and discovered that his deed was known and would surely get back to Pharaoh. We here see a passion for Israel and for justice in Moses that was not learned through his Egyptian education.

2:13 And when he went out the second day, behold, two men of the Hebrews strove together: and he said to him that did the wrong, Wherefore smitest thou thy fellow? **2:14** And he said, **Who made thee a prince and a judge over us?** intendest thou to kill me, as thou killedst the Egyptian? And Moses feared, and said, Surely this thing is known.

Moses with a basic knowledge from his natural parents and an education in all the knowledge of Egypt; chose God. Moses then fled to the wilderness of Sinai where he was educated in godliness by the priest of God, Jethro.

Meanwhile Thutmose III had been fully educated as a priest of Amun-Ra as well as trained to rule.

For the next forty years Thutmose III became Egypt's greatest pharaoh and conqueror, attaining a huge empire in the name of the hidden god. At that time Egypt ruled all the surrounding nations as a great empire and Thutmose III was truly the god-king of the known world.

When Thutmose III became pharaoh he was a devotee of the "secret god" Amun who's manifestation was the sun god Ra [the sun being a symbol of Lucifer/Satan in all sun worship and occult material].

The contest between Thutmose III and Moses was truly a contest between the god Amun-Ra [Satan] and the Eternal.

Bringing down this pharaoh who was the champion of the god Lucifer / Satan by God's emissary Moses makes the allegory of this pharaoh as a type of Satan complete; and God's power to deliver from Satan was established indelibly.

When Moses cast down his rod and it became a serpent, it was the priests of Amun-Ra who cast down their rods and they became serpents. When God's serpent swallowed the serpents of Amun it should have been clear that God had full power over the serpent Satan.

The empty tomb of Thutmose III has been found and contains images of the priests of Amun-Ra throwing down sticks which turned into serpents.

Immediately after the Exodus God said to Moses:

> **Exodus 13:17** And it came to pass, when Pharaoh had let the people go, **that God led them not through the way of the land of the Philistines, although that was near; for God said, Lest peradventure the people repent when they see war, and they return to Egypt: 13:18** But God led the people about, through the way of the wilderness of the Red sea: and the children of Israel went up harnessed out of the land of Egypt.

We know that God planned for Israel to go through the Red Sea. The slaves called out of Egypt symbolically dying and being resurrected as an allegory of baptism, death and resurrection

> **1 Corinthians 10:2** And were all **baptized** unto Moses **in the cloud and in the sea**;

The entering into the Red Sea represented death and the rising up out of the Red Sea represented a resurrection of those who follow and live by the Word of God. Israel by obeying and following God was saved from the watery grave, while the followers of Amun-Ra [Satan] were destroyed.

The lesson being that those who sincerely repent of past sin and follow God to live by every Word of God, shall be saved in a resurrection to life, but the unrepentant who will not live by every Word of God will perish.

We know these spiritual things, but God also gave a physical reason for the route he took: **that God led them not through the way of the land of the Philistines, although that was near; for God said, Lest peradventure the people repent when they see war, and they return to Egypt:**

God knew that Israel would see war if they went by the main highway out of Egypt proper!

The fascinating history is that while the first born and heir to the throne of Thutmose III, Amenemhat and all the Egyptian firstborn were killed in Egypt on Passover; pharaoh's second born son was alive and well and was returning to Egypt by the coast highway from a battle in Syria Palestine.

> **Exodus 11:5** And all the firstborn in the land of Egypt shall die, from the **first born of Pharaoh that sitteth upon his throne,** even unto the firstborn of the maidservant that is behind the mill; and all the firstborn of beasts.

The second born son of Pharaoh Thutmose III, Amenhotep II was NOT in Egypt! He had been away putting down an insurrection in Syria and was returning to Egypt by the main highway along the Mediterranean Sea!

If Israel on leaving Egypt with a mighty Egyptian army in pursuit had met another Egyptian army coming right at them head on, they may indeed have panicked and fled.

Here is a point of interest in Egyptian history

Amenhotep II, the second son of Thutmose III was journeying back to Egypt as Israel was coming out of Egypt!

When he arrived back in Egypt he found his heritage devastated, the land destroyed, the government crushed and the main army totally destroyed.

Amenhotep II went into a fury, blaming and outlawing the religion of Amun-Ra [direct Satan worship] for the debacle, and swept through Egypt destroying the religion of Amun-Ra and killing its priests and priestesses.

The destruction of Egypt by the plagues, followed by the loss of its most powerful army and then this rage of Amenhotep II in destroying the religion of Amun-Ra, resulted in the total prostration of Egypt and the independence of its tributary peoples, including the Philistines, Canaanites, Ammon, Moab, Midian and Syria.

This Egyptian of Amun Ra would continue as a small thing and over time would reassert itself until during the time of Solomon, Solomon himself was led by his Egyptian wife into this apostasy.

Today Masonry and Kabbalah [practitioners claim that Kabbalah, a key part of modern Rabbinic Judaism, came from the angel Metraton the Lord of serpent wisdom] claim to be restorations of the "wisdom" of ancient Egypt as preserved by Solomon. This "wisdom" of Solomon was the ancient Egyptian Satan worship that Moses defeated through the power of God and for which apostasy the ten tribes were torn away from the line of David and Solomon.

Pharaoh hears that Moses killed an Egyptian

Pharaoh did hear of the matter and being a case of an Egyptian being killed in favor of an Israelite; Pharaoh had his excuse to be rid of his main potential rival for the throne of Egypt, Moses.

Moses then fled to Midian [the modern Bedouin] where he met a priest of God. Remember that Midian was descended from Abraham by Keturah and Abraham would have taught godliness to all of his children. It seems that God preserved godliness in Midian so that there would be a man of God to teach godliness to the Egyptian educated Moses.

Exodus 2:15 Now when Pharaoh heard this thing, he sought to slay Moses. But Moses fled from the face of Pharaoh, and dwelt in the land of Midian: and he sat down by a well.

Again Moses shows his passion for justice and fairness, and stands up to help the women being pushed aside by the men.

2:16 Now the priest of Midian had seven daughters: and they came and drew water, and filled the troughs to water their father's flock. **2:17** And the shepherds came and drove them away: but Moses stood up and helped them, and watered their flock.

Then the daughters of this priest of God in Midian told their father of the kindness of this "Egyptian."

2:18 And when they came to Reuel their father, he said, How is it that ye are come so soon to day? **2:19** And they said, An Egyptian delivered us out of the hand of the shepherds, and also drew water enough for us, and watered the flock.

Reuel [Jethro] then opens the hospitality of his home to Moses.

2:20 And he said unto his daughters, And where is he? why is it that ye have left the man? call him, that he may eat bread.

Moses was pleased to dwell with this man of God and to keep sheep for him; and in due course he fell for one of Reuel's daughters taking her in marriage.

2:21 And Moses was content to dwell with the man: and he gave Moses Zipporah his daughter. **2:22** And she bare him a son, and he called his name Gershom: for he said, I have been a stranger in a strange land.

Summation verse, recalling the beginning of the persecution and the subsequent cries of Israel for deliverance.

2:23 And it came to pass in process of time, that the king of Egypt died [the pharaoh who had known Joseph]: and the children of Israel sighed by reason of the bondage [of Thutmose III], and they cried, and their cry came up unto God by reason of the bondage.

God heard the cries for deliverance from Israel; and after forty years of being educated in all the wisdom of Egypt in Pharaoh's court, and then another forty years being humbled in the wilderness and educated in all that the priest of God could teach him; Moses was ready to be called of God to lead Israel out of Egypt under the leadership of the Lamb of God, the Messiah the Christ.

2:24 And God heard their groaning, and God remembered his covenant with Abraham, with Isaac, and with Jacob. **2:25** And God looked upon the children of Israel, and God had respect unto them.

God listened to the cries of Israel because the time of God's promise to Abram to deliver them was at hand.

Exodus 3

Jethro [Ruel] was a priest of God before Israel was called out of Egypt and before the Levitical priesthood was made at Sinai, and he obviously believed in the Eternal (Ex 18). How could Jethro be the priest of a strange god if he worshiped God with Moses at Sinai?

God was training Moses for his future responsibility and God led Moses to Jethro, who was a man filled with wisdom [See Exodus 18], and Jethro became very close to Moses.

Jethro sent Moses back to Egypt and he was the man who later met Moses at Sinai and offered sacrifices to God there, and who's advice Moses valued and sought even when God was speaking personally to him.

Moses takes the flocks of Jethro [Reuel] to Mount Sinai

Exodus 3:1 Now Moses kept the flock of Jethro his father in law, the priest of Midian: and he led the flock to the backside of the desert, and came to the mountain of God, even to Horeb.

Christ appears to Moses as a fire burning in a bush on Mount Sinai.

3:2 And the angel of the LORD appeared unto him in a flame of fire out of the midst of a bush: and he looked, and, behold, the bush burned with fire, and the bush was not consumed. **3:3** And Moses said, I will now turn aside, and see this great sight, why the bush is not burnt.

Moses is told to show respect, for the ground was holy because of the presence of God.

3:4 And when the LORD saw that he turned aside to see, God called unto him out of the midst of the bush, and said, Moses, Moses. And he said, Here am I. **3:5** And he said, Draw not nigh hither: put off thy shoes from off thy feet, for the place whereon thou standest is holy ground.

The Creator then identifies himself as the God of Moses' forefathers and Moses greatly feared. Without doubt Moses had been told of these things by his parents as a child and later learned more from Jethro.

God had guided Moses to the home of Jethro and there over forty years Moses would have learned all that Jethro knew.

> Later Jethro would go out to meet Moses at Mt Sinai [Horeb] after Israel had left Egypt, and Jethro was faithful in supporting Moses and giving Moses wise advice about teaching the people the Word of God.

3:6 Moreover he said, I am the God of thy father, the God of Abraham, the God of Isaac, and the God of Jacob. And Moses hid his face; for he was afraid to look upon God [that is the fire of God].

The Creator tells Moses that he has heard the cries of the people of Israel and is about to deliver them. This God who later gave up his God-hood to be made flesh as Jesus Christ, besides hearing the cries of the people was also ready to fulfill his prophecy to deliver Israel 400 years after the birth of Isaac.

3:7 And the LORD said, I have surely seen the affliction of my people which are in Egypt, and have heard their cry by reason of their taskmasters; for I know their sorrows; **3:8** And I am come down to deliver them out of the hand of the Egyptians, and to bring them up out of that land unto a good land and a large, unto a land flowing with milk and honey; unto the place of the Canaanites, and the Hittites, and the Amorites, and the Perizzites, and the Hivites, and the Jebusites. **3:9** Now therefore, behold, the cry of the children of Israel is come unto me: and I have also seen the oppression wherewith the Egyptians oppress them.

Then the Creator proposed to send Moses to act as his agent in Egypt; and of course the Creator had been working with, preparing and training Moses for this very responsibility all of his life; just like he has been working with, molding and training his called out through the millennia.

The Creator also trained up Joseph before exalting him to responsibility, as a physical example of how he trains up his called out to prepare them for spiritual responsibilities.

3:10 Come now therefore, and I will send thee unto Pharaoh, that thou mayest bring forth my people the children of Israel out of Egypt.

Moses humbly asks why he should be given such a responsibility. Moses did not try to exalt himself as very many leaders and elders do today. This Moses was an example of righteousness and humility, which to our great shame most of the ministry has not followed today.

3:11 And Moses said unto God, Who am I, that I should go unto Pharaoh, and that I should bring forth the children of Israel out of Egypt?

Moses is told that he will bring the children of Israel out of Egypt and take them to the very mount of Sinai; then Moses would fully know that God is with him.

I ask here: Who ordained Moses? Did not God ordain Moses spiritually by sending him on this mission?

Today people exalt ordination by men and close their eyes to ordination by God. People look at ordination by men, and ignore the fruits of many such men; whether they be faithful to the whole Word of God, or whether they are evil doers (Mat 7).

3:12 And he said, Certainly I will be with thee; and **this shall be a token unto thee, that I have sent thee:** When thou hast brought forth the people out of Egypt, ye shall serve God upon this mountain.

Jesus then tells Moses to say that his name is "I Am" [YHVH].

3:13 And Moses said unto God, Behold, when I come unto the children of Israel, and shall say unto them, The God of your fathers hath sent me unto you; and they shall say to me, What is his name? what shall I say unto them? **3:14** And God said unto Moses, I AM THAT I AM: and he said, Thus shalt thou say unto the children of Israel, I AM hath sent me unto you.

Moses was told to say that "I AM" was the name of the God of Abraham, even though they had not known God by that name before.

3:15 And God said moreover unto Moses, Thus shalt thou say unto the children of Israel, the LORD God of your fathers, the God of Abraham, the God of Isaac, and the God of Jacob, hath sent me unto you: this is my name for ever, and this is my memorial unto all generations.

Moses was told to present himself to the elders of Israel and to say to them that the God of their fathers had appeared to them and commanded them to leave Egypt.

3:16 Go, and gather the elders of Israel together, and say unto them, The LORD God of your fathers, the God of Abraham, of Isaac, and of Jacob, appeared unto me, saying, I have surely visited you, and seen that which is done to you in Egypt: **3:17** And I have said, I will bring you up out of the affliction of Egypt unto the land of the Canaanites, and the Hittites, and the Amorites, and the Perizzites, and the Hivites, and the Jebusites, unto a land flowing with milk and honey.

In the presence of Pharaoh, Moses is not to speak his own words but is to speak the words that God has told him to say.

3:18 And they shall hearken to thy voice: and thou shalt come, thou and the elders of Israel, unto the king of Egypt, and ye shall say unto him, The LORD God of the Hebrews hath met with us: and now let us go, we beseech thee, three days' journey into the wilderness, that we may sacrifice to the LORD our God. **3:19** And I am sure that the king of Egypt will not let you go, no, not by a mighty hand. **3:20** And I will stretch out my hand, and smite Egypt with all my wonders which I will do in the midst thereof: and after that he will let you go.

God tells Moses that he [God] will smite Egypt, and Israel will be delivered with great riches.

This is an allegory of how God will smite the wicked in the day of the Lord, and give rich rewards to his chosen at the resurrection of the faithful.

3:21 And I will give this people favour in the sight of the Egyptians: and it shall come to pass, that, when ye go, ye shall not go empty. **3:22** But every woman shall borrow of her neighbour, and of her that sojourneth in her house, jewels of silver, and jewels of gold, and raiment: and ye shall put them upon your sons, and upon your daughters; and ye shall spoil the Egyptians.

Exodus 4

God then gives Moses certain signs to convince Israel that he speaks the truth

Very soon now God will send his two servants to call spiritual Israel out of this society with mighty signs and miracles; and as in the days of the Pharisees, only a few faithful will respond.

The proud modern spiritual Pharisees called Laodiceans will not respond and will, like the ancient Pharisees, claim that God's two servants are of the devil because they do not bow to the false traditions of men.

The vast majority in today's Ekklesia will not respond positively to the warnings of God and will fall into great tribulation. Then in much tribulation they will remember that they had been warned by a merciful God.

Exodus 4:1 And Moses answered and said, But, behold, they will not believe me, nor hearken unto my voice: for they will say, The LORD hath not appeared unto thee.

Moses is given awesome signs to convince Israel of his calling.

4:2 And the LORD said unto him, What is that in thine hand? And he said, A rod. **4:3** And he said, Cast it on the ground. And he cast it on the ground, and it became a serpent; and Moses fled from before it. **4:4** And the LORD said unto Moses, Put forth thine hand, and take it by the tail. And he put forth his hand, and caught it, and it became a rod in his hand: **4:5** That they may believe that the LORD God of their fathers, the God of Abraham, the God of Isaac, and the God of Jacob, hath appeared unto thee.

A second sign

4:6 And the LORD said furthermore unto him, Put now thine hand into thy bosom. And he put his hand into his bosom: and when he took it out, behold, his hand was leprous as snow. **4:7** And he said, Put thine hand into thy bosom again. And he put his hand into his bosom again; and plucked it out of his bosom, and, behold, it was turned again as his other flesh. **4:8** And it shall come to pass, if they will not believe thee, neither hearken to the voice of the first sign, that they will believe the voice of the latter sign.

The third sign

4:9 And it shall come to pass, if they will not believe also these two signs, neither hearken unto thy voice, that thou shalt take of the water of the river, and pour it upon the dry land: and the water which thou takest out of the river shall become blood upon the dry land.

Moses points out that he is not eloquent to speak.

4:10 And Moses said unto the LORD, O my LORD, I am not eloquent, neither heretofore, nor since thou hast spoken unto thy servant: but I am slow of speech, and of a slow tongue.

God then promises to give Moses the words that he must say, and God promises us that he will also put his words in our mouths when we are rejected by the assemblies and and later before civil judges, because of our Christ-like zeal to live by the righteousness of the whole Word of God.

> **Matthew 10:17** But beware of men: for they will deliver you up to the councils, and they will scourge you in their synagogues; **10:18** And ye shall be brought before governors and kings for my sake, for a testimony against them and the Gentiles. **10:19** But when they deliver you up, take no thought how or what ye shall speak: for it shall be given you in that same hour what ye shall speak.

Exodus 4:11 And the LORD said unto him, Who hath made man's mouth? or who maketh the dumb, or deaf, or the seeing, or the blind? have not I the LORD? **4:12** Now therefore go, and I will be with thy mouth, and teach thee what thou shalt say.

Jesus Christ rebukes this apparent lack of willingness to serve and informs Moses that Aaron is already on his way to meet him.

4:13 And he said, O my LORD, send, I pray thee, by the hand of him whom thou wilt send. **4:14** And the anger of the LORD was kindled against Moses, and he said, Is not Aaron the Levite thy brother? I know that he can speak well. And also, **behold, he cometh forth to meet thee: and when he seeth thee, he will be glad in his heart.**

God will tell Moses what to say and then Moses will tell Aaron what to say.

In this historical allegory, Moses is the mediator of the Mosaic Covenant and a type of Jesus Christ the Mediator of the New Covenant.

Aaron as the physical high priest [beginning at Sinai] is also an allegory of Jesus Christ our spiritual High Priest. Therefore it is appropriate that both Moses and Aaron [as intended by YHVH from the beginning], as types of Christ, speak to Pharaoh the type of the god-king enslaving this world.

4:15 And thou shalt speak unto him, and put words in his mouth: and I will be with thy mouth, and with his mouth, and will teach you what ye shall do. **4:16** And he shall be thy spokesman unto the people: and he shall be, even he shall be to thee instead of a mouth, and thou shalt be to him instead of God.

Moses is to take the rod with him.

4:17 And thou shalt take this rod in thine hand, wherewith thou shalt do signs.

Moses then asks his father in law for his approval to return to Egypt. Clearly this is a limited report of the conversation and Moses must have been bursting to tell of his experience and the burning bush. Yet Jethro believed and did nothing to try to dissuade Moses but simply said: GO! Yes, Jethro was a man of God!

4:18 And Moses went and returned to Jethro his father in law, and said unto him, Let me go, I pray thee, and return unto my brethren which are in Egypt, and see whether they be yet alive. And Jethro said to Moses, Go in peace.

God then tells Moses that the men who sought to kill him in Egypt were dead, and bids him return to Egypt. So Moses takes his wife and two sons and the rod of God and starts out on his journey.

4:19 And the LORD said unto Moses in Midian, Go, return into Egypt: for all the men are dead which sought thy life.

The relatives and avengers of the dead Egyptian would have died and pharaoh himself would have forgotten Moses after forty years of war and empire building.

4:20 And Moses took his wife and his sons, and set them upon an ass, and he returned to the land of Egypt: and Moses took the rod of God in his hand.

God tells Moses that he [God] will harden Pharaoh's heart that God might show forth God's power on Egypt.

4:21 And the LORD said unto Moses, When thou goest to return into Egypt, see that thou do all those wonders before Pharaoh, which I have put in thine hand: but I will harden his heart, that he shall not let the people go.

Here even at the beginning, God says that he plans to institute Passover and slay the first born of Egypt.

4:22 And thou shalt say unto Pharaoh, Thus saith the LORD, Israel is my son, even my firstborn: **4:23** And I say unto thee, Let my son go, that he may serve me: and if thou refuse to let him go, behold, **I will slay thy son, even thy firstborn** [Yes, the first born son of pharaoh died in Egypt on Passover].

Then Christ appears to Moses and would have slain the family because of their uncircumcision.

Perhaps at this time Moses sent his wife and sons back to Jethro, because later they went to Moses at Sinai:

> **Exodus 18:2** Then Jethro, Moses' father in law, took Zipporah, Moses' wife, after he had sent her back, **18:3** And her two sons;

Exodus 4:24 And it came to pass by the way in the inn, that the LORD met him, and sought to kill him. **4:25** Then Zipporah took a sharp stone, and cut off the foreskin of her son, and cast it at his feet, and said, Surely a bloody husband art thou to me. **4:26** So he let him go: then she said, A bloody husband thou art, because of the circumcision.

God then told Aaron where to meet Moses.

4:27 And the LORD said to Aaron, Go into the wilderness to meet Moses. And he went, and met him in the mount of God [Sinai, Horeb], and kissed him.

Moses then told Aaron all the words of God and Aaron took Moses to meet the elders of Israel.

4:28 And Moses told Aaron all the words of the LORD who had sent him, and all the signs which he had commanded him. **4:29** And Moses and Aaron went and gathered together all the elders of the children of Israel: **4:30** And Aaron spake all the words which the LORD had spoken unto Moses, and did the signs in the sight of the people.

The people believed for they were desperate for deliverance from the burden of Egypt, which is a type of our bondage to Sin.

Sadly today the called out people do not want deliverance from their sins; instead they are lustful after the pleasures of sin, and love their idols of men, false traditions and corporate entities above any zeal for the Word of God; and they will reject the warnings of God.

4:31 And the people believed: and when they heard that the LORD had visited the children of Israel, and that he had looked upon their affliction, then they bowed their heads and worshipped.

Exodus 5

After Aaron had introduced Moses to the elders and they had been convinced of the mission of Moses, Moses went to the court of Pharaoh.

One might ask in our day: Will God send his two servants to the elders of the Ekklesia first before sending them to the worldly? I would not be surprised; in fact I would be very surprised if God's two servants did not go to the leaders of the Ekklesia first, at the appointed time

Exodus 5:1 And afterward Moses and Aaron went in, and told Pharaoh, Thus saith the LORD God of Israel, Let my people go, that they may hold a feast unto me in the wilderness.

Pharaoh then asked: Who is this God?

5:2 And Pharaoh said, Who is the LORD, that I should obey his voice to let Israel go? I know not the LORD, neither will I let Israel go.

Aaron and Moses then identified the God of the Hebrews and repeated their request.

5:3 And they said, The God of the Hebrews hath met with us: let us go, we pray thee, three days' journey into the desert, and sacrifice unto the LORD our God; lest he fall upon us with pestilence, or with the sword.

Pharaoh then reprimands Aaron and Moses for turning the people from their labors.

5:4 And the king of Egypt said unto them, Wherefore do ye, Moses and Aaron, let the people from their works? get you unto your burdens. **5:5** And Pharaoh said, Behold, the people of the land now are many, and ye make them rest from their burdens.

Pharaoh them increases the burdens on the people.

Spiritually when people are called out of this world's bondage to sin, the pharaoh god-king of this world also persecutes and burdens us to discourage us from seeking freedom from his bondage.

The Word of God is easy and the burden of godliness is light; it is the burden that the pharaoh god king of this world [Satan] places upon us for our zeal for freedom from bondage to him that afflicts us. Yet if we continue in learning and living by every Word of God with passionate enthusiasm; our Mighty One will deliver us just as he delivered Israel from Pharaoh!

Just like Jesus Christ raised his called out of bondage in physical Egypt and from the Red Sea of death, at the end of the sixth day of the Feast of Unleavened Bread, raising physical Israel up to the seventh day of rejoicing: Jesus Christ will resurrect his chosen called out of spiritual Israel at the end of six thousand years, to a millennial Sabbath of rest for all humanity!

> **Matthew 11:28** Come unto me, all ye that labour and are heavy laden, and I will give you rest. **11:29** Take my yoke upon you, and learn of me; for I am meek and lowly in heart: and ye shall find rest unto your souls. **11:30** For my yoke is easy, and my burden is light.

Exodus 5:6 And Pharaoh commanded the same day the taskmasters of the people, and their officers, saying, **5:7** Ye shall no more give the people straw to make brick, as heretofore: let them go and gather straw for themselves. **5:8** And the tale of the bricks, which they did make heretofore, ye shall lay upon them; ye shall not diminish ought thereof: for they be idle; therefore they cry, saying, Let us go and sacrifice to our God.

God's words of deliverance are NOT vain; our Mighty One will perform all his promises to his faithful. It is the words and actions of Satan and his minions that are vain, they shall not profit, but will bring destruction on all who chose to reject God's deliverance from the bondage of sin.

5:9 Let there more work be laid upon the men, that they may labour therein; and let them not regard vain words. **5:10** And the taskmasters of the people went out, and their officers, and they spake to the people, saying, Thus saith Pharaoh, I will not give you straw. **5:11** Go ye, get you straw where ye can find it: yet not ought of your work shall be diminished. **5:12** So the people were scattered abroad throughout all the land of Egypt to gather stubble instead of straw. **5:13** And the taskmasters hasted them, saying, Fulfil your works, your daily tasks, as when there was straw.

Then Israel complained to Moses that they were not delivered and that their burdens were increased.

When we are burdened with temptations to remain in sin, or burdened by persecutions and trials designed to make us turn aside from the Word of God: We must redouble and redouble again our dedication to learn and to fully live by every Word of God! We must RUN to our Deliverer and ask him to help us to learn whatever he is teaching us by the situation, we must ask for faith and courage to take a stand for the Word of God. We must ask for the courage of Daniel and his three friends and acquit ourselves like people of God Almighty!

Whether we live or die in the flesh is of no consequence if we lose our eternal life! Nothing physical matters whatsoever in comparison to being like our Father for all eternity!

> **Matthew 16:26** For what is a man profited, if he shall gain the whole world, and lose his own soul [spirit, eternal life]? or what shall a man give in exchange for his soul [spirit, eternal life]?

Exodus 5:14 And the officers of the children of Israel, which Pharaoh's taskmasters had set over them, were beaten, and demanded, Wherefore have ye not fulfilled your task in making brick both yesterday and to day, as heretofore? **5:15** Then the officers of the children of Israel came and cried unto Pharaoh, saying, Wherefore dealest thou thus with thy servants? **5:16** There is no straw given unto thy servants, and they say to us, Make brick: and, behold, thy servants are beaten; but the fault is in thine own people.

When we seek to worship and obey God, the enemy attacks and burdens us.

We need to understand that our trials, temptations and afflictions are not from obeying God; they come from our own errors and from Satan to discourage us in following and keeping every Word of God.

5:17 But he said, Ye are idle, ye are idle: therefore ye say, Let us go and do sacrifice to the LORD. **5:18** Go therefore now, and work; for there shall no straw be given you, yet shall ye deliver the tale of bricks.**5:19** And the officers of the children of Israel did see that they were in evil case, after it was said, Ye shall not minish ought from your bricks of your daily task.

Now Israel falls for a satanic lie common throughout history, and blames the Word of God for all their troubles; instead of placing the blame on Pharaoh [a type of Satan] where it belongs.

When facing trials physical Israel always blamed God instead of placing the blame on Satan and on their own sinfulness where it belonged.

5:20 And they met Moses and Aaron, who stood in the way, as they came forth from Pharaoh: **5:21** And they said unto them, The LORD look upon you, and judge; because ye have made our savour [we stink in pharaoh's nose] to be abhorred in the eyes of Pharaoh, and in the eyes of his servants, to put a sword in their hand to slay us.

Even Moses begins to blame God and must still learn the lesson that God is good and it is the sins of the people and the attacks of Satan that are to be blamed for our afflictions. That said, it is also true that God allows us to experience trials for our own good, to mature us into the people he wants us to be.

In this case God did harden Pharaoh in order to fulfill his purpose of teaching us these lessons. The lesson of Job is that God is far wiser than man, and we should not question his actions; but should trust in him and understand that what he does is for our long term good.

5:22 And Moses returned unto the LORD, and said, LORD, wherefore hast thou so evil entreated this people? why is it that thou hast sent me? **5:23** For since I came to Pharaoh to speak in thy name, he hath done evil to this people; neither hast thou delivered thy people at all.

We need to break out of our tradition of idolizing men, we need to stop idolizing the heroes of scripture. They were only men like ourselves, their greatness was not their own, but their enormous trust and faith and fidelity to the Word of God made them great.

This man worship has been deeply ingrained in us by our leaders, and it needs to be totally rooted out.

The Being who became flesh as Jesus Christ gave up his God-hood to become flesh, and while in the flesh clearly taught that no man in the flesh is good, only God is good.

Moses was probably the closest to godly goodness of anyone except Christ himself, but that is because of Moses's willingness to learn and to keep the whole Word of God.

Moses was flesh as we are flesh, and Moses had to learn, just as we must continually learn and grow. Jesus himself learned as he suffered and we must also learn through suffering.

> **Hebrews 5:8** Though he were a Son, yet learned he obedience by the things which he suffered;

While in the flesh we are all unfinished products; let us not idolize any man, no not our elders or leaders, and no not even the champions in scripture; rather let us work to become overcomers of sin with God as they were, so that we might attain as they did.

> **Matthew 19:17** And he said unto him, Why callest thou me good? there is none good but one, that is, God: but if thou wilt enter into life, keep the commandments.

Exodus 6

Moses and Aaron visited the elders of Israel and told them of their mission, and then they went to pharaoh who refused to let the people go and increased their burdens. Israel then complained to Moses and God told Moses to stand fast in his mission and go before pharaoh again.

The Egyptians had a pantheistic religion and believed that all physical things had a little bit of God in them. That being the case they worshiped the creation in place of the Creator.

With Amun-Ra as the sun and chief god, all other things from cats to crocodiles, from dung beetles to the bull god Apis were worshipped as gods.

The sin of Aaron and Israel and later of Jeroboam in setting up golden calves as gods, came from the Egyptian worship of Apis the bull god.

The superstitious Egyptian common folk literally worshipped these physical things, while the high level initiates understood that these things were only symbols of spirit entities.

The sun god Ra was a symbol of Lucifer [Satan] called Apollo, Saturn or Baal in other languages.

From this point on every sign and every plague given in Egypt, used the gods of Egypt themselves either to afflict the Egyptians by their own gods, or to demonstrate the power of the Eternal over all other gods.

Then God said, stand back and see what I shall do to Pharaoh, for God had hardened Pharaoh's heart that God might show forth his power as the Deliverer of physical and spiritual Israel!

This was for us as well as those people, so that we might know the power of our Mighty God and always be zealous and faithful to his Word in the flesh and in the spirit.

Exodus 6:1 Then the LORD said unto Moses, Now shalt thou see what I will do to Pharaoh: for with a strong hand shall he let them go, and with a strong hand shall he drive them out of his land.

Then Messiah the Christ informed Moses that he would keep his promises to their fore-bearer Abram and deliver them out of Egypt on schedule exactly 430 years after his promise to Abraham in Ur.

Even so the Mighty God whose dwelling is eternity; will keep his promises to the spiritually called out of bondage to sin; and he will come to resurrect God's faithful at the appointed time!

If we follow HIM faithfully and live by EVERY Word of God always, we will enter be resurrected from death to enter the spiritual Promised Land of eternal life!

The Eternal IS God Almighty and beside him there are NO other gods!

6:2 And God spake unto Moses, and said unto him, I am the LORD: **6:3** And I appeared unto Abraham, unto Isaac, and unto Jacob, by the name of God Almighty, but by my name JEHOVAH [YHVH] was I not known to them. **6:4** And I have also established my covenant with them, to give them the land of Canaan, the land of their pilgrimage, wherein they were strangers. **6:5** And I have also heard the groaning of the children of Israel, whom the Egyptians keep in bondage; and I have remembered my covenant.

Today the whole earth groans under the bondage of Satan and sin; soon God will deliver his spiritually called out and after that he will deliver the whole earth from Satan the god-king Pharaoh who holds this world in bondage!

Our Deliverer will keep his promises and deliver his faithful of spiritual Israel into the Promised Land of eternal life and all good things. Then Christ will also deliver all humanity, grafting then into spiritual Israel his collective bride!

Just as physical Israel had God's promise of deliverance from bondage in Egypt; God has given mankind a promise of deliverance from Satan and sin!

6:6 Wherefore say unto the children of Israel, I am the LORD, and I will bring you out from under the burdens of the Egyptians, and I will rid you out of their bondage, and I will redeem you with a stretched out arm, and with great judgments: **6:7** And I will take you to me for a people, and I will be to you a God: and ye shall know that I am the LORD your God, which bringeth you out from under the burdens of the Egyptians [a type of deliverance from bondage to sin and Satan]. **6:8** And I will bring you in unto the land, concerning the which I did swear to give it to Abraham, to Isaac, and to Jacob; and I will give it you for an heritage: I am the LORD.

The people could not believe because they focused on the cruelty of their bondage; even so many of us lose faith in the midst of afflictions in this life.

It is very hard to think of a wonderful future when we are faced with present distress. Yet to overcome the present distress, we must remain focused on the end result of our calling, and on the power of our God to deliver us in his own good time!

As our Great God made an example of Pharaoh in Egypt; in these last days he is making an example of his power to accomplish his purposes against Satan.

Messiah the Christ will come to resurrect his chosen and then he will return with his collective bride in great power and glory to bring the millennial Sabbath of rest and freedom from the burden of sin to this world!

6:9 And Moses spake so unto the children of Israel: but they hearkened not unto Moses for anguish of spirit, and for cruel bondage.

Then God sent Moses to speak unto Pharaoh again

6:10 And the LORD spake unto Moses, saying, **6:11** Go in, speak unto Pharaoh king of Egypt, that he let the children of Israel go out of his land.

Moses discouraged, asked the one who later gave up his God-hood to be made flesh as Jesus Christ: "What is the point of going back to Pharaoh?"

6:12 And Moses spake before the LORD, saying, Behold, the children of Israel have not hearkened unto me; how then shall Pharaoh hear me, who am of uncircumcised lips?

God commissioned Aaron and Moses with the responsibility to bring Israel out of Egypt.

It is so easy to get discouraged and to have a crisis of faith when we focus on the present distress and do not focus on the power of our Mighty God. Even Moses got discouraged many times, but nevertheless God kept all of his promises and demonstrated his mighty power to deliver his people if they will only trust him and keep his Word.

Brethren, these things were recorded for us so that in times of trials we would not be discouraged; but remember these things and have faith in the Word, promises and power of our God to raise us up from the pit to the birthright of our calling; which is eternal life if we faint not in following our Mighty One!

6:13 And the LORD spake unto Moses and unto Aaron, and gave them a charge unto the children of Israel, and unto Pharaoh king of Egypt, to bring the children of Israel out of the land of Egypt.

Exodus 7

An important thing to observe is that Moses and Aaron did not decide for themselves what to say to Pharaoh or what to do in Egypt. Instead they said what God had told them to say and proclaimed the plagues that God had commanded them to warn that God would bring. This was not about Moses, but was about revealing God and his power to Israel and Egypt and all the nations of that time.

The serpent was a symbol of the god Amun-Ra and God showed that he had power over the serpent god Amun-Ra

Exodus 7:1 And the LORD said unto Moses, See, I have made thee a god to Pharaoh: and Aaron thy brother shall be thy prophet. **7:2** Thou shalt speak all that I command thee: and Aaron thy brother shall speak unto Pharaoh, that he send the children of Israel out of his land.

The One who became Messiah explained that Pharaoh will not let the people go until he, YHVH, has made his power and glory known.

In the same way at this end time, the power and glory of Messiah will be made known by God's two prophets and all His mighty works at His coming.

Just as God delivered his called out bride from bondage to sin with many mighty deeds in physical Egypt: He will also deliver his spiritual Bride from bondage to sin and raise up his faithful chosen to be a part of his collective spiritual Bride on that day.

7:3 And I will harden Pharaoh's heart, and multiply my signs and my wonders in the land of Egypt. **7:4** But Pharaoh shall not hearken unto you, that I may lay my hand upon Egypt, and bring forth mine armies, and my people the children of Israel, out of the land of Egypt by great judgments.

The Egyptians were made to fear God in ancient times and all of the world will be made to know God at the coming of Messiah the Christ.

7:5 And **the Egyptians shall know that I am the LORD**, when I stretch forth mine hand upon Egypt, and bring out the children of Israel from among them.

Moses and Aaron now knew the purpose of God and the reason for the actions of Christ in hardening Pharaoh's heart, and the mighty miracles that Messiah would perform for Israel.

We of spiritual Israel should also begin to understand the reason for the trials and afflictions in our lives; which is to bring us toward the perfection of our Father!

7:6 And Moses and Aaron did as the LORD commanded them, so did they. **7:7** And Moses was fourscore [80] years old, and Aaron fourscore and three [83] years old, when they spake unto Pharaoh.

Christ commands Moses and Aaron to visit Pharaoh and to show him the first miracle that was shown to the elders of Israel.

7:8 And the LORD spake unto Moses and unto Aaron, saying, **7:9** When Pharaoh shall speak unto you, saying, Shew a miracle for you: then thou shalt say unto Aaron, **Take thy rod, and cast it before Pharaoh, and it shall become a serpent.**

The wise men [priests of Amun] of Egypt duplicated this miracle by the power of Amun [Satan] whom they worshiped.

Here we have a short duel between the miracle workers of Egypt and the servants of God, between Amun [Satan] and the Eternal.

7:10 And Moses and Aaron went in unto Pharaoh, and they did so as the LORD had commanded: and Aaron cast down his rod before Pharaoh, and before his servants, and it became a serpent. **7:11** Then Pharaoh also called the wise men and the sorcerers: now the magicians of Egypt, they also did in like manner with their enchantments. **7:12** For they cast down every man his rod, and they became serpents: **but Aaron's rod swallowed up their rods. 7:13** And he hardened Pharaoh's heart, that he hearkened not unto them; as the LORD had said.

Pharaoh saw the miracles of his own people and maybe thought that the God of Moses and Aaron was not greater than his god Amun-Ra.

7:14 And the LORD said unto Moses, Pharaoh's heart is hardened, he refuseth to let the people go.

Then God sent Moses and Aaron to meet Pharaoh at the riverside to turn the water into blood to show the power of God, but the magicians of Egypt [Satan] were again able to duplicate the miracle.

7:15 Get thee unto Pharaoh in the morning; lo, he goeth out unto the water; and thou shalt stand by the river's brink against he come; and the rod which was turned to a serpent shalt thou take in thine hand.

Moses and Aaron are then told by the One who later gave up his God-hood to become flesh and die like a Lamb for his creation, to speak against the Nile River [which was worshiped as the goddess Anuket] unto Pharaoh.

7:16 And thou shalt say unto him, The LORD God of the Hebrews hath sent me unto thee, saying, Let my people go, that they may serve me in the wilderness: and, behold, hitherto thou wouldest not hear. **7:17** Thus saith the LORD, In this thou shalt know that I am the LORD: behold, I will smite with the rod that is in mine hand upon the waters which are in the river, and they shall be turned to blood. **7:18** And the fish that is in the river shall die, and the river shall stink; and the Egyptians shall lothe to drink of the water of the river.

After Moses and Aaron had thus addressed the god-king of Egypt; the God who became Messiah the Christ commanded them to lift up the rod against the Nile and all its tributaries and streams in the delta.

7:19 And the LORD spake unto Moses, Say unto Aaron, Take thy rod, and stretch out thine hand upon the waters of Egypt, upon their streams, upon their rivers, and upon their ponds, and upon all their pools of water, that they may become blood; and that there may be blood throughout all the land of Egypt, both in vessels of wood, and in vessels of stone.

They obeyed the spiritual Lamb of God, and all was fulfilled as Messiah had declared.

7:20 And Moses and Aaron did so, as the LORD commanded; and he lifted up the rod, and smote the waters that were in the river, in the sight of Pharaoh, and in the sight of his servants; and all the waters that were in the river were turned to blood. **7:21** And the fish that was in the river died; and the river stank, and the Egyptians could not drink of the water of the river; and there was blood throughout all the land of Egypt.

Then the Egyptian magicians turned pots of well water into blood.

7:22 And the magicians of Egypt did so with their enchantments: and Pharaoh's heart was hardened, neither did he hearken unto them; as the LORD had said. **7:23** And Pharaoh turned and went into his house, neither did he set his heart to this also.

The river was like blood for seven days, and the Egyptians dug wells for water.

7:24 And all the Egyptians digged round about the river for water to drink; for they could not drink of the water of the river. **7:25** And seven days were fulfilled, after that the LORD had smitten the river.

Exodus 8

After seven days God commanded Moses and Aaron to go to Pharaoh and ask him to let the people of Israel go; and if he refused God would bring a curse of frogs across Egypt. The frog being a goddess of Egypt, would be used to afflict the Egyptians.

Hequet was the frog goddess of childbirth of the Egyptians and it was only appropriate that frogs were summoned to afflict the Egyptians, after they had sought to cast the sons of Israel into the Nile to drown as offerings to this god.

Exodus 8:1 And the LORD spake unto Moses, Go unto Pharaoh, and say unto him, Thus saith the LORD, Let my people go, that they may serve me. **8:2** And if thou refuse to let them go, behold, I will smite all thy borders with frogs: **8:3** And the river shall bring forth frogs abundantly, which shall go up and come into thine house, and into thy bedchamber, and upon thy bed, and into the house of thy servants, and upon thy people, and into thine ovens, and into thy kneadingtroughs: **8:4** And the frogs shall come up both on thee, and upon thy people, and upon all thy servants.

Then Messiah the Christ commanded Moses and Aaron to stretch out the rod and bring the curse of frogs on the nation.

8:5 And the LORD spake unto Moses, Say unto Aaron, Stretch forth thine hand with thy rod over the streams, over the rivers, and over the ponds, and cause frogs to come up upon the land of Egypt. **8:6** And Aaron stretched out his hand over the waters of Egypt; and the frogs came up, and covered the land of Egypt.

The Egyptian magicians then replicated the miracle.

8:7 And the magicians did so with their enchantments, and brought up frogs upon the land of Egypt.

Then Pharaoh begged Moses to remove the frogs, and Moses perhaps believing Pharaoh rejoiced.

8:8 Then Pharaoh called for Moses and Aaron, and said, Intreat the LORD, that he may take away the frogs from me, and from my people; and **I will let the people go, that they may do sacrifice unto the LORD. 8:9** And Moses said unto Pharaoh, Glory over me: when shall I intreat for thee, and for thy servants, and for thy people, to destroy the frogs from thee and thy houses, that they may remain in the river only? **8:10** And he said, To morrow. And he said, Be it according to thy word: that thou mayest know that there is none like unto the LORD our God. **8:11** And the frogs shall depart from thee, and from thy houses, and from thy servants, and from thy people; they shall remain in the river only.

Moses then asked God to take away the frogs from Egypt and the One who became Christ heard and fulfilled the matter.

8:12 And Moses and Aaron went out from Pharaoh: and Moses cried unto the LORD because of the frogs which he had brought against Pharaoh. **8:13** And the LORD did according to the word of Moses; and the frogs died out of the houses, out of the villages, and out of the fields.

Christ caused all the frogs to die out and they were gathered by the people out of their houses into stinking heaps so the people could see the truth about their god of child birth.

8:14 And they gathered them together upon heaps: and the land stank.

Pharaoh then went back on his word

8:15 But when Pharaoh saw that there was respite, he hardened his heart, and hearkened not unto them; as the LORD had said.

Then the one who became Jesus Christ brought up a plague of lice out of the dust of the land.

The word "lice" is rendered as "sand flies" or "fleas" in some translations. The Hebrew word "kinnim" comes from a root word meaning "to dig"; it is probable that the insect in question would burrow under the skin.

This plague would have been an embarrassment to Geb, the Egyptian god of the earth. Egyptians gave offerings to Geb for the bounty of the soil -- yet it was from "the dust of the soil" that this plague originated.

8:16 And the LORD said unto Moses, Say unto Aaron, Stretch out thy rod, and smite the dust of the land, that it may become lice throughout all the land of Egypt. **8:17** And they did so; for Aaron stretched out his hand with his rod, and smote the dust of the earth, and it became lice in man, and in beast; all the dust of the land became lice throughout all the land of Egypt.

The priests and enchanters of Egypt could not replicate this miracle.

8:18 And the magicians did so with their enchantments to bring forth lice, but they could not: so there were lice upon man, and upon beast.

The magicians then openly told Pharaoh that this could not be duplicated because it was from God the Eternal.

8:19 Then the magicians said unto Pharaoh, This is the finger of God: and Pharaoh's heart was hardened, and he hearkened not unto them; as the LORD had said.

The Messiah, our physical and spiritual Deliverer, then commanded Moses to again call on Pharaoh to let his people go; and if he will not, then swarms shall fill the land.

The word fly is not in the text but is the conjecture of the translators. The swarms could be mosquitoes, biting flies or even hornets.

We must be careful not to let the translation mislead us into thinking of the common house fly here. These Egyptian swarms were not a mere nuisance, but were most likely stinging insects or biting mosquitoes and flies like the deer, horse and black flies in the North American wilderness and the biting flies of Africa. This was a very real and terrible plague.

The "swarms" in this passage could have also been swarms of the scarab beetle, the Egyptian god Khepri.

The scarab was actually a dung beetle -- an insect that feeds on the dung in the fields. The plague of swarms of scarabs, with mandibles that can saw through wood, would be terrible and the scarab was another god of Egypt!

8:20 And the LORD said unto Moses, Rise up early in the morning, and stand before Pharaoh; lo, he cometh forth to the water; and say unto him, Thus saith the LORD, Let my people go, that they may serve me. **8:21** Else, if thou wilt not let my people go, behold, I will send swarms of flies upon thee, and upon thy servants, and upon thy people, and into thy houses: and the houses of the Egyptians shall be full of swarms of flies, and also the ground whereon they are.

God separates out Goshen from Egypt in terms of this curse.

8:22 And I will sever in that day the land of Goshen, in which my people dwell, that no swarms of flies shall be there; to the end thou mayest know that I am the LORD in the midst of the earth.

In this end time Christ is dividing his faithful from the lukewarm, so that God may deliver his faithful from the strong correction to come upon the lukewarm.

8:23 And I will put a division between my people and thy people: to morrow shall this sign be.

Then the land of Egypt was overwhelmed by vast swarms of biting stinging flying insects, from which there was no escape.

Such swarms have been known to drive animals and men mad in the wilderness, often the only relief being to dive under water or to coat themselves with thick mud. If you have no experience with this, just imagine yourself continually swarmed by thousands of hungry mosquitoes even inside your home.

8:24 And the LORD did so; and there came a grievous swarm of flies into the house of Pharaoh, and into his servants' houses, and into all the land of Egypt: the land was corrupted by reason of the swarm of flies.

Pharaoh then seeks a compromise and tells Moses to sacrifice within Egypt.

8:25 And Pharaoh called for Moses and for Aaron, and said, Go ye, sacrifice to your God in the land.

Moses rejects this offer of Pharaoh to sacrifice to God within Egypt. God's people must come OUT of Egypt, as an allegory that we MUST come OUT of sin and spiritual Egypt to meet the Eternal.

8:26 And Moses said, It is not meet so to do; for we shall sacrifice the abomination of the Egyptians to the LORD our God: lo, shall we sacrifice the abomination of the Egyptians before their eyes, and will they not stone us? **8:27** We will go three days' journey into the wilderness, and sacrifice to the LORD our God, as he shall command us.

Then Pharaoh gives in temporarily

8:28 And Pharaoh said, I will let you go, that ye may sacrifice to the LORD your God in the wilderness; only ye shall not go very far away: intreat for me.

Moses then agrees to ask the one who later gave up his Godhood to become Jesus Christ to remove the flies but warns Pharaoh not to change his word this time.

8:29 And Moses said, Behold, I go out from thee, and I will intreat the LORD that the swarms of flies may depart from Pharaoh, from his servants, and from his people, to morrow: but **let not Pharaoh deal deceitfully any more in not letting the people go to sacrifice to the LORD.**

8:30 And Moses went out from Pharaoh, and intreated the LORD. **8:31** And the LORD did according to the word of Moses; and he removed the swarms of flies from Pharaoh, from his servants, and from his people; there remained not one.

The Pharaoh changed his mind and would not let the people go.

8:32 And Pharaoh hardened his heart at this time also, neither would he let the people go.

Exodus 9

The Egyptians worshiped the creation and these plagues on Egypt were designed to show the absolute power of God over all the gods of Egypt, and that these gods were not really gods at all: The Eternal has absolute power over his creation and that includes Satan today.

Exodus 9:1 Then the LORD said unto Moses, Go in unto Pharaoh, and tell him, Thus saith the LORD God of the Hebrews, Let my people go, that they may serve me.

Murrain is not some specific disease but means: Heb. deber, "destruction," a "great dying," which was the fifth plague that fell upon the Egyptians.

The cow goddess Hathor was the symbolic mother of Pharaoh while the bull god Apis was worshiped throughout the land. Remember Aaron's and later Jeroboam's golden calves.

9:2 For if thou refuse to let them go, and wilt hold them still, **9:3** Behold, the hand of the LORD is upon thy cattle which is in the field, upon the horses, upon the asses, upon the camels, upon the oxen, and upon the sheep: there shall be a very grievous murrain [dying].

Many of the flocks and herds of lesser [sheep and goats] cattle and greater [beeves] cattle of Egypt died, but the lesser and greater cattle of Israel remained alive.

9:4 And the LORD shall sever between the cattle of Israel and the cattle of Egypt: and there shall nothing die of all that is the children's of Israel. **9:5** And the LORD appointed a set time, saying, To morrow the LORD shall do this thing in the land.

The plague killed the lesser and greater cattle of Egypt as the Eternal had said, but in Israel none died. This would have been a disaster for Egypt because not only were these animals good for food but they were used to plough the fields for planting the grain.

The loss of working cattle would have reduced the farmers to digging with mattocks reducing the harvest greatly for many years.

9:6 And the LORD did that thing on the morrow, and all the cattle of Egypt died: but of the cattle of the children of Israel died not one. **9:7** And Pharaoh sent, and, behold, there was not one of the cattle of the Israelites dead. And the heart of Pharaoh was hardened, and he did not let the people go.

This was about the god of medicine Imhotep who could not heal the priests or the people.

9:8 And the LORD said unto Moses and unto Aaron, Take to you handfuls of ashes of the furnace, and let Moses sprinkle it toward the heaven in the sight of Pharaoh. **9:9** And it shall become small dust in all the land of Egypt, and shall be a boil breaking forth with blains upon man, and upon beast, throughout all the land of Egypt.

Encyclopedia – International Standard Bible Encyclopedia – Blains

> **BLAINS**
>
> blanz (abha`bu`ah: only in **Exodus 9:9,10**): Pustules containing fluid around a boil or inflamed sore. It is an Old English word "bleyen," used sometimes as a synonym for boil. Wyclif (1382) uses the expression "stinkende bleyne" for Job's sores. The Hebrew word is from a root which means that which bubbles up.

Painful boils filled with leaking pus spread to people and beasts in Egypt and afflicted the magicians so that they were brought low just like Job had been.

9:10 And they took ashes of the furnace, and stood before Pharaoh; and Moses sprinkled it up toward heaven; and it became a boil breaking forth with blains upon man, and upon beast. **9:11** And the magicians could not stand before Moses because of the boils; for the boil was upon the magicians, and upon all the Egyptians.

It was the Eternal who had hardened the heart of Pharaoh so that God might make an example of him for our instruction.

The Eternal loves the physical bride that was called out of physical Egypt whom he married at Sinai; and he loves the collective spiritual Bride that God the Father has called out for HIM!

As the Eternal destroyed Egypt and delivered physical Israel out of bondage; he will also fight for and deliver spiritual Israel out from the bondage of sin with mighty deeds.

We need not fear what this world can do, neither should we hesitate to fully follow our Deliverer OUT of the bondage of sin; for he will deliver the faithful of spiritual Israel out of the pit of death as he delivered physical Israel out of the Red Sea of death.

Our espoused Husband is Mighty, he is Holy, he is Righteous in all his ways; let us follow him and God the Father forever!

9:12 And the LORD hardened the heart of Pharaoh, and he hearkened not unto them; as the LORD had spoken unto Moses.

Now the Eternal brings a plague of great hail upon the land, yet he warns all who would listen that if they and their animals take shelter they shall live; the plague will only kill all who reject the warnings and remain out in the fields.

All of these plagues are to teach the Egyptians AND physical Israel, AND the called of spiritual Israel; that the Eternal God the Father and God the Son are God indeed and there is NO OTHER god besides the mighty God family.

It seems strange to say it, but we of the called out of spiritual Israel have forgotten any zeal for our Deliverer and have idolized men.

9:13 And the LORD said unto Moses, Rise up early in the morning, and stand before Pharaoh, and say unto him, Thus saith the LORD God of the Hebrews, Let my people go, that they may serve me. **9:14** For I will at this time send all my plagues upon thine heart [the desire of your heart], and upon thy servants, and upon thy people; **that thou mayest know that there is none like me in all the earth. 9:15** For now I will stretch out my hand, that I may smite thee and thy people with pestilence; and thou shalt be cut off from the earth.

The Eternal has hardened the heart of Pharaoh for the express purpose of demonstrating his power and greatness to all the earth; and the Eternal will yet allow Satan to raise up a miracle working son of perdition in the Vatican and a bestial king emperor over the New Europe; for the express purpose of demonstrating the power of the Eternal God and humbling and preparing humanity to receive Messiah the Christ at his coming!

9:16 And in very deed **for this cause have I raised thee up, for to shew in thee my power; and that my name may be declared throughout all the earth.**

9:17 As yet exaltest thou thyself against my people, that thou wilt not let them go? **9:18** Behold, to morrow about this time I will cause it to rain a very grievous hail, such as hath not been in Egypt since the foundation thereof even until now.

In this plague the flax and barley crops were destroyed (Exodus. 9:31) in Egypt, which means this must have taken place about late February.

Since this plague originated from the sky, it would have shown the impotence of Nut, the sky goddess. Nut was also considered by the Egyptians to be the mother of five other gods: Osiris, Hathor, Set, Isis, and Nephthys.

Before the plague of destruction, God gave a merciful warning to all who would listen and take heed.

9:19 Send therefore now, and gather thy cattle, and all that thou hast in the field; for upon every man and beast which shall be found in the field, and shall not be brought home, the hail shall come down upon them, and they shall die.

9:20 He that feared the word of the LORD among the servants of Pharaoh made his servants and his cattle flee into the houses: **9:21** And he that regarded not the word of the LORD left his servants and his cattle in the field.

Moses did NOT do what he himself wanted, he did not do what seemed right to him: Moses did as God commanded him. So it is with all godly men, and so it will be with God's two servants; they will serve the Eternal and not their own ways.

9:22 And the LORD said unto Moses, Stretch forth thine hand toward heaven, that there may be hail in all the land of Egypt, upon man, and upon beast, and upon every herb of the field, throughout the land of Egypt.

9:23 And Moses stretched forth his rod toward heaven: and the LORD sent thunder and hail, and the fire ran along upon the ground; and the LORD rained hail upon the land of Egypt. **9:24** So there was hail, and fire [lightening and great thunder] mingled with the hail, very grievous, such as there was none like it in all the land of Egypt since it became a nation. **9:25** And the hail smote throughout all the land of Egypt all that was in the field, both man and beast; and the hail smote every herb of the field, and brake every tree of the field.

Those who heeded the warning in Egypt were spared.

9:26 Only in the land of Goshen, where the children of Israel were, was there no hail.

Pharaoh repented in words only, as very many of us also do.

Pharaoh's heart was set on keeping these people as his slaves; and our hearts are set upon the pleasures of spiritual Egypt [sin]. Today many of us say and do not, as did Pharaoh in Egypt.

> **Luke 6:46** And why call ye me, Lord, Lord, and do not the things which I say?
>
> **6:47** Whosoever cometh to me, and heareth my sayings, and **doeth them,** I will shew you to whom he is like: **6:48** He is like a man which built an house, and digged deep, and laid the foundation on a rock: and when the flood arose, the stream beat vehemently upon that house, and could not shake it: for it was founded upon a rock. **6:49** But he that heareth, and **doeth not**, is like a man that without a foundation built an house upon the earth; against which the stream did beat vehemently, and immediately it fell; and the ruin of that house was great.

Exodus 9:27 And Pharaoh sent, and called for Moses and Aaron, and said unto them, I have sinned this time: the LORD is righteous, and I and my people are wicked. **9:28** Intreat the LORD (for it is enough) that there be no more mighty thunderings and hail; and I will let you go, and ye shall stay no longer.

The thunder, lightning and great hail demonstrated the power of God, but the cutting off of the same demonstrated that God had the power to send and to stop plagues upon the earth.

9:29 And Moses said unto him, As soon as I am gone out of the city, I will spread abroad my hands unto the LORD; and the thunder shall cease, neither shall there be any more hail; **that thou mayest know how that the earth is the LORD's. 9:30** But as for thee and thy servants, I know that ye will not yet fear the LORD God. **9:31** And the flax and the barley was smitten: for the barley was in the ear [the barley matures earlier in Egypt then in Israel], and the flax was bolled. **9:32** But the wheat and the rie were not smitten: for they were not grown up.

9:33 And Moses went out of the city from Pharaoh, and spread abroad his hands unto the LORD: and the thunders and hail ceased, and the rain was not poured upon the earth. **9:34** And when Pharaoh saw that the rain and the hail and the thunders were ceased, he sinned yet more, and hardened his heart, he and his servants.

Isn't this just like us; when we have a need we cry out to God and repent with our words to follow him; and when the crisis is past we turn away from any zeal to live by the Word of God, returning to live as we want?

9:35 And the heart of Pharaoh was hardened, neither would he let the children of Israel go; as the LORD had spoken by Moses.

Exodus 10

God hardened the heart of Pharaoh so that all peoples would learn that the Eternal is God and is Mighty above ALL gods.

This is the very reason why in our time God will correct his called out in great tribulation when the abomination goes to the holy mount (Mat 24:15). To teach us and to teach all humanity that the Eternal is God indeed!

Exodus 10:1 And the LORD said unto Moses, Go in unto Pharaoh: for I have hardened his heart, and the heart of his servants, that I might shew these my signs before him: **10:2** And that thou mayest tell in the ears of thy son, and of thy son's son, what things I have wrought in Egypt, and my signs which I have done among them; **that ye may know how that I am the LORD.**

Moses and Aaron make it very clear to Pharaoh that he is to bow down and humble himself before the Eternal. We need to learn this same lesson and humble ourselves before the Eternal and his Word to learn it and to keep it, instead of clinging to our own ways and our idols of men and our false traditions.

10:3 And Moses and Aaron came in unto Pharaoh, and said unto him, Thus saith the LORD God of the Hebrews, How long wilt thou refuse to humble thyself before me? let my people go, that they may serve me.

God warns Pharaoh through Moses that her will send a plague of locusts to eat up every green thing in Egypt, except in Goshen.

10:4 Else, if thou refuse to let my people go, behold, to morrow will I bring the locusts into thy coast: **10:5** And they shall cover the face of the earth, that one cannot be able to see the earth: and they shall eat the residue of that which is escaped, which remaineth unto you from the hail, and shall eat every tree which groweth for you out of the field: **10:6** And they shall fill thy houses, and the houses of all thy servants, and the houses of all the Egyptians; which neither thy fathers, nor thy fathers' fathers have seen, since the day that they were upon the earth unto this day. And he turned himself, and went out from Pharaoh.

Then Pharaoh's servants and advisers recommended to him to let the people go; spiritually this means that Satan cannot stand against God.

10:7 And Pharaoh's servants said unto him, How long shall this man be a snare unto us? let the men go, that they may serve the LORD their God: knowest thou not yet that Egypt is destroyed?

Moses demanded that all Israel and all their animals must go to worship God. Notice carefully that physical Israel was called out of Egypt to worship [the Hebrew word "worship" means "to obey!"] GOD!

Spiritually some are called out of the spiritual Egypt of this world to worship [which means to obey] GOD! Not to do what we think is right, or to do what some man or group of men says is right: But to live by EVERY Word of God!

10:8 And Moses and Aaron were brought again unto Pharaoh: and he said unto them, Go, serve the LORD your God: but who are they that shall go? **10:9** And Moses said, We will go with our young and with our old, with our sons and with our daughters, with our flocks and with our herds will we go; for we must hold a feast unto the LORD. **10:10** And he said unto them, Let the LORD be so with you, as I will let you go, and your little ones: look to it; for evil is before you.

Pharaoh then permits the males only to leave, for he intends to keep the women hostage against the return of the males.

10:11 Not so: go now ye that are men, and serve the LORD; for that ye did desire. And they were driven out from Pharaoh's presence.

Then Messiah the Christ called for Moses to stretch out his rod so that the locusts would come and cover the land.

10:12 And the LORD said unto Moses, Stretch out thine hand over the land of Egypt for the locusts, that they may come up upon the land of Egypt, and eat every herb of the land, even all that the hail hath left.

The locusts came the next morning

This would have been a few days or weeks after the hail destroyed the crops and now the locusts would be eating up every green thing that was sprouting anew.

Nepri, the god of grain could not save the grain, Isis is silent once again. Thermuthis, the goddess of fertility and the harvest was speechless. Seth, another god of crops, was also mute.

10:13 And Moses stretched forth his rod over the land of Egypt, and the LORD brought an east wind upon the land all that day, and all that night; and when it was morning, the east wind brought the locusts. **10:14** And the locust went up over all the land of Egypt, and rested in all the coasts of Egypt: very grievous were they; **before them there were no such locusts as they, neither after them shall be such. 10:15** For they covered the face of the whole earth, so that the land was darkened; and they did eat every herb of the land, and all the fruit of the trees which the hail had left: and there remained not any green thing in the trees, or in the herbs of the field, through all the land of Egypt.

Moses who had been driven out the day before is called back by Pharaoh who begs for relief from the locusts.

10:16 Then Pharaoh called for Moses and Aaron in haste; and he said, I have sinned against the LORD your God, and against you. **10:17** Now therefore forgive, I pray thee, my sin only this once, and intreat the LORD your God, that he may take away from me this death only.

Moses than entreats God and the Eternal removes the locusts.

10:18 And he went out from Pharaoh, and intreated the LORD. **10:19** And the LORD turned a mighty strong west wind, which took away the locusts, and cast them into the Red sea; there remained not one locust in all the coasts of Egypt.

Then once again Pharaoh changes his mind as God hardens his heart. Now Pharaoh was a mere man with the weaknesses of a man and he would probably have let the people go after all this; but God wanted to make him an example of the hardness of Satan, and make God's power over Satan known to all people.

10:20 But the LORD hardened Pharaoh's heart, so that he would not let the children of Israel go.

Then God sent a deep darkness over all the land so that there was no light at all. This is symbolic of the spiritual darkness and ignorance of sin and the eternal death which swallows up sinners.

The greatest god of Egypt was the sun god which was the symbol of the god Amun-Ra [Lucifer Satan]. Bringing total darkness demonstrated the power of the Eternal over the supreme sun god to the people, and God's power over Satan himself.

10:21 And the LORD said unto Moses, Stretch out thine hand toward heaven, that there may be darkness over the land of Egypt, even darkness which may be felt. **10:22** And Moses stretched forth his hand toward heaven; and there was a thick darkness in all the land of Egypt three days: **10:23** They saw not one another, neither rose any from his place for three days: but all the children of Israel had light in their dwellings.

Pharaoh then lets the people of Israel go but tries to withhold their flocks and herds for himself, the physical mind trying to salvage something for Egypt.

10:24 And Pharaoh called unto Moses, and said, Go ye, serve the LORD; only let your flocks and your herds be stayed: let your little ones also go with you.

Moses says no and demands that all the flocks and herds also be released.

10:25 And Moses said, Thou must give us also sacrifices and burnt offerings, that we may sacrifice unto the LORD our God. **10:26** Our cattle also shall go with us; there shall not an hoof be left behind; for thereof must we take to serve the LORD our God; and we know not with what we must serve the LORD, until we come thither.

Then God hardened the heart of Pharaoh one more time so that Exodus 4:22-23 might be fulfilled.

10:27 But the LORD hardened Pharaoh's heart, and he would not let them go. **10:28** And Pharaoh said unto him, Get thee from me, take heed to thyself, see my face no more; for in that day thou seest my face thou shalt die. **10:29** And Moses said, Thou hast spoken well, I will see thy face again no more.

Exodus 11

We now come to the last plague which is the destruction of the firstborn of man and beast in Egypt; with the destroyer passing over the called out of Egypt at midnight on the fourteenth day of the first month.

Exodus 11:1 And the LORD said unto Moses, Yet will I bring one plague more upon Pharaoh, and upon Egypt; afterwards he will let you go hence: when he shall let you go, he shall surely thrust you out hence altogether.

God then commanded Moses to tell the people to spoil the Egyptians, and the Egyptians willingly give all that was asked of them to the called out.

Brethren, this is NOT an example for us to borrow without an intent to pay back. This is an allegory of how at the coming of Christ spiritual Israel will inherit all things and become the rulers of the whole earth.

11:2 Speak now in the ears of the people, and let every man borrow of his neighbour, and every woman of her neighbour, jewels of silver and jewels of gold. **11:3** And the LORD gave the people favour in the sight of the Egyptians.

The Egyptians were in awe of Moses and those called out from Egypt, and gave whatever they had for fear of God and the people. Even so, Satan fears our Mighty God and knows that he cannot stand before him!

James 2:19 Thou believest that there is one God; thou doest well: the devils also believe, and tremble

Exodus 11:3 Moreover the man Moses was very great in the land of Egypt, in the sight of Pharaoh's servants, and in the sight of the people.

Moses then tells Pharaoh the Word of God

11:4 And Moses said, Thus saith the LORD, About midnight will I go out into the midst of Egypt: **11:5** And all the firstborn in the land of Egypt shall die, from the first born of Pharaoh that sitteth upon his throne, even unto the firstborn of the maidservant that is behind the mill; and all the firstborn of beasts. **11:6** And there shall be a great cry throughout all the land of Egypt, such as there was none like it, nor shall be like it any more.

All the Called Out from Egypt, who were faithful to obey God were spared!

God gave Israel instructions as to what to do to be spared, and those who did not follow those instructions were destroyed in the plague with the Egyptians. ONLY those who kept the whole Word of God and all of God's instructions were passed over!

Even so, it is with spiritual Israel who are the spiritually Called Out from this worldly spiritual Egypt of bondage to Satan and sin; ONLY those who obey and follow the whole Word of God, will be delivered from bondage to sin and death, and cross over the Red Sea of death into the resurrection to eternal life; given as the birthright of the chosen.

11:7 But against any of the children of Israel shall not a dog move his tongue, against man or beast: that ye may know how that the LORD doth put a difference between the Egyptians and Israel.

Moses tells Pharaoh that Pharaoh will send his servants to demand that Israel leave Egypt.

11:8 And all these thy servants shall come down unto me, and bow down themselves unto me, saying, Get thee out, and all the people that follow thee: and after that I will go out. And he went out from Pharaoh in a great anger.

Then the Eternal [YHVH] told Moses that Pharaoh would not let them go until after the Passover.

This was because God was using this physical history as an allegory to teach us about the deliverance of spiritual Israel, and the spiritual Passover sacrifice of the Lamb of God; which is applied ONLY to those who sincerely repent and commit to follow God and his Word, forever.

11:9 And the LORD said unto Moses, Pharaoh shall not hearken unto you; that my wonders may be multiplied in the land of Egypt. **11:10** And Moses and Aaron did all these wonders before Pharaoh: and the LORD hardened Pharaoh's heart, so that he would not let the children of Israel go out of his land.

Exodus 12

The one who became Jesus Christ proclaimed the first month of the year to begin in the SPRING; and proclaimed that the Passover, the Feast of Unleavened Bread and the Wave Sheaf lifting must take place in that month. As we see in the Calendar lessons, the barley harvest must be ripening for cutting and grinding into flour for the Wave Offering in order to sanctify the first month.

Exodus 12:1 And the LORD spake unto Moses and Aaron in the land of Egypt saying, **12:2** This month shall be unto you the beginning of months: it shall be the first month of the year to you.

On the tenth day of the month they were to take a lamb to live with each of the families of physical Israel in Egypt; then it was to be sacrificed after sunset ending the 13th day of the first month. The number of people needed to completely consume a whole lamb in its first year is about 20.

The Passover lambs were lambs which had been born in early spring, as those which had been born during the previous year's spring lambing would be too old to be in their first year.

12:3 Speak ye unto all the congregation of Israel, saying, In **the tenth day of this month they shall take to them every man a lamb,** according to the house of their fathers, a lamb for an house: **12:4** And if the household be too little for the lamb, let him and his neighbour next unto his house take it according to the number of the souls; every man according to his eating shall make your count for the lamb.

The Passover sacrifice must be a lamb of the sheep flocks, or a kid of the goat herds. Please remember that the Passover can be a kid of the goat herds in your further studies, as in some places "herds" are mentioned and this has confused some people.

The lamb pictures the sacrifice of Christ being applied to the called out of spiritual Egypt and the spring or early harvest; and the goat kid pictures the sacrifice of Christ as being applied in the autumn to the main harvest; think of the Day of Atonement here.

However the sacrifice of Christ was done ONLY ONCE! The Lamb of God was pictured by the Passover sacrifice, but the one who became flash as Jesus Christ, being the very Creator was of much more value than a physical lamb.

12:5 Your lamb shall be without blemish, a male of the first year [in its first year]: ye shall take it out from **the sheep, or from the goats**: **12:6** And ye shall keep it up until [up to the beginning of the 14th, or to the end of the 13th day] the fourteenth day of the same month: and the whole assembly of the congregation of Israel shall kill it in the evening.

The blood of the sacrifice must be on the top and on the two sides of the door posts of their homes. This pictures the atoning blood of the sacrifice of Christ covering the door of our hearts and minds.

The blood on the door posts in Egypt was a sign that the people were God's people and that the destroyer should pass over them in peace. In the same way the application of the sacrifice of Christ to atone for the sincerely repentant and God's gift of his Holy Spirit marks out the spiritual people of God.

While not mentioned here, the Passover sacrifice and all sacrifices were to be accompanied by a Drink Offering of Wine, representing the shed blood of Christ.

Physical Israel was to eat the lamb with unleavened bread. The lamb picturing the total and complete innocence, meekness and submission of Messiah the Lamb of God to God the Father which we are to also have.

The unleavened bread pictures absolute purity from leaven [a type of sin] and the body of Christ which was to be broken for humanity. The bitter herbs represent the bitter sorrows and death that the Lamb of God must endure, and the of bitterness in our converted lives of overcoming as he overcame.

This whole meal was an allegory that we must eat [internalize] every Word of God, which was inspired by Jesus Christ who is the Logos. If we are lax or reject any point such as zeal for the sanctity of the Sabbath; we are apostate from Christ.

12:7 And they shall take of the blood, and strike it on the two side posts and on the upper door post of the houses, wherein they shall eat it. **12:8 And they shall eat the flesh in that night, roast with fire, and unleavened bread; and with bitter herbs they shall eat it.**

The Passover lamb or kid must be roasted whole; which represented the sacrifice of the Lamb of God, Jesus Christ as being wholly complete.

12:9 Eat not of it raw, nor sodden at all with water, but roast with fire; his head with his legs, and with the purtenance thereof. **12:10** And ye shall let nothing of it remain until the morning; and that which remaineth of it until the morning ye shall burn with fire.

The meal is to be eaten in haste in Egypt, thus representing physical Israel leaving Egypt in haste after the deaths in Egypt on the Passover.

This is a picture that once we sincerely repent and have the sacrifice of Christ applied to us; we must make haste to diligently study the scriptures and remove all sin in passionate zeal to internalize every Word of God, to learn and to live by every Word of God; working to become perfect as God our Father is perfect!

Anyone who is not passionately zealous to internalize the nature of God by faithfully rooting out all error and to live by the whole Word of God, is in grave danger of severe correction.

12:11 And thus shall ye eat it; with your loins girded, your shoes on your feet, and your staff in your hand; and ye shall eat it in haste: it is the LORD's passover.

Then the one who became Jesus Christ tells them that HE will go through the land and kill all the first born of Egypt.

12:12 For I will pass through the land of Egypt this night, and will smite all the firstborn in the land of Egypt, both man and beast; and against all the gods of Egypt I will execute judgment: I am the LORD.

Those with the token of blood on their doorposts will be spared but none of the wicked will be spared. This is an instructional example that only those who diligently live by every Word of God will be resurrected to eternal life while the unrepentant wicked will be destroyed.

12:13 And the blood shall be to you for a token upon the houses where ye are: and when I see the blood, I will pass over you, and the plague shall not be upon you to destroy you, when I smite the land of Egypt.

God's people are commanded to keep the Passover forever; it is an ordinance of God.

12:14 And this day shall be unto you for a memorial; and ye shall keep it a feast to the LORD throughout your generations; **ye shall keep it a feast by an ordinance for ever**.

At this point there is an inset concerning the Feast of Unleavened Bread.

Putting out leaven pictures putting out all sin from our lives, and the eating of unleavened bread every day as commanded further on, pictures internalizing the Bread of Life Jesus Christ and every Word of God throughout our entire lives.

12:15 Seven days shall ye eat unleavened bread; even the first day ye shall put away leaven out of your houses: for whosoever eateth leavened bread from the first day until the seventh day, that soul shall be cut off from Israel.

As the six day week with a seventh day of rest at its end, pictures a complete six day physical creation followed by a Sabbath of rest: The seven days of the Feast of Unleavened Bread pictures a six thousand year SPIRITUAL creation followed by a millennial rest!

The first day being a High Day because God the Father began his spiritual work in calling a people to himself through the Son with righteous Abel; then the calling out of an early harvest continued until the end of the sixth day [the six thousandth year], followed by the resurrection and a millennial Sabbath of rest during which God's Spirit will be poured out upon all flesh completing the full early seven day [seven thousand year] harvest of first fruits!

The called out from Egypt came out as the first day of the Feast of Unleavened Bread began, and they journeyed through the wilderness; picturing the spiritually called out journeying through this world's wilderness of sin for six thousand years.

Then the called out from Egypt crossed the Red Sea at the end of the sixth day; to rejoice at their deliverance on the seventh and High Holy Day of that Feast of Unleavened Bread, thus picturing the resurrection of the spiritually called out at the end of the six thousandth year followed by the millennial Sabbath!

12:16 And in the first day there shall be an holy convocation, and in the seventh day there shall be an holy convocation to you; no manner of work shall be done in them, save that which every man must eat, that only may be done of you. **12:17** And ye shall observe the feast of unleavened bread; for **in this selfsame day have I brought your armies out of the land of Egypt: therefore shall ye observe this day in your generations by an ordinance for ever.**

Verse 15 tells us that we must eat unleavened bread for seven days; therefore if we count back from the 21st day we will see the High Day on which this Feast begins is the day after Passover on the 15 day of the first month. 21, 20, 19, 18, 17, 16, 15.

Therefore the Passover is on the 14th day of the month beginning at sunset ending the 13th day, and the Feast of Unleavened Bread begins at the end of the 14th on the 15th day the next day after Passover when the people leave Egypt.

Here we have a direct and explicit COMMAND to eat unleavened bread every day of the whole Feast, and the spiritual significance of the unleavened bread makes it obvious that we should indeed eat it EVERY DAY of the feast. Indeed this is not a five day feast, nor is it a three day feast; it is the seven day Feast of Unleavened Bread and therefore we are to eat unleavened bread every day for a full seven days!

12:18 In the first month, on the fourteenth day of the month at even, ye shall eat unleavened bread, until the one and twentieth day of the month at even.

The person who eats any leaven during this feast is cut off from God and cut off from the Ekklesia the spiritual assembly of the called out.

Spiritually, if we pollute ourselves with willful sin after our calling and commitment to go and sin no more, we have also separated ourselves from God and lost out on the early [spring] resurrection of the chosen.

12:19 Seven days shall there be no leaven found in your houses: for whosoever eateth that which is leavened, even that soul shall be cut off from the congregation of Israel, whether he be a stranger, or born in the land.

Here is the positive command again. This represents that we are to eat, consume, hunger and thirst after, internalize and become one with God the Father and Jesus Christ by filling ourselves [eating] with learning and living by every Word of God.

12:20 Ye shall eat nothing leavened [we must not internalize a sinful nature]; **in all your habitations shall ye eat unleavened bread** [Internalizing the nature of God.].

Then God commanded Moses and the elders of Israel to choose lambs on the tenth day for killing after sunset ending the 13th day. God also commanded that hyssop be used as a brush to paint the blood on the doorposts. Hyssop is a plant which has soap like cleansing properties, and it is most appropriate to apply the blood representing the cleansing from sin properties of the blood of the Lamb of God.

The people were commanded not to go out during the night because the destroyer would be in the land and would kill any first born not marked out by the blood. Spiritually this is a sign to us that any person who is not sincerely repentant and under the sacrificial stoning blood of the Lamb of God and is not passionately committed to be faithful to God in all things, will surely be corrected and if unrepentant will surely spiritually perish.

12:21 Then Moses called for all the elders of Israel, and said unto them, Draw out and take you a lamb according to your families, and kill the passover. **12:22** And ye shall take a bunch of hyssop, and dip it in the blood that is in the bason, and strike the lintel and the two side posts with the blood that is in the bason; and none of you shall go out at the door of his house until the morning.

12:23 For the LORD will pass through to smite the Egyptians; and when he seeth the blood upon the lintel, and on the two side posts, the LORD will pass over the door, and will not suffer the destroyer to come in unto your houses to smite you.

12:24 And ye shall observe this thing for an ordinance to thee and to thy sons for ever.

Physical Israel is to keep the Passover forever in memory of how they were called out of Egypt and delivered by the strong arm of God. The New Covenant called out of Spiritual Israel are also to keep the Passover forever on the fourteenth day of the first month in memory of the sacrifice of the Lamb of God and his deliverance of us out of our bondage to sin.

12:25 And it shall come to pass, when ye be come to the land which the LORD will give you, according as he hath promised, that ye shall keep this service. **12:26** And it shall come to pass, when your children shall say unto you, What mean ye by this service? **12:27** That ye shall say, It is the sacrifice of the LORD's passover, who passed over the houses of the children of Israel in Egypt, when he smote the Egyptians, and delivered our houses. And the people bowed the head and worshipped.

Then Israel obeyed, killing the lambs and kids immediately after the sun set ending the 13th day of the first month; and at midnight on the 14 day of the first month the destroyer went through Egypt killing every first born of man and beast; only those who obeyed God were spared.

Just like the physical lambs died to save Israel's first born in Egypt; The Messiah the Lamb of God, died to save God's spiritually Called Out from bondage to Satan, sin and death.

12:28 And the children of Israel went away, and did as the LORD had commanded Moses and Aaron, so did they. **12:29** And it came to pass, that **at midnight the LORD smote all the firstborn** in the land of Egypt, from the firstborn of Pharaoh that sat on his throne unto the firstborn of the captive that was in the dungeon; and all the firstborn of cattle.

The Called Out of Egypt are an analogy of the spiritually Called Out of bondage to Satan and sin [spiritual Egypt], and called to God the Father and the marriage of the Lamb.

The firstborn of man and beast in physical Israel belonged to God having been redeemed by the physical sacrifice. Those firstborn of physical Israel represent the first fruits of spiritual Israel which belong to God, having been redeemed by the sacrifice of the Lamb of God.

The Passover occurred at midnight on the 14th day of the first month, the day having begun at the previous sunset. Pharaoh then insisted with all of Egypt, that Israel leave the land as soon as possible.

12:30 And Pharaoh rose up in the night, he, and all his servants, and all the Egyptians; and there was a great cry in Egypt; for there was not a house where there was not one dead. **12:31** And he called for Moses and Aaron by night, and said, Rise up, and get you forth from among my people, both ye and the children of Israel; and go, serve the LORD, as ye have said. **12:32** Also take your flocks and your herds, as ye have said, and be gone; and bless me also. **12:33** And the Egyptians were urgent upon the people, that they might send them out of the land in haste; for they said, We be all dead men.

Joseph had settled Israel in Goshen and over the years the people had grown and overspread the area so that there were many towns and villages of Israel in Goshen. It would have been early morning on the 14th day that the word came to leave and Israel then came out of their towns and villages to gather at their central city of Avaris [later renamed Ramses].

12:34 And the people took their dough before it was leavened, their kneadingtroughs being bound up in their clothes upon their shoulders. **12:35** And the children of Israel did according to the word of Moses; and they borrowed of the Egyptians jewels of silver, and jewels of gold, and raiment: **12:36** And the LORD gave the people favour in the sight of the Egyptians, so that they lent unto them such things as they required. And they spoiled the Egyptians.

Then as the sun set on the 14th day of the first month, at the beginning of the 15 day of the first month, Israel journeyed from Ramses to Succoth.

So they began the journey out of Egypt as the sun set on the Passover day of the 14th and on the beginning of the first day of Unleavened Bread the 15 day of the first month. For this reason this is a night to be much observed [remembered].

This is an allegory that all of the spiritually Called Out from bondage to Satan and sin, begin a journey AWAY from bondage to sin; and they must actively journey out of sin by hungering and thirsting to internalize Jesus Christ and God the Father, and to live by every Word of God.

Anyone who says that we need not obey God and eat unleavened bread every day of the Feast, is saying that we need not have any zeal to internalize the Word of God; they are of the spirit of antichrist.

12:37 And the children of Israel journeyed from Rameses to Succoth, about six hundred thousand on foot that were men, beside children.

Here we are told that a large number of others not called out by God, journeyed with Israel. These are typical of the tares that cleave to the spiritually Called Out in this age.

They did considerable damage in discouraging Israel from any zeal for God in the wilderness, just as we are also tested by the well meaning and sincere but unconverted and uncalled within our midst.

12:38 And a mixed multitude went up also with them; and flocks, and herds, even very much cattle.

The day after sunset ends the 14th day and begins the 15 day of the first month: Begins the first day of the Feast of Unleavened Bread.

This first day of the Feast of Unleavened Bread is a High Holy Day because on this day God led Israel out of Egypt, and because this day is symbolic of the beginning of God calling out a spiritual first fruits people for six thousand years and removing the leaven of bondage to sin, and leading them into godliness.

12:39 And they baked unleavened cakes of the dough which they brought forth out of Egypt, for it was not leavened; because they were thrust out of Egypt, and could not tarry, neither had they prepared for themselves any victual.

12:40 Now the sojourning of the children of Israel, who dwelt in Egypt, was four hundred and thirty years. **12:41** And it came to pass at the end of the four hundred and thirty years, even the selfsame day it came to pass, that all the hosts of the LORD went out from the land of Egypt.

It is because our Lord has kept his promises and delivered physical Israel that we know that he is able to and will keep his promises to spiritual Israel!

It has become a tradition to observe this night by having a big meal and talking about everything EXCEPT the thing we are supposed to be remembering. That is wrong and it is a sin.

This is a night to be much observed in memory of the deliverance of the called out of both physical and spiritual Israel. On this first High Day of Unleavened Bread we should be remembering and rehearsing the deliverance of Israel by the Mighty Arm of our Great Deliverer, the Lamb of God!

Besides being the day that Israel began the journey out of Egypt, and besides representing the need to remove sin and replace it with the Word of

God; the Feast of Unleavened Bread is also prophetic. This Feast represents that God the Father has been calling out a certain early harvest for six thousand years, beginning with righteous Abel, to Noah, Moses, Elijah, David and John Baptist along with many others.

Just as Israel journeyed for six days and then came up out of the Red Sea at the end of the sixth day, to rejoice over their final deliverance on the seventh day, a High Holy Day. Even so, spiritual Israel has been called out of sin for six thousand years, and at the end of the sixth thousandth year the chosen will be resurrected from the grave of death and changed to spirit and they will rejoice in a millennial Sabbath of Rest on the earth!

There is so much information and meaning on God's Holy Days and Festivals!

12:42 It is a night to be much observed unto the LORD for bringing them out from the land of Egypt: this is that night of the LORD to be observed of all the children of Israel in their generations.

Back to the Passover

No physically unclean person, or in the New Covenant no person unclean by unrepented sin may take the Passover. Only the circumcised in heart [sincerely repentant] may lawfully partake of the Passover.

12:43 And the LORD said unto Moses and Aaron, This is the ordinance of the passover: There shall no stranger eat thereof: **12:44** But every man's servant that is bought for money, when thou hast circumcised him, then shall he eat thereof. **12:45** A foreigner and an hired servant shall not eat thereof.

The lamb must be eaten wholly in the house of the family that made the sacrifice, with no part being taken outside. This symbolized that the sacrifice of Christ the Lamb of God, is applied ONLY to the sincerely repentant and is not applied to those who have NOT been called by God the Father to become part of the faithful family of God.

The lamb or kid represents Jesus Christ the Lamb of God and no bone may be broken, this to symbolize that no bone of Christ would be broken at his sacrifice.

12:46 In one house shall it be eaten; thou shalt not carry forth ought of the flesh abroad out of the house; neither shall ye break a bone thereof.

Every person spiritually Called Out to the New Covenant of spiritual Israel, MUST take the Passover with sincere repentance on the 14th day of the first month.

Later it was commanded by God that physical sacrifices including the Passover could only be made at the Temple.

At this time we are in a period between the destruction of the Temple in 70 A.D. and the building of the new Ezekiel Temple after Christ comes; therefore lambs may not be sacrificed at this time and we continue to take the Unleavened Bread and Wine without the lamb as instructed until the new Temple is built.

12:47 All the congregation of Israel shall keep it.

No uncircumcised in heart unconverted or unrepentant person may take the New Covenant Passover, but if a person is called by God the Father and is sincerely repentant, then let him be spiritually circumcised in a baptismal commitment to STOP sinning; and then partake of the Passover.

12:48 And when a stranger shall sojourn with thee, and will keep the passover to the LORD, let all his males be circumcised, and then let him come near and keep it; and he shall be as one that is born in the land: for **no uncircumcised person shall eat thereof.**

The laws that God gave to Israel were to apply to ALL those in their congregations and assemblies. Therefore no person may remain in the congregations of the Ekklesia of the Called Out, unless he is zealous to live by every Word of God.

12:49 One law shall be to him that is homeborn, and unto the stranger that sojourneth among you.

After the Passover day just as the sun set ending the 14th day of the first month, on the beginning of the 15th day of the first month; the physically called out began their journey out of Egypt!

12:50 Thus did all the children of Israel; as the LORD commanded Moses and Aaron, so did they.

It must be understood that this was the beginning of the journey out of Egypt, and that the journey was only completed at the end of the sixth day, as they came up out of the Red Sea of Death.

Technically at that time, Egypt ruled Sinai and Canaan, however the plagues broke the back of Egyptian hegemony over the region.

12:51 And it came to pass the selfsame day, that the LORD did bring the children of Israel out of the land of Egypt by their armies

Exodus 13

Exodus 13 begins with instructions to the people late on Passover day just before the sunset beginning the 15th day of the first month and the beginning of the march out of Egypt on the Night to be Much Remembered.

Exodus 13:1 And the LORD spake unto Moses, saying, **13:2** Sanctify unto me all the firstborn, whatsoever openeth the womb among the children of Israel, both of man and of beast: it is mine.

> **1 Corinthians 7:23** Ye are bought with a price; be not ye the servants of men.

Moses then commanded Israel to remember the exodus from Egypt on the evening beginning the fifteenth day of the first month as an annual observance forever.

Exodus 13:3 And Moses said unto the people, Remember this day, in which ye came out from Egypt, out of the house of bondage; for by strength of hand the LORD brought you out from this place: there shall no leavened bread be eaten.

13:4 This day came ye out in the month Abib.

13:5 And it shall be when the LORD shall bring thee into the land of the Canaanites, and the Hittites, and the Amorites, and the Hivites, and the Jebusites, which he sware unto thy fathers to give thee, a land flowing with milk and honey, that thou shalt keep this service in this month.

Here is a direct and specific command to eat unleavened bread every day of the seven day Feast.

13:6 Seven days thou shalt eat unleavened bread, and in the seventh day shall be a feast to the LORD. **13:7 Unleavened bread shall be eaten seven days**; and there shall no leavened bread be seen with thee, neither shall there be leaven seen with thee in all thy quarters.

We must diligently teach our children the meaning of this Feast of Unleavened Bread and the mighty deeds that Christ did in delivering ancient physical Israel from bondage in Egypt; and we are to remember the sacrifice of Christ and his deliverance from the bondage of spiritual Egypt, to Satan, to sin and death, through the giving up of the very life of the Creator.

13:8 And thou shalt shew thy son in that day, saying, This is done because of that which the LORD did unto me when I came forth out of Egypt.

We are commanded to keep the Feast annually year by year, and to remember these things and understand them; so that we may remember what happened in Egypt and the power that God has over all things to deliver us from Satan, just as God delivered physical Israel from the god king of physical Egypt.

WHY? So that we may remember the delivering power of our LORD and never depart from living by every Word of God!

13:9 And it shall be for a sign unto thee upon thine hand, and for a memorial between thine eyes, **that the LORD's law may be in thy mouth**: for with a strong hand hath the LORD brought thee out of Egypt. **13:10** Thou shalt therefore keep this ordinance in his season from year to year.

13:11 And it shall be when the LORD shall bring thee into the land of the Canaanites, as he sware unto thee and to thy fathers, and shall give it thee, **13:12** That thou shalt set apart unto the LORD all that openeth the matrix, and every firstling that cometh of a beast which thou hast; the males shall be the LORD's.

13:13 And every firstling of an ass thou shalt redeem with a lamb; and if thou wilt not redeem it, then thou shalt break his neck: and all the firstborn of man among thy children shalt thou redeem.

13:14 And it shall be when thy son asketh thee in time to come, saying, What is this? that thou shalt say unto him, By strength of hand the LORD brought us out from Egypt, from the house of bondage: **13:15** And it came to pass, when Pharaoh would hardly let us go, that the LORD slew all the firstborn in the land of Egypt, both the firstborn of man, and the firstborn of beast: therefore I sacrifice to the LORD all that openeth the matrix, being males; but all the firstborn of my children I redeem.

13:16 And it shall be for a token upon thine hand, and for frontlets between thine eyes: for by strength of hand the LORD brought us forth out of Egypt.

The first born were redeemed by the blood of the lamb in physical Egypt, and the spiritually first born [those called out from bondage to sin] of God are redeemed by the blood sacrifice of the Lamb of God. Being redeemed by the blood of the Lamb of God: We BELONG to GOD!

The Called Out of Egypt are an analogy of the spiritually Called Out of bondage to Satan and sin [spiritual Egypt], and called to God the Father and the marriage of the Lamb.

The firstborn of man and beast in physical Israel belonged to God having been redeemed by the physical sacrifice. Those firstborn of physical Israel represent the first fruits of spiritual Israel, which belong to God having been redeemed by the sacrifice of the Lamb of God.

> **1 Corinthians 6:19** What? know ye not that your body is the temple of the Holy Ghost which is in you, which ye have of God, and ye are not your own? **6:20** For ye are bought with a price: therefore glorify God in your body, and in your spirit [live by every Word of God who has purchased (redeemed) us], which are God's.

Exodus 13:17 And it came to pass, when Pharaoh had let the people go, that God led them not through the way of the land of the Philistines, although that was near; for God said, Lest peradventure the people repent when they see war, and they return to Egypt: **13:18** But God led the people about, through the way of the wilderness of the Red sea: and the children of Israel went up harnessed [laden with their goods] out of the land of Egypt.

13:19 And Moses took the bones of Joseph with him: for he had straitly sworn the children of Israel, saying, God will surely visit you; and ye shall carry up my bones away hence with you.

13:20 And they took their journey from Succoth, and encamped in Etham, in the edge of the wilderness.

13:21 And the LORD went before them by day in a pillar of a cloud, to lead them the way; and by night in a pillar of fire, to give them light; to go by day and night: **13:22** He took not away the pillar of the cloud by day, nor the pillar of fire by night, from before the people.

Exodus 14

At Etham, the Elohim member who later gave up his God-hood to be made flesh as Jesus Christ; told Moses to command the people to turn from their eastward journey and head to the south to camp by the sea.

Exodus 14:1 And the LORD spake unto Moses, saying, **14:2** Speak unto the children of Israel, that they turn and encamp before Pihahiroth, between Migdol and the sea, over against Baalzephon: before it shall ye encamp by the sea.

When Israel became trapped between the mountains and the sea at the close of the third day's journey, Pharaoh realized that he has Israel "in the bag" and resolved to pursue them.

14:3 For Pharaoh will say of the children of Israel, They are entangled in the land, the wilderness hath shut them in. **14:4** And I will harden Pharaoh's heart, that he shall follow after them; and I will be honoured upon Pharaoh, and upon all his host; that the Egyptians may know that I am the LORD. And they did so.

God had led Israel into a trap to bait Pharaoh to pursue them, and Pharaoh with his horses and chariots pursued Israel. Pharaoh's army had to cover the same ground although they were much faster without flocks and herds and the old and young, and could easily have made the journey in less than two days.

Israel became entrapped after only three days of travel and then stayed trapped in the same place on the fourth and fifth days. Pharaoh began to pursue them on the third day; arriving on the fifth day.

14:5 And it was told the king of Egypt that the people fled: and the heart of Pharaoh and of his servants was turned against the people, and they said, Why have we done this, that we have let Israel go from serving us? **14:6** And he made ready his chariot, and took his people with him: **14:7** And he took six hundred chosen chariots, and all the chariots of Egypt, and captains over every one of them.

Then the Egyptian army pursued Israel arriving on the fifth day.

14:8 And the LORD hardened the heart of Pharaoh king of Egypt, and he pursued after the children of Israel: and the children of Israel went out with an high hand. **14:9** But the Egyptians pursued after them, all the horses and chariots of Pharaoh, and his horsemen, and his army, and overtook them encamping by the sea, beside Pihahiroth, before Baalzephon.

Here we are told that Pharaoh himself was with the army and Israel feared greatly.

14:10 And **when Pharaoh drew nigh,** the children of Israel lifted up their eyes, and, behold, the Egyptians marched after them; and they were sore afraid: and the children of Israel cried out unto the LORD. **14:11** And they said unto Moses, Because there were no graves in Egypt, hast thou taken us away to die in the wilderness? wherefore hast thou dealt thus with us, to carry us forth out of Egypt? **14:12** Is not this the word that we did tell thee in Egypt, saying, Let us alone, that we may serve the Egyptians? For it had been better for us to serve the Egyptians, than that we should die in the wilderness.

This fear of the Egyptian army was representative of the fear of persecution and trials that drives many a new convert back into the bondage of sin out of which they came.

This was a deliberate act of God to demonstrate to physical and to spiritual Israel the power of God over Pharaoh and all his power, as an example of the great power of Christ to overcome Satan and all his power!

14:13 And Moses said unto the people, Fear ye not, stand still, and see the salvation of the LORD, which he will shew to you to day: for the

Egyptians whom ye have seen to day, ye shall see them again no more for ever.

When faced with temptations and trials we are to RUN to our Beloved and trust in him to deliver us; we are never to try and deal with the situation by our own ways and by compromising with any part of the Word of God. We are to trust in our God and GO FORWARD in enthusiastic zeal for his Word!

14:14 The LORD shall fight for you, and ye shall hold your peace.

This is the key to overcoming all our fears. We are not in the fight alone! The Eternal will fight for us, and all we need do is to faithfully follow HIM!

14:15 And the LORD said unto Moses, Wherefore criest thou unto me? **speak unto the children of Israel, that they go forward: 14:16** But lift thou up thy rod, and stretch out thine hand over the sea, and divide it: and the children of Israel shall go on dry ground through the midst of the sea.

Again Pharaoh is mentioned as being present.

Yes, let us go forward and continue on the path of faith in our Deliverer; never fearing, never compromising; being always faithful DOERS of the Word and FOLLOWERS of God our Father in heaven!

14:17 And I, behold, I will harden the hearts of the Egyptians, and they shall follow them: and I will **get me honour upon Pharaoh, and upon all his host, upon his chariots, and upon his horsemen.**

14:18 And the Egyptians shall know that I am the LORD, when I have gotten me honour upon Pharaoh, upon his chariots, and upon his horsemen.

Then the fire and cloud were moved to the rear of Israel, separating Pharaoh from Israel on that fifth night as the wind blew all night.

14:19 And the angel of God, which went before the camp of Israel, removed and went behind them; and the pillar of the cloud went from before their face, and stood behind them: **14:20** And it came between the camp of the Egyptians and the camp of Israel; and it was a cloud and darkness to them, but it gave light by night to these: so that the one came not near the other all the night.

The wind blew all night separating the sea into two parts so that Israel could pass through dry shod. Wind is also a type of the Holy Spirit which opens the way to salvation and eternal life in the spirit, if we passionately please our Beloved by following him and keeping his Word.

14:21 And Moses stretched out his hand over the sea; and the LORD caused the sea to go back by a strong east wind all that night, and made the sea dry land, and the waters were divided.

The Egyptian army arrived on the fifth day and the wind blew all that night, and early in the morning of the sixth day Israel entered the Red Sea and crossed that sea on the SIXTH DAY of Unleavened Bread.

Then the called out of physical Egypt rose up out of the Sea of Death, picturing the resurrection of the chosen called out from sin: While Pharaoh and his army perished as a type of the end of the unrepentant wicked.

14:22 And the children of Israel went into the midst of the sea upon the dry ground: and the waters were a wall unto them on their right hand, and on their left.

The called Out passed through the sea and the Egyptians could not do so as an analogy that the faithful zealous called out and chosen shall pass through the sea of death into a resurrection to spirit and eternal life; while those who reject zeal to live by every Word of God cannot cross from flesh into spirit.

14:23 And the Egyptians pursued, and went in after them to the midst of the sea, even all Pharaoh's horses, his chariots, and his horsemen.

Jesus Christ troubled this professional army in order to deliver his people; just as he will deliver his spiritual people from the power of Satan, sin and from the power of death itself!

14:24 And it came to pass, that in the morning watch the LORD looked unto the host of the Egyptians through the pillar of fire and of the cloud, and troubled the host of the Egyptians, **14:25** And took off their chariot wheels, that they drave them heavily: so that the Egyptians said, Let us flee from the face of Israel; for the LORD fighteth for them against the Egyptians.

The Egyptians, being a type of bondage to sin, could not cross through the sea representing the grave; and those who are not zealous to follow the Lamb withersoever he goeth, will not be in the resurrection to spirit.

14:26 And the LORD said unto Moses, Stretch out thine hand over the sea, that the waters may come again upon the Egyptians, upon their chariots, and upon their horsemen. **14:27** And Moses stretched forth his hand over the sea, and the sea returned to his strength when the morning appeared; and the Egyptians fled against it; and the LORD overthrew the Egyptians in the midst of the sea. **14:28** And the waters returned, and covered the chariots, and the horsemen, and all the host of Pharaoh that came into the sea after them; there remained not so much as one of them.

Those who passionately love their LORD enough to learn and to live by every Word of God will be lifted from the grave and given a new and incorruptible body of spirit in eternal life.

14:29 But the children of Israel walked upon dry land in the midst of the sea; and the waters were a wall unto them on their right hand, and on their left.

The Eternal saved physical Israel and he will save all those who love him with the passionate love of the Shulamite [the beloved of God, the Song of Songs]: While those who do wickedly and refuse to sincerely repent will go down to destruction.

14:30 Thus the LORD saved Israel that day out of the hand of the Egyptians; and Israel saw the Egyptians dead upon the sea shore.

When a resurrection of the faithful and chosen dead comes in the next few years; then all the earth will SEE and KNOW the power of God and they will believe and turn to God in the millennial rest.

14:31 And Israel saw that great work which the LORD did upon the Egyptians: and the people feared the LORD, and believed the LORD, and his servant Moses.

Exodus 15

After Israel came up out of the sea which the Egyptians could not cross, Moses wrote this song of deliverance which Israel sang in rejoicing on the seventh day of the Feast of Unleavened Bread. This is the very same song that will be sung at the Wedding Feast of the Lamb of God and the resurrected bride in heaven.

> **Revelation 15:1** And I saw another sign **in heaven**, great and marvellous, seven angels having the seven last plagues; for in them is filled up the wrath of God.
>
> **15:2** And I saw as it were a sea of glass mingled with fire [An expanse of crystal paving the heavenly Temple courtyard, refracting and reflecting the light of God like multi colored flames.]: and **them that had gotten the victory over the beast, and over his image, and over his mark, and over the number of his name, stand on the sea of glass**, having the harps of God.
>
> **15:3** And they sing the song of Moses the servant of God, and the song of the Lamb, saying, Great and marvellous are thy works, Lord God Almighty; just and true are thy ways, thou King of saints.

15:4 Who shall not fear thee, O Lord, and glorify thy name? for thou only art holy: for all nations shall come and worship before thee; for thy judgments are made manifest.

The Song of Moses

If you have prepared yourself and have been passionately zealous for our Beloved and every Word of God and overcome all worldliness; then you too will stand before the throne of God the Father and sing this song of rejoicing at the Marriage of the Lamb!

Exodus 15:1 Then sang Moses and the children of Israel this song unto the LORD, and spake, saying,

I will sing unto the LORD, for he hath triumphed gloriously: the horse and his rider hath he thrown into the sea.

Just as God defeated pharaoh, our Lord has defeated the armies of Satan, the god-king of this world!

15:2 The LORD is my strength and song, and he is become my salvation: he is my God, and I will prepare him an habitation; my father's God, and I will exalt him.

We must trust ONLY in our God who is Mighty to Deliver, and he will build us into a Temple [a dwelling place] for our God through the gift of God's Spirit dwelling in us!

15:3 The LORD [Who later gave up his God-ho0d to be made flesh as Jesus Christ] is a man of war: the LORD [YHVH, the Eternal] is his name.

The Eternal is our defense and our Deliverer, NO ONE can stand before him!

15:4 Pharaoh's chariots and his host hath he cast into the sea: his chosen captains also are drowned in the Red sea. **15:5** The depths have covered them: they sank into the bottom as a stone. **15:6** Thy right hand, O LORD, is become glorious in power: thy right hand, O LORD, hath dashed in pieces the enemy. **15:7** And in the greatness of thine excellency thou hast overthrown them that rose up against thee: thou sentest forth thy wrath, which consumed them as stubble. **15:8** And with the blast of thy nostrils the waters were gathered together, the floods stood upright as an heap, and the depths were congealed in the heart of the sea.

15:9 The enemy said, I will pursue, I will overtake, I will divide the spoil; my lust shall be satisfied upon them; I will draw my sword, my hand shall destroy them.

15:10 Thou didst blow with thy wind, the sea covered them: they sank as lead in the mighty waters.

Who is like God the Father and Jesus Christ?

15:11 Who is like unto thee, O LORD, among the gods? who is like thee, glorious in holiness, fearful in praises, doing wonders? **15:12** Thou stretchedst out thy right hand, the earth swallowed them.

15:13 Thou in thy mercy hast led forth the people which thou hast redeemed: thou hast guided them in thy strength unto thy holy habitation.

15:14 The people shall hear, and be afraid: sorrow shall take hold on the inhabitants of Palestina.

15:15 Then the dukes of Edom shall be amazed; the mighty men of Moab, trembling shall take hold upon them; all the inhabitants of Canaan shall melt away.

The Canaanites were types of wickedness and rebellion against God!

15:16 Fear and dread shall fall upon them; by the greatness of thine arm they shall be as still as a stone; till thy people pass over, O LORD, till the people pass over, which thou hast purchased.

The sincerely repentant spiritual people which Christ has purchased with his blood; will pass through the Sea of Death [the grave] into eternal life, and they will be given an inheritance as kings and priests over all the earth!

15:17 Thou shalt bring them in, and plant them in the mountain of thine inheritance, in the place, O LORD, which thou hast made for thee to dwell in, in the Sanctuary, O LORD, which thy hands have established.

15:18 The LORD shall reign for ever and ever.

Oh, what a great rejoicing in Israel on that High Holy Day of the Seventh Day of Unleavened Bread!

Oh, what a fantastic millennium of rejoicing the resurrected chosen saints will have as they bring the millennial harvest of first fruits into the family of God, in the very presence of the Creator himself!

Then Miriam led all Israel in a Song of Rejoicing at the deliverance and power of the Eternal from physical Egypt; and the resurrected chosen will also sing a Song of Rejoicing at the deliverance and power of the Eternal to deliver from bondage to Satan, sin and death!

15:20 And Miriam the prophetess, the sister of Aaron, took a timbrel in her hand; and all the women went out after her with timbrels and with dances.

15:21 And Miriam answered them, Sing ye to the LORD, for he hath triumphed gloriously; the horse and his rider hath he thrown into the sea.

Israel then had a day of rejoicing a Sabbath of Rest, representing a Millennial Sabbath of Rest, in the Feast of Unleavened Bread allegory.

Now a new allegory comes into view about the trials and difficulties of the period of espousal before the marriage of the Lamb to physical Israel at Sinai; these trials are a lesson for the spiritually called out that their espousal will be filled with trials; and that their deliverance in a resurrection to spirit as part of the collective bride depends on their fidelity to their espoused Husband and God the Father.

This pictures the journey of espousal of physical Israel to their marriage to God on Pentecost at Sinai.

The Wave Offering pictures the spiritual harvest of Christ as the first of many, and the establishment of the spiritual New Covenant Kingdom of God in its fullness on a future Feast of Pentecost.

After the seventh day of Unleavened Bread, Israel traveled three days without water.

15:22 So Moses brought Israel from the Red sea, and they went out into the wilderness of Shur; and they went three days in the wilderness, and found no water.

The water they found at Marah was bitter [salty water] and could not be drunk. Then the people complained bitterly and wanted to go back into Egypt because of the trial. The issue is one of attitude because the people blamed God and Moses, instead of seeking God's deliverance.

15:23 And when they came to Marah, they could not drink of the waters of Marah, for they were bitter: therefore the name of it was called Marah. **15:24** And the people murmured against Moses, saying, What shall we drink? **15:25** And he cried unto the LORD; and the LORD shewed him a tree, which when he had cast into the waters, the waters were made sweet:

Then God promised them that none of the plagues of Egypt would come upon his faithful; clearly implying that if they were NOT faithful to the whole Word of God that they would be subject to correction.

. . . there he made for them a statute and an ordinance, and there he proved them, **15:26** And said, **If thou wilt diligently hearken to the voice of the LORD thy God, and wilt do that which is right in his sight, and wilt give ear to his commandments, and keep all his statutes,** I will put none of these diseases upon thee, which I have brought upon the Egyptians: for I am the LORD that healeth thee.

God then led Israel to a well watered land

15:27 And they came to Elim, where were twelve wells of water, and threescore and ten palm trees: and they encamped there by the waters.

The Mediators of the Covenants

Moses was the mediator of the covenant called by his name and was a type of Christ the ONLY MEDIATOR of the New Covenant. Jesus [Hebrew: Yeshua] Christ is the Way and the Door to salvation and the resurrection of the dead.

> **John 10:9** I am the door: by me if any man enter in, he shall be saved, and shall go in and out, and find pasture.

> **John 11:25** Jesus said unto her, I am the resurrection, and the life: he that believeth in me, though he were dead, yet shall he live:

Only by following HIM "whithersoever he goeth" will any person be chosen to have a part on the coming resurrection to spirit.

> **Revelation 14:4** These are they which were not defiled with women; for they are virgins. These are they which **follow the Lamb whithersoever he goeth**. These were redeemed from among men, being the firstfruits unto God and to the Lamb.

We should also remember that Daniel was told not once, but twice; that the prophecies were sealed until the very end; and that at the end knowledge would increase (Dan 12). Many think that it was only physical knowledge which was to increase and that certainly has happened; however the clear context is spiritual knowledge.

The High Holy Days are prophetic and therefore could not be fully understood until the end of the age; for they, like the other prophecies, were sealed until there was a genuine need to know.

The Spring Festivals are a kind of foundation for the Fall Festivals and to properly understand the Fall Festivals it is important to remember the profound meaning of the Early or Spring Festivals.

We should understand that the Passover is a type of the sacrifice of the Lamb of God for his creation, the Passover lamb being identified with the Creator who died for his creation (1 Cor 5:7).

The blood of that Passover lamb covering and protecting the first born of Israel from the destroyer in Egypt; was a symbol of the blood of the Creator which atones for the sin of the sincerely repentant and protects them from ultimate destruction in the lake of fire.

> **Matthew 10:28 And fear not them which kill the body, but are not able to kill the soul: but rather fear him which is able to destroy both soul** [pneuma spirit] **and body in hell.** [gehenna]

The Passover lamb was eaten showing that we must internalize the true Passover Lamb, Jesus Christ. We must turn from disobeying God the Father and internalize the attitude of Jesus Christ who did obey his Father (John 13:10). We must become like him, allowing him to dwell within us through the agency of the Spirit of God.

Besides becoming our sacrifice, the Lamb of God also set us an example that we should walk [live] as he walked [lived].

> **1 John 2:6** He that saith he abideth in him ought himself also so to walk, even as he walked.

On the Wave Offering day, the resurrected Christ ascended to God the Father to "be accepted for us" (Lev 23:10-14). At the moment that his sacrifice was accepted by the Father; he became a High Priest forever, after the order of Melchizedek. He became our eternal spirit High Priest, the ONLY mediator between men and God the Father.

> **1 Timothy 2:5** For there is one God, and **one mediator** between God and men, the man Christ Jesus; and he became the **mediator of the New Covenant** through the sprinkling of his blood,

> **Hebrews 12:24** And to Jesus the **mediator of the new covenant**, and to the blood of sprinkling

During the Feast of Unleavened Bread, leaven is used as a picture of sin is to be removed and unleavened bread is to be eaten every day during the Feast, picturing the internalizing of Jesus Christ, the living Word of God and the Unleavened Bread of Life, (John 6:33, 6:35, 6:48 and 6:51); and leavening of any type becomes symbolic of sin and is to be avoided for that week.

The Unleavened Bread is a symbol of the purity and freedom from sin of Jesus Christ, and the eating of this Unleavened Bread each day pictures our need to internalize the true Bread of Life, Jesus Christ: day by day.

The seven days of the Unleavened Bread Festival show that for six thousand years God has been calling out a kind of first fruits starting with righteous Abel and including all the ancient men of God; until the resurrection of first fruits at the end of the sixth day. The sixth day is then followed by a Sabbath of rest or millennium represented by the seventh day High Holy Day of the Feast.

The first day is a High Holy Day, since it pictures the beginning of God's plan to call out an early harvest beginning with Abel, symbolized by God's calling of physical Israel out of Egypt as an allegory of God called a people out of bondage to Satan, sin and death.

The seventh day of this Feast is a High Holy Day, because it pictures a Sabbath of rest and victory for Israel after they had passed through the Red Sea and Pharaoh's armies had been destroyed. These events being an instructional allegory of a resurrection of the godly and a Millennial Sabbath of rest with Satan removed and humanity at peace in the presence of his Creator.

Remember that the first fruits resurrection must be in the Spring because a Spring Harvest MUST be reaped in the Spring. If it is reaped in the Fall, it would be a Fall Harvest; and not a Spring Harvest! Any farm boy can tell you that.

Exodus 16

One month after leaving Egypt, Israel came to a wilderness [desert] called Sin. The obvious word SIN cannot be overlooked and this desert was typical of the dry desert waste and the decay and death that sin brings in our lives.

Exodus 16:1 And they took their journey from Elim, and all the congregation of the children of Israel came unto the wilderness of Sin, which is between Elim and Sinai, **on the fifteenth day of the second month after their departing out of the land of Egypt.**

The people complain against God instead of seeking His deliverance, and they long to return to the bondage of Egypt. This is a lesson that Satan tries his best to discourage us to give up the fight against sin, but if we are faithful to live by every Word of God, God will deliver us.

16:2 And the whole congregation of the children of Israel murmured against Moses and Aaron in the wilderness: **16:3** And the children of Israel said unto them, Would to God we had died by the hand of the LORD in the land of Egypt, when we sat by the flesh pots, and when we did eat bread to the full; for ye have brought us forth into this wilderness, to kill this whole assembly with hunger.

Then the Eternal rains bread down from heaven; this being an obvious analogy of the spiritual Bread of Life, Jesus Christ and the Word of God; given to men from God in the spiritual wilderness of this world.

16:4 Then said the LORD unto Moses, Behold, I will rain bread from heaven for you; and the people shall go out and gather a certain rate every day, **that I may prove [test] them, whether they will walk in my law, or no.**

God does not prepare food for the people on the Sabbath, revealing by God's own example that we should also NOT prepare food on the Sabbath. We are to prepare our food on the day BEFORE the Sabbath and Holy Days and we are not to cook on God's Sabbaths and Annual High Days.

16:5 And it shall come to pass, that **on the sixth day they shall prepare that which they bring in; and it shall be twice as much as they gather daily.**

16:6 And Moses and Aaron said unto all the children of Israel, At even, then ye shall know that the LORD hath brought you out from the land of Egypt: **16:7** And in the morning, then ye shall see the glory of the LORD; for that he heareth your murmurings against the LORD: and what are we, that ye murmur against us? **16:8** And Moses said, This shall be, when the LORD shall give you in the evening flesh to eat, and in the morning bread to the full; for that the LORD heareth your murmurings which ye murmur against him: and what are we? your murmurings are not against us, but against the LORD.

Then the God who later gave up his Godhood to become flesh as Jesus Christ appeared to all Israel in his glory hidden inside a cloud.

16:9 And Moses spake unto Aaron, Say unto all the congregation of the children of Israel, Come near before the LORD: for he hath heard your murmurings. **16:10** And it came to pass, as Aaron spake unto the whole congregation of the children of Israel, that they looked toward the wilderness, and, behold, the glory of the LORD appeared in the cloud.

Christ promises Israel quails in the evening and heavenly bread in the morning.

16:11 And the LORD spake unto Moses, saying, **16:12** I have heard the murmurings of the children of Israel: speak unto them, saying, At even ye shall eat flesh, and in the morning ye shall be filled with bread; and ye shall know that I am the LORD your God. **16:13** And it came to pass, that at even the quails came up, and covered the camp: and in the morning the dew lay round about the host.

In the morning Israel found small grains and called it: "What's this?" And Moses told them that it was the food that God had supplied.

16:14 And when the dew that lay was gone up, behold, upon the face of the wilderness there lay a small round thing, as small as the hoar frost [a grainy pebbly material] on the ground. **16:15** And when the children of Israel saw it, they said one to another, It is manna: for they wist not what it was. And Moses said unto them, This is the bread which the LORD hath given you to eat.

Moses commanded the people to gather up this bread according to the needs of each person every morning, with double on the sixth day, to eat on the Sabbath as well as on the sixth day.

16:16 This is the thing which the LORD hath commanded, Gather of it every man according to his eating, an omer for every man, according to the number of your persons; take ye every man for them which are in his tents. **16:17** And the children of Israel did so, and gathered, some more, some less. **16:18** And when they did mete it with an omer, he that gathered much had nothing over, and he that gathered little had no lack; they gathered every man according to his eating.

If the regular daily gathering was left in their tents overnight until the following morning it would rot and breed worms [maggots].

16:19 And Moses said, Let no man leave of it till the morning.

Yet, some could not follow even these simple instructions which were given to set apart God's Sabbaths, and teach the people to properly prepare for the Sabbath on the day before the Sabbath.

16:20 Notwithstanding they hearkened not unto Moses; but some of them left of it until the morning, and it bred worms [maggots, flies], and stank: and Moses was wroth with them. **16:21** And they **gathered it every morning**, every man according to his eating: and when the sun waxed hot, it melted [evaporated on the open ground in the sun like the dew].

On the sixth day they were to prepare for the seventh day Sabbath by collecting one portion for the sixth day and one portion for the Sabbath day.

This was to teach us that we are to follow the example of God and that we are NOT to cook and prepare food on any Sabbath or Annual High Day, and we are NOT to pay others to do this sin for us!

16:22 And it came to pass, that on the sixth day they gathered twice as much bread, two omers for one man: and all the rulers of the congregation came and told Moses. **16:23** And he said unto them, **This is that which the LORD hath said, To morrow is the rest of the holy sabbath unto the LORD: bake that which ye will bake to day, and seethe that ye will seethe; and that which remaineth over lay up for you to be kept until the morning.**

16:24 And they laid it up till the morning, as Moses bade: and it did not stink, neither was there any worm therein. **16:25** And Moses said, **Eat that to day; for to day is a sabbath unto the LORD: to day ye shall not find it in the field.**

16:26 Six days ye shall gather it; but on the seventh day, which is the sabbath, in it there shall be none.

Then some people did not prepare for the Sabbath on the preparation day and went out to gather food to cook on the Sabbath day; many today also commit this same sin in the Ekklesia of God.

16:27 And it came to pass, that there went out some of the people on the seventh day for to gather, and they found none.

Then Jesus Christ was very angry with the people who refused to obey him regarding the Sabbath and Annual Holy Days. Later he sent Israel and then Judah into captivity mainly for breaking God's Sabbaths. How much angrier with us of spiritual Israel who are supposed to love and live by every Word of God?

16:28 And the LORD said unto Moses, **How long refuse ye to keep my commandments and my laws? 16:29 See, for that the LORD hath given you the sabbath, therefore he giveth you on the sixth day the bread of two days; abide ye every man in his place, let no man go out of his place on the seventh day. 16:30** So the people rested on the seventh day.

16:31 And the house of Israel called the name thereof Manna [What's this?]: and it was like coriander seed, white; and the taste of it was like wafers made with honey.

A pot of manna was gathered to be kept in the tabernacle as a reminder of the bread from God.

16:32 And Moses said, This is the thing which the LORD commandeth, Fill an omer of it to be kept for your generations; that they may see the bread wherewith I have fed you in the wilderness, when I brought you forth from the land of Egypt. **16:33** And Moses said unto Aaron, Take a pot, and put an omer full of manna therein, and lay it up before the LORD, to be kept for your generations.

16:34 As the LORD commanded Moses, so Aaron laid it up before the Testimony, to be kept.

16:35 And the children of Israel did eat manna forty years, until they came to a land inhabited; they did eat manna, until they came unto the borders of the land of Canaan.

16:36 Now an omer [3.64 US quarts or liters] is the tenth part of an ephah.

Exodus 17

Exodus 17:1 And all the congregation of the children of Israel journeyed from the wilderness of Sin, after [according to] their journeys, according to the commandment of the LORD, and pitched in Rephidim: and there was no water for the people to drink.

God could have led the people to water, instead he led them to a dry place to make them thirst exceedingly. This being a lesson for us that we should exceedingly thirst for the water of the Spirit and Word of God.

17:2 Wherefore the people did chide with Moses, and said, Give us water that we may drink. And Moses said unto them, Why chide ye with me? wherefore do ye tempt the LORD? **17:3** And the people thirsted there for water; and the people murmured against Moses, and said, Wherefore is this that thou hast brought us up out of Egypt, to kill us and our children and our cattle with thirst? **17:4** And Moses cried unto the LORD, saying, What shall I do unto this people? they be almost ready to stone me.

Moses is commanded to smite the rock; as a picture of Jesus Christ the ROCK of our Salvation dying for the sins of the world. Being smitten to death as the Lamb of God so that the waters of salvation - the Holy Spirit of God - could flow from him to fill a spiritually thirsty people.

John 4:10 Jesus answered and said unto her, If thou knewest the gift of God, and who it is that saith to thee, Give me to drink; thou wouldest have asked of him, and he would have given thee living water. **4:11** The woman saith unto him, Sir, thou hast nothing to draw with, and the well is deep: from whence then hast thou that living water?

John 7:37 In the last day, that great day of the feast, Jesus stood and cried, saying, If any man thirst, let him come unto me, and drink.

7:38 He that believeth on me, as the scripture hath said, out of his belly shall flow rivers of living water.

7:39 (But this spake he of the Spirit, which they that believe on him should receive: for the Holy Ghost was not yet given; because that Jesus was not yet glorified.)

Exodus 17:5 And the LORD said unto Moses, Go on before the people, and take with thee of the elders of Israel; and thy rod, wherewith thou smotest the river, take in thine hand, and go. **17:6** Behold, I will stand before thee there upon the rock in Horeb; and **thou shalt smite the rock,** [As a type of the smiting and death of the Rock of our Salvation for our sins, so that the water of the Holy Spirit might be poured out.] and there shall come water out of it, that the people may drink. And Moses did so in the sight of the elders of Israel.

17:7 And he called the name of the place Massah, and Meribah, because of the chiding of the children of Israel, and because they tempted the LORD, saying, Is the LORD among us, or not?

Then the enemy came out to fight the people, just like the spiritually called out are also confronted by many trials from the Adversary.

17:8 Then came Amalek [a tribe of Essau], and fought with Israel in Rephidim.

Here we find that Joshua [an elder of Ephraim] was a leader of Israel and a disciple of Moses from the very time that Israel left Egypt.

17:9 And Moses **said unto Joshua,** Choose us out men, and go out, fight with Amalek: to morrow I will stand on the top of the hill with the rod of God in mine hand. **17:10** So Joshua did as Moses had said to him, and fought with Amalek: and Moses, Aaron, and Hur went up to the top of the hill.

When Moses held up his hands in supplication to God, the people overcame; and when his hands fell from supplicating God, the people failed and were overcome. This was a example lesson that only by our appeals and loyalty to our God, will we be delivered from Satan the Adversary.

In continually raising his hands to God in supplication for deliverance Moses became physically exhausted; just as we may become spiritually tired and need strengthening from our God to seek him.

Aaron and Hur helped Moses to hold up his hands; and God made Israel victorious at the end of the day when the sun went down. We shall also be victorious over Satan and sin through the deliverance of God if we faint not.

17:11 And it came to pass, when Moses held up his hand, that Israel prevailed: and when he let down his hand, Amalek prevailed. **17:12** But Moses hands were heavy; and they took a stone, and put it under him, and he sat thereon; and **Aaron and Hur stayed up his hands**, the one on the one side, and the other on the other side; and his hands were steady until the **going down of the sun.**

17:13 And Joshua discomfited Amalek [a descendant of Esau] and his people with the edge of the sword.

Jesus Christ promises the total destruction of Amalek. Saul later lost his kingdom by not destroying that wicked people and all that they had (1 Sam 15).

17:14 And the LORD said unto Moses, Write this for a memorial in a book, and rehearse it in the ears of Joshua: for I will utterly put out the remembrance of Amalek from under heaven.

17:15 And Moses built an altar, and called the name of it Jehovahnissi [YHVH our Banner, or Champion]: **17:16** For he said, Because the LORD hath sworn that the LORD will have war with Amalek from generation to generation.

Exodus 18

Moses' father in law brings Moses his wife and two sons to him at Sinai and worships God with Moses there

Exodus 18:1 When Jethro, the priest of Midian, Moses' father in law, heard of all that God had done for Moses, and for Israel his people, and that the LORD had brought Israel out of Egypt; **18:2** Then Jethro, Moses' father in law, took Zipporah, Moses' wife, after he had sent her back, **18:3** And her two sons; of which the name of the one was **Gershom**; for he said, I have been an alien in a strange land: **18:4** And the name of the other was **Eliezer**; for the God of my father, said he, was mine help, and delivered me from the sword of Pharaoh:

18:5 And Jethro, Moses' father in law, came with his sons and his wife unto Moses into the wilderness, where he encamped at the mount of God: **18:6** And he said unto Moses, I thy father in law Jethro am come unto thee, and thy wife, and her two sons with her.

Moses went out to see his family and tells them of all the things that had happened since he last saw them.

18:7 And Moses went out to meet his father in law, and did obeisance, and kissed him; and they asked each other of their welfare; and they came into the tent. **18:8** And Moses told his father in law all that the LORD had done unto Pharaoh and to the Egyptians for Israel's sake, and all the travail that had come upon them by the way, and how the LORD delivered them.

Jethro the man of God from Midian rejoiced and praised God.

18:9 And Jethro rejoiced for all the goodness which the LORD had done to Israel, whom he had delivered out of the hand of the Egyptians. **18:10** And Jethro said, Blessed be the LORD, who hath delivered you out of the hand of the Egyptians, and out of the hand of Pharaoh, who hath delivered the people from under the hand of the Egyptians.

Jethro then proclaimed the Eternal to be the God above all gods, and sacrificed to him; and a great feast was made with Jethro and all the elders of Israel before the LORD.

18:11 Now I know that the LORD is greater than all gods: for in the thing wherein they dealt proudly he was above them. **18:12** And Jethro, Moses' father in law, took a burnt offering and sacrifices for God: and Aaron came, and all the elders of Israel, to eat bread with Moses' father in law before God.

Jethro wisely advises Moses.

This concerned an administrative body of godly men OUTSIDE of the priesthood!

The priesthood was of the sons of Aaron, but this body consisted of Godly men from all tribes, called by God and given his spirit to form a civil judicial system or Sanhedrin [70 elders] of Israel.

18:13 And it came to pass on the morrow, that Moses sat to judge the people: and the people stood by [many people came to Moses for decisions] Moses from the morning unto the evening.

18:14 And when Moses' father in law saw all that he did to the people, he said, What is this thing that thou doest to the people? why sittest thou thyself alone, and all the people stand by thee from morning unto even? **18:15** And Moses said unto his father in law, Because the people come unto me to enquire of God: **18:16** When they have a matter, they come unto me; and I judge between one and another, and I do make them know the statutes of God, and his laws.

18:17 And Moses' father in law said unto him, The thing that thou doest is not good. **18:18 Thou wilt surely wear away, both thou, and this people that is with thee: for this thing is too heavy for thee; thou art not able to perform it thyself alone.**

The very Jesus Christ who inspired this through Jethro to Moses, also sent out 70 teachers during his physical life just as he had sent 70 men to help Moses.

> **Luke 10:1** After these things the Lord appointed other **seventy also**, and sent them two and two before his face into every city and place, whither he himself would come.

Exodus 18:19 Hearken now unto my voice, I will give thee counsel, and God shall be with thee: Be thou for the people to God-ward, that thou mayest bring the causes unto God: **18:20** And thou shalt teach them ordinances and laws, and shalt shew them the way wherein they must walk, and the work that they must do.

God placed those men into this body in Moses day; and Jesus ordained his disciples (Mark 3:14, 1 Ti 2:7) who ordained godly elders (Acts 14:23, Titus 1:5).

There is nothing wrong with organization in the Ekklesia. The problem arises when:

1. The wrong men are ordained for the wrong reasons, and are not loyal to God.
2. When the ordained people seek to exalt themselves above the Word of God instead of focusing the brethren on God to live by every Word of God.

All authority comes from God and when men depart from any part of the Word of God; they lose all godly authority and become the adversaries of God.

Today most elders are chosen by men because they proved to be loyal to those men above any loyalty to God; and therefore - no matter how sincere they may be - they have NO authority, because they are not of God!

18:21 Moreover thou shalt provide out of all the people **able men, such as fear God, men of truth, hating covetousness; and place such over them,** to be rulers of thousands, and rulers of hundreds, rulers of fifties, and rulers of tens: **18:22** And let them judge the people at all seasons: and it shall be, that every great matter they shall bring unto thee, but every small matter they shall judge: so shall it be easier for thyself, and they shall bear the burden with thee.

18:23 If thou shalt do this thing, and God command thee so, then thou shalt be able to endure, and all this people shall also go to their place in peace.

18:24 So Moses hearkened to the voice of his father in law, and did all that he had said. **18:25** And Moses chose able men out of all Israel, and made them heads over the people, rulers of thousands, rulers of hundreds, rulers of fifties, and rulers of tens. **18:26** And they judged the people at all seasons: the hard causes they brought unto Moses, but every small matter they judged themselves.

Oh how different the godly attitude of Moses was from the attitude of most of today's ministry!

A civil government was established to manager civil affairs according to the whole law and Word of God; as separate from the priesthood which was to teach the Word of God and to fulfill the role of Mediator between God and repentant humanity.

18:27 And Moses let his father in law depart; and he went his way into his own land.

Exodus 19

On the fifteenth day of the third month Israel arrived at Sinai where she would be married to God.

Exodus 19:1 In the **third month,** when the children of Israel were gone forth out of the land of Egypt, **the same day** came they into the wilderness of Sinai. **19:2** For they were departed from Rephidim, and were come to the desert of Sinai, and had pitched in the wilderness; and there Israel camped before the mount.

There, the Mosaic Marriage Covenant took place with the Eternal declaring his requirement that they live by every Word of God ,and physical Israel accepting and binding themselves together with their Deliverer to live by every Word of God in a Marriage Covenant.

19:3 And Moses went up unto God, and the LORD called unto him out of the mountain, saying, **Thus shalt thou say to the house of Jacob, and tell the children of Israel; 19:4 Ye have seen what I did unto the Egyptians, and how I bare you on eagles' wings, and brought you unto myself. 19:5 Now therefore, if ye will obey my voice indeed, and keep my covenant, then ye shall be a peculiar treasure unto me above all people: for all the earth is mine: 19:6 And ye shall be unto me a kingdom of priests, and an holy nation.**

God commanded Moses to speak all these words to Israel. In this, Moses was the mediator of the marriage between God and Israel.

. . . These are the words which thou shalt speak unto the children of Israel. **19:7** And Moses came and called for the elders of the people, and laid before their faces all these words which the LORD commanded him.

Then Israel responded to the Word of God and entered into a Marriage Covenant with him. All marriages are the same agreement; the husband vows to care for and love his wife, and the wife vows to love and obey her husband in all things.

This is precisely the same agreement that we make with Jesus Christ by being baptized! We agree to love him and to do all that our espoused Husband says and He agrees to fulfill the duties of a husband, and if we continue and are faithful in our spiritual espousal we will be fully married before the throne of God the Father in heaven at the resurrection (Rev 15).

When we compromise with the Word of God and pollute his Sabbaths or idolize any man or organization above our love for our espoused Husband: Then we have BROKEN our baptismal marriage vows!

19:8 And all the people answered together, and said, All that the LORD hath spoken we will do. And Moses returned the words of the people unto the LORD.

Then the Being who married Israel and was later made flesh as Jesus Christ, instructed Moses to prepare the people to hear his voice so that they will always remember him and their marriage agreement with him.

19:9 And the LORD said unto Moses, Lo, I come unto thee in a thick cloud, that the people may hear when I speak with thee, and believe thee for ever. And Moses told the words of the people unto the LORD.

God told Moses to sanctify the people because he would speak to them on the third day.

19:10 And the LORD said unto Moses, Go unto the people, and sanctify them to day and to morrow, and let them wash their clothes, **19:11** And be ready against the third day: **for the third day the LORD will come down in the sight of all the people upon mount Sinai.**

19:12 And thou shalt set bounds unto the people round about, saying, Take heed to yourselves, that ye go not up into the mount, or touch the border of it: whosoever toucheth the mount shall be surely put to death: **19:13** There shall not an hand touch it, but he shall surely be stoned, or shot through;

whether it be beast or man, it shall not live: when the trumpet soundeth long, they shall come up to the mount.

19:14 And Moses went down from the mount unto the people, and sanctified the people; and they washed their clothes. **19:15** And he said unto the people, Be ready against the third day: come not at your wives.

19:16 And it came to pass **on the third day in the morning, that there were thunders and lightnings, and a thick cloud upon the mount, and the voice of the trumpet** [Shofar] **exceeding loud**; so that all the people that was in the camp trembled.

The awesome meeting between God the Husband and his new bride!

19:17 And Moses brought forth the people out of the camp to meet with God; and they stood at the nether [distant from the camp] part of the mount.

19:18 And mount Sinai was altogether on a smoke, because the LORD descended upon it in fire: and the smoke thereof ascended as the smoke of a furnace, and the whole mount quaked greatly. **19:19** And when the voice of the trumpet sounded long, and waxed louder and louder, Moses spake, and God answered him by a voice.

Christ called Moses up to the top of the Mount to meet with him.

19:20 And the LORD came down upon mount Sinai, on the top of the mount: and the LORD called Moses up to the top of the mount; and Moses went up.

The Eternal then commanded Moses to get back down and to warn the people not to approach the Mount; Moses protested that he had already done so, but the Eternal demanded that Moses go back down and warn the people again.

19:21 And the LORD said unto Moses, Go down, charge the people, lest they break through unto the LORD to gaze, and many of them perish. **19:22** And let the priests also, which come near to the LORD, sanctify themselves, lest the LORD break forth upon them.

19:23 And Moses said unto the LORD, The people cannot come up to mount Sinai: for thou chargedst us, saying, Set bounds about the mount, and sanctify it. **19:24** And the LORD said unto him, **Away, get thee down, and thou shalt come up, thou, and Aaron with thee**: but let not the priests and the people break through to come up unto the LORD, lest he break forth upon them.

19:25 So Moses went down unto the people, and spake unto them.

Exodus 20

Then the Husband of Israel, to whom Israel had pledged obedience, THUNDERED his basic will from the mount to his collective bride!

The Eternal is the God who has brought us out of spiritual bondage to Satan and sin!

Exodus 20:1 And God spake all these words, saying, **20:2** I am the LORD thy God, which have brought thee out of the land of Egypt, out of the house of bondage.

We are not to allow anything to come between us and our God; no, not family, or church organizations, or elders, or friends; nor money nor any temptation to do any sin, nor fear of any threat against us!

20:3 Thou shalt have no other gods before me.

20:4 Thou shalt not make unto thee any graven image, or any likeness of any thing that is in heaven above, or that is in the earth beneath, or that is in the water under the earth. **20:5** Thou shalt not bow down thyself to them, nor serve them: for I the LORD thy God am a jealous God, visiting the iniquity of the fathers upon the children unto the third and fourth generation of them that hate me; **20:6** And shewing mercy unto thousands of them that love me, and keep my commandments.

The true spiritual Ekklesia are those who follow the Lamb of God and live by EVERY WORD of GOD. Calling organizations the "Church of God" when NO physical organization is the Church of God is a LIE and takes God's name in vain!

20:7 Thou shalt not take the name of the LORD thy God in vain; for the LORD will not hold him guiltless that taketh his name in vain.

20:8 Remember the sabbath day, to keep it holy. **20:9** Six days shalt thou labour, and do all thy work: **20:10** But the seventh day is the sabbath of the LORD thy God: **in it thou shalt not do any work, thou, nor thy son, nor thy daughter, thy manservant, nor thy maidservant, nor thy cattle, nor thy stranger that** [anyone that you are responsible for] **is within thy gates: 20:11** For in six days the LORD made heaven and earth, the sea, and all that in them is, and rested the seventh day: wherefore the LORD blessed the sabbath day, and hallowed it.

20:12 Honour thy father and thy mother: that thy days may be long upon the land which the LORD thy God giveth thee.

First and foremost we are to honour God our Father in heaven by enthusiastically learning and living by his every Word (Mat 4:4). We are also to honour our physical parents and the elders in the faith the best we can, while always putting our Father in heaven above all else.

20:13 Thou shalt not kill [shed innocent blood].

The word kill as used here refers to murder, the shedding of innocent blood. Our authorities and governments are commanded to kill the wicked.

20:14 Thou shalt not commit adultery.

Adultery is sex of any type with a woman engaged or married to another man. This does not specifically forbid fornication which is forbidden elsewhere in the statutes.

Spiritually adultery refers to exalting anyone or anything above the husband of our baptismal espousal by following them contrary to the Word of God.

20:15 Thou shalt not steal.

We are to take nothing which belongs to others and which we have no right to take.

20:16 Thou shalt not bear false witness against thy neighbour.

False witness can be outright lies or it can be taking points out of context to make them seem to mean something different than what they were intended to mean. It can be subtle twists of the truth to deceive. False witness is to be deceitful, to deceive about anything.

20:17 Thou shalt not covet thy neighbour's house, thou shalt not covet thy neighbour's wife, nor his manservant, nor his maidservant, nor his ox, nor his ass, nor any thing that is thy neighbour's.

Covet means to unlawfully desire. If you want something belonging to another then offer to buy it lawfully and if the answer is no, then give it up and do not dwell on your desire which has become unlawful.

The people saw the awesomeness of God and greatly feared.

20:18 And all the people saw the thunderings, and the lightnings, and the noise of the trumpet, and the mountain smoking: and when the people saw it, they removed, and stood afar off.

Then the people asked Moses to be their intercessor or mediator between them and God.

20:19 And they said unto Moses, Speak thou with us, and we will hear: but let not God speak with us, lest we die. **20:20** And Moses said unto the people, Fear not: for God is come to prove you, and that his fear may be before your faces, that ye sin not.

Moses approached God.

20:21 And the people stood afar off, and Moses drew near unto the thick darkness where God was.

God tells Moses to command the people not to make idols of any thing, but to worship God alone. He speaks of idols of gold and silver; and in our day many make idols of money and wealth or physical things and personal advantage, or we make idols of men, church leaders and corporate church organizations.

An idol is ANYTHING that comes between us and God.

Today this world is full of idols and the Ekklesia is filled with the idolizing of men and corporate entities which they place above the whole Word of God!

20:22 And the LORD said unto Moses, Thus thou shalt say unto the children of Israel, Ye have seen that I have talked with you from heaven.

20:23 Ye shall not make with me gods of silver, neither shall ye make unto you gods of gold.

Our spiritual altar is the Rock of our Salvation, even Jesus Christ the true Lamb of God! The Stone, the Rock that is made without hands (Dan 2) which is the Chief Corner Stone!

> **Daniel 2:34** Thou sawest till that a stone was cut out without hands, which smote the image upon his feet that were of iron and clay, and brake them to pieces.

> **Ephesians 2:20** And are built upon the foundation of the apostles and prophets, Jesus Christ himself being the chief corner stone;

Exodus 20:24 An altar of earth [stone] thou shalt make unto me, and shalt sacrifice thereon thy burnt offerings, and thy peace offerings, thy sheep, and thine oxen: in all places where I record my name I will come unto thee, and I will bless thee. **20:25** And if thou wilt make me **an altar of stone** [signifying Jesus Christ the stone (Rock) of our salvation], **thou shalt not build it of hewn stone: for if thou lift up thy tool upon it, thou hast polluted it.**

20:26 Neither shalt thou go up by steps unto mine altar, that thy nakedness be not discovered thereon.

Exodus 21

The foundations of a successful society are:

1. Security of our person from harm and security of our lives,
2. Security of our families,
3. Security of our property, and
4. Security of our livelihood, or ability to make a living.

God's judgments and statutes, many of which [such as divorce] were for a physical unconverted people to maintain peace and order among a hardhearted people; fulfill the foundational principles on which successful societies can be built.

All of the commandments, laws, statutes, precepts and judgments of the Word of God have spiritual applications as well as physical applications; and EVERY WORD OF GOD is to be obeyed in both its physical and its spiritual aspects.

The Ten Commandments represent the whole law gelled down to the very basic principles of the nature of God.

The Statutes define the commandments a little further, by explaining how we should keep the commandments under various circumstances. The Statutes are also principles by which we may make other judgments; for example the issue of "if an ox gore a person" is directly applicable to us if our dog or any other [owned] animal is not properly controlled and attacks a person.

Exodus 21:1 Now these are the judgments which thou shalt set before them.

In those days it was common to sell oneself to a period of service in payment for a debt. This is a form of what we might call indentured servitude today, such as when an immigrant sold himself for a certain number of years of servitude in exchange for passage and land in the new world from the big companies who had received crown land grants.

This is about maximum six years of allowed service by males and the Land Sabbath year of release from all debt (Deu 15:1-3).

21:2 If thou buy an Hebrew servant, six years he shall serve: and in the seventh he shall go out free for nothing. **21:3** If he came in by himself, he shall go out by himself: if he were married, then his wife shall go out with him.

The following presents women servants who were bought by the master to be a wife for his male servant. A maidservant is not to be released on the seventh year, because she is owned by the master. This would be a powerful incentive for the male servant to remain with his master.

21:4 If his master have given him a wife, and she have born him sons or daughters; the wife and her children shall be her master's, and he shall go out by himself.

The servant may make a personal decision to remain with his master.

21:5 And if the servant shall plainly say, I love my master, my wife, and my children; I will not go out free: **21:6** Then his master shall bring him unto the judges; he shall also bring him to the door, or unto the door post; and his master shall bore his ear through with an aul; and he shall serve him for ever.

Concubinage

Many of these are cases where a family is very poor and deep in debt and a rich neighbour offers to pay off the debt if they will agree to give their daughter in marriage to him or his son etc.

This is about concubinage where the lady is forced by circumstances into a relationship, as opposed to entering into a marriage of her own full free will.

The sale of a female was not an outright sale on the auction block but the giving to wife in exchange for debt relief or for a sum; and the woman is to be secure from being sold to others as chattel by the first master.

21:7 And if a man sell his daughter to be a maidservant, she shall not go out as the menservants do. **21:8** If she please not her master, who hath betrothed her to himself, then shall he let her be redeemed: to sell her unto a strange nation he shall have no power, seeing he hath dealt deceitfully with her.

If she is rejected by her husband, she may be redeemed by her father back to her own family [just like a divorcee would return a woman to her father's house], but she may not be sold to another.

21:9 And if he have betrothed her unto his son, he shall deal with her after the manner of daughters.

If a man purchase a woman for his son; she shall be the purchaser's daughter and he must treat her as such [as his daughter in law].

The purchased concubine or the wife of freewill are both considered to be legal wives because they have become one flesh with their husband; the term wife or concubine is only referring to the original circumstances of the marriage.

Neither divorce nor polygamy were intended by the Creator, but because the Mosaic Covenant was only physical and because of the hardness of their hearts, God allowed these things and made rules to soften the evil.

21:10 If he take him another wife; her food, her raiment, and her duty of marriage, shall he not diminish. **21:11** And if he do not these three unto her, then shall she go out free without money.

The difference between manslaughter and willful murder

21:12 He that smiteth a man, so that he die, shall be surely put to death. **21:13** And if a man lie not in wait, but God deliver him into his hand; then I will appoint thee a place whither he shall flee. **21:14** But if a man come presumptuously upon his neighbour, to slay him with guile; thou shalt take him from mine altar, that he may die.

To strike one's parents is an act worthy of death. In the spiritual sense this is about eternal loyalty to God our Father in heaven and the penalty of death for any rebellion against HIM.

21:15 And he that smiteth his father, or his mother, shall be surely put to death.

Willful kidnapping is a crime meriting death.

21:16 And he that stealeth a man, and selleth him, or if he be found in his hand, he shall surely be put to death.

To curse one's parents is the same as cursing our Creator and merits death.

21:17 And he that curseth his father, or his mother, shall surely be put to death.

The following statute is to help people avoid jumping to conclusions about the cause of a death. It states that if after a fight a person is well for several days, we are not to assume that a subsequent death was the result of the earlier fight. This was given at a time when there were no methods of determining the cause of death [postmortems, autopsies] in such circumstances.

21:18 And if men strive together, and one smite another with a stone, or with his fist, and he die not, but keepeth his bed: **21:19** If he rise again, and walk abroad upon his staff, then shall he that smote him be quit: only he shall pay for the loss of his time, and shall cause him to be thoroughly healed.

Even servants are protected by the law.

21:20 And if a man smite his servant, or his maid, with a rod, and he die under his hand; he shall be surely punished [with death].

The master of a servant is protected by the same law regarding the assumption of the cause of death just like anyone else.

21:21 Notwithstanding, if he continue a day or two, he shall not be punished: for he is his money [the master has already lost the value of his servant].

The law concerning ACCIDENTAL abortion: Deliberate abortion is murder since at the instant of the meeting of the living egg and the living sperm a completely new and living organism has been created. For this reason the fertilization of several eggs outside of the body and then deliberately experimenting with them or killing the unwanted ones: Is murder.

21:22 If men strive, and hurt a woman with child, so that her fruit depart from her, and yet no mischief [she recovers] follow: he shall be surely punished, according as the woman's husband will lay upon him; and he shall pay as the judges determine.

The term "mischief" refers to the injury or death of the woman. Later the Rabbins reasoned that it would be better to pay the value of an eye than for a man to give up an eye. This may seem wiser than God to the mind of man, but it removes the obstacle to abuse for a rich man and allows a rich man to maim others for a price of money.

If God had wanted rich men to be allowed to perform such wickedness, God would have said so; instead God made the law applicable to all and make equal punishment for these things so that the potential victims would have strong protection.

21:23 And if any mischief follow, then thou shalt give life for life, **21:24** Eye for eye, tooth for tooth, hand for hand, foot for foot, **21:25** Burning for burning, wound for wound, stripe for stripe.

Servants are to go free if any physical harm is inflicted on them. This law of mercy was thousands of years ahead of its time.

21:26 And if a man smite the eye of his servant, or the eye of his maid, that it perish; he shall let him go free for his eye's sake. **21:27** And if he smite out his manservant's tooth, or his maidservant's tooth; he shall let him go free for his tooth's sake.

If an animal kills a person it must also surely die.

21:28 If an ox gore a man or a woman, that they die: then the ox shall be surely stoned, and his flesh shall not be eaten; but the owner of the ox shall be quit.

If the owner of a known vicious animal does not take care to keep it under control, then that owner is responsible for the acts of that animal just as if he had committed murder himself. Today this statute would be more common with vicious dogs than with an ox. However the owner may redeem himself from the death penalty for the acts of his animals with money by paying compensation to the afflicted family.

21:29 But if the ox were wont to push with his horn in time past, and it hath been testified to his owner, and he hath not kept him in, but that he hath killed a man or a woman; the ox shall be stoned, and his owner also shall be put to death. **21:30** If there be laid on him a sum of money, then he shall give for the ransom of his life whatsoever is laid upon him.

The price of redemption is set at thirty shekels of silver and the death of the offending animal.

21:31 Whether he have gored a son, or have gored a daughter, according to this judgment shall it be done unto him. **21:32** If the ox shall push a manservant or a maidservant; he shall give unto their master thirty shekels of silver, and the ox shall be stoned.

We are to take great care to make all we do safe for others and if an accident should happen we are responsible and must make the loss good.

21:33 And if a man shall open a pit, or if a man shall dig a pit, and not cover it, and an ox or an ass fall therein; **21:34** The owner of the pit shall make it good, and give money unto the owner of them; and the dead beast shall be his.

The law if one animal should kill another.

21:35 And if one man's ox hurt another's, that he die; then they shall sell the live ox, and divide the money of it; and the dead ox also they shall divide. **21:36** Or if it be known that the ox hath used to push in time past, and his owner hath not kept him in; he shall surely pay ox for ox; and the dead shall be his own.

Exodus 22

Laws to protect property from theft

Exodus 22:1 If a man shall steal an ox, or a sheep, and kill it, or sell it; he shall restore five oxen for an ox, and four sheep for a sheep.

Despite the law against murder, Biblically we have the right to defend our homes with lethal force if broken into during the night. However we must use good judgment and this right is not always respected by the law of the land in today's world.

This law was made as a law for a whole nation in physical Israel. Today spiritual Israel is only scattered individuals and while it is lawful by God's Word to defend with lethal force against a night time intruder; all things that are lawful are not always expedient, and today you can get into a world of trouble for doing so. Focus on prevention and secondarily on non lethal force to protect your home.

22:2 If a thief be found breaking up, and be smitten that he die, there shall no blood be shed for him.

However even in the Mosaic Covenant time, any killing of a thief in the daylight is forbidden. A thief must make full restitution for his theft and damage, and if he cannot restore because of personal poverty, he must be sold to work up to six years for his damage and theft.

22:3 If the **sun be risen upon him, there shall be blood shed for him**; for he should make full restitution; if he have nothing, then he shall be sold for his theft.

If the stolen things be found with the thief, then he must restore double.

22:4 If the theft be certainly found in his hand alive, whether it be ox, or ass, or sheep; he shall restore double.

Concerning restoring a harvest

22:5 If a man shall cause a field or vineyard to be eaten, and shall put in his beast, and [it] shall feed in another man's field; of the best of his own field, and of the best of his own vineyard, shall he make restitution.

22:6 If fire break out, and catch in thorns, so that the stacks of corn [grain], or the standing corn [grain], or the field, be consumed therewith; he that kindled the fire shall surely make restitution.

Things in safe keeping with others

22:7 If a man shall deliver unto his neighbour money or stuff to keep, and it be stolen out of the man's house; if the thief be found, let him pay double. **22:8** If the thief be not found, then the master of the house shall be brought unto the judges, to see whether he have put his hand unto his neighbour's goods.

If any such matter cannot be resolved privately then it should be brought before the legal judges.

22:9 For all manner of trespass, whether it be for ox, for ass, for sheep, for raiment, or for any manner of lost thing which another challengeth to be his, the cause of both parties shall come before the judges; and whom the judges shall condemn, he shall pay double unto his neighbour.

Restitution of a lost animal

22:10 If a man deliver unto his neighbour an ass, or an ox, or a sheep, or any beast, to keep; and it die, or be hurt, or driven away, no man seeing it: **22:11** Then shall an oath of the LORD be between them both, that he hath not put his hand unto his neighbour's goods; and the owner of it shall accept thereof, and he shall not make it good.

The entrusted person must restore that which was stolen from him to the owner.

22:12 And if it be stolen from him, he shall make restitution unto the owner thereof.

If an animal is torn by wild beasts, [or die on its own] no restitution is required because this is a natural peril.

22:13 If it be torn in pieces, then let him bring it for witness, and he shall not make good that which was torn.

Borrowed animals and things lost by the borrower must be restored by the borrower.

22:14 And if a man borrow ought of his neighbour, and it be hurt, or die, the owner thereof being not with it, he shall surely make it good.

If a person is working for the owner using the owners tools; than the user is not responsible for the tools because they remain in the owners control.

22:15 But if the owner thereof be with it, he shall not make it good: if it be an hired thing, it came for his hire.

Fornication is to be controlled by the command that the fornicators marry if they were indeed lovers; however this has a safety exit in that the father may refuse the marriage if the man is a scoundrel but the man must still pay the normal dowry which would have been substantial. It appears that the dowry price was 50 shekels of silver as stated in Deuteronomy 22:28-29, or about two years unskilled wages.

22:16 And if a man entice a maid that is not betrothed, and lie with her, he shall surely endow her to be his wife. **22:17** If her father utterly refuse to give her unto him, he shall pay money according to the dowry of virgins.

The sin of witchcraft is any rebellion against the keeping of any part of the Word of God.

> **1 Samuel 15:23** For rebellion is as the sin of witchcraft, and stubbornness is as iniquity and idolatry. Because thou hast rejected the word of the LORD, he hath also rejected thee from being king.

Exodus 22:18 Thou shalt not suffer a witch to live.

Lying with a beast is equivalent to becoming one flesh with it and totally degrades the image of God into the image of the brute beast.

22:19 Whosoever lieth with a beast shall surely be put to death.

Serving any god other than the Eternal is spiritual adultery and idolatry, this includes obeying some minister or priest contrary to the Word of God.

A prime example of this is cooking or paying others to cook [patronizing restaurants or having catered meals] on God's holy weekly and annual

Sabbath days, which sin is rebellion against the Word of God and is the same as witchcraft.

22:20 He that sacrificeth unto any god, save unto the LORD only, he shall be utterly destroyed.

We are not to afflict any person

22:21 Thou shalt neither vex a stranger, nor oppress him: for ye were strangers in the land of Egypt.

22:22 Ye shall not afflict any widow, or fatherless child. **22:23** If thou afflict them in any wise, and they cry at all unto me, I will surely hear their cry; **22:24** And my wrath shall wax hot, and I will kill you with the sword; and your wives shall be widows, and your children fatherless.

22:25 If thou lend money to any of my people that is poor by thee, thou shalt not be to him as an usurer, neither shalt thou lay upon him usury.

22:26 If thou at all take thy neighbour's raiment to pledge, thou shalt deliver it unto him by that the sun goeth down: **22:27** For that is his covering only, it is his raiment for his skin: wherein shall he sleep? and it shall come to pass, when he crieth unto me, that I will hear; for I am gracious.

22:28 Thou shalt not revile the gods [Elohim; rulers], nor curse the ruler of thy people.

God is to be respected and all authorities among the people are to be respected and obeyed in the Lord.

22:29 Thou shalt not delay to offer the first of thy ripe fruits, and of thy liquors: the firstborn of thy sons shalt thou give unto me. **22:30** Likewise shalt thou do with thine oxen, and with thy sheep: seven days it shall be with his dam; on the eighth day thou shalt give it me.

The eighth day pictures a new beginning and the first born of man and beast are to be presented to the Eternal and all human males are to be circumcised on the eighth day.

22:31 And ye shall be holy men unto me: neither shall ye eat any flesh that is torn of beasts in the field; ye shall cast it to the dogs.

Exodus 23

We are not to willfully speak falsely and if we are found to be in error we are to correct ourselves.

Exodus 23:1 Thou shalt not raise a false report: put not thine hand with the wicked to be an unrighteous witness. **23:2** Thou shalt not follow a multitude to do evil; neither shalt thou speak in a cause to decline after many to wrest judgment: **23:3** Neither shalt thou countenance a poor man in his cause.

We are to be faithful to God and to the truth; we are NOT to follow a crowd to turn aside from the truth. We are NOT to wrest judgment for either the rich or the poor. Godly righteous judgment must be given without regard for riches and position, and without pity for a wicked man who is poor.

23:4 If thou meet thine enemy's ox or his ass going astray, thou shalt surely bring it back to him again.

If you find a stray ox, means in principle; that if you find anything belonging to another, you must return it to its rightful owner.

23:5 If thou see the ass of him that hateth thee lying under his burden, and wouldest forbear to help him, thou shalt surely help with him.

We are to help even the animals of our enemies.

23:6 Thou shalt not wrest the judgment of thy poor in his cause.

We should not pity the poor so as to wrest his judgment and account a wicked man not guilty based on sympathy.

Our judgment is to be just and we should never justify the wicked or condemn the righteous.

> **Proverbs 17:15** He that justifieth the wicked, and he that condemneth the just, even they both are abomination to the Lord.

Exodus 23:7 Keep thee far from a false matter; and the innocent and righteous slay thou not: for I will not justify the wicked.

We are to never take any bribe to pervert justice.

23:8 And thou shalt take no gift: for the gift blindeth the wise, and perverteth the words of the righteous.

Do not oppress the foreigner and always be hospitable to him.

23:9 Also thou shalt not oppress a stranger: for ye know the heart of a stranger, seeing ye were strangers in the land of Egypt.

The seventh year is to be a Sabbath of rest from regular labors.

23:10 And six years thou shalt sow thy land, and shalt gather in the fruits thereof: **23:11** But the seventh year thou shalt let it rest and lie still; that the poor of thy people may eat: and what they leave the beasts of the field shall eat. In like manner thou shalt deal with thy vineyard, and with thy oliveyard.

23:12 Six days thou shalt do thy work, and on the seventh day thou shalt rest: that thine ox and thine ass may rest, and the son of thy handmaid, and the stranger, may be refreshed.

Be always totally unshakably faithful to the Eternal and do not let the false gods and idols of the wicked be even mentioned except to warn against them.

23:13 And in all things that I have said unto you be circumspect: and make no mention of the name of other gods, neither let it be heard out of thy mouth.

We are to appear before God in the three harvest seasons:

1. For Passover and the Feast of Unleavened Bread,
2. When the grain harvest is concluded at Pentecost, and

3. When the main fall harvest comes at the Feast of Tabernacles.

These are the three specifically mentioned times when an offering is required because of the bounty of the harvests. No offering is required by God on the Memorial of Trumpets, the Fast of Atonement, and the Feast of the Eighth Day.

A congregation may be asked for an offering on these other scripturally unmentioned days, but one is NOT REQUIRED by God and should be totally voluntary. If anyone tells you that an offering is required by God on any other Festival or Appointed Time; they are lying, and I would not give God's money to liars.

23:14 Three times thou shalt keep a feast unto me in the year.

23:15 Thou shalt keep the **feast of unleavened bread**: (thou shalt eat unleavened bread seven days, as I commanded thee, in the time appointed of the month Abib; for in it thou camest out from Egypt: and none shall appear before me empty:) **23:16** And **the feast of harvest, the firstfruits of thy labours** [Pentecost], which thou hast sown in the field: and the **feast of ingathering** [Tabernacles], which is in the end of the year, when thou hast gathered in thy labours out of the field.

These are the three pilgrim feasts when all the males and as many of their family members as possible are to travel to the place that God dwells. In those days God placed his name in the tabernacle and later in the temple, but right now God dwells in each of those individual people who are faithful to Him.

23:17 Three times in the year all thy males shall appear before the LORD God.

Physical sacrifices may not be made with any leaven which represents sin; because the physical sacrifices represent the sinless Christ the spiritual Lamb of God.

23:18 Thou shalt not offer the blood of my sacrifice with leavened bread; neither shall the fat of my sacrifice remain until the morning.

The first born of beasts belong to God; the firstborn human males also belong to God and are to be redeemed, because God spared the first born of Israel in Egypt by later giving up his own first born to be sacrificed in our place. The first fruits of the harvest also belong to God.

Simmering a kid in its own mother's milk was a local pagan fertility rite. This does not forbid the eating of meat with milk as some Rabbins suppose. Abraham ate milk, butter and meat with God and the angels:

> **Genesis 18:8** And he took butter, and milk, and the calf which he had dressed, and set it before them; and he stood by them under the tree, and they did eat.

Exodus 23:19 The first of the firstfruits of thy land thou shalt bring into the house of the LORD thy God. Thou shalt not seethe a kid in his mother's milk.

Christ then said that he will leave Israel because of their sins but that his angel [Messenger] bearing his authority to lead the people and that God Almighty must be obeyed in all things.

23:20 Behold, I send an Angel [Messenger] before thee, to keep thee in the way, and to bring thee into the place which I have prepared.

Do NOT provoke the Spirit of God by polluting his commanded Sabbaths and exalting and obeying men contrary to the Word of God.

23:21 Beware of him, and obey his voice, provoke him not; for he will not pardon your transgressions: for my name is in him. **23:22** But if thou shalt indeed obey his voice, and do all that I speak; then I will be an enemy unto thine enemies, and an adversary unto thine adversaries.

Those who are full of passionate love for our espoused Husband and obey his voice will surely be beloved of him. Let the beloved of the LORD rejoice in all adversity, for they are with their Beloved and He is with them!

The Canaanites were a physical type of unrepentant sin and they are given over to destruction as an example that the unrepentant sinner will be totally destroyed in the second death.

23:23 For mine Angel shall go before thee, and bring thee in unto the Amorites, and the Hittites, and the Perizzites, and the Canaanites, the Hivites, and the Jebusites: and I will cut them off.

We are not to bow before any god but the Eternal, that includes making idols of men and corporate church organizations. Godly men can be a help to focus us on the Eternal, but they are NEVER to replace the Eternal as a supposed moral authority above the whole Word of God.

23:24 Thou shalt not bow down to their gods, nor serve them, nor do after their works: but thou shalt utterly overthrow them, and quite break down their images.

If physical Israel would faithfully serve God they would be greatly blessed; and spiritually if we faithfully serve God we would be greatly blessed in spiritual things and will inherit God's gift of eternal life in the spirit.

In the same way that God went before physical Israel and gave them physical victories when they were faithful; Almighty God will go before his New Covenant faithful who live by every Word of God in the letter and the spirit, and give them victory over Satan, sin and death.

23:25 And ye shall serve the LORD your God, and he shall bless thy bread, and thy water; and I will take sickness away from the midst of thee. **23:26** There shall nothing cast their young, nor be barren, in thy land: the number of thy days I will fulfil.

23:27 I will send my fear before thee, and will destroy all the people to whom thou shalt come, and I will make all thine enemies turn their backs unto thee. [and flee] **23:28** And I will send hornets before thee, which shall drive out the Hivite, the Canaanite, and the Hittite, from before thee.

23:29 I will not drive them out from before thee in one year; lest the land become desolate, and the beast of the field multiply against thee. **23:30** By little and little I will drive them out from before thee, until thou be increased, and inherit the land.

The promised ultimate border of Israel is from the Red Sea to the Euphrates. This border was achieved by David and Solomon, and is a type of the millennial border of Israel.

23:31 And I will set thy bounds from the Red sea even unto the sea of the Philistines, and from the desert [of Egypt] unto the river: [Euphrates] for I will deliver the inhabitants of the land into your hand; and thou shalt drive them out before thee.

Today New Covenant spiritual Israel is to make no agreement with false teachers. We are to have nothing to do with them except to condemn their sin.

23:32 Thou shalt make no covenant with them, nor with their gods. **23:33** They shall not dwell in thy land, lest they make thee sin against me: for if thou serve their gods, it will surely be a snare unto thee.

Exodus 24

Moses is called to approach God

Exodus 24:1 And he said unto Moses, Come up unto the LORD, thou, and Aaron, Nadab, and Abihu, and seventy of the elders of Israel; and worship ye afar off.

The seventy elders with Aaron and his sons were told to worship God at a certain distance from the mount while Moses approached God.

24:2 And Moses alone shall come near the LORD: but they shall not come nigh; neither shall the people go up with him.

When Moses returned he told the people all the statutes and judgments that God had given them. This is called the Book of the Covenant, which book contained the words that God spoke to the people in Genesis 20 and the words that God dictated to Moses as recorded in Genesis 20:22-23:32.

24:3 And Moses came and **told the people all the words of the LORD, and all the judgments**: and all the people answered with one voice, and said, **All the words which the LORD hath said will we do. 24:4** And Moses wrote all the words of the LORD, and rose up early in the morning, and builded an altar under the hill, and twelve pillars, according to the twelve tribes of Israel.

Moses made sacrifices to confirm the Covenant.

24:5 And he sent young men of the children of Israel, which offered burnt offerings, and sacrificed peace offerings of oxen unto the LORD. **24:6** And Moses took half of the blood, and put it in basons; and half of the blood he sprinkled on the altar.

Moses read the Book of the Covenant to the people and the people committed themselves to a Marriage Covenant with Christ their Deliverer.

24:7 And he took **the book of the covenant,** and read in the audience of the people: and **they said, All that the LORD hath said will we do, and be obedient.**

24:8 And Moses took the blood, and sprinkled it on the people, and said, Behold the blood of the covenant, which the LORD hath made with you concerning all these words.

The blood of the physical sacrifice, symbolizing the blood of Christ shed for the New Covenant Called Out Bride; was then sprinkled on the people of the Mosaic Covenant physical bride of Christ.

> The marriage of physical Israel at Pentecost was symbolic of the ultimate calling out of all humanity who will then also commit to live by every Word of God in a New Covenant. The Holy Spirit will then be poured out on a repentant humanity to begin the Millennial Kingdom of God, on a future Feast of First Fruits [Pentecost] (Joel 2:28).
>
> We have been deceived into thinking that only those in the first mass resurrection to spirit are the first fruits; when all who live during the millennium are also a part of the first fruits, because the seventh day is still a part of the overall week!
>
> It is only AFTER the millennium that the main harvest is reaped. The first six thousand years pictures the spiritually Called Out of the New Covenant struggling to overcome, while the millennial rest pictures the resurrected chosen bringing in the remaining first fruits of the last day of the week of Unleavened Bread.

Then the elders went up before God and stopped a short way from the mount.

24:9 Then went up Moses, and Aaron, Nadab, and Abihu, and seventy of the elders of Israel: **24:10** And they saw the God of Israel: and there was under his feet as it were a paved work of a sapphire stone, and as it were the body of heaven [the sky] in his clearness.

24:11 And upon the nobles of the children of Israel he [God did not destroy them for coming close] laid not his hand: also they saw God, and did eat and drink.

They saw God, the one who became the Son and NOT God the Father; and lived.

Moses is called up to God in the mount after reading the Book of the Covenant to the people; this time to receive the tables of stone.

24:12 And the LORD said unto Moses, Come up to me into the mount, and be there: and I will give thee tables of stone, and a law, and commandments which I have written; that thou mayest teach them.

Here we see Joshua going with Moses; this begins to show the background of Joshua and his training under Moses which helped him to be so faithful to God in conquering the land and leading the people to be faithful to God like Moses did.

God had carefully prepared Joshua for his responsibility in succeeding Moses as the physical leader of Israel.

24:13 And Moses rose up, and his minister [assistant] Joshua: and Moses went up into the mount of God.

Moses went up the mount again while Aaron, his sons and the seventy remained below.

24:14 And he said unto the elders, Tarry ye here for us, until we come again unto you: and, behold, Aaron and Hur are with you: if any man have any matters to do, let him come unto them.

Moses went up the mount only to wait for six days for God to speak to him. Then on the seventh day God spoke to Moses.

24:15 And Moses went up into the mount, and a cloud covered the mount. **24:16** And the glory of the LORD abode upon mount Sinai, and the cloud covered it six days: and the seventh day he called unto Moses out of the midst of the cloud.

The people in the plain below the mount saw a very bright light, like a huge fire or the sun itself burning on the mountain.

24:17 And the sight of the glory of the LORD was like devouring fire on the top of the mount in the eyes of the children of Israel.

Moses was up on the mount in the presence of God for forty days and nights, sustained by the power and glory of God.

During those forty days God gave Moses the two tablets of stone on which the ten commandments were written and Moses wrote out a much more extensive book of the Word of God as dictated by God, including the commandments, laws, statutes, precepts, judgments and the instructions for the tabernacle, and very probably including the book of Genesis.

24:18 And Moses went into the midst of the cloud, and gat him up into the mount: and Moses was in the mount forty days and forty nights.

First God spoke to the people, and then Moses approached God and wrote a Book of the Covenant containing Exodus 20 to Exodus 23:32. Then in Exodus 24 Moses goes up on the mount to receive the two tablets of stone and to write out many more words that God dictated to him.

Exodus 25

The details of the tabernacle

God, a member of the YHVH [meaning: I exist] family who later became flesh as Jesus Christ [Hebrew: Yeshua Mashiach]; told Moses to take an offering from the people to build the tabernacle.

The tabernacle was very carefully laid out as a copy of God the Father's Temple and throne in heaven in a movable format to accompany Israel on their journeys. Later the permanent Temple was very carefully laid out in the same pattern which is full of significance.

Exodus 25:1 And the LORD spake unto Moses, saying, **25:2** Speak unto the children of Israel, that they bring me an offering: of every man that giveth it willingly with his heart ye shall take my offering.

25:3 And this is the offering which ye shall take of them; gold, and silver, and brass, **25:4** And blue, and purple, and scarlet, and fine linen, and goats' hair, **25:5** And rams' skins dyed red, and badgers' [rams skins dyed blue] skins, and shittim [acacia] wood, **25:6** Oil for the light, spices for anointing oil, and for sweet incense, **25:7** Onyx stones, and stones to be set in the ephod, and in the breastplate.

Moses was to make a physical tabernacle according to the plan of God; and The New Covenant faithful are to become the tabernacle of God's Spirit.

25:8 And let them make me a sanctuary; that I may dwell among them. **25:9** According to all that I shew thee, after the pattern of the tabernacle, and the pattern of all the instruments thereof, even so shall ye make it.

The Ark of the Covenant

25:10 And they shall make an ark of shittim [acacia] wood: two cubits and a half shall be the length thereof, and a cubit and a half the breadth thereof, and a cubit and a half the height thereof. **25:11** And thou shalt overlay it with pure gold, within and without shalt thou overlay it, and shalt make upon it a crown of gold round about.

Two carrying poles were placed one on each side of the Ark, and were to remain there permanently so that the Ark might be moved.

25:12 And thou shalt cast four rings of gold for it, and put them in the four corners thereof; and two rings shall be in the one side of it, and two rings in the other side of it. **25:13** And thou shalt make staves of shittim wood, and overlay them with gold. **25:14** And thou shalt put the staves into the rings by the sides of the ark, that the ark may be borne with them. **25:15** The staves shall be in the rings of the ark: they shall not be taken from it.

Certain things to be put inside the box of the Ark when it was completed

25:16 And thou shalt put into the ark the testimony which I shall give thee.

The Ark was called the Mercy Seat and represented the Throne of God the Father in heaven, it was about 45 inches long, 27 inches wide and 18 inches high.

25:17 And thou shalt make a **mercy seat of pure gold: two cubits and a half shall be the length thereof, and a cubit and a half the breadth thereof.**

One cherub was placed on each side of the Ark with its wings stretched out over the throne and both faces looking inward at the Throne.

25:18 And thou shalt make two cherubims of gold, of beaten work shalt thou make them, in the two ends of the mercy seat. **25:19** And make one cherub on the one end, and the other cherub on the other end: even of the mercy seat shall ye make the cherubims on the two ends thereof. **25:20** And the cherubims shall stretch forth their wings on high, covering the mercy seat with their wings, and their faces shall look one to another; toward the mercy seat shall the faces of the cherubims be.

25:21 And **thou shalt put the mercy seat above upon the ark**; and in the ark thou shalt put the testimony that I shall give thee. **25:22** And there I will meet with thee, and **I will commune with thee from above the mercy seat, from between the two cherubims which are upon the ark of the testimony, of all things which I will give thee in commandment** unto the children of Israel.

The Table of the LORD for the Bread of Presence was 36 inches long, 18 inches wide and 27 inches high.

25:23 Thou shalt also make a table of shittim [acacia] wood: two cubits shall be the length thereof, and a cubit the breadth thereof, and a cubit and a half the height thereof. **25:24** And thou shalt overlay it with pure gold, and make thereto a crown of gold round about.

A crown or raised lip of about 6 inches high ran around the edge of the table.

25:25 And thou shalt make unto it a border of an hand breadth round about, and thou shalt make a golden crown to the border thereof round about.

Rings and staves for carrying the table.

25:26 And thou shalt make for it four rings of gold, and put the rings in the four corners that are on the four feet thereof. **25:27** Over against the border shall the rings be for places of the staves to bear the table. **25:28** And thou shalt make the staves of shittim [acacia] wood, and overlay them with gold, that the table may be borne with them.

Dishes for the Shewbread, the bread of presence

25:29 And thou shalt make the dishes thereof, and spoons thereof, and covers thereof, and bowls thereof, to cover withal: of pure gold shalt thou make them.

25:30 And thou shalt set upon the table shewbread before me [inside the tabernacle] alway.

The heavenly lamp stand for the tabernacle. The seven branched lamp stand pictured the seven churches shining the light of God through the burning pure olive oil representing the Spirit of God.

25:31 And thou shalt make a candlestick of pure gold: of beaten work shall the candlestick be made: his shaft, and his branches, his bowls, his knops [buds], and his flowers, shall be of the same. **25:32** And six branches shall come out of the sides of it; three branches of the candlestick out of the one side, and three branches of the candlestick out of the other side: **25:33** Three bowls made like unto almonds, with a knop and a flower in one branch; and three bowls made like almonds in the other branch, with a knop and a flower: so in the six branches that come out of the candlestick.

25:34 And in the candlesticks shall be four bowls made like unto almonds, with their knops and their flowers. **25:35** And there shall be a knop under two branches of the same, and a knop under two branches of the same, and a knop under two branches of the same, according to the six branches that proceed out of the candlestick. **25:36** Their knops and their branches shall be of the same: all it shall be one beaten work of pure gold.

25:37 And thou shalt make the seven lamps thereof: and they shall light the lamps thereof, that they may give light over against it. **25:38** And the tongs thereof, and the snuffdishes thereof, shall be of pure gold. **25:39** Of a talent of pure gold shall he make it, with all these vessels.

25:40 And look that thou make them after their pattern, which was shewed thee in the mount.

Exodus 26

The tabernacle [tent] was an enclosure of ten different curtains placed end to end, each one 42 feet in length and six feet high; dyed purple and scarlet with art work of cherubims on them.

Exodus 26:1 Moreover thou shalt make the tabernacle with ten curtains of fine twined linen, and blue, and purple, and scarlet: with cherubims of cunning work shalt thou make them. **26:2** The length of one curtain shall be eight and twenty cubits, and the breadth of one curtain four cubits: and every one of the curtains shall have one measure.

Five curtains were linked together for a total of 210 feet; that section was then linked with a second five curtain section.

26:3 The five curtains shall be coupled together one to another; and other five curtains shall be coupled one to another. **26:4** And thou shalt make loops of blue upon the edge of the one curtain from the selvedge in the coupling; and likewise shalt thou make in the uttermost edge of another curtain, in the coupling of the second. **26:5** Fifty loops shalt thou make in the one curtain, and fifty loops shalt thou make in the edge of the curtain that is in the coupling of the second; that the loops may take hold one of another.**26:6** And thou shalt make fifty taches of gold, and couple the curtains together with the taches: and it shall be one tabernacle.

26:7 And thou shalt make curtains of goats' hair to be a covering upon the tabernacle: eleven curtains shalt thou make. **26:8** The length of one curtain shall be thirty cubits, and the breadth of one curtain four cubits: and the eleven curtains shall be all of one measure. **26:9** And thou shalt couple five curtains by themselves, and six curtains by themselves, and shalt double the sixth curtain in the forefront of the tabernacle.

26:10 And thou shalt make fifty loops on the edge of the one curtain that is outmost in the coupling, and fifty loops in the edge of the curtain which coupleth the second. **26:11** And thou shalt make fifty taches of brass, and put the taches into the loops, and couple the tent together, that it may be one. **26:12** And the remnant that remaineth of the curtains of the tent, the half curtain that remaineth, shall hang over the backside of the tabernacle.

26:13 And a cubit on the one side, and a cubit on the other side of that which remaineth in the length of the curtains of the tent, it shall hang over the sides of the tabernacle on this side and on that side, to cover it.

26:14 And thou shalt make a covering for the tent of rams' skins dyed red, and a covering above of badgers' [rams skins dyed blue] skins.

Board frames were to be set up upon which to hang the curtains surrounding the tabernacle.

26:15 And thou shalt make boards for the tabernacle of shittim wood standing up. **26:16** Ten cubits [a cubit being about 18 inches] shall be the length of a board, and a cubit and a half shall be the breadth of one board. **26:17** Two tenons shall there be in one board, set in order one against another: thus shalt thou make for all the boards of the tabernacle.

26:18 And thou shalt make the boards for the tabernacle, twenty boards on the south side southward. **26:19** And thou shalt make forty sockets of silver under the twenty boards; two sockets under one board for his two tenons, and two sockets under another board for his two tenons.

26:20 And for the second side of the tabernacle on the north side there shall be twenty boards: **26:21** And their forty sockets of silver; two sockets under one board, and two sockets under another board.

26:22 And for the sides of the tabernacle westward thou shalt make six boards. **26:23** And two boards shalt thou make for the corners of the tabernacle in the two sides. **26:24** And they shall be coupled together beneath, and they shall be coupled together above the head of it unto one ring: thus shall it be for them both; they shall be for the two corners. **26:25**

And they shall be eight boards, and their sockets of silver, sixteen sockets; two sockets under one board, and two sockets under another board.

26:26 And thou shalt make bars of shittim wood; five for the boards of the one side of the tabernacle, **26:27** And five bars for the boards of the other side of the tabernacle, and five bars for the boards of the side of the tabernacle, for the two sides westward. **26:28** And the middle bar in the midst of the boards shall reach from end to end.

26:29 And thou shalt overlay the boards with gold, and make their rings of gold for places for the bars: and thou shalt overlay the bars with gold. **26:30** And thou shalt rear up the tabernacle according to the fashion thereof which was shewed thee in the mount.

26:31 And thou shalt make a vail [curtain] of blue, and purple, and scarlet, and fine twined linen of cunning work: with cherubims shall it be made: **26:32** And thou shalt hang it upon four pillars of shittim wood overlaid with gold: their hooks shall be of gold, upon the four sockets of silver. **26:33** And thou shalt hang up the vail under the taches, that thou mayest bring in thither within the vail the ark of the testimony: and the vail shall divide unto you between the holy place and the most holy.

26:34 And thou shalt put the mercy seat upon the ark of the testimony in the most holy place. **26:35** And thou shalt set the table without the vail, and the candlestick over against the table on the side of the tabernacle toward the south: and thou shalt put the table on the north side.

26:36 And thou shalt make an hanging for the door of the tent, of blue, and purple, and scarlet, and fine twined linen, wrought with needlework [embroidered] .

26:37 And thou shalt make for the hanging five pillars of shittim wood, and overlay them with gold, and their hooks shall be of gold: and thou shalt cast five sockets of brass for them.

Exodus 27

The things concerning the altar of Burnt Offerings and the priestly garments

The altar of burnt offering consisted of an enclosure of acacia wood coated with brass, on the top of which was to be a grate of brass on which to place the sacrifice to be burned.

Inside the enclosure of brass coated acacia wood and under the brass grate were pans made of brass, on which the firewood was placed, so that when the firewood was burned the fire would rise up through the grate and consume the sacrifice. The brass pans could then be removed to remove the ashes.

This was far superior to placing an animal on a simple pile of burning wood, because this system made a VERY hot fire which could consume the entire burnt offering quickly.

Exodus 27:1 And thou shalt make an altar of **shittim** [acacia] **wood**, five cubits long, and five cubits broad; the altar shall be foursquare: and the height thereof shall be three cubits. **27:2** And thou shalt make the horns of it upon the four corners thereof: his horns shall be of the same: and thou shalt **overlay it with brass**.

27:3 And thou shalt make his pans to receive his ashes, and his shovels, and his basons, and his fleshhooks, and his firepans: all the vessels thereof thou shalt make of brass.

27:4 And thou shalt make for it a grate of network of brass; and upon the net shalt thou make four brasen rings in the four corners thereof. **27:5** And thou shalt put it under the compass of the altar beneath, that the net may be even to the midst of the altar. **27:6** And thou shalt make staves for the altar, staves of shittim wood, and overlay them with brass. **27:7** And the staves shall be put into the rings, and the staves shall be upon the two sides of the altar, to bear it.

The altar was to be made like a hollow box with boards overlaid with brass.

27:8 Hollow with boards shalt thou make it: as it was shewed thee in the mount, so shall they make it.

The altar would have looked somewhat like this

27:9 And thou shalt make the court of the tabernacle: for the south side southward there shall be hangings for the court [the actual tabernacle] of fine twined linen of an hundred cubits long for one side:

27:10 And the twenty pillars thereof and their twenty sockets shall be of brass; the hooks of the pillars and their fillets shall be of silver. **27:11** And likewise for the north side in length there shall be hangings of an hundred cubits long, and his twenty pillars and their twenty sockets of brass; the hooks of the pillars and their fillets of silver.

27:12 And for the breadth of the court on the west side shall be hangings of fifty cubits: their pillars ten, and their sockets ten. **27:13** And the breadth of the court on the east side eastward shall be fifty cubits.

27:14 The hangings of one side of the gate shall be fifteen cubits: their pillars three, and their sockets three. **27:15** And on the other side shall be hangings fifteen cubits: their pillars three, and their sockets three.

27:16 And for the gate of the court shall be an hanging of twenty cubits, of blue, and purple, and scarlet, and fine twined linen, wrought with needlework: and their pillars shall be four, and their sockets four. **27:17** All the pillars round about the court shall be filleted with silver; their hooks shall be of silver, and their sockets of brass.

The tabernacle court of the priests

The later Temple building of Solomon was a duplicate of the tabernacle but built with permanent materials, and with the addition of an outer courtyard for the people surrounding the Temple building and its inner courtyard for the priests.

27:18 The length of the court[yard] shall be an hundred cubits [150 feet], and the breadth fifty [75 feet] every where, and the height five cubits [7.5 feet] of fine twined linen, and their sockets of brass.

27:19 All the vessels of the tabernacle in all the service thereof, and all the pins thereof, and all the pins of the court, shall be of brass.

27:20 And thou shalt command the children of Israel, that they bring thee **pure oil olive beaten for the light, to cause the lamp to burn always.**

27:21 In the tabernacle of the congregation without the vail, which is before the testimony, Aaron and his sons shall order it from evening to morning before the LORD: it shall be a statute for ever unto their generations on the behalf of the children of Israel.

Exodus 28

The commandments concerning the physical priestly garments

Exodus 28:1 And take thou unto thee Aaron thy brother, and his sons with him, from among the children of Israel, that he may minister unto me in the priest's office, even Aaron, Nadab and Abihu, Eleazar and Ithamar, Aaron's sons.

Moses was a type of Jesus Christ as a mediator between God and the people, while Aaron the high priest of the Mosaic Covenant, was also a type of Christ as the High Priest of the New Covenant.

28:2 And thou shalt make holy garments for Aaron thy brother for glory and for beauty. **28:3** And thou shalt speak unto all that are wise hearted, whom I have filled with the spirit of wisdom, that they may make Aaron's garments to consecrate him, that he may minister unto me in the priest's office.

28:4 And these are the garments which they shall make; a breastplate, and an ephod, and a robe, and a broidered coat, a mitre, and a girdle: and they shall make holy garments for Aaron thy brother, and his sons, that he may minister unto me in the priest's office.

There are some issues with the choice of descriptive words in the KJV. The robe is the white linen shirt next to the skin which comes down to the ankles, to hide the loins and thighs; which is then covered by the Ephod, which is the blue robe hanging from the pieces on the shoulders; these are covered with the embroidered coat; then the breastplate is the square of stones on the chest; and finally the sash embroidered the same as the vest; and the headwear.

The Blue Ephod

28:5 And they shall take gold, and blue, and purple, and scarlet, and fine linen. **8:6** And they shall make the ephod of gold, of blue, and of purple, of scarlet, and fine twined linen, with cunning work.

The ephod is the blue coat or girdle with the two shoulder pieces to be worn on top of the white linen robe. There is more on the ephod beginning verse 31.

28:7 It shall have **the two shoulderpieces** thereof joined at the two edges thereof; and so it shall be joined together. **28:8** And the curious girdle of the ephod, which is upon it, shall be of the same, according to the work thereof; even of gold, of blue, and purple, and scarlet, and fine twined linen.

28:9 And thou shalt take two onyx stones, and grave on them the names of the children of Israel: **28:10** Six of their names on one stone, and the other six names of the rest on the other stone, according to their birth. **28:11** With the work of an engraver in stone, like the engravings of a signet, shalt thou engrave the two stones with the names of the children of Israel: thou shalt make them to be set in ouches of gold. **28:12** And thou shalt put the two stones upon the shoulders of the ephod for stones of memorial unto the children of Israel: and Aaron shall bear their names before the LORD upon his two shoulders for a memorial.

The Breastplate

28:13 And thou shalt make ouches of gold; **28:14** And two chains of pure gold at the ends; of wreathen work shalt thou make them, and fasten the wreathen chains to the ouches.

28:15 And thou shalt make the breastplate of judgment with cunning work; after the work of the ephod thou shalt make it; of gold, of blue, and of purple, and of scarlet, and of fine twined linen, shalt thou make it. **28:16** Foursquare it shall be being doubled; a span shall be the length thereof, and a span shall be the breadth thereof.

28:17 And thou shalt set in it settings of stones, even four rows of stones: the first row shall be a sardius, a topaz, and a carbuncle: this shall be the first row. **28:18** And the second row shall be an emerald, a sapphire, and a diamond. **28:19** And the third row a ligure, an agate, and an amethyst. **28:20** And the fourth row a beryl, and an onyx, and a jasper: they shall be set in gold in their inclosings.

This brings to mind the twelve stones of the New Jerusalem

> **Revelation 21:19** And the foundations of the wall of the city were garnished with all manner of precious stones. The first foundation was jasper; the second, sapphire; the third, a chalcedony; the fourth, an emerald; **21:20** The fifth, sardonyx; the sixth, sardius; the seventh, chrysolyte; the eighth, beryl; the ninth, a topaz; the tenth, a chrysoprasus; the eleventh, a jacinth; the twelfth, an amethyst.

Exodus 28:21 And the stones shall be with the names of the children of Israel, twelve, according to their names, like the engravings of a signet; every one with his name shall they be according to the twelve tribes.

28:22 And thou shalt make upon the breastplate chains at the ends of wreathen work of pure gold. **28:23** And thou shalt make upon the breastplate two rings of gold, and shalt put the two rings on the two ends of the breastplate. **28:24** And thou shalt put the two wreathen chains of gold in the two rings which are on the ends of the breastplate.

The breastplate was fastened to the shoulder pieces of the ephod by gold writhen chains.

28:25 And the other two ends of the two wreathen chains thou shalt fasten in the two ouches, and put them on the shoulderpieces of the ephod before it. **28:26** And thou shalt make two rings of gold, and thou shalt put them upon the two ends of the breastplate in the border thereof, which is in the side of the ephod inward. **28:27** And two other rings of gold thou shalt make, and shalt put them on the two sides of the ephod underneath, toward the forepart thereof, over against the other coupling thereof, above the curious girdle of the ephod. **28:28** And they shall bind the breastplate by the rings thereof unto the rings of the ephod with a lace of blue, that it may be above the curious girdle of the ephod, and that the breastplate be not loosed from the ephod.

Aaron is always to bear the names of the tribes on his own person next to his heart; just as Jesus Christ has the names of his beloved always in his heart as he intercedes for them with God the Father.

28:29 And Aaron shall bear the names of the children of Israel in the breastplate of judgment upon his heart, when he goeth in unto the holy place, for a memorial before the LORD continually.

The black and white Urim and Thummim by which the Aaronic high priest was to cast lots before the LORD, to determine the will of God in any difficult matter.

28:30 And thou shalt put in the breastplate of judgment the Urim and the Thummim; and they shall be upon Aaron's heart, when he goeth in before the LORD: and Aaron shall bear the judgment of the children of Israel upon his heart before the LORD continually.

The Blue Ephod

28:31 And thou shalt make the robe **of the ephod** all of blue. **28:32** And there shall be an hole in the top of it, in the midst thereof: it shall have a binding of woven work round [a reinforced seam around the neck hole] about the hole of it, as it were the hole of an habergeon, that it be not rent.

The white linen floor length shirt was prophetic of the purity from sin of the priesthood of Jesus Christ and the resurrected kings and priests of his priesthood; and covering it is the blue ephod representing the royal nature of the priests

On the bottom of the blue ephod were bells of gold, so that the physical high priest may be heard as he walks about.

These gold bells alternated with gold pomegranates hanging on the gold border of the garment.

The gold pomegranates: Pomegranates are filled to bursting with seeds and this represents the seed of the Word of God (Mat 13).

28:33 And beneath upon the hem of it thou shalt make **pomegranates of blue, and of purple, and of scarlet, round about the hem thereof; and bells of gold between them round about: 28:34 A golden bell and a pomegranate, a golden bell and a pomegranate, upon the hem of the robe round about.**

28:35 And it shall be upon Aaron to minister: and **his sound shall be heard when he goeth in unto the holy place before the LORD, and when he cometh out, that he die not.**

The Crown

28:36 And thou shalt make **a plate of pure gold, and grave upon it**, like the engravings of a signet, **HOLINESS TO THE LORD.**

28:37 And thou shalt **put it on a blue lace,** that it may be upon the mitre; upon the forefront of the mitre it shall be.

The physical high priest was to bear the repented physical iniquities of the Mosaic Covenant people; and the spiritual High Priest Jesus Christ [Melchizedek] bears the sincerely repented iniquities of the Called Out of the New Covenant faithful.

The mitre on the head being a crown of high priesthood and significant of having HOLINESS TO THE LORD always on his mind as the high priest serves God.

28:38 And it shall be upon Aaron's forehead, that Aaron may bear the iniquity of the holy things, which the children of Israel shall hallow in all their holy gifts; and it shall be always upon his forehead, that they [the Covenant faithful] may be accepted before the LORD.

The fabric of the garments was of fine linen.

28:39 And thou shalt embroider the coat of fine linen, and thou shalt make the mitre of fine linen, and thou shalt make the girdle of needlework.

Aaron's sons, the priesthood of the Mosaic Covenant under the high priest; were to have priestly garments of fine while linen covered by colorful garments of their office.

The white linen floor length shirt was prophetic of the purity from sin of the priesthood of Jesus Christ and the resurrected kings and priests of his priesthood; and covering it is the blue ephod representing the royal nature of the priests

> **Revelation 19:7** Let us be glad and rejoice, and give honour to him: for the marriage of the Lamb is come, and his wife hath made herself ready. **19:8** And to her was granted that she should be arrayed in fine linen, clean and white: for the fine linen is the righteousness of saints.

Exodus 28:40 And for Aaron's sons thou shalt make coats, and thou shalt make for them girdles, and bonnets shalt thou make for them, for glory and for beauty.

God Speaking to Moses

28:41 And thou shalt put them upon Aaron thy brother, and his sons with him; and shalt anoint them, and consecrate them, and sanctify them, that they may minister unto me in the priest's office.

Linen breeches is an awkward translation and refers to the linen shirt upon the skin and under the blue ephod that extends from the neck down to the ankles and covers the loins and thighs.

28:42 And thou shalt make them linen breeches to cover their nakedness; from the loins even unto the thighs they shall reach: **28:43** And they shall be upon Aaron, and upon his sons, when they come in unto the tabernacle of the congregation, or when they come near unto the altar to minister in the holy place; that they bear not iniquity, and die: it shall be a statute for ever unto him and his seed after him.

Exodus 29

The consecration of the priests

Exodus 29:1 And this is the thing that thou shalt do unto them to hallow them, to minister unto me in the priest's office: Take one young bullock, and two rams without blemish, **29:2** And unleavened bread, and cakes unleavened tempered with oil, and wafers unleavened anointed with oil: of wheaten flour shalt thou make them. **29:3** And thou shalt put them into one basket, and bring them in the basket, with the bullock and the two rams.

They shall be washed clean [referring allegorically to being washed clean from sin], and then dressed in the priestly garments. First Aaron the physical high priest and then his sons the physical priests.

Even so Jesus Christ ascended to God the Father to be accepted for us as a High Priest and the ONLY Intercessor between man and God the Father, and we shall also be made priests of the High Priesthood of Jesus Christ [Melchizedek] at our change to spirit and marriage to Him.

First we must be cleansed from all uncleanness and sin; and only then can the Holy Spirit be poured out upon us like the holy oil.

29:4 And Aaron and his sons thou shalt bring unto the door of the tabernacle of the congregation, and shalt wash them with water. **29:5** And thou shalt take the garments, and put upon Aaron the coat, and the robe of the ephod, and the ephod, and the breastplate, and gird him with the curious girdle of the ephod: **29:6** And thou shalt put the mitre upon his head, and put the holy crown upon the mitre. **29:7** Then shalt thou take the anointing oil, and pour it upon his head, and anoint him.

The regular priests were to be dressed in white linen coats and blue ephods and headgear [crowns] of office. This pertains to the spiritual priesthood of Jesus Christ after the resurrection to spirit, as well as to the physical priesthood of Aaron.

29:8 And thou shalt bring his sons, and put coats upon them. **29:9** And thou shalt gird them with girdles, Aaron and his sons, and put the bonnets on them: and the priest's office shall be theirs for a perpetual statute: and thou shalt consecrate Aaron and his sons.

A bullock [young bull] was be killed for the physical priests as a sin offering; representing the strength of Christ as our spiritual sin offering. The placing of the hands on the bullock to confess sins over it, is reminiscent of the fast of Atonement when the sins of the people are confessed with a laying on of hands on the sacrificial goat.

In this case the patience and strength of the bullock in the bearing of the sins of the physical priesthood is a reference to the strength and power of Jesus Christ to bear the sins of the called out and sincerely repentant.

29:10 And thou shalt cause a bullock to be brought before the tabernacle of the congregation: and Aaron and his sons shall put their hands upon the head of the bullock. **29:11** And thou shalt kill the bullock before the LORD, by the door of the tabernacle of the congregation.

29:12 And thou shalt take of the blood of the bullock, and put it upon the horns of the altar with thy finger, and pour all the blood beside the bottom of the altar. **29:13** And thou shalt take all the fat that covereth the inwards, and the caul that is above the liver, and the two kidneys, and the fat that is upon them, and burn them upon the altar.

29:14 But the flesh of the bullock, and his skin, and his dung, shalt thou burn with fire without the camp: **it is a sin offering.**

After the sin offering has atoned for the sins of the priests, a burnt offering is made representing the wholehearted service of Jesus Christ to God the Father and our own expected wholehearted Christ-like service to God the Father.

The burnt offering pictures Jesus Christ serving God the Father with his whole being; and is an example that we are to follow.

The priests are to lay their hands on the head of the ram to symbolize the wholehearted service of the Lamb of God to God the Father in heaven. The ram representing leadership of the flock and leading the flock to God.

29:15 Thou shalt also take one ram; and Aaron and his sons shall put their hands upon the head of the ram. **29:16** And thou shalt slay the ram, and thou shalt take his blood, and sprinkle it round about upon the altar. **29:17** And thou shalt cut the ram in pieces, and wash the inwards of him, and his legs, and put them unto his pieces, and unto his head.

Wholehearted Christ-like service to God the Father and the learning and living by every Word of God, are a pleasant pleasing perfume to God the Father in heaven!

29:18 And thou shalt burn the whole ram upon the altar: it is a burnt offering unto the LORD: it is a sweet savour, an offering made by fire unto the LORD.

Another ram was to be killed and its blood placed on the right ear, thumb and toe of Aaron and the priests; this to open the hearing with the ear, the doing with the hand and the walking [living], in the same godly life of our Spiritual High Priest Jesus Christ: Who died so that the Holy Spirit could be given to the sincerely repentant enabling us to hear with understanding, do with strength and to live as Christ lived, walking as he walked.

29:19 And thou shalt take the other ram; and Aaron and his sons shall put their hands upon the head of the ram. **29:20** Then shalt thou kill the ram, and take of his blood, and put it upon the tip of the right ear of Aaron, and upon the tip of the right ear of his sons, and upon the thumb of their right hand, and upon the great toe of their right foot, and sprinkle the blood upon the altar round about.

The rest of the ram's blood was to be poured out on the altar, representative of the sacrifice and poured out blood of Jesus Christ, the Lamb of God the Father.

Then the blood was taken from the altar and sprinkled on every part of the priests and their garments, to show that they were reconciled to God the Father by the blood sacrifice of the Lamb of God, Jesus Christ.

29:21 And thou shalt take of the blood that is upon the altar, and of the anointing oil, and sprinkle it upon Aaron, and upon his garments, and upon his sons, and upon the garments of his sons with him: and he shall be hallowed, and his garments, and his sons, and his sons' garments with him.

The fat which represents the energy of the ram along with the strength of the right shoulder, and a piece of unleavened bread picturing Jesus Christ as the Bread of Life, with which the priests were to feed the people [by zealously teaching the whole Word of God], and a piece of unleavened bread [picturing purity from all sin] covered in olive oil [picturing the Holy Spirit]; was lifted up to God the Father in heaven for a wave offering. Which was offered to be accepted for the called out of Levi so that they might be accepted and consecrated as part of the priesthood of Aaron as a type of the spiritual priesthood of Jesus Christ.

29:22 Also thou shalt take of the ram the fat and the rump, and the fat that covereth the inwards, and the caul above the liver, and the two kidneys, and the fat that is upon them, and the right shoulder; for it is a ram of consecration: **29:23** And one loaf of bread, and one cake of oiled bread, and one wafer out of the basket of the unleavened bread that is before the LORD: **29:24** And thou shalt put all in the hands of Aaron, and in the hands of his sons; and shalt wave them for a wave offering before the LORD.

After being lifted up and waved before God the Father, the articles were to be burned on the altar; for they represented the powerful service to God the Father of Jesus Christ; and the ceremony for these physical priests of Aaron represented those who would become spiritual priests of the High Priesthood of Christ.

29:25 And thou shalt receive them of their hands, and burn them upon the altar for a burnt offering, for a sweet savour before the LORD: it is an offering made by fire unto the LORD.

Moses as the mediator in the establishment of the priesthood of Aaron is then given the breast of the Ram, after he waves it before the Father to be accepted; after which in future time the Peace Offering breast and shoulder would belong to the priests who make the sacrifices.

29:26 And thou shalt take the breast of the ram of Aaron's consecration, and wave it for a wave offering before the LORD: and it shall be thy part.

The breast and right shoulder of the Peace Offerings belongs to the officiating priest.

29:27 And thou shalt sanctify the **breast of the wave offering, and the shoulder of the heave offering,** which is waved, and which is heaved up, of the ram of the consecration, even of that which is for Aaron, and of that which is for his sons: **29:28** And it shall be Aaron's and his sons' by a statute for ever from the children of Israel: for it is an heave offering: and it shall be an heave offering from the children of Israel of the sacrifice of **their peace offerings**, even their heave offering unto the LORD.

The descendants of the physical Aaronic high priest who hold a priestly office must also wear the same holy garments.

29:29 And the holy garments of Aaron shall be his sons' after him, to be anointed therein, and to be consecrated in them. **29:30** And that son that is priest in his stead shall put them on seven days, when he cometh into the tabernacle of the congregation to minister in the holy place.

After the fat is burned and the breast and right shoulder have been waved; the remaining flesh was to be simmered and eaten by the consecrated priests, as a type of them internalizing godliness.

29:31 And thou shalt take the ram of the consecration, and seethe his flesh in the holy place. **29:32** And Aaron and his sons shall eat the flesh of the ram, and the [unleavened] bread that is in the basket by the door of the tabernacle of the congregation. **29:33** And they shall eat those things wherewith the atonement was made, to consecrate and to sanctify them: but a stranger shall not eat thereof, because they are holy.

This unleavened bread and the ram of consecration must be eaten as a picture of internalizing of the Lamb of God, [like Passover] and anything left until the morning must be burned.

29:34 And if ought of the flesh of the consecrations, or of the bread, remain unto the morning, then **thou shalt burn the remainder with fire**: it shall not be eaten, because it is holy.

The consecration of the altar

The sin offerings are to be made every day for seven days to picture a complete consecration of the new priests.

29:35 And thus shalt thou do unto Aaron, and to his sons, according to all things which I have commanded thee: seven days shalt thou consecrate them. **29:36** And thou shalt **offer every day a bullock for a sin offering**

for atonement: and thou shalt cleanse the altar, when thou hast made an atonement for it, and thou shalt anoint it, to sanctify it.

29:37 Seven days thou shalt make an atonement for the altar, and sanctify it; and it shall be an altar most holy: whatsoever toucheth the altar shall be holy.

The Daily Sacrifice

29:38 Now this is that which thou shalt offer upon the altar; two lambs of the first year [a year or less old, in the first year of life] day by day continually.

A lamb was to be offered in the morning and this service began very early with the lamb being killed and prepared and then offered [burned] at sunrise. The lamb was to be offered with flour mingled with oil; representing the purity from sin of the lamb and the presence of the Holy Spirit; as a type of the Lamb of God, Jesus Christ. The wine represented the poured out blood of the Lamb of God, Jesus Christ.

29:39 The one lamb thou shalt offer in the morning; and the other lamb thou shalt offer at even: **29:40** And with the one lamb a tenth deal of flour mingled with the fourth part of an hin of beaten oil; and the fourth part of an hin of wine for a drink offering.

Another lamb was to be offered at the evening [at sunset and before full dark]. The service actually began much earlier as prayers were made and the lamb killed and then the lamb was offered [burned] at sunset.

Up until the destruction of the temple in the Roman wars; whenever it was offered, the evening sacrifice was killed and prepared in the afternoon and was always offered [burned] immediately after sunset.

The lamb was to be offered with flour mingled with oil; representing the unleavened [sinless purity] nature of the lamb and the presence of the Holy Spirit; as a type of the Lamb of God, Jesus Christ. The wine represented the poured pout blood of the Lamb of God, Jesus Christ.

29:41 And the other lamb thou shalt offer at even, and shalt do thereto according to the meat offering of the morning, and according to the drink offering thereof, for a sweet savour, an offering made by fire unto the LORD.

29:42 This shall be a continual burnt offering throughout your generations at the door of the tabernacle of the congregation before the LORD: where I will meet you, to speak there unto thee. **29:43** And there I will meet with the children of Israel, and the tabernacle shall be sanctified by my glory.

29:44 And I will sanctify [set apart for holiness] the tabernacle of the congregation, and the altar: I will sanctify also both Aaron and his sons, to minister to me in the priest's office.

29:45 And I will dwell among the children of Israel, and will be their God. **29:46** And they shall know that I am the LORD [YHVH] their God, that brought them forth out of the land of Egypt, that I may dwell among them: I am the LORD their God.

Exodus 30

The Altar of Incense

Exodus 30:1 And thou shalt make an altar to burn incense upon: of shittim [acacia] wood shalt thou make it.

Three feet high and 18 inches square

30:2 A cubit shall be the length thereof, and a cubit the breadth thereof; foursquare shall it be: and two cubits shall be the height thereof: the horns thereof shall be of the same. **30:3** And thou shalt overlay it with pure gold, the top thereof, and the sides thereof round about, and the horns thereof; and thou shalt make unto it a crown [lip or edge] of gold round about.

30:4 And two golden rings shalt thou make to it under the crown of it, by the two corners thereof, upon the two sides of it shalt thou make it; and they shall be for places for the staves to bear it withal. **30:5** And thou shalt make the staves of shittim wood, and overlay them with gold.

The altar of incense was placed in the Holy Place with the lamp stand just outside of the curtain covering the Most Holy Place.

30:6 And thou shalt put it before **the vail** that is by the ark of the testimony [ark of the covenant], before the mercy seat that is over the testimony, where I will meet with thee.

Incense as it burns rises up in a pleasant smelling smoke, which is representative of the rising up to heaven of the prayers of the faithful.

The pagans use this same allegory in the various burning ceremonies of witchcraft **like birthday candles**.

The priests burned incense on this altar each time the daily morning and evening sacrifices were offered [burned], once in the morning at sunrise and once just after sunset in the evening. Each of these two offerings begin the Daily Sacrifice [evening and morning] with the symbolic sweetness of the rising prayer of the faithful.

The daily Burnt Offering represents the daily ministering of the resurrected High Priest Jesus Christ, for the whole nation with God the Father in heaven.

30:7 And Aaron shall burn thereon sweet incense every morning: when he dresseth the lamps, he shall burn incense upon it. **30:8** And when Aaron lighteth the lamps at even, he shall burn incense upon it, a perpetual incense before the LORD throughout your generations.

Only the special incense that God commanded was be offered on this Altar of Incense and nothing else.

30:9 Ye shall offer no strange incense thereon, nor burnt sacrifice, nor meat offering; neither shall ye pour drink offering thereon.

On the fast of Atonement each year, the blood of the sin offering is to be sprinkled on the horns of the Altar of Incense; symbolizing the acceptance of the prayers of the sincerely repentant by God the Father through the sacrifice of the Lamb of God

30:10 And Aaron shall make an atonement upon the horns of it once in a year with the blood of the sin offering of atonements: once in the year shall he make atonement upon it throughout your generations: it is most holy unto the LORD.

Every Israelite twenty years old and above gave ten gerahs [atonement money] for the maintenance of the tabernacle.

30:11 And the LORD spake unto Moses, saying, **30:12** When thou takest the sum of the children of Israel after their number, then shall they give every man a ransom for his soul unto the LORD, when thou numberest them; that there be no plague among them, when thou numberest them.

30:13 This they shall give, every one that passeth among them that are numbered, half a shekel after the shekel of the sanctuary: (a shekel is twenty gerahs:) an half shekel shall be the offering of the LORD.

30:14 Every one that passeth among them that are numbered, from twenty years old and above, shall give an offering unto the LORD. **30:15** The rich shall not give more, and the poor shall not give less than half a shekel, when they give an offering unto the LORD, to make an atonement for your souls.

30:16 And thou shalt take the atonement money of the children of Israel, and shalt appoint it for the service of the tabernacle of the congregation; that it may be a memorial unto the children of Israel before the LORD, to make an atonement for your souls.

A laver or sea, is a very large basin of water. The basin would be filled with water for the priests to wash their hands and feet before entering the tabernacle tent.

30:17 And the LORD spake unto Moses, saying, **30:18** Thou shalt also make a laver of brass, and his foot also of brass, to wash withal: and thou shalt put it between the tabernacle of the congregation and the altar, and **thou shalt put water therein**.

Water was placed in the top section and flowed down to faucets at the bottom section where the washing took place. The washing to be clean physically was an allegory that we need to be spiritually clean by the washing of the Holy Spirit and the Word of God.

30:19 For Aaron and his sons shall wash their hands and their feet thereat: **30:20** When they go into the tabernacle of the congregation, they shall wash with water, that they die not; or when they come near to the altar to minister, to burn offering made by fire unto the LORD: **30:21** So they shall wash their hands and their feet, that they die not: and it shall be a statute for ever to them, even to him and to his seed throughout their generations.

The holy anointing oil which was to be used to anoint all the holy things including the priests.

30:22 Moreover the LORD spake unto Moses, saying, **30:23** Take thou also unto thee principal spices, of **pure myrrh** five hundred shekels, and of **sweet cinnamon** half so much, even two hundred and fifty shekels, and of **sweet calamus** two hundred and fifty shekels, **30:24** And **of cassia** five hundred shekels, after the shekel of the sanctuary, and of **oil olive** an hin:

30:25 And thou shalt make it an oil of holy ointment, an ointment compound after the art of the apothecary: it shall be an holy anointing oil.

This oil represented the Holy Spirit

30:26 And thou shalt anoint the tabernacle of the congregation therewith, and the ark of the testimony, **30:27** And the table and all his vessels, and the candlestick and his vessels, and the altar of incense, **30:28** And the altar of burnt offering with all his vessels, and the laver and his foot. **30:29** And thou shalt sanctify them, that they may be most holy: whatsoever toucheth them shall be holy.

30:30 And **thou shalt anoint Aaron and his sons, and consecrate them, that they may minister unto me in the priest's office.**

30:31 And thou shalt speak unto the children of Israel, saying, This shall be an holy anointing oil unto me throughout your generations. **30:32** Upon [the common non priest] man's flesh shall it not be poured, neither shall ye make any other like it, after the composition of it: it is holy, and it shall be holy unto you. **30:33** Whosoever compoundeth any like it, or whosoever putteth any of it upon a stranger, shall even be cut off from his people.

A perfume was made to put inside the tabernacle holy place [NOT the Most Holy Place], typifying the pleasant odor [perfume] of holiness and godliness.

30:34 And the LORD said unto Moses, Take unto thee sweet spices, **stacte, and onycha, and galbanum**; these sweet spices with **pure frankincense**: of each shall there be a like weight: **30:35** And thou shalt make it a perfume, a confection after the art of the apothecary, tempered together, pure and holy: **30:36** And thou shalt beat some of it very small, and put of it before the testimony [place it just outside the Most Holy Place, inside the tabernacle] in the tabernacle of the congregation, where I will meet with thee: it shall be unto you most holy.

30:37 And as for the perfume which thou shalt make, ye shall not make to yourselves according to the composition thereof: it shall be unto thee holy for the LORD. **30:38** Whosoever shall make like unto that, to smell thereto, shall even be cut off from his people.

Exodus 31

While on the mount God informs Moses that Bezaleel and Aholiab have been called by God and given skill to work on the things of the priesthood and the tabernacle.

Exodus 31:1 And the LORD spake unto Moses, saying, **31:2** See, I have called by name Bezaleel the son of Uri, the son of Hur [Hur who had helped to hold up Moses' arms during the battle with the Amalekites.], of the tribe of Judah: **31:3** And I have filled him with the spirit of God, in wisdom, and in understanding, and in knowledge, and in all manner of workmanship, **31:4** To devise cunning works, to work in gold, and in silver, and in brass, **31:5** And in cutting of stones, to set them, and in carving of timber, to work in all manner of workmanship.

31:6 And I, behold, I have given with him Aholiab, the son of Ahisamach, of the tribe of Dan: and in the hearts of all that are wise hearted I have put wisdom, that they may make all that I have commanded thee; **31:7** The tabernacle of the congregation, and the ark of the testimony, and the mercy seat that is thereupon, and all the furniture of the tabernacle, **31:8** And the table and his furniture, and the pure candlestick with all his furniture, and the altar of incense, **31:9** And the altar of burnt offering with all his furniture, and the laver and his foot, **31:10** And the cloths of service, and the holy garments for Aaron the priest, and the garments of his sons, to minister in the priest's office, **31:11** And the anointing oil, and sweet incense for the holy place: according to all that I have commanded thee shall they do.

On the mount God dictates his Word and them makes a particular emphasis concerning his Holy Sabbath Day to Moses.

31:12 And the LORD spake unto Moses, saying, **31:13** Speak thou also unto the children of Israel, saying, **Verily my sabbaths ye shall keep: for it is a sign between me and you throughout your generations; that ye may know that I am the LORD that doth sanctify you.**

Zeal for keeping the Sabbath is emphasized as a very important sign between God and his people. This sign is also for us today, so that we may have this weekly time to spend with God and learn about him: **"that ye may know that I am the LORD that doth sanctify you.**

31:14 Ye shall keep the sabbath therefore; for it is holy unto you: **every one that defileth it shall surely be put to death: for whosoever doeth any work therein, that soul shall be cut off from among his people.**

Today the Assemblies proclaim the Set Apartness of the Sabbath, and then go out to pollute it on a weekly basis: FOR SHAME! They cook and they do menial work around the home and they pay others to cook and work for them! For Shame that the brethren for the most part, speak their own words about business and gossip, and do not discuss the Word of the Eternal on his Holy Sabbath Day!

For this God proclaims that they are cut off from HIM and are cut off from being accounted among his people as a part of his collective bride!

The apostate Called Out of today's Spiritual Israel will surely be rejected by Jesus Christ (Rev 3:16) and vomited out of his body into great tribulation, where they will be strongly corrected for defiling the sanctity of the Sabbath and Annual Holy Days.

31:15 Six days may work be done; but **in the seventh is the sabbath of rest, holy to the LORD: whosoever doeth any work in the sabbath day, he shall surely be put to death. 31:16** Wherefore the children of Israel shall keep the sabbath, to observe the sabbath throughout their generations, for a perpetual covenant.

Keeping the Sabbath, the New Moons and Festivals on God's schedule in the way that God has said, acknowledges the absolute authority of God and His Word.

31:17 It is a sign between me and the children of Israel for ever: for in six days the LORD made heaven and earth, and on the seventh day he rested, and was refreshed.

Then the one who became Jesus Christ [Hebrew: Yeshua Mashiach] gave Moses two tables of stone written with the ten foundational commandments.

31:18 And he gave unto Moses, when he had made an end of communing with him upon mount Sinai, two tables of testimony, tables of stone, written with the finger of God.

Exodus 32

Moses was up on the mount and hidden in clouds for 40 days and the people grew impatient. They went to Aaron and asked him to make them statues representing spiritual things so that they could worship before them.

Exodus 32:1 And when the people saw that Moses delayed to come down out of the mount, the people gathered themselves together unto Aaron, and said unto him, Up, make us gods, which shall go before us; for as for this Moses, the man that brought us up out of the land of Egypt, we wot not what is become of him.

Aaron then took gold from the people and made them idols of calves after the likeness of Apis the bull god of Egypt. Later Jeroboam was to commit this same sin, setting up the bull god of Egypt in Samaria.

32:2 And Aaron said unto them, Break off the golden earrings, which are in the ears of your wives, of your sons, and of your daughters, and bring them unto me. **32:3** And all the people brake off the golden earrings which were in their ears, and brought them unto Aaron.

A calf of gold was then formed and declared to be the likeness of God, and Aaron built an altar to it.

This demonstrates how quickly men go astray: Israel which had just walked through the Sea was turned aside from their God who they had just married them proclaiming: "All that the LORD has said; we will do." In fact the people were deceived, for not having seen God they imagined him as being like a strong bull calf! They worshiped God by their own ways and imaginations just like most of the brethren try to worship God today!

The spiritually Called Out of the today's spiritual Ekklesia have gone astray just like physical Israel at Sinai: being misled into thinking that they are worshiping God, while following idols of men, corporate organizations and of numbers and mammon! Doing what they think is right by their own imaginations, instead of being zealous to live by every Word of God!

32:4 And he received them at their hand, and fashioned it with a graving tool, after he had made it a molten calf: and they said, These be thy gods, O Israel, which brought thee up out of the land of Egypt. **32:5** And when Aaron saw it, he built an altar before it; and Aaron made proclamation, and said, To morrow is a feast to the LORD. **32:6** And they rose up early on the morrow, and offered burnt offerings, and brought peace offerings; and the people sat down to eat and to drink, and rose up to play.

YHVH then commanded Moses to run down to the people because of this terrible sin; which is the same sin perpetrated by the majority of today's brethren.

32:7 And the LORD said unto Moses, Go, get thee down; for thy people, which thou broughtest out of the land of Egypt, have corrupted themselves: **32:8** They have turned aside quickly out of the way which I commanded them: they have made them a molten calf, and have worshipped it, and have sacrificed thereunto, and said, These be thy gods, O Israel, which have brought thee up out of the land of Egypt.

Then the one who became Jesus Christ resolved to destroy the people!

Even so, the Called Out of today's spiritual Israel, calling themselves God's people; have committed this same sin in a spiritual manner. Worshiping and exalting men and corporate organizations above the Word of God, blindly following the words of men contrary to the Word of God and worshiping [following and obeying] organizational golden calves and the opinions of men!

Most assuredly if Jesus Christ decided to reject and kill those people who did not have his Spirit; how much more will he be angry and reject those today who are supposed to have his Spirit and still commit the same sins on a spiritual level! See the message to Laodicea (Rev 3).

32:9 And the LORD said unto Moses, I have seen this people, and, behold, it is a stiffnecked people: **32:10** Now therefore let me alone, that my wrath may wax hot against them, and that I may consume them: and I will make of thee a great nation.

Moses the Mosaic Mediator pleads for the people, and YHVH who later became Jesus Christ accepted his plea, but today Jesus Christ is our Mediator and he will not plead for us any longer. He will stop his Daily Intercession for us before the throne of God the Father because of the abominations committed by today's spiritual Ekklesia in rejecting God's Word to follow our own false traditions.

32:11 And Moses besought the LORD his God, and said, LORD, why doth thy wrath wax hot against thy people, which thou hast brought forth out of the land of Egypt with great power, and with a mighty hand? **32:12** Wherefore should the Egyptians speak, and say, For mischief did he bring them out, to slay them in the mountains, and to consume them from the face of the earth? Turn from thy fierce wrath, and repent of this evil against thy people.

32:13 Remember Abraham, Isaac, and Israel, thy servants, to whom thou swarest by thine own self, and saidst unto them, I will multiply your seed as the stars of heaven, and all this land that I have spoken of will I give unto your seed, and they shall inherit it for ever.

The Eternal repented of his thoughts against Israel, because of the mediatorial pleadings of Moses.

Today God will not hold back and many of spiritual New Covenant Israel will be thrown into the fire of affliction.

32:14 And the LORD repented of the evil which he thought to do unto his people.

The stone tablets were written by the hand of God on BOTH sides.

32:15 And Moses turned, and went down from the mount, and the two tables of the testimony were in his hand: **the tables were written on both their sides**; on the one side and on the other were they written. **32:16** And the tables were the work of God, and the writing was the writing of God, graven upon the tables.

As Moses came down from the mount Joshua met him, and they heard the noise of the people partying before the calf.

32:17 And when Joshua heard the noise of the people as they shouted, he said unto Moses, There is a noise of war in the camp. **32:18** And he said, It is not the voice of them that shout for mastery, neither is it the voice of them that cry for being overcome: but the noise of them that sing do I hear.

Moses was hot with anger at this sin; while today's Assemblies fail to condemn this same sin within their congregations. Why? Because we have made the leaders and organizations: Our golden calves!

Today most elders and leaders will not correct the people for exalting them [the corporate churches and elders] as little gods, blindly following them without question.

32:19 And it came to pass, as soon as he [Moses] came nigh unto the camp, that he saw the calf, and the dancing: and Moses' anger waxed hot, and he cast the tables out of his hands, and brake them beneath the mount.

Just as Moses destroyed those idols; so I speak out, calling all brethren to turn from our corporate idols, to turn men back to a genuine zeal for learning and living by every Word of God and exalt the Mighty One of Jacob!

32:20 And he took the calf which they had made, and burnt it in the fire, and ground it to powder, and strawed it upon the water, and made the children of Israel drink of it.

Then Moses inquired of Aaron, and Aaron blamed the people and justified himself.

Oh, how like Aaron we are today; for the brethren say that "We were only obeying the elders;" and the elders will say "we were only obeying our employers;" and the leaders will say "we are only following what we thought was right." Is there no one who will take responsibility for his own actions?

I tell you true that our Judge will not buy into such self-justification; he will judge every person for their own actions according to the whole Word of God. We are all personally responsible for proving all things and living by every Word of God!

32:21 And Moses said unto Aaron, What did this people unto thee, that thou hast brought so great a sin upon them? **32:22** And Aaron said, Let not the anger of my lord wax hot: thou knowest the people, that they are set on mischief. **32:23** For they said unto me, Make us gods, which shall go before us: for as for this Moses, the man that brought us up out of the land of Egypt, we wot not what is become of him. **32:24** And I said unto them, Whosoever hath any gold, let them break it off. So they gave it me: then I cast it into the fire, and there came out this calf.

The people were naked, revealed as sinners and exposed to their enemies. Even so today's spiritual Israel stands naked of godliness and we have lost the protection of the Eternal by our idolatry. The time of our rejection into great tribulation is almost at hand.

Very many who consider themselves Elijah's today, will find that Jesus Christ has thrown them into the furnace of affliction to humble them for their pride and sin.

Moses separated and divided the people; those who were zealous for God on one side and the faithless on the other side.

The very same thing is being done today, as God is sifting out those individuals who are zealous for Him and his Word from the spiritually lax, lukewarm and sinful.

32:25 And when Moses saw that the people were naked; (for Aaron had made them naked unto their shame among their enemies:) **32:26** Then Moses stood in the gate of the camp, and said, Who is on the LORD's side? let him come unto me. And **all the sons of Levi gathered themselves together unto him**.

Just as the Levites slew many on that day so very many of today's Ekklesia will fall during the imminent tribulation; for they are rejected from God's protection because of the overspreading of their idolatries.

32:27 And he said unto them, Thus saith the LORD God of Israel, Put every man his sword by his side, and go in and out from gate to gate throughout the camp, and slay every man his brother, and every man his companion, and every man his neighbour. **32:28** And the children of Levi did according to the word of Moses: and there fell of the people that day about three thousand men.

The Called Out of Spiritual Israel, today's Church of God groups, are being called to consecrate [by sincerely repenting and turning from our sin] themselves to the Eternal, and to turn away from their blind unquestioning idolatrous following of men and false traditions.

32:29 For Moses had said, Consecrate yourselves today to the LORD, even every man upon his son, and upon his brother; that he may bestow upon you a blessing this day.

I expect that when the Levites began to kill the wicked the living quickly repented; even as most of today's Called Out will quickly repent when they find themselves in tribulation.

Then the next day Moses as mediator goes to make an atonement for the people, and pleads with God on their behalf.

32:30 And it came to pass on the morrow, that Moses said unto the people, Ye have sinned a great sin: and now I will go up unto the LORD; peradventure I shall make an atonement for your sin.

32:31 And Moses returned unto the LORD, and said, Oh, this people have sinned a great sin, and have made them gods of gold. **32:32** Yet now, if thou wilt forgive their sin--; and if not, blot me, I pray thee, out of thy book which thou hast written.

God then tells Moses that every person must die for his own unrepented sin. This was true then and it is true today: Anyone who justifies himself and refuses to sincerely repent will be blotted out of the book of life!

32:33 And the LORD said unto Moses, **Whosoever hath sinned against me, him will I blot out of my book.**

The Eternal corrected the people and the people returned to the LORD to move forward. Today a powerful correction is at hand for physical and spiritual Israel and Judah.

32:34 Therefore now go, lead the people unto the place of which I have spoken unto thee: behold, mine Angel shall go before thee: nevertheless in the day when I visit I will visit their sin upon them. **32:35** And the LORD plagued the people, because they made the calf, which Aaron made.

Exodus 33

Then the YHVH Elohim who later gave up his God-hood to be made flesh as Jesus Christ the Lamb of God the Father, instructed the people to go in and possess the land; only he said that he would not be with them, but would send an angel in his place; because the people were continually provoking him and if he were with them he might destroy them

Exodus 33:1 And the LORD said unto Moses, Depart, and go up hence, thou and the people which thou hast brought up out of the land of Egypt, unto the land which I sware unto Abraham, to Isaac, and to Jacob, saying, Unto thy seed will I give it: **33:2** And **I will send an angel before thee;** and I will drive out the Canaanite, the Amorite, and the Hittite, and the Perizzite, the Hivite, and the Jebusite: **33:3** Unto a land flowing with milk and honey: for **I will not go up in the midst of thee; for thou art a stiffnecked people: lest I consume thee in the way.**

This statement by their Deliverer caused the people to repent of their sin of idolatry with the gold calves.

33:4 And when the people heard these evil tidings, they mourned: and no man did put on him his ornaments.

The people repented and did not adorn themselves because of their shame

33:5 For the LORD had said unto Moses, Say unto the children of Israel, Ye are a stiffnecked [very stubborn, self-willed, hardhearted] people: **I will**

come up into the midst of thee in a moment, and consume thee: therefore now put off thy ornaments [put off your pleasant things and repent in sackcloth and fasting] **from thee, that I may know what to do unto thee. 33:6** And the children of Israel stripped themselves of their ornaments by the mount Horeb.

Moses then built the tabernacle according to the plan that God gave him, and set it up a distance outside the camp because of the sins of the people.

33:7 And Moses took the tabernacle, and pitched it without the camp, afar off from the camp, and called it the Tabernacle of the congregation. And it came to pass, that every one which sought the LORD went out unto the tabernacle of the congregation, which was without the camp.

Then those who sought God had to leave the camp to come to the tabernacle. This is a picture that we need to leave our worldliness behind to seek and find God.

Now when Moses had set up the tabernacle all the people looked out of their tents to see what would happen.

33:8 And it came to pass, when Moses went out unto the tabernacle, that all the people rose up, and stood every man at his tent door, and looked after Moses [watched to see], until he was gone into the tabernacle.

When Moses entered the tabernacle, the cloud came down and rested at the tabernacle entrance and God spoke with Moses. The people saw this with their own eyes [not having seen Moses on the top of Sinai] and the people fell down to worship God.

This coming of Jesus Christ to the tabernacle DOOR was representative of Jesus Christ as the DOOR to Salvation.

> **John 10:9** I am the door: by me if any man enter in, he shall be saved, and shall go in and out, and find pasture.

Exodus 33:9 And it came to pass, as **Moses entered into the tabernacle, the cloudy pillar descended, and stood at the door of the tabernacle, and the Lord talked with Moses. 33:10 And all the people saw the cloudy pillar stand at the tabernacle door: and all the people rose up and worshipped, every man in his tent door.**

Then YHVH spoke to Moses and Joshua out of the cloud.

33:11 And the LORD spake unto Moses face to face, as a man speaketh unto his friend. And he turned again into the camp: but his servant Joshua, the son of Nun, a young man, departed not out of the tabernacle.

Moses reasoned that God should be with them, and not just an angel as God had said. Moses argued that God had abandoned him by turning away from the people.

33:12 And Moses said unto the LORD, See, thou sayest unto me, Bring up this people: and thou hast not let me know whom thou wilt send with me. Yet thou hast said, I know thee by name, and thou hast also found grace in my sight.

Moses asked God to remain with him and with the people to teach, guide and lead them.

33:13 Now therefore, I pray thee, if I have found grace in thy sight, **shew me now thy way, that I may know thee, that I may find grace in thy sight: and consider that this nation is thy people.**

God then promised to remain with Moses and the people.

33:14 And he said, **My presence shall go with thee**, and I will give thee rest.

Moses replied asking God to let them remain at Sinai and not command them to enter the land if God will not go with them.

This is an example that spiritual Israel may not enter the spiritual Promised Land of eternal life if we are not zealously faithful to God. God will be with us and bring us into the Promised Land of eternal life, ONLY if we are with him and if we are quick to obey and follow him in all things.

33:15 And he said unto him, If thy presence go not with me, carry us not up hence If God will not be with them then they would rather stay in the wilderness and not go without God into the physical land of promise.

Moses declared that it is the presence of God that sets Israel apart from all others.

It is the same in spiritual Israel; for if we do not diligently follow our God and live by every Word of God; HOW are we different from any other people?

33:16 For wherein shall it be known here that I and thy people have found grace in thy sight? is it not in that thou goest with us? so shall we be separated, I and thy people, from all the people that are upon the face of the earth.

Then YHVH agreed to remain with the people for Moses sake. Moses had interceded for physical Israel as the mediator of the Mosaic Marriage

Covenant, which was an allegory that today the resurrected Jesus Christ intercedes for Spiritual Israel with God the Father as the ONLY Mediator of the New Covenant. The Daily Sacrifice also teaching that the spirit High Priest the resurrected Jesus Christ now intercedes day and night as the Mediator Intercessor for Spiritual Israel before the throne of God the Father in heaven.

33:17 And the LORD said unto Moses, I will do this thing also that thou hast spoken: for thou hast found grace in my sight, and I know thee by name.

Then Moses asked to see the Creator in his glory, for before this Moses had only heard his voice God being hidden by the cloud

33:18 And he said, I beseech thee, shew me thy glory.

Then the God Being who later became flesh as Jesus Christ showed Moses his glory in part; someday when changed to spirit Moses and the resurrected chosen will see Him in His full glory.

> **John 17:5** And now, O Father, glorify thou me with thine own self with the glory which I had with thee before the world was.

After our resurrection we shall see him as he is.

> **John 17:24** Father, I will that they also, whom thou hast given me, **be with me where I am** [he went to heaven]; **that they may behold my glory**, which thou hast given me: for thou lovedst me before the foundation of the world.

The resurrected chosen will be given the same kind of glory but to a lessor degree when changed to spirit! Jesus Christ the Door of our Salvation will give us a glorious spiritual body like his own.

> **John 17:22** And the glory which thou gavest me I have given them; that they may be one, even as we are one:

Exodus 33:19 And he said, I will make all my goodness pass before thee, and I will proclaim the name of the LORD before thee; and will be gracious to whom I will be gracious, and will shew mercy on whom I will shew mercy. **33:20** And he said, Thou canst not see my face: for there shall no man see me, and live.

Moses was then taken and placed in a cleft of rock so that he would see only a small part of God in his glory.

33:21 And the LORD said, Behold, there is a place by me, and thou shalt stand upon a rock: **33:22** And it shall come to pass, while my glory passeth by, that I will put thee in a clift of the rock, and will cover thee with my hand while I pass by: **33:23** And I will take away mine hand, and thou shalt see my back parts: but my face shall not be seen.

Exodus 34

Then God commanded Moses to make two tablets of stone like the first two and says that HE, God, would write on them.

Exodus 34:1 And the LORD said unto Moses, Hew thee two tables of stone like unto the first: and **I will write** upon these tables the words that were in the first tables, which thou brakest.

Moses was to come to God at the top of the mount alone, no other living man or creature was to be seen on the mount. The top of Sinai represented the heaven of God the Father, and Moses as the mediator of the Mosaic Covenant was to physically climb the mount as an allegory that in future the Spiritual Mediator of the New Covenant would ascend to the heaven of God the Father to intercede for us!

34:2 And be ready in the morning, and come up in the morning unto mount Sinai, and present thyself there to me in the top of the mount. **34:3** And no man shall come up with thee, neither let any man be seen throughout all the mount; neither let the flocks nor herds feed before that mount.

Moses obeyed God and made the two tablets of stone and in the morning he went up into the mount to meet God.

34:4 And he hewed two tables of stone like unto the first; and Moses rose up early in the morning, and went up unto mount Sinai, as the LORD had commanded him, and took in his hand the two tables of stone. **34:5** And the LORD descended in the cloud, and stood with him there, and proclaimed the name of the LORD.

The Eternal who became Jesus Christ then proclaimed his mercy for the sincerely repentant and his wrath on all unrepentant sinners.

34:6 And the LORD passed by before him, and proclaimed, The LORD, The LORD God, merciful and gracious, longsuffering, and abundant in goodness and truth, **34:7** Keeping mercy for thousands, forgiving iniquity and transgression and sin, [Forgiving the sincerely repentant who STOP breaking God's Word.] and **that will by no means clear the guilty;** visiting the iniquity of the fathers upon the children, and upon the children's children, unto the third and to the fourth generation.

34:8 And Moses made haste, and bowed his head [prostrated himself before God in an act of total submission] toward the earth, and worshipped.

Moses begged God's mercy for the people.

34:9 And he said, If now I have found grace in thy sight, O LORD, let my LORD, I pray thee, go among us; for it is a stiffnecked people; and pardon our iniquity and our sin, and take us for thine inheritance

Then God promised marvels for his people; this being an allegory of the spiritual marvels that God performs to deliver the spiritually called out of the New Covenant.

34:10 And he [God] said, Behold, I make a covenant: before all thy people I will do marvels, such as have not been done in all the earth, nor in any nation: and all the people among which thou art shall see the work of the LORD: for it is a terrible thing that I will do with thee.

God promises to drive out the Canaanites as a type of removing all sin from the sincerely repentant. Our God will drive out all sin from his people, if they will only obey his Word and follow him.

34:11 Observe thou that which I command thee this day: behold, I drive out before thee the Amorite, and the Canaanite, and the Hittite, and the Perizzite, and the Hivite, and the Jebusite.

Israel was to make no covenant with the Canaanites because they were a type of sin and we are to keep ourselves clean from all sin and compromise with the Word of God!

34:12 Take heed to thyself, lest thou make a covenant with the inhabitants of the land whither thou goest, lest it be for a snare in the midst of thee:

Spiritually we are to destroy all sin out of our lives; including our idols of mammon, men and organizational entities. We are to exalt the Eternal above all else!

Organizing is not wrong as long as the organizations help us to focus on God: It is when those organizations seek to come between us and God that they become an abomination to God!

Just as physical Israel was not to become of one flesh with the daughters of the Canaanites, we are NOT to marry the unconverted; nor are we to become spiritually one with sin by learning the ways of the heathen to worship God according to our own ways: We are to worship God according to HIS commandments!

34:13 But ye shall destroy their altars, break their images, and cut down their groves: **34:14** For thou shalt worship no other god: for the LORD, whose name is Jealous, is a jealous God: **34:15** Lest thou make a covenant with the inhabitants of the land, and they go a whoring after their gods, and do sacrifice unto their gods, and one call thee, and thou eat of his sacrifice; **34:16** And thou take of their daughters unto thy sons, and their daughters go a whoring after their gods, and make thy sons go a whoring after their gods.

Physical Israel was not to make idols of any thing and we are not to make idols in either the physical or spiritual sense!

34:17 Thou shalt make thee no molten gods.

Here we have a specific command to eat unleavened bread for seven days. How is it that some claim it is not sin to disobey God in this matter? It is because they have no zeal to live by every Word of God and they will face the same condemnation as other stubborn stiff-necked self-willed persons who rebel against the Word of God!

34:18 The feast of unleavened bread shalt thou keep. **Seven days thou shalt eat unleavened bread,** as I commanded thee, in the time of the month Abib: for in the month Abib thou camest out from Egypt.

All the first born belong to God because he delivered Israel's first born in Egypt, and because God the Father gave up HIS firstborn the Lamb of God for sinners. The first born of the clean animals were to be given to the priests and were then used for the Daily Sacrifices and the National Sacrifices on behalf of the nation.

The first born males of Israel were to be redeemed with money, and the first born of the unclean creatures are to be redeemed with a lamb.

34:19 All that openeth the matrix [the first born] is mine; and every firstling among thy cattle, whether ox or sheep, that is male. **34:20** But the firstling of an ass thou shalt redeem with a lamb: and if thou redeem him not, then shalt thou break his neck. **All the firstborn of thy sons thou shalt redeem. And none shall appear before me empty.**

We are to rest on the weekly Sabbath even during harvest time

The Pentecost and Fall Harvest commandments are repeated.

34:21 Six days thou shalt work, but on the seventh day thou shalt rest: in earing time and in harvest thou shalt rest. **34:22** And thou shalt observe **the feast of weeks, of the firstfruits of wheat harvest**, and **the feast of ingathering at the year's end. 34:23** Thrice in the year shall all your menchildren appear before the LORD God, the God of Israel.

Only if we are zealous for the weekly and annual Sabbaths and Festivals to keep them as God has commanded [including on the correct day that God's Biblical Calendar requires]; will Spiritual Israel be blessed!

34:24 For I will cast out the nations before thee, and enlarge thy borders: neither shall any man desire thy land, when thou shalt go up to appear before the LORD thy God thrice in the year.

No sacrifice may be offered with leaven, for leaven is used as a type of sin. A whole Bible word study on the subject of "leaven" would be rewarding.

34:25 Thou shalt not offer the blood of my sacrifice with leaven; neither shall the sacrifice of the feast of the passover be left unto the morning.

The first of the first fruits, here refers to the Wave Offering on the Sunday during the Feast of Unleavened Bread.

Simmering a kid in its own mother's milk was a fertility rite of the Canaanites, and has nothing to do with eating milk products with meat.

34:26 The first of the firstfruits of thy land thou shalt bring unto the house of the LORD thy God. Thou shalt not seethe a kid in his mother's milk.

Previously God had written all these words on BOTH sides of the two tablets of stone, then later God wrote the same Ten Commandments on two new tables of stone a second time (Deu 10:4).

Note that God wrote the words of the Ten Commandments TWICE, and now God is telling Moses to write the rest of God's words of instruction, which Moses does over forty days.

34:27 And the LORD said unto Moses, Write thou these words: for after the tenor of these words I have made a covenant with thee and with Israel.

Moses was on the mount for forty days and nights writing the words that Almighty God dictated to him, and the Eternal sustained him.

34:28 And he was there with the LORD forty days and forty nights; he did neither eat bread, nor drink water. And he wrote upon the tables the words of the covenant, the ten commandments.

Moses spent forty days writing so he must have also written other words of God on papyrus or vellum, including the first three books of Moses.

Moses face shone with light from his exposure to God, which was typical that God's faithful will shine with the glory of God in our conduct, like a Light on a Hill; through enthusiastically learning and living by every Word of God.

> **Matthew 5:13** Ye are the salt [our zeal for godliness preserves the earth from utter destruction] of the earth: but if the salt have lost his savour, wherewith shall it be salted? it is thenceforth good for nothing, but to be cast out, and to be trodden under foot of men.
>
> **5:14** Ye are the light of the world. A city that is set on an hill cannot be hid. **5:15** Neither do men light a candle, and put it under a bushel, but on a candlestick; and it giveth light unto all that are in the house
>
> **5:16** Let your light so shine before men, that they may see your good works, and glorify your Father which is in heaven.
>
> **5:17** Think not that I am come to destroy the law, or the prophets: I am not come to destroy, but to fulfill [to keep fully, live by every Word of God as a shining example, for us to also keep as an example for others] .

Exodus 34:29 And it came to pass, when Moses came down from mount Sinai with the two tables of testimony in Moses' hand, when he came down from the mount, that Moses wist not that the skin of his face shone while he talked with him. **34:30** And when Aaron and all the children of Israel saw Moses, behold, the skin of his face shone; and they were afraid to come nigh him.

Then Moses taught the elders and all the people the Words that God gave to him on Sinai.

34:31 And Moses called unto them; and Aaron and all the rulers of the congregation returned unto him: and Moses talked with them. **34:32** And afterward all the children of Israel came nigh: and he gave them in commandment **all that the LORD had spoken with him in mount Sinai.**

NO, there are no hidden or secret instructions from God as some false teachers claim in the hope of leading the people away from the revealed Word of God!

Moses covered his face until the shining glory had diminished, because the people feared; but when Moses went into the tabernacle to speak to God he removed the veil.

34:33 And till Moses had done speaking with them, he put a vail on his face. **34:34** But when Moses went in before the LORD to speak with him, he took the vail off, until he came out. And he came out, and spake unto the children of Israel that which he was commanded. **34:35** And the children of Israel saw the face of Moses, that the skin of Moses' face shone: and Moses put the vail upon his face again, until he went in to speak with him.

Exodus 35

After the people had repented Moses went up on the mount for the second time (Ex 34) and now Moses comes down for the second time and instructs the people concerning the words that God has dictated to him on the mount.

To recap:

- God spoke to the people and being afraid they asked for a mediator (Ex 20),
- God then spoke to Moses at the foot of the mount and Moses wrote the Book of the Covenant (Ex 24) which was then read out to the people
- Moses went up the mount for the first time and received instructions for the tabernacle (Ex 25-32), and while he was away Israel sinned only to be rebuked when Moses returned and then to repent
- The tabernacle was then built (Ex 33)
- Then Moses went up the mount for the second time (Ex 34)

After returning from the mount for the second time Moses reminds the people of the Sabbath and then remembers the building of the

Tabernacle. The instructions for the tabernacle are recorded in Exodus 25-32 and now Moses explains the details of the work which was done.

Exodus 35:1 And Moses gathered all the congregation of the children of Israel together, and said unto them, These are the words which the LORD hath commanded, that ye should do them.

The very first thing commanded here is to sanctify the Sabbath to keep it holy: The seventh day which runs from Friday sunset to Saturday sunset is holy to God, it is God's time and it is NOT our own time.

35:2 Six days shall work be done, but on the seventh day there shall be to you an holy day, a sabbath of rest to the LORD: whosoever doeth work therein shall be put to death.

The following refers to kindling a fire from scratch without matches, a major effort. This is not about throwing a stick on an already burning fire, nor does it refer to using modern heating on a cold winter's night.

35:3 Ye shall kindle no fire throughout your habitations upon the sabbath day.

Moses rehearses that when he had come down from the mount the first time and corrected the people the people were sincerely repentant and highly motivated to please God, giving very generous offering for the building of the tabernacle.

35:4 And Moses spake unto all the congregation of the children of Israel, saying, This is the thing which the LORD commanded, saying, **35:5** Take ye from among you an offering unto the LORD: whosoever is of a willing heart, let him bring it, an offering of the LORD; gold, and silver, and brass, **35:6** And blue, and purple, and scarlet, and fine linen, and goats' hair, **35:7** And rams' skins dyed red, and badgers' ["Tachash" Blue Ram's skins] skins, and shittim wood, **35:8** And oil for the light, and spices for anointing oil, and for the sweet incense, **35:9** And onyx stones, and stones to be set for the ephod, and for the breastplate.

35:10 And every wise hearted among you shall come, and make all that the LORD hath commanded; **35:11** The tabernacle, his tent, and his covering, his taches, and his boards, his bars, his pillars, and his sockets, **35:12** The ark, and the staves thereof, with the mercy seat, and the vail of the covering, **35:13** The table, and his staves, and all his vessels, and the shewbread, **35:14** The candlestick also for the light, and his furniture, and his lamps, with the oil for the light, **35:15** And the incense altar, and his staves, and the anointing oil, and the sweet incense, and the hanging for the door at the entering in of the tabernacle, **35:16** The altar of burnt offering, with his brasen grate, his staves, and all his vessels, the laver and his foot, **35:17** The hangings of the court, his pillars, and their sockets, and the hanging for the door of the court, **35:18** The pins of the tabernacle, and the pins of the court, and their cords, **35:19** The cloths of service, to do service in the holy place, the holy garments for Aaron the priest, and the garments of his sons, to minister in the priest's office.

Moses remembers the offerings for the tabernacle

35:20 And all the congregation of the children of Israel departed from the presence of Moses.

35:21 And they came, every one whose heart stirred him up, and every one whom his spirit made willing, and they brought the LORD's offering to the work of the tabernacle of the congregation, and for all his service, and for the holy garments. **35:22** And they came, both men and women, as many as were willing hearted, and brought bracelets, and earrings, and rings, and tablets, all jewels of gold: and every man that offered offered an offering of gold unto the LORD.

35:23 And every man, with whom was found blue, and purple, and scarlet, and fine linen, and goats' hair, and red skins of rams, and badgers' [Blue ram's skins] skins, brought them. **35:24** Every one that did offer an offering of silver and brass brought the LORD's offering: and every man, with whom was found shittim wood for any work of the service, brought it.

35:25 And all the women that were wise hearted did spin with their hands, and brought that which they had spun, both of blue, and of purple, and of scarlet, and of fine linen. **35:26** And all the women whose heart stirred them up in wisdom spun goats' hair. **35:27** And the rulers brought onyx stones, and stones to be set, for the ephod, and for the breastplate; **35:28** And spice, and oil for the light, and for the anointing oil, and for the sweet incense.

A large offering was willingly provided by the people for the tabernacle.

35:29 The children of Israel brought a willing offering unto the LORD, every man and woman, whose heart made them willing to bring for all manner of work, which the LORD had commanded to be made by the hand of Moses.

Moses tells the people that Bezaleel and Aholiab would be in charge of the things for tabernacle and its construction.

35:30 And Moses said unto the children of Israel, See, the LORD hath called by name Bezaleel the son of Uri, the son of Hur, of the tribe of Judah; **35:31** And he hath filled him with the spirit of God, in wisdom, in understanding, and in knowledge, and in all manner of workmanship; **35:32** And to devise curious works, to work in gold, and in silver, and in brass, **35:33** And in the cutting of stones, to set them, and in carving of wood, to make any manner of cunning work.

35:34 And he [God] hath put in his heart that he may teach, both he, and Aholiab, the son of Ahisamach, of the tribe of Dan. **35:35** Them hath he filled with wisdom of heart, to work all manner of work, of the engraver, and of the cunning workman, and of the embroiderer, in blue, and in purple, in scarlet, and in fine linen, and of the weaver, even of them that do any work, and of those that devise cunning work.

Exodus 36

The offerings of the people for the tabernacle were given to Bezaleel and Aholiab and the skilled workers to build the tabernacle, and the people continued to bring more offerings daily.

Exodus 36:1 Then wrought Bezaleel and Aholiab, and every wise hearted man, in whom the LORD put wisdom and understanding to know how to work all manner of work for the service of the sanctuary, according to all that the LORD had commanded. **36:2** And Moses called Bezaleel and Aholiab, and every wise hearted man, in whose heart the LORD had put wisdom, even every one whose heart stirred him up to come unto the work to do it: **36:3** And they received of Moses all the offering, which the children of Israel had brought for the work of the service of the sanctuary, to make it withal. And they brought yet unto him free offerings every morning.

The people brought more than was needed and were asked to cease bringing offerings for the tabernacle.

36:4 And all the wise men, that wrought all the work of the sanctuary, came every man from his work which they made; **36:5** And they spake unto Moses, saying, The people bring much more than enough for the service of the work, which the LORD commanded to make. **36:6** And Moses gave commandment, and they caused it to be proclaimed throughout the camp, saying, Let neither man nor woman make any more work for the offering of the sanctuary. So the people were restrained from bringing. **36:7** For the stuff they had was sufficient for all the work to make it, and too much.

At this point Moses repeats the instructions for the tabernacle given to him by God, in Exodus 25-52. This time in terms of what they actually built: Adding a few details as for example that the board framework of the tabernacle was to be overlaid with pure gold.

36:8 And every wise hearted man among them that wrought the work of the tabernacle made ten curtains of fine twined linen, and blue, and purple, and scarlet: with cherubims of cunning work made he them. **36:9** The length of one curtain was twenty and eight cubits, and the breadth of one curtain four cubits: the curtains were all of one size. **36:10** And he coupled the five curtains one unto another: and the other five curtains he coupled one unto another.

36:11 And he made loops of blue on the edge of one curtain from the selvedge in the coupling: likewise he made in the uttermost side of another curtain, in the coupling of the second. **36:12** Fifty loops made he in one curtain, and fifty loops made he in the edge of the curtain which was in the coupling of the second: the loops held one curtain to another. **36:13** And he made fifty taches of gold, and coupled the curtains one unto another with the taches: so it became one tabernacle.

36:14 And he made curtains of goats' hair for the tent over the tabernacle: eleven curtains he made them. **36:15** The length of one curtain was thirty cubits, and four cubits was the breadth of one curtain: the eleven curtains were of one size. **36:16** And he coupled five curtains by themselves, and six curtains by themselves.

36:17 And he made fifty loops upon the uttermost edge of the curtain in the coupling, and fifty loops made he upon the edge of the curtain which coupleth the second. **36:18** And he made fifty taches of brass to couple the tent together, that it might be one. **36:19** And he made a covering for the tent of rams' skins dyed red, and a covering of badgers' skins ["Tachash" Ram's skins dyed blue] above that.

36:20 And he made boards for the tabernacle of shittim wood, standing up. **36:21** The length of a board was ten cubits, and the breadth of a board one cubit and a half. **36:22** One board had two tenons, equally distant one from another: thus did he make for all the boards of the tabernacle. **36:23** And he made boards for the tabernacle; twenty boards for the south side southward: **36:24** And forty sockets of silver he made under the twenty boards; two sockets under one board for his two tenons, and two sockets under another board for his two tenons.

36:25 And for the other side of the tabernacle, which is toward the north corner, he made twenty boards, **36:26** And their forty sockets of silver; two sockets under one board, and two sockets under another board.

36:27 And for the sides of the tabernacle westward he made six boards. **36:28** And two boards made he for the corners of the tabernacle in the two sides. **36:29** And they were coupled beneath, and coupled together at the head thereof, to one ring: thus he did to both of them in both the corners. **36:30** And there were eight boards; and their sockets were sixteen sockets of silver, under every board two sockets.

36:31 And he made bars of shittim wood; five for the boards of the one side of the tabernacle, **36:32** And five bars for the boards of the other side of the tabernacle, and five bars for the boards of the tabernacle for the sides westward. **36:33** And he made the middle bar to shoot through the boards from the one end to the other.

The frame of boards on which the curtains of the tabernacle were placed was overlaid with gold.

36:34 And he overlaid the boards with gold, and made their rings of gold to be places for the bars, and overlaid the bars with gold.

36:35 And he made a vail of blue, and purple, and scarlet, and fine twined linen: with cherubims made he it of cunning work. **36:36** And he made thereunto four pillars of shittim wood, and overlaid them with gold: their hooks were of gold; and he cast for them four sockets of silver.

36:37 And he made an hanging for the tabernacle door of blue, and purple, and scarlet, and fine twined linen, of needlework; **36:38** And the five pillars of it with their hooks: and he overlaid their chapiters and their fillets with gold: but their five sockets were of brass.

Exodus 37

The work in building the tabernacle was completed by Bezaleel and Aholiab exactly as inspired by the God who later gave up his Godhood to be made flesh as Jesus Christ. The tabernacle was built according to the specifications provided by God to Moses.

This is an example of how the spiritually called out are to remove all sin and internalize godliness until we become a suitable tabernacle [Temple] for God to dwell in through the agency of the Holy Spirit: And how do we build ourselves up into a spiritual Temple? By doing exactly what Moses, Bezaleel and Aholiab did! By keeping and following every Word of God precisely and exactly!

The tabernacle was a movable Temple that was later replaced by a permanent structure in Jerusalem. The tabernacle was the dwelling place of God as was the later Jerusalem Temple; and IF we faithfully and zealously live by every Word of God in Christ-like passion we will grow and be built into a dwelling place of God through his Spirit!

> **Ephesians 2:19** Now therefore ye are no more strangers and foreigners, but fellowcitizens with the saints, and of the household of God;

Paul refers to the whole of scripture by referring to the offices of the men who wrote the scriptures; at no time does he mean that some later day claimant of one of these offices has any right to turn aside from the Holy Scriptures.

Some have later come along and claimed to be apostles, prophets or representatives of Christ and have told people to believe and obey themselves! We are commanded to prove all things (1 Thess 5:21) by the Word of God, including those who claim to be apostles (Rev 2:2); and we are NEVER to follow any man or corporate church without questioning what they say by the scriptures.

> **2:20** And **are built upon the foundation of the apostles and prophets, Jesus Christ himself being the chief corner stone**; **2:21** In whom all the building fitly framed together groweth unto an holy temple in the Lord: **2:22** In whom ye also are builded together for an habitation of God through the Spirit.

We are to follow the example of Jesus Christ and we are to reject and cast out with their false teachings, all those who teach contrary to any part of the whole Word of God!

Today the major Assemblies of the spiritual Ekklesia have indeed become dens of idolatry deceiving the brethren and condemning those who are zealous to live by every Word of God!

Yes, they use the name of God and they say some right things along with their errors; but they use the name of God to deceive and lead men after themselves.

They teach in many subtle ways to be zealous for men and they condemn any zeal to live by every Word of God, for they know that zeal for God means the loss of their personal following because they teach for doctrine the commandments of men.

I will be bold and state plainly that any elder who condemns zeal for the sanctity of the Sabbath and Holy Days, or any other part of the whole Word of God and claims to be a man of God: Is a LIAR and a HYPOCRITE! For he claims to be godly, while rejecting the zealous keeping of the whole Word of God!

> **Matthew 15:7 Ye hypocrites, well did Esaias prophesy of you, saying, 5:8** This people draweth nigh unto me with their mouth, and honoureth me with their lips; but their heart is far from me. **5:9** But

> **in vain they do worship me, teaching for doctrines the commandments of men.**

If you follow men in their sins, you will also have a part in their judgment and will be cast out of the presence of God with them!

> **Matthew 21:12** And Jesus went into the temple of God, and cast out all them that sold and bought in the temple, and overthrew the tables of the moneychangers, and the seats of them that sold doves, **21:13** And said unto them, It is written, My house shall be called the house of prayer; but ye have made it a den of thieves.

The builders of the tabernacle did what Almighty God said, and they followed fully his instructions; they did not begin to do what they thought was right, but followed the whole Word of God exactly in building the tabernacle [and later the Temple] of God.

The spiritual Ekklesia are to be building themselves into a spiritual Tabernacle, a spiritual Temple; and to accomplish that we must learn, keep and live by every Word the comes from the mouth of God!

Many blindly follow human deceivers and do what they say without question, polluting the Sabbath day and committing many other sins.

> **1 Corinthians 3:16** Know ye not that ye are the temple of God, and that the Spirit of God dwelleth in you? **3:17** If any man defile the temple of God [with sin], him shall God destroy; for the temple of God is holy, which temple ye are.

Exodus 37:1 And Bezaleel made the ark of shittim [acacia] wood: two cubits and a half was the length of it, and a cubit and a half the breadth of it, and a cubit and a half the height of it: **37:2** And he overlaid it with pure gold within and without, and made a crown of gold to it round about. **37:3** And he cast for it four rings of gold, to be set by the four corners of it; even two rings upon the one side of it, and two rings upon the other side of it. **37:4** And he made staves of shittim wood, and overlaid them with gold. **37:5** And he put the staves into the rings by the sides of the ark, to bear the ark.

37:6 And he made the mercy seat [the Ark] of pure gold: two cubits and a half was the length thereof, and one cubit and a half the breadth thereof. **37:7** And he made two cherubims of gold, beaten out of one piece made he them, on the two ends of the mercy seat; **37:8** One cherub on the end on this side, and another cherub on the other end on that side: out of the mercy seat made he the cherubims on the two ends thereof. **37:9** And the cherubims spread out their wings on high, and covered with their wings over the mercy seat, with their faces one to another; even to the mercy seatward were the faces of the cherubims.

37:10 And he made the table of shittim [acacia] wood: two cubits was the length thereof, and a cubit the breadth thereof, and a cubit and a half the height thereof: **37:11** And he overlaid it with pure gold, and made thereunto a crown of gold round about. **37:12** Also he made thereunto a border of an handbreadth round about; and made a crown of gold for the border thereof round about. **37:13** And he cast for it four rings of gold, and put the rings upon the four corners that were in the four feet thereof. **37:14** Over against the border were the rings, the places for the staves to bear the table. **37:15** And he made the staves of shittim wood, and overlaid them with gold, to bear the table.

37:16 And he made the vessels which were upon the table, his dishes, and his spoons, and his bowls, and his covers to cover withal, of pure gold.

37:17 And he made the candlestick [lamp stand] of pure gold: of beaten work made he the candlestick; his shaft, and his branch, his bowls, his knops, and his flowers, were of the same: **37:18** And six branches going out of the sides thereof; three branches of the candlestick out of the one side thereof, and three branches of the candlestick out of the other side thereof: **37:19** Three bowls made after the fashion of almonds in one branch, a knop [bud] and a flower; and three bowls made like almonds in another branch, a knop [bud] and a flower: so throughout the six branches going out of the candlestick.

37:20 And in the candlestick [lamp stand] were four bowls made like almonds, his knops [buds], and his flowers: **37:21** And a knop [bud] under two branches of the same, and a knop under two branches of the same, and a knop under two branches of the same, according to the six branches going out of it. **37:22** Their knops [buds] and their branches were of the same: all of it was one beaten work of pure gold. **37:23** And he made his seven lamps, and his snuffers, and his snuffdishes, of pure gold. **37:24** Of a talent of pure gold made he it, and all the vessels thereof.

37:25 And he made the incense altar of shittim wood: the length of it was a cubit, and the breadth of it a cubit; it was foursquare; and two cubits was the height of it; the horns thereof were of the same. **37:26** And he overlaid it with pure gold, both the top of it, and the sides thereof round about, and the horns of it: also he made unto it a crown of gold round about. **37:27** And he made two rings of gold for it under the crown thereof, by the two corners of it, upon the two sides thereof, to be places for the staves to bear it withal. **37:28** And he made the staves of shittim wood, and overlaid them with gold.

37:29 And he made the holy anointing oil, and the pure incense of sweet spices, according to the work of the apothecary.

Exodus 38

Exodus 38:1 And he made the altar of burnt offering of shittim [acacia] wood: five cubits was the length thereof, and five cubits the breadth thereof; it was foursquare; and three cubits the height thereof. **38:2** And he made the horns thereof on the four corners of it; the horns thereof were of the same: and he overlaid it with brass.

38:3 And he made all the vessels of the altar, the pots, and the shovels, and the basons, and the fleshhooks, and the firepans: all the vessels thereof made he of brass.

38:4 And he made for the altar a brasen grate of network under the compass thereof beneath unto the midst of it. **38:5** And he cast four rings for the four ends of the grate of brass, to be places for the staves. **38:6** And he made the staves of shittim wood, and overlaid them with brass. **38:7** And he put the staves into the rings on the sides of the altar, to bear it withal; he made the altar hollow with boards.

38:8 And he made the laver of brass [basin of water], and the foot of it of brass, of the lookingglasses of the women assembling, which assembled at the door of the tabernacle of the congregation.

38:9 And he made the court[yard]: on the south side southward the hangings of the court [the tapestry around the courtyard] were of fine twined linen, an hundred cubits: **38:10** Their pillars were twenty, and their brasen sockets twenty; the hooks of the pillars and their fillets were of silver. **38:11** And for the north side the hangings were an hundred cubits, their pillars were twenty, and their sockets of brass twenty; the hooks of the pillars and their fillets of silver. **38:12** And for the west side were hangings of fifty cubits, their pillars ten, and their sockets ten; the hooks of the pillars and their fillets of silver. **38:13** And for the east side eastward fifty cubits.

38:14 The hangings of the one side of the gate were fifteen cubits; their pillars three, and their sockets three. **38:15** And for the other side of the court gate, on this hand and that hand, were hangings of fifteen cubits; their pillars three, and their sockets three. **38:16** All the hangings of the court round about were of fine twined linen. **38:17** And the sockets for the pillars were of brass; the hooks of the pillars and their fillets of silver; and the overlaying of their chapiters of silver; and all the pillars of the court were filleted with silver.

38:18 And the hanging for the gate of the court[yard] was needlework, of blue, and purple, and scarlet, and fine twined linen: and twenty cubits was the length, and the height in the breadth was five cubits, answerable to the hangings of the court. **38:19** And their pillars were four, and their sockets of brass four; their hooks of silver, and the overlaying of their chapiters and their fillets of silver. **38:20** And all the pins of the tabernacle, and of the court round about, were of brass.

38:21 This is the sum of the tabernacle, even of the tabernacle of testimony, as it was counted, according to the commandment of Moses, for the service of the Levites, by the hand of Ithamar, son to Aaron the priest.

38:22 And Bezaleel the son Uri, the son of Hur, of the tribe of Judah, made all that the LORD commanded Moses. **38:23** And with him was Aholiab, son of Ahisamach, of the tribe of Dan, an engraver, and a cunning workman, and an embroiderer in blue, and in purple, and in scarlet, and fine linen.

A talent was about fifty pounds.

38:24 All the gold that was occupied for the work in all the work of the holy place, even the gold of the offering, was twenty and nine talents, and seven hundred and thirty shekels, after the shekel of the sanctuary.

38:25 And the silver of them that were numbered of the congregation was an hundred talents, and a thousand seven hundred and threescore and fifteen shekels, after the shekel of the sanctuary: **38:26** A bekah for every man, that is, half a shekel, after the shekel of the sanctuary, for **every one that went to be numbered, from twenty years old and upward,** for six hundred thousand and three thousand and five hundred and fifty men.

38:27 And of the hundred talents of silver were cast the sockets of the sanctuary, and the sockets of the vail; an hundred sockets of the hundred talents, a talent for a socket. **38:28** And of the thousand seven hundred seventy and five shekels he made hooks for the pillars, and overlaid their chapiters, and filleted them.

38:29 And the brass of the offering was seventy talents, and two thousand and four hundred shekels. **38:30** And therewith he made the sockets to the door of the tabernacle of the congregation, and the brasen altar, and the brasen grate for it, and all the vessels of the altar, **38:31** And the sockets of the court round about, and the sockets of the court gate, and all the pins of the tabernacle, and all the pins of the court round about.

Exodus 39

Moses continues explaining the tabernacle and the priestly garments

Exodus 39:1 And of the blue, and purple, and scarlet, they made cloths of service [the priestly clothes for their service], to do service in the holy place, and made the holy garments for Aaron; as the LORD commanded Moses.

39:2 And he made the ephod of gold, blue, and purple, and scarlet, and fine twined linen.

They embroidered the linen with thread of pure gold.

39:3 And they did beat the gold into thin plates, and cut it into wires, to work it in the blue, and in the purple, and in the scarlet, and in the fine linen, with cunning work. **39:4** They made shoulderpieces for it, to couple it together: by the two edges was it coupled together.

39:5 And the curious girdle of his ephod, that was upon it, was of the same, according to the work thereof; of gold, blue, and purple, and scarlet, and fine twined linen; as the LORD commanded Moses. **39:6** And they wrought onyx stones inclosed in ouches of gold, graven, as signets are graven, with the names of the children of Israel. **39:7** And he put them on the shoulders of the ephod, that they should be stones for a memorial to the children of Israel; as the LORD commanded Moses.

39:8 And he made the breastplate of cunning work, like the work of the ephod; of gold, blue, and purple, and scarlet, and fine twined linen. **39:9** It was foursquare; they made the breastplate double: a span was the length thereof, and a span the breadth thereof, being doubled. **39:10** And they set in it four rows of stones: the first row was a sardius, a topaz, and a carbuncle: this was the first row. **39:11** And the second row, an emerald, a sapphire, and a diamond. **39:12** And the third row, a ligure, an agate, and an amethyst. **39:13** And the fourth row, a beryl, an onyx, and a jasper: they were inclosed in ouches of gold in their inclosings.

39:14 And the stones were according to the names of the children of Israel, twelve, according to their names, like the engravings of a signet, every one with his name, according to the twelve tribes.

39:15 And they made upon the breastplate chains at the ends, of wreathen work of pure gold. **39:16** And they made two ouches of gold, and two gold rings; and put the two rings in the two ends of the breastplate. **39:17** And they put the two wreathen chains of gold in the two rings on the ends of the breastplate. **39:18** And the two ends of the two wreathen chains they fastened in the two ouches, and put them on the shoulderpieces of the ephod, before it.

39:19 And they made two rings of gold, and put them on the two ends of the breastplate, upon the border of it, which was on the side of the ephod inward. **39:20** And they made two other golden rings, and put them on the two sides of the ephod underneath, toward the forepart of it, over against the other coupling thereof, above the curious girdle of the ephod. **39:21** And they did bind the breastplate by his rings unto the rings of the ephod with a lace of blue, that it might be above the curious girdle of the ephod, and that the breastplate might not be loosed from the ephod; as the LORD commanded Moses.

39:22 And he made the robe of the ephod of woven work, all of blue. **39:23** And there was an hole in the midst of the robe, as the hole of an habergeon, with a band round about the hole, that it should not rend. **39:24** And they made upon the hems of the robe pomegranates of blue, and purple, and scarlet, and twined linen.

39:25 And they made bells of pure gold, and put the bells between the pomegranates upon the hem of the robe, round about between the pomegranates; **39:26** A bell and a pomegranate, a bell and a pomegranate, round about the hem of the robe to minister in; as the LORD commanded Moses.

39:27 And they made coats of fine linen of woven work for Aaron, and for his sons, **39:28** And a mitre of fine linen, and goodly bonnets of fine linen, and linen breeches of fine twined linen, **39:29** And a girdle of fine twined linen, and blue, and purple, and scarlet, of needlework; as the LORD commanded Moses.

39:30 And they made the plate of the holy crown of pure gold, and wrote upon it a writing, like to the engravings of a signet, **HOLINESS TO THE LORD. 39:31** And they tied unto it a lace of blue, to fasten it on high upon the mitre; as the LORD commanded Moses.

39:32 Thus was all the work of the tabernacle of the tent of the congregation finished: and the children of Israel did according to all that the LORD commanded Moses, so did they.

All these things were completed and brought to Moses for his approval before being set up.

39:33 And they brought the tabernacle unto Moses, the tent, and all his furniture, his taches, his boards, his bars, and his pillars, and his sockets, **39:34** And the covering of rams' skins dyed red, and the covering of badgers' skins, and the vail of the covering, **39:35** The ark of the testimony, and the staves thereof, and the mercy seat, **39:36** The table, and all the vessels thereof, and the shewbread, **39:37** The pure candlestick, with the lamps thereof, even with the lamps to be set in order, and all the vessels thereof, and the oil for light,

39:38 And the golden altar [of incense], and the anointing oil, and the sweet incense, and the hanging for the tabernacle door, **39:39** The brasen altar, and his grate of brass, his staves, and all his vessels, the laver and his foot, **39:40** The hangings of the court, his pillars, and his sockets, and the hanging for the court gate, his cords, and his pins, and all the vessels of the service of the tabernacle, for the tent of the congregation, **39:41** The cloths [clothing, garments] of service to do service in the holy place, and the holy garments for Aaron the priest, and his sons' garments, to minister in the priest's office.

39:42 According to all that the LORD commanded Moses, so the children of Israel made all the work.

Moses as the mediator of the Mosaic Covenant blessed the workers who had fashioned these things faithfully according to the whole Word of God; Even as Jesus Christ our spiritual Mediator of the New Covenant will bless all those who are fully faithful to internalize and live by every Word of God!

39:43 And Moses did look upon all the work, and, behold, they had done it as the LORD had commanded, even so had they done it: and Moses blessed them.

Exodus 40

The tabernacle was set up on the beginning of the biblical year in the spring.

Exodus 40:1 And the LORD spake unto Moses, saying, **40:2** On the first day of the first month shalt thou set up the tabernacle of the tent of the congregation. **40:3** And thou shalt put therein the ark of the testimony, and cover the ark with the vail.

40:4 And thou shalt bring in the table, and set in order the things that are to be set in order upon it; and thou shalt bring in the candlestick [lamp stand], and light the lamps thereof.

40:5 And thou shalt set the altar of gold for the incense before the ark of the testimony, and put the hanging of the door to the tabernacle.

40:6 And thou shalt set the altar of the burnt offering before the door of the tabernacle of the tent of the congregation.

40:7 And thou shalt set the laver between the tent of the congregation and the altar, and shalt put water therein.

40:8 And thou shalt set up the court round about, and hang up the hanging at the court gate.

When all these things were set up they were sanctified by the anointing oil, picturing the Spirit of God dwelling in the faithful who re the spiritual temple of God.

> **1 Corinthians 3:16** Know ye not that ye are the temple of God, and that the Spirit of God dwelleth in you? **3:17** If any man defile the temple of God, him shall God destroy; for the temple of God is holy, which temple ye are.

> **1 Corinthians 6:19** What? know ye not that your body is the temple of the Holy Ghost which is in you, which ye have of God, and ye are not your own?

Exodus 40:9 And thou shalt take the anointing oil, and anoint the tabernacle, and all that is therein, and shalt hallow it, and all the vessels thereof: and it shall be holy. **40:10** And thou shalt anoint the altar of the burnt offering, and all his vessels, and sanctify the altar: and it shall be an altar most holy. **40:11** And thou shalt anoint the laver and his foot, and sanctify it.

Aaron then put on his holy garments and was anointed with the oil. This was a physical allegory of the Wave Offering Day picturing the acceptance of Jesus Christ as the High Priest of the New Covenant and being anointed into office by God the Father.

The term "Christ" is an English derivative of the New Testament Greek word christos, which means "anointed." The equivalent Hebrew word in the Old Testament is Mashiach. This term is transliterated in the King James New Testament as Messias (John:1:41; 4:25), a word that has come down into modern English, including many Bible versions, as "Messiah." Both *Christ* [Greek] and *Messiah* [Hebrew] mean "anointed" or "anointed one."

In a prophecy of Messiah David writes:

> **Psalm 45:6** Thy throne, O God, is for ever and ever: the sceptre of thy kingdom is a right sceptre. **45:7** Thou lovest righteousness, and hatest wickedness: therefore God, thy God, hath anointed thee [Messiah, Christ] with the oil of gladness above thy fellows.

The physical priests must be washed with water so that they may be made clean; and those called to become spiritual priests must be baptized with physical water and then washed with the water of the whole Word of God;

having their sins washed away by replacing their evil conduct with the righteousness of the Whole Word of God.

> **Ephesians 5:25...** even as Christ also loved the church, and gave himself for it; **5:26 That he might sanctify and cleanse it with the washing of water by the word, 5:27 That he might present it to himself a glorious church, not having spot, or wrinkle, or any such thing; but that it should be holy and without blemish.**

The physical priests were washed at the DOOR of the tabernacle, BEFORE they were allowed inside; just as we must be cleansed from all spiritual uncleanness and sin, BEFORE we may be changed to spirit and enter the heavenly places through the DOOR of Jesus Christ, the Lamb of God.

Exodus 40:12 And thou shalt bring Aaron and his sons unto the door of the tabernacle of the congregation, and **wash them with water.**

When we think of the Wave Offering we think of the waving of a cake of unleavened bread, but what actually went on in heaven before the throne of God the Father was the anointing of Jesus Christ to be God the Father's High Priest and the ONLY Mediator and Intercessor between God the Father and humanity!

In like fashion the resurrected overcomers will also be arrayed in the holy robes of the priesthood of Melchizedek before the door of the heavenly temple!

> **Revelation 19:7** Let us be glad and rejoice, and give honour to him: for the marriage of the Lamb is come, and **his wife hath made herself ready. 19:8 And to her was granted that she should be arrayed in fine linen** [An white ankle length white shirt which is worn underneath the embroidered blue ephod.], **clean and white: for the fine linen is the righteousness of saints.**

Exodus 40:13 And thou shalt put upon Aaron the holy garments, and anoint him, and sanctify him; that he may minister unto me in the priest's office. **40:14** And thou shalt bring his sons, and clothe them with [linen] coats: **40:15** And thou shalt anoint them, as thou didst anoint their father, that they may minister unto me in the priest's office: for their anointing shall surely be an everlasting priesthood throughout their generations.

40:16 Thus did Moses: according to all that the LORD commanded him, so did he.

40:17 And it came to pass in the first month in the second year, on the first day of the month, that the tabernacle was reared up. **40:18** And Moses reared up the tabernacle, and fastened his sockets, and set up the boards thereof, and put in the bars thereof, and reared up his pillars.

40:19 And he spread abroad the tent over the tabernacle, and put the covering of the tent above upon it; as the LORD commanded Moses. **40:20** And he took and put the testimony into the ark, and set the staves on the ark, and put the mercy seat above upon the ark: **40:21** And he brought the ark into the tabernacle, and set up the vail of the covering, and covered the ark of the testimony; as the LORD commanded Moses.

40:22 And he put the table in the tent of the congregation, upon the side of the tabernacle northward, without the vail.

40:23 And he set the [unleavened bread] bread in order upon it before the LORD; as the LORD had commanded Moses. **40:24** And he put the candlestick [lamp stand] in the tent of the congregation, over against the table, on the side of the tabernacle southward. **40:25** And he lighted the [olive oil] lamps before the LORD; as the LORD commanded Moses.

40:26 And he put the golden altar in the tent of the congregation before the vail: **40:27** And he burnt sweet incense thereon; as the LORD commanded Moses. **40:28** And he set up the hanging at the door of the tabernacle.

40:29 And he put the altar of burnt offering by the door of the tabernacle of the tent of the congregation, and offered upon it the burnt offering and the meat offering; as the LORD commanded Moses. **40:30** And he set the laver between the tent of the congregation and the altar, and put water there, to wash withal.

They washed at the laver ["sea" or huge basin full of water] before the door of the tent of meeting or tabernacle.

40:31 And Moses and Aaron and his sons washed their hands and their feet thereat: **40:32** When they went into the tent of the congregation, and when they came near unto the altar, they washed; as the LORD commanded Moses.

40:33 And he reared up the [outer] court[yard] [The courtyard of the people which was immediately outside the inner courtyard of the priests.] round about the tabernacle and the altar, and set up the hanging of the court gate. So Moses finished the work.

Then when all was finished the God being who later became flesh as Jesus Christ came down to the tabernacle in a cloud by day and in fire by night.

40:34 Then a cloud covered the tent of the congregation, and the glory of the LORD filled the tabernacle. **40:35** And Moses was not able to enter into the tent of the congregation, because the cloud abode thereon, and the glory of the LORD filled the tabernacle.

40:36 And when the cloud was taken up from over the tabernacle, the children of Israel went onward in all their journeys: **40:37** But if the cloud were not taken up, then they journeyed not till the day that it was taken up.

40:38 For the cloud of the LORD was upon the tabernacle by day, and fire was on it by night, in the sight of all the house of Israel, throughout all their journeys.

Visit Our Website

theshininglight.info

www.ingramcontent.com/pod-product-compliance
Lightning Source LLC
Chambersburg PA
CBHW060503300426
44112CB00017B/2533